THE HUNGER OF THE REPUBLIC

How did we get here? As the twenty-first century unfolds, several seemingly unprecedented phenomena evoke ghosts of past histories that suggest we may have been here before. Forms and arguments gone acquire new relevance, as retrospective signposts for the contemporary. **India Since the 90s** assembles texts and images from diverse academic disciplines and cultural practices, to look again at the millennial turn that is shaping our present.

Series Editor
Ashish Rajadhyaksha

IN THE SERIES

VOLUME 1 The Hunger of the Republic: Our Present in Retrospect
Editor: **Ashish Rajadhyaksha**

VOLUME 2 Improvised Futures: Encountering the Body in Performance
Editor: **Ranjana Dave**

VOLUME 3 The Vanishing Point: Moving Images After Video
Editor: **Rashmi Sawhney**

VOLUME 4 Cities on the Ground: The New 'Urban' Experience
Editors: **Solomon Benjamin and the Frozen Fish Collective**

VOLUME 5 Another Lens: Photography Practices and Image Cultures
Editor: **Rahaab Allana**

VOLUME 6 Ghosts of Future Nations: Gods, Migrants and Tribals in the Late-Modern Museum
Editor: **Kavita Singh**

Set up in 2010, **West Heavens** (http://westheavens.net/) is an integrated cross-cultural exchange programme aiming to disentangle and compare the different paths of modernity taken by India and China. It promotes several layers of interaction across intellectual and art practices, and social thought, between the two countries. In its ten years of existence, the project has organized numerous forums, exhibitions, film screenings and workshops, and has published more than twenty books.

India Since the 90s

THE HUNGER OF THE REPUBLIC

OUR PRESENT IN RETROSPECT

Edited by
Ashish Rajadhyaksha

Tulika Books

WEST HEAVENS

India Since the 90s
is a collaborative bilingual project between

Tulika Books, New Delhi and **West Heavens**, Shanghai

Tulika Books

WEST HEAVENS

supported by
Moonchu Foundation, Hong Kong

夢周文教基金會
Moonchu Foundation

The Hunger of the Republic: Our Present in Retrospect

First published in India in 2021 by
Tulika Books
44 (first floor), Shahpur Jat, New Delhi 110 049, India
tulikabooks.in

ISBN: 978-81-945348-1-5

Design, visual concepts, original photography, montages: Gauri Nagpal

Printed in India at Chaman Offset, Delhi 110 002

INTRODUCTION TO THE SERIES

India Since the 90s

India Since the 90s is a series of six volumes published in English and Chinese, intended to provide a historical frame for our present. Barring very few exceptions, all texts and images used here are reprints of existing material. What is *new* is how they are presented here. They are assembled into an interpretative mash-up that reframes, estranges and refamiliarizes India's recent past and, in some instances, its actual present, to a different gaze.

As 2019-20 unfolded, as we began implementing our project, it often appeared that we had chosen a particularly inauspiciously time to attempt something like this. Simply put, it wasn't a great moment from where to seek historical distance. As it evolved, however, the circumstances of the project did yield two unexpected opportunities that recast its ambition.

One: as we saw totalitarian state apparatuses roll out emergency measures of extraordinary control, including nationwide lockdowns, in the name of the public good, we were incessantly reminded of the longer histories of several of the concepts invoked. We were reminded that, notwithstanding their overwhelming immediacy, the radically new phenomena at play – the new viruses, new technologies, new modes of organization and 'occupation', new systems of regulation and surveillance – required that even 'unprecedented' situations do allow larger historical frames to emerge for our time.

Two: as we went on, however, some clarity emerged around the 'new normal'. The uncertainty gave us a glimpse of what lay beneath the usual cover-ups of the everyday. It was almost as though the emphasis on social distancing came in inverse proportion to the impossibility of *historical* distance. Every step forward required a few steps backwards. Even as our capacity to imagine stable utopian futures drained away, it was reinvigorated by a *textual prescience*. Texts and images from times past appeared to want to say something to these conditions, in ways their original authors and makers may never have anticipated.

We discovered a new, or at least previously undiagnosed, ability to read uncanny significances into the familiar, thereby reinvigorating many of our received systems of interpretation and meaning-making. *Meaning* emerged through a fusing of three interpretative moves: one from present to past, a second from past to future, a third purely in the present in the way texts circulated horizontally, from hand to hand. As these vectors combined into one hallucinatory amalgam of hindsight and retrofuturism, they revealed a consciousness that we, their readers/ viewers, appeared to share with makers often far removed in time and space: a textual solidarity through a process of re-presentation and re-circulation, as if pre-designed to address future historical uncertainty, even as the uncertainty generated unexpected creative and analytical opportunity.

A ceaseless movement, the 'new normal', threw new light on the constitutive role of normalcy itself. This redefined 'normal' takes us, this book series argues, back to other moments that had similarly encountered the unprecedented everyday. This was not a return to origins. Rather, it was the discovery, in such moments, of the ghosts of other moments. Today's stories, however things pan out, cannot be told without recognizing in them the specters of the 1990s, the decade that launched a globalization whose end might well have been signalled in 2020. And the 1990s in turn could not, it further appeared, be comprehended without accessing another equally 'new' moment in history, the 1970s – and so forth, so that even immediate questions took us back to times when the Indian state was imagined and reimagined, politically and administratively.

Perhaps the key textual challenge was to the founding text of modern India, its Constitution, and the battles over its interpretation fifty years later, amid the political challenges of the 1990s and 2000s. The 1990s were defined, arguably, by three events that took place within the first four years of that decade, framed within Articles 14 (equality before law), 15 (right to the public domain), 19 (freedom of speech) and 21 (life and liberty). The first was in 1990, when a year after a new government took charge, having defeated the Congress and set up a Left-supported coalition against the pro-Hindu right, key recommendations of the Mandal Commission were implemented enabling reservation for the category of 'Other Backward Classes'. The second, in 1992, a year after the assassination of Prime Minister Rajiv Gandhi, the pro-Hindu Bharatiya Janata Party (BJP) brought down a Mughal mosque that they said had been erected at the birthplace of the Hindu god Rama (of the Ramayana), attempting a political programme based on pan-national majoritarianism. And third, in Bombay in 1993, a retaliation for the riots that followed the destruction of the mosque, a series of bomb blasts that inaugurated a long trajectory of 'terrorism' with events such as the attack on the Indian Parliament on 13 December 2001 and the attacks in Mumbai on 26 November 2008.

These events defined the spaces of overt political action. Parallelly, however, other spaces of *covert* political action pluralized the support of the Constitution: such as urban pavements (slum-dwellers living on these pavements claiming a fundamental right to shelter), urban safety for women (and movements such as 'Take Back the Night') and spaces for intimacy. While several of the technologies associated with the regulation and ordering of covert space saw battles over state action (several e-governance initiatives, the Aadhaar biometric identity project), perhaps the most significant battle was over social media. Key Supreme Court judgements abolishing the draconian Section 66A of the Information Technology Act of 2000 (state surveillance of all electronic communication including social media) and Section 377 of the Indian Penal Code ('carnal intercourse against the order of nature'), and upholding the Right to Privacy – interpreting equality before law, freedom of speech and the right to liberty – may well be among the defining political actions of the early twenty-first century, as also the astonishing movement protesting the Citizenship Amendment Act and the National Population Register that is literally taking place as we write.

Each of the volumes in this book series exists on its own, as conceived by its editor. A common feature across the volumes is the introduction of a glossary of keywords. Several keywords are Indian words, some are acronyms or abbreviations, while others are English words used in India in ways that diverge sharply from dictionary definitions. While they serve the purpose of introducing them to those unfamiliar with Indian political debate, they also extend the estrangement and refamiliarization project even to those acquainted with their conventional 'Indian' meaning.

Perhaps the only other element common to all the volumes, apart from an interest in the period following the 1990s in India, is in a triad of concepts that we may name *politics*, *space*, *technology*. In all of these volumes, we will see a pendular movement within political spaces: a movement between physical and virtual, between the local and the planetary. Technology, connected with how space is occupied, is *apparatus*, *frame*, *mediation* and *surveillance*. Three further terms, in turn, produce the habitus for these concepts: *democracy*, the *body* and the *text*. Even as key democratic concepts such as freedom need to be defined anew in times when bodies – both physical and virtual – occupy complex political domains, the prescient text, re-interpreted, too finds itself bearing new responsibilities.

Ashish Rajadhyaksha
Series Editor
Bangalore, 1 June 2020

CONTENTS

INTRODUCTION

ASHISH RAJADHYAKSHA

> India is a deviant case in a much more fundamental sense: most threats to democracy in India arise from the sector that promotes modernity.
>
> – Rajni Kothari, 'Democracy in Search of a Theory'

WE, THE PEOPLE: THE NARRATIVE DEVICE

In 1985, a year after the deadly industrial disaster occurred at the Union Carbide plant in Bhopal, the Government of India declared itself as *parens patriae* – or parent of the nation – to become the unilaterally authorized single representative of all those affected by that disaster.

It did so, says Veena Das in her essay included in this volume, in the name of the people. The people were declared incapable of speaking for themselves, and were thus judicially incompetent or *non sui juris*. When the victims contested such a labelling in the Supreme Court and claimed their right to represent themselves, a 'narrative device' came into play, says Das, to explain just why the victims were never consulted, and how their protests over the settlement, decided in their absence, could be recast as the actions of irresponsible and ignorant people. Such a device also served to justify the fact that the judges had not allowed public scrutiny over what the government or its medical establishment had done by way of relief and help. It was, in the end, able to 'obfuscate the fact that they had completely failed to fix the responsibility for the accident and had thus converted the issue of multinational liability into that of multinational charity'.

The narrative operation, which has become increasingly familiar as the millennium has worn on, was in brief this: the people's suffering became, on its own, 'sufficient reason to justify the settlement and uphold the usurpation of power by the government'. The problem was not with the people when seen as a whole – there was 'no lack of concern for the impact of a hazardous industry on *society in general*'. The problem only lay when such a concept of society translated into a particular set of victims. 'Every reference to victims and their suffering only served to reify "suffering" while dissolving the real victims in order that they could be reconstituted into nothing more than verbal objects.'

Utsa Patnaik provides a somewhat different example, from another historical moment, for what may be an uncannily similar narrative twist. In her famous essay, 'The Republic of Hunger', also in this volume, she speaks of a moment when people facing drought and deepening hunger were claimed to have 'voluntarily agreed', in Finance Ministry and allied reports, to a 'dietary diversification'. Even as 33 million tonnes of grain were procured through distress sales, one survey described them as *excess stocks*, a 'surplus over what people voluntarily wish to consume', and said that they represented a 'problem of plenty'. Another, trying to explain the 'falling share of cereals in the spending on food', said that this was because 'not only the well-to-do, but all segments of the population were voluntarily diversifying their diets to high-value foods away from cereals'. That year, 2001–02, saw 12 million tonnes exported to other countries and another 6 million tonnes sold in the open market. 'For a country which has been seeing sharp deceleration of agricultural growth in the 1990s,' writes Patnaik, 'arguments on voluntary dietary diversification for all rural population segments are illogical to the point of being foolish.' 'We now know why the central government undertook massive food exports last year in a situation of steeply falling food availability, and despite a severe drought: it has all been justified and rationalized already, simply by interpreting deepening hunger and starvation as "voluntary choice".'

The present assemblage comprises numerous works that writers, artists and activists generously made available to this project, montaged into what may be a potentially large argument traversing diverse political positions. I hasten to add that I cannot assume that all, or even any, of the contributors agree with either the montage or my editorial interpretation of what it may mean, and in presenting this assemblage thus, I rely more than usual on their generosity while also offering the usual caveats.

Its central contention, which can be read (I argue) into the texts and images that follow, is that the 1990s inaugurated a major narrative operation upon the category of 'the people'. What occurred was an *abstraction* of the concept in two senses of the term, to *make abstract* in order to *usurp*, and it has had a devastating impact across law, economics and aesthetics. Citizenship, over these decades, has increasingly been taken away from actual people, becoming the property of the state which has more and more attributed to itself the sole right to speak for them. 'People' no longer receive benefits because they possess the universal social rights of *citizens*, but as needy *beneficiaries*. Actual people, thus no longer 'people' in an older sense of the term, have become segregated into diverse categories of need and victimhood, identified and targeted through technologies of enumeration (as well as of social othering) that have taken on greater aspects of surveillance. This approach has effectively signalled the end of the principle of welfare, replaced, in the words of Partha Chatterjee, by 'multifarious biopolitical techniques of governmentality'.[1]

Populist state authoritarianism – the appropriation of the concept of 'people' and its use against actual people – has been a major topic of political debate in many parts of the world, perhaps belying Kothari's assumption of Indian deviancy. In India, the debate has moved from law to economics to technology and, to some extent, to aesthetics. In law, the fight for people to retain the right to citizenship has defined key battles over the past two decades around Articles 14, 15, 19 and 21 (equality, non-discrimination, freedom of speech, and the right to life and livelihood);[2] in economics, in questions around the shift away from universal to targeted public distribution, most specifically in the area of direct cash transfers;[3] and in technology, in the areas of surveillance and data protection.[4] In the arts, the most direct impact of the usurping of 'the people' by the state has been the wide and indiscriminate attribution of *sedition* (Section 124A of the Penal Code) to *dissent*, arguably the cornerstone of art practice.[5]

Here I attempt not so much to reprise that debate but to amalgamate the cumulative energy of this book, to allow us to step back and view in real time the unravelling of what I call, after Veena Das, a 'narrative device' that appeared to come into full view from the early 1990s. The choice of texts and visuals is admittedly subjective, but I should assert that the assemblage came first, the argument later, driven by a clarity that only hindsight can bring. Several very well-known and even foundational works combine here with others that may be new to readers; old texts are reprised (overcoming the reluctance of authors who have wondered about their obsolescence), juxtaposed and sometimes montaged, revealing, I propose, new significance and perhaps a new means of entering into the present.

A NARRATIVE, NOT FOR ALL TO HEAR

> Narrative does not . . . aspire to be a universal form of discourse. It draws lines, it distributes people, unlike rational theoretical discourse which attempts to unite them in an abstract universe of ideal consensus. Narratives are not for all to hear, for all to participate in to an equal degree.
>
> – Sudipta Kaviraj, 'The Imaginary Institution of India'

In his well-known essay included in this book, Sudipta Kaviraj, speaking of how the institution of India came to be imagined, produces a radically new concept of narrative itself. While nations are, he admits, indeed objective entities, he wants readers to 'soften' their concept of objectivity when dealing with such phenomena, because 'things that exist in history are often objective only in this way, and only to this extent', unsatisfactory though it may be to 'grimly scientific minds'.

Such 'softened' objective entities are produced, he says, in narrative. But narrative here exists only for a particular purpose, namely to enable communities to reproduce themselves by telling stories about themselves. Narratives are above all 'practical things', 'interpretations of the world and its history which issue in a call to change it'; they are a *transaction*, a *contract* between a self and an audience. Narratives of the nation, therefore, have a strictly curtailed function – while they are able to speak with eloquence about freedom, sacrifice and glory, they are 'vague about the more concrete and contestable questions of distribution, equality, power, the actual unequal ordering of the past society or of the future one'.

Kaviraj is here not creating an exceptionalist Indian narrative; instead he *redefines narrative itself*. The purpose of narrative is of course to open meaning out, to make it universally comprehensible: this is the basis of its egalitarian claim. The idea of *non-universalism* as a *fundamental property* of narrative is surely a major departure from the definition of the term. Kaviraj indeed offers the caution that such narratives of the nation must be seen to have done their work when Independence is achieved, for, 'if pressed into the service of providing an order to the nation and its state, they begin to falter'.

The appropriations of state populism in the name of the nation, able to pick and choose parts of the story precisely because of its basic feature of transactional non-universality, may well be viewed as a Benjaminian afterlife of Kaviraj's imaginary institution of India. Inevitably, narratives faltered, as Gyanendra Pandey shows when he juxtaposes a classic history textbook on Indian nationalism with a report on a particular gruesome incident of violence in the town of Bhagalpur in 1989, and discusses the difficulties that a human rights document faced in trying to explain just what had happened. But they also diversified, went underground, so to say, into grey areas where the state could not always follow – like those Sharmila Rege names as *counterpublics*, where Ambedkarite literature, poetry and consumption, alongside interventions into national time through the making of calendars with an entirely independent list of holidays, festivals and pilgrimages create and collectively maintain a 'record that links time past and the crises of the present'. A counterpublic is, she says, 'notional and empirical, and is never just the sum total of persons . . . it is different from crowds or audience which require co-presence'. It is, in the end, 'a way of organizing oneself'.

Such organization occurs at multiple invisible, quasi-legal levels as forms of 'structural violence', show Sunil Mohan and Rumi Harish, speaking of sexual minorities. While much violence, such as 'family violence, racial violence, hate crimes, terrorism, genocide and war' are overt and have legal visibility, Mohan and Harish's interest, outlined in a landmark report on violence produced by Bangalore's Alternative Law Forum, lies in bringing legal visibility to forms of violence that 'are not loud. Structural violence brings in a certain kind of silence.'

One (admittedly somewhat audacious) insertion here is the famous essay on the 'Colonial Mode of Production' by British–Pakistani sociologist and activist Hamza Alavi, alongside the iconic human rights activist and political commentator K. Balagopal's well-known 'Rich Peasant, Poor Peasant'.[6] This insertion is to propose a possible genealogy: between our populist 'abstraction' and a 'mode' that Alavi names 'disarticulation' and says was invented during late colonialism. Under this mode, internal links between major agrarian economies were destroyed and made to relate to each other only through their separate ties with the colonial–metropolitan economy. There was a basic economic purpose to this rigid centre–periphery apparatus, Alavi says: to transform small landholders into becoming cheap labour both in the countryside and in the city. This transformation could however only be enabled through (what we might now call) a narrative operation, and one that may have a curious ancestry in the early twenty-first century segregation of 'the people', when this smallholder class was dis- and re-articulated into capitalism in a certain way and at a certain level, and with only certain rights. Disagreeing with a common description of this class as 'pre-capitalist', Alavi proposes instead that it was on the backs of its labour that a properly capitalist 'expanded reproduction' was enabled, in turn enabling metropolitan economies to go beyond feudalism. Such an expansion had a curiously 'deformed' aspect, however, which forced this very class into economic destitution by forcing them to 'sell their land to big farmers and descend into the ranks of the landless poor'.

Alavi would take the debate into the post-Independence period, proposing an updated colonial mode in the further disarticulation of feudalism under Congress rule. For Balagopal, it would define the far more recent 1980s–90s, whose central feature was to him the growing dominance of a new and explicitly post-Independence class of rural elite produced in collusion with the Indian state: 'dominant landholders in villages, who range all the way from old-style landlords holding 100 acres or more, to their modern progeny of ex-tenants holding smaller but usually technologically modernized and highly productive holdings'. This, even as smaller tenants got evicted and converted into the new labour force – 'unrecorded tenants, farm servants (and) wage labourers'.

The first section of this book, and its explication of the narrative device in texts by Kaviraj, Pandey, Patnaik, Alavi and Balagopal, begins with *democracy* and ends with *modernism*. Political theorist Rajni Kothari makes a flat assertion that we have 'no theory of democracy' left any longer (needing us to remember that we are speaking of one who virtually defined the meaning of politics in India). The theory we have worked with so far, now defunct, was based on an 'inordinately atomistic view of both the individual and the state' alongside a 'disproportionately homogeneous conception of social and cultural reality'. A new theory of democracy, if we can at all put one together, would need to 'accept the great diversity of human situations and yet provide coherence to them through an active political process'. New and creative spaces would have to be able to 'restructure the state to realize these ends'. Kothari appears unsure that this is any longer possible.

In a trenchant essay central to her longstanding engagement with modernism as received in the non-western world,[7] Geeta Kapur outlines a condition that may actually bear similarity to Alavi's colonial mode – of being coterminous with the modern but outside it, or, as she says, 'struggling with the processes of modernization [but] excluded from modernism *per se*'. She proposes a possible way out, of sidestepping the 'unitary logic of advancement' through a move away from the 'modern' and into the 'contemporary'. The modern, as conceived in nineteenth-century Europe, assumes 'in the metropolitan concentration of culture [and its] centre and periphery' that 'one or the other among the peoples of the world are always seen to be out of step'. Her *side*stepping move therefore, of which the artist Bhupen Khakhar would be the quintessential example, may (I argue) well be viewed in hindsight as precisely enabled by the underside of non-universality – an 'appropriating' of tradition through acts of transgression, creating a politicized 'tradition-in-use' that could, first and foremost, resist the 'reification to which the artefacts of "other" civilizations succumb in the wake of western modernism'.

THE LABYRINTH OF SHADOWS

> We may learn to become inured to the tug of an uncomfortable and persistent memory of things and people that went amiss. Like the 'out-takes' in footage that never quite made it into a film, about which we can say that we have a memory of being present as witnesses at the shooting, but little or no recall of ever having seen them on screen, like papers, documents, transcripts, bodies and memories that turn to dust and are scattered, the history of the attack on the Parliament of India too will in all likelihood become a

> hazy recollection with only the words and images of 'terrorists' and 'martyrs' and 'threat to national security' thrown up in bold relief, and with all else obscured within a labyrinth of shadows.
>
> – Shuddhabrata Sengupta, 'Media Trials and Courtroom Tribulations'

> Respectable citizens phoned each other to find out if all was well, while labourers on the footpath stayed under the sky with their eyes open, spending the night like ghosts. Laughter was banned on the streets. Looking someone in the eye was banned. Schools wore the silence of hospitals.
>
> – Jayant Kaikini, 'The Unframed'

The second section of this book is pivoted around a startling disappearance, perhaps an abduction, of a statue. On a fine morning in December 2001, on Chennai's Marina Beach waterfront, the familiar statue of Kannagi is found missing. Kannagi is of course the quintessential figurehead of Tamil politics: protagonist of the epic *Silappathikaram*, icon of Tamil womanhood, key figure in Dravidian nationalism, incarnated in the twentieth century by P. Kannamba's enactment in the classic 1942 movie of the same name, and a statue familiar to Chennai's denizens since it was first put up in 1968 by (then) Chief Minister C.N. Annadurai. M.S.S. Pandian's short tale of the gaping hole, an actual hole on the Marina and, more devastatingly, a *discursive* void created within Tamil public life, spans an astonishing mix of politics, popular culture, conspiracy theory and history, as frantic efforts are made to fill in the vacuum.

To disappear, to make invisible, to go underground – over recent decades these have become survival strategies, physical and discursive. As 'the people' disappear, the vacuum created by the poisoning of the public sphere also signals the end of a logic of representation, as it does the loss of citizenship, the erasure of the author and the collapse of a stable narratorial standpoint from where stories make sense. Among the protagonists of such confused narratives with no beginning or end are the Delhi University professor S.A.R. Geelani, accused of terrorism by a grey amalgam of law, police procedure, popular fiction, cheap true-life thrillers and late night television, and the anonymous person whose framed photograph becomes different things to people in Jayant Kaikini's short story. And they are the imaginations of a Dalit concept of death that does not share either the idea of an end or that of an afterlife of eternal bliss in Kancha Ilaiah's testament to emotional sedition, *Why I am not a Hindu*.

'Are we... dealing with an older state form, or some as-yet unrecognized new one?' asks Madhava Prasad. In 'The Republic of Babel', Prasad asserts the centrality of language but at the same time repositions its very location. It is the 'only concrete universal that can bridge the gap between the ethnic particularity of a group and the featureless abstraction of the citizen'. Language, if redefined away from its traditional boundaries and into a vastly expanded sphere of *political* language, and thus also an expanded space occupied by all those who speak it, requires us to recognize the need for a state even as there is a reinvention of the very idea of a state. Our state shall now not be 'some elusive reality which escapes the normative demands of nation-state discourse', he writes, but something that is 'inescapably determined by the mutually impacting coexistence of the norm and the reality'. To him, such a 'state of in-betweenness' must be taken to 'constitute a state in itself for purposes of description'.

This state of in-betweenness would become a linguistic condition as well as a technological one as the millennium turned. Prasad includes the *cinema* as a possible presence in this idea of an expanded space of political language. What we got, as the twentieth century shaded into the twenty-first, was both an expanded cinema and an expanded state. Ravi Sundaram's 'Beyond the Nationalist Panopticon' was written in 1996, at a time when, to quote a cyber-activist in 2020, the 'toxic cocktail of NPR+Aadhaar+NRC'[8] could hardly have been imagined. At the time, virtuality had brought new value to diverse peripheral 'cyberpublics', no longer disadvantaged by their analogue marginality but empowered to such an extent that they could end – in their very peripherality – the 'great western millennium'; what would also end, perhaps once and for all, was the 'old state-system of modernity based on secure borders and sovereignty', and with it, 'canonical notions of subjectivity, representation and freedom'. For, even in 1996, a quarter-century ago, they had 'taken a battering from which one suspects they will never fully recover'. Yet Sundaram envisaged a condition in which the 'social cartographies' of nationalism could lead to a vast new era of digital surveillance, for which, even at the time, he cast a wide net. Perhaps the curious truth of that 'battering' is revealed in our expanded state: an all-seeing condition of surveillance on the one hand, and the citizen-speaker becoming a self-absented data shadow on the other.

NOT JUST RE-TELLING BUT RE-BUILDING: THE HEROIC AND THE ORDINARY

> Survivors' stories, narratives of neighbourhoods, all need not just re-telling but re-building. What happens to those who have been used as foot soldiers, fed on tales of enemy-othering and hate, even as the chief architects fast ascend the pyramid of state power?
>
> – Teesta Setalvad, 'Being their Target',
> in *Footsoldier of the Constitution: A Memoir*

Teesta Setalvad is of course very well known for her extraordinary struggle seeking justice for the victims of the massacre that followed the riots of 2002 in Gujarat – and for the extent to which she was targeted and hounded by the entire machinery of the state for more than a decade thereafter. The text that figureheads the third and final section of the book, taken from her autobiographical description of this period, tells a part of the story. The story is also of significance for another reason. Setalvad personifies, together with a small number of colleagues and co-defendants, the kind of high-visibility constitutional subject that is directly under threat at the millennial turn: a threat of populist abstraction to which many contributors to this book make direct reference, but nobody embodies quite as directly as she does. Her description of her struggle is also presented as an invitation to reprise what used to be the properties of such a citizen-subject, and what may happen – at the experiential, bodily levels, as much as the legal and symbolic level – when the Constitution is faced with situations that were probably inconceivable to its framers.

Setalvad's fight is thus 'for the heart and soul of India'; it will take place 'out there and in our homes', will be fought 'on the streets, within our homes and classrooms armed with arsenal from history, culture, poetry, music, literature', and we 'do not know yet, who shall win'. Inevitably there is heroism, but there is also the unheroic pragmatism of the everyday. 'Committed politics' needs to work alongside 'everyday-lived reality', for 'the struggle for justice has become multiple things'. It is 'to make yourself vulnerable and threatened', to 'fight the good fight even when others tire . . . to relentlessly pursue, gather and cull through evidence while protecting my own back'.

The possible link between a heroism of gestural signification and another register of the pragmatic and the elusive defines the visible–invisible subject of this book. Anita Dube's manifesto-statement for a short-lived group of radical artists presents, for what may well be the last time in our history, the artist as heroic subject. The artists in her collective consciously reject the practices of the arts mainstream, and declare that they will 'turn the compound questioning eye on everything, seize the present moment, stand crude, naked and knife-sharp, and will not allow anyone to pass'.

The problem, inevitably, is twofold – and it is not, as Dube writes, an easy decision. In not allowing anyone to pass, the collective wants a gatekeeping 'politicization of consciousness', but as the last decades have moved, such politicization has taken an opposite turn to the conventional idea of consciousness. Conscious speech, traceable to a speaker responsible for his/her speech under Article 19 of the Constitution, has been replaced by an increasing fascination with covert authorship, or even the elision of the speaking subject. Speech-forms – even art works – do not any more trace to any artist–auteur–speaker, but are increasingly those of shadowy forms, like anonymous trolls, that also arise from the invisibilization of 'the people'. They dissolve, sometimes intentionally, into popular culture or, more likely, the digital ether.

Heroic speech in such times can be leavened, as conscious strategy, by the unheroic. Dube herself has elsewhere spoken of the artist K.P. Krishnakumar, founder and leader of the Radical Painters and Sculptors collective, and his fascination with the radicalism of figures who are 'not the glorious figures of labour, as in the modernist sculpture of Ramkinkar Baij in the discourse of the left', but 'edgy, naked, sexual, cunning proletarians'.[9]

VISUAL REFERENCES

The visuals that accompany these texts comprise several sources. These have however often been combined into what, to use a term from cognitive design, we may call mashups: unstable assemblages harvesting a diversity of resources to produce a visual that simulates consistency. Several memes have been introduced that intervene into, and walk over, authorial works. Montage forms re-frame and re-present existing art works. Several of the mashups are further created on the ultimate '90s window to the world, the square Samsung 740N Syncmaster monitor, here buried, covered, painted and plastered.

Documentary, in both film and photography, is represented in the works of filmmakers Rakesh Sharma, Sanjay Kak and Paromita Vohra, and photographers Anushka Jain, Julian Nyca and one photographer who does not wish to be named. The book has made extensive use of works by artists Riyas Komu, Moinak Biswas, Bhupen Khakhar, Raqs Media Collective, Karthick K.G., Atul Dodiya, K.P. Reji, Navjot Altaf and K.P. Krishnakumar. Synced to these named, authored sources, are found objects including book covers, human rights documents, legal judgments, jackets of music albums, maps, letters, and images from Hindi, Tamil and Telugu films.

The overarching meme defining this assemblage comes from the final sequence of Ritwik Ghatak's last testament film, *Jukti Takko aar Gappo* (1977), where the drunken Neelkantha Bagchi falls over, caught in the crossfire of police and radical guerrilla fighters. Ghatak did not live to see the turn of the millennium, of course, and yet his falling spectral presence spreads like an Angelus Novus over the devastations of the millennial turn. The image is in part from Ghatak's film but primarily from Moinak Biswas's iteration in his two-channel installation, *Across the Burning Tracks* (2016). A second image is adapted from the prone Dalit figure, the *Thumbingal Chathan* or 'spirit of Thumbingal' from K.P. Reji's painting of 2012, that appears most prominently alongside Kancha Ilaiah's

'Hindu Death and Our Death'. And there is finally the protagonist of K.P. Krishnakumar's *The Thief* (1985), the edgiest, most cunning and most moral of Krishnakumar's 'proletarians', pointing his finger at someone.

A NOTE ON USAGE

Permission to reproduce has been received wherever possible. Use of all content here falls within the purview of fair use as stated in Sec. 52 of the Indian Copyright Act, 1957 (together with subsequent amendments). Use intended for research, criticism and review is within Article 13 of the Agreement on Trade-Related Aspects of Intellectual Property Rights (TRIPS), which includes fair use in cases that do not conflict with a normal exploitation of the work and do not unreasonably prejudice the legitimate interests of the right-holder as per Article 9(2) of the Berne Convention for the Protection of Literary and Artistic Works (1967), the WIPO Copyright Treaty and the EU Copyright Directive (1996). Such use is also protected by Section 107 of the Copyright Law of the United States of America as 'criticism, comment, scholarship, or research' that in no way damages the 'potential market for or value of the copyrighted work', and by Britain's 1988 Copyright, Designs and Patents Act (Chapter III, Section 28–29).

SECTION I

NARRATIVES OF STATE

SyncMaster 740n
KAR SEVAKS DESTROY BABRI MASJID
President's rule in U.P. ● Assembly dissolved ● Imam appeals for peace
The Republic Besmirched
SAMSUNG

Political theorist Rajni Kothari (1928–2015) wrote his final book, **Rethinking Democracy**, in 2005 as something of a *fin de siècle* testament on what democracy could possibly mean. The term, linked to the equally widespread (and equally amorphous) concept of 'freedom', is in wider circulation today than ever in history: both as a single-point solution for political organization in the 'free' world, and as a stick with which to beat seemingly non- or anti-democratic societies and nations. The apparently self-explanatory concept may, however, have gone over a definitional tipping-point, at the same time as it survives, like all memes, through circulation. Even as democratic states appear increasingly unwilling to carry out their constitutional obligations and people do not know what else to turn to, the stage is being set for 'violence, inequity, destruction of natural resources, contraction of institutional spaces and the consequent decline in more moderate and constructive modes of dissent'. On one side of the polarization is a 'techno-managerial response from the elite'; on the other, an 'ethnic response from social peripheries'. The 'crisis of the state' has entered a new stage as it becomes increasingly difficult to find solutions to challenges to the state from within its own framework.

Images: Falling man from Ritwik Ghatak's last film, **Jukti Takko aar Gappo (Reason, Debate and a Story**, 1977), placed over newspaper images of key developments that transformed democracy in India in the 1990s: the 1991 budget of Finance Minister Manmohan Singh that inaugurated the era of globalization; the 1992 destruction of the Babri Masjid and subsequent riots that rocked the country; the anti-reservation agitations also from 1992; the nuclear (Pokharan-II) tests of 1998; and the event in Godhra that inaugurated the 2002 Gujarat pogrom.

1

RAJNI KOTHARI

2005

DEMOCRACY: IN SEARCH OF A THEORY

We have entered a phase of human history when long-cherished ideals of liberty, equality and fraternity appear increasingly difficult to realize. The ideals themselves are no doubt worth pursuing, as are values such as social justice, individual freedom and the idea of a state that could liberate people from the shackles of both tradition and modernity. These ideals and values together provide humankind with a vision of a utopian social order – humane and just. But how do we translate this utopia into reality? For long, it has been imagined that a 'democratic way of life' will provide humanity with the necessary framework at once institutional and ideological – through which this utopia could be realized. It is only in the recent decades that the faith in such an ideological-cum-institutional framework for 'delivering the goods' is being questioned. To address the theme of the prospects for democracy in India with a broad societal rather than just political perspective, we have to ask where the country is headed, what the possibilities are for enhancing individual freedom and moving towards collective goals of social justice and emancipation.

India is already undergoing a massive process of inner change involving the very womb of its culture and civilization – from the awakening of the inner self of each individual being to the democratizing of civil society as a whole. India is also experiencing an opening up of the polity and the state, both in respect of their inner constituents and in their relation to other cultures, nationalities and civilizations. India faces the challenge of not just pursuing a set of social and political ideals; a deeper and more comprehensive involvement is necessary – to engage in *acts of human imagination* for dealing with the vast diversity of situations facing it; to perceive the diverse goals facing the country as part of one large, religious order. Religion should be seen as a pluralistic *and* monistic discipline of discovering oneself, one's community, one's spiritual essence. And through the discoveries, one engages in tasks of social–political–moral transformation and emancipation. These tasks will extend the self all the way from inner intuitive drives to larger engagements in the socio-political arena, and further external involvements vis-à-vis diverse nationalities, states and the globalizing drives of transnational and corporate entities.

The challenges contemporary India faces are – how to relate and join the deeper, i.e. the inner, drives of citizens and communities to the broader challenge of sociopolitical transformation and the still larger challenge of emancipation; how to engage in the preservation of freedom and autonomy in the face of external confrontations of both corporate and transnational varieties, and confrontations found *within* the nation-state, such as economic divides based on class and caste, and the more threatening communal and fundamentalist drives that are overtaking a vast variety of religious constellations, castes and communities.

Viewing Indian reality as it unfolds in our time, of all the domains impinging on contemporary India – from the personal in the considerable diversity characterizing civil society to that of the state and its political processes – it is the political that dominates. It penetrates all other domains. This politicization applies as much to religion and caste as to the highly personalized domains of families, friendships and neighbourhoods, and close-knit circles of clubs, professional groups and peer groups. In the recent past, it has been argued that religious loyalties and social structures are emerging as alternative foci to those more clearly political in nature. This is no longer the case [...]

With (the) distortion of Hinduism by Hindutva,[1] there is an atmosphere of growing alienation and intolerance between majority and minority communities. Even in other parts of the world, ruling structures are coming under the influence of strong-armed mafia and lumpen elements, accompanied by the rise of money-power, criminalization and corruption, producing anxiety about terrorism and the increasing influence of security and paramilitary forces. These are the ultimate consequences of perverse forms of politicization of life, whether this be in the domain of civil society and the grassroots level at which right-wing groups are gaining ascendancy (in place of left and liberal groups that had initiated the grassroots perspective), or in the arena of militant religious groupings and their search for omnipotence in place of what was once a pluralist framework. India's real misfortune lies in this hijacking of pluralist structures by monotheist and centripetal social and political ideologies. The same has happened in Sri Lanka, Pakistan, Bangladesh, Nepal, the rest of South East Asia and beyond. The roles played by institutions of corporate capitalism – consisting on the one hand of Bretton Woods institutions like the World Bank, the International Monetary Fund (IMF) and other such global bodies, and on the other hand, the array of transnational corporations – have also contributed to the destruction of pluralism. A plethora of non-governmental organizations (NGOs) operating within individual countries, including the so-called grassroots groups as well as the newly empowered party and party-like formations at decentralized levels, are now being drawn into the vortex.

I have, for long, been a believer in the political process, its inherent dynamics, its capacity to correct imbalances and institutional erosions, its basic thrust towards empowering people, even in those found in underprivileged and oppressed social terrains. Even today, I want to work towards the restorative ethics of basic political processes leading to ever-growing possibilities of *change*; indeed, the very ideas of change, and the prospect of turning what is currently a crisis in the idea change into a real challenge of change. This has to be done in the full spirit of transformative and emancipatory politics. Nothing outside of politics can do this, not even religion, despite its inherent humanizing and service-oriented potential. For religion to work towards change, or let us say for castes and communities to do this, they will need to develop discreet strategies for restoring pluralism – and diversity-enhancing possibilities. Religion is fast ceasing to be available for such restructuring. Caste still has the possibility for such restructuring provided it is transformed in ways that lead to new realignments in the social structure starting from the bottom. Even traditional institutions of family and kinship, caste and community are being subjected to churning, leading either to violence, or on the positive side, to a restructuring of the institutional framework of civil society. Underlying it all is the role of dissent at various levels, dissent being the operative core of the political process. Indeed, underneath the surface stillness, much is on the boil, only waiting to find institutional or societal expression.

For, the crux of real change lies in the bottom-up processes inherent in democratic politics that have yet remained latent. Many of the new stirrings at the bottom indicate the growth of a new democratic process. A new revolution is unfolding leading to a growing consciousness and political activism among the masses. New social formations are under way; class as a factor, producing fresh turbulence amongst castes and tribal groups; the rise of a new middle class in the form of other backward castes (OBCs) that own land and are relatively prosperous even though they may have been left behind in the social arena. Then, there are new types of movements found to be growing among the women, the youth, the unemployed, the migrants – the whole spectrum of what can be called the underclass of history.

DEMOCRACY: IN SEARCH OF A THEORY

A broader perspective on the issues raised in the introduction will be provided in this essay. We live in an age of democratic consciousness. Age-old hegemonies are being challenged or have crumbled. Ideological doctrines fashioned to perpetuate dominance and control are being widely questioned.

Recognition

It is not well recognized that we also live in an age of growing backlash and crushing onslaught against democratic forces; an age of cooptation of the voices of protest and intellectual dissent. New hegemonies are being configured and perpetuated. Widely held beliefs and deeply ingrained doctrines – of security, stability and unity – are being used to pursue patterns of governance that are clearly anti-democratic. It is even less clearly recognized that the very structures that have been conceived for promoting the democratic process and providing liberation from traditional constraints – political parties, representative institutions and the judiciary – are becoming vulnerable to the influence of anti-democratic forces. Democratic structures are proving incapable of dealing with these forces. There are some major exceptions to be found among the judiciary, the press and the intellectuals.

Perhaps the least recognized are the deep forces of erosion, uncertainty and anomie that are taking hold of the middle-class mind at a time when the vacuums created by the undermining of institutions and the decline of democratic temper are being filled by specialists in violence, corruption, private arms trade and gang warfare. All of which is leading up to a sharp decline in the role of the political process set up in motion by conscientious members of political parties and administrative services. Their ability to mediate social conflicts and restore faith in the democratic process among the people and the 'operators of the system' has been severely limited. The result has not only been political instability, but also a tendency to engage in activities that fragment and destabilize the social order. Disruptions in

SyncMaster 740N
NEWS DIGEST
Mob attacks train in Gujarat, 58 killed
Vajpayee links Godhra incident to temple issue, Advani warns VHP of stern action
Prevent entry of 'Ram sevaks' into Ayodhya: Centre
VHP calls for Maharashtra bandh on Friday
Vajpayee cancels visit to Australia
Goa house dissolved
Malaysia stuns India
Suspend temple campaign, PM tells VHP
YOU SAID IT
100% job assurance
I'LL CARRY OUR LUGGAGE YOU CARRY OUR RAIL FARE
SAMSUNG

the functioning of the democratic system and a wide range of conflicts in the social arena have been the consequences of such erosion. The conflicts include social violence, the rise of negativist identities (communal and otherwise), and the growth of doctrines of exclusion and dispensability according to which entire populations are dismissed as unwanted.

Finally, the real actors and movements that have been struggling for the civil and democratic rights of various segments are being engulfed by new vulnerabilities of the communal or ethnic kind, or are being pushed out of public consciousness. As the public is overwhelmed by immediate issues of stability and survival, the challenges of economic survival, gender inequities, ecological destruction and human rights are neglected. Institutional channels that had been devised for dealing with these challenges are choked and all manner of narrow and selfish interests are exploiting state power.

Erosion

Central to this scenario of social and political erosion is the sharp decline in the legitimacy and authority of what was considered until recently the key institution of civil society – the modern state. Both the conception of the state as a negative good where authoritative assumption of disproportionate power was considered essential for providing order and security, and the more positive conception of the state as an instrument of liberation and transformation have suffered a decline in credibility.

There are many reasons for the erosion of the authority and legitimacy of the state. First, the erstwhile vision in making the state a condition for civilized existence has been under attack from two antagonistic forces – those who would subject every institution to the homogenizing impulse of economic development and technology; and those who would insistently defend the autonomy of diverse cultures and identities. Pitchforked between these globalist and decentralist thrusts, the institutions of the state have been found to be doubly vulnerable.

Second, a marked change has taken place in the growth of both left-wing and right-wing ideologies which have had a direct bearing on the role of the state. The left-wing perspective has moved from a statist conception of power for reordering society to a grassroots conception of rights for deprived classes, genders and environments. There has also been a change in the very conception of rights, with the colour having shifted from red to green. The rightist idea of making the state a defender of order and security in diverse national settings has given way to the principle of the market as the new integrative ideology at the global level. Once again the state is caught between globalist and localist pressures.

Third, a completely new set of interests has emerged in the public arena. There are global corporate interests arising from the latest phase of capitalism with transnational corporations as key factors. These interests are not merely economic and technological. For there are new extensions of the state and the corporate structure that are rooted in world militarization, impinging on the nation-state in the guise of providing it muscle. At a deeper level, there are revivalist and fundamentalist pressures emanating from the social and cultural terrain that are also challenging the authority of the state. The traditional institutions of the state and polity – legislatures and courts, political parties and the bureaucracy – are unable to cope with these new and powerful interests and pressures.

Fourth, as the institutions of the state are overwhelmed by these opposing tendencies and interests, political leadership becomes increasingly uncertain of itself and gives way to catalysts of money and muscle power, negotiators of overt and covert deals, and commissions and kickbacks at the higher reaches of the state apparatus. As these become public knowledge, the credibility of governing structures and ultimately of the state take a sharp plunge. The result is bewilderment commonly expressed in outbursts such as 'We do not know what is happening!' It is the average citizen's lack of comprehension that accounts for the current predicament of the state.

Reassertion

Despite the erosion of institutional spaces, in fact during the period of erosion, major assertions of people's rights have taken place from many vantage points. These range from class-based struggles against upper-caste and upper-class hegemonies to the struggle for women's rights, new assertions of peripheral and forcibly displaced communities against the destruction of their environments, tribal uprisings for safeguarding their locations and lifestyles, and strident defences of cultures, regional identities and nationalities. These assertions constitute a broad range of popular awakenings, protests and social movements. People's commitment to and faith in democratic values have been rising simultaneous with the decline of these values among the elite. The result is a marked transformation in the social basis of democracy – from the early liberal defence of incremental diffusion of institutional spaces to the more radical assertion of civil liberties and democratic rights. Paradoxically, most of these struggles and demands are directed at the state, the same state that is under attack from both global and local forces. The result is that the mass of the people are still committed to the state even though the state has fallen prey to interests that have no commitment to, or even compassion for, the people.

Increasingly, shorn of its earlier autonomy from dominant interests, the state is proving incapable of responding to these various awakenings and movements, and unwilling to expand its own social base. Instead, it assumes confrontational postures vis-à-vis various sections of the people described by the media in terms of their caste, ethnicity and region, and branded by the ruling elitists as extremist, anti-social and even anti-national. The perception of the state being subjected to challenges has increased; this perception is now being used as a cover for repressive measures perpetuated by both agents of the state (police, paramilitary and armed forces) and agents of ruling juntas or parties (politicians, private armies of industrialists or landlords, and armed lumpens employed by dominant factions or communities).

It is this polarization – between a state increasingly unwilling to carry out its constitutional obligations and a people not knowing what else to turn to – that is setting the stage for the growing incidence of violence, inequity, destruction of natural resources, contraction of institutional spaces and the consequent decline in more moderate and constructive modes of dissent. Two opposing tendencies have been set in motion as a result of this polarization – a techno-managerial response from the elite (both governing and oppositional) and an ethnic (that is communal, caste or religious) response from the diverse social peripheries. The 'crisis of the state' therefore enters a critical stage as it becomes increasingly difficult to find solutions to the diverse situations facing the state *within* its own framework.

Civil society also enters a critical stage and the tendency among diverse social strata to seek frameworks outside the state and civil society grows. Meanwhile, just as a new breed of corporatism takes charge of the state, replacing the bureaucratic with the technocratic, a new breed of voluntarism takes root among the ethnic and religious minorities, deprived social groups and various non-amalgamated communities like the tribals and inhabitants of hills and forests. It is a type of voluntarism based on a combination of alienation from the state and assertion of exclusivist identities.

All these tendencies get highlighted in plural and multi-ethnic societies like India. Here democracy is expressed in and through a diversified social terrain while the state faces the task of restructuring its internal composition along lines that are quite different from those obtaining in western democracies. This accounts for the continuous stress on decentralization and, as a step in the direction of decentralization, on federalism. The advantage of a decentralized perspective is that it is conceived within the framework of the state, but is sensitive to the plurality of civil society. This perspective is as integral to the institutional model of democracy, just as it is an attempt to transform the nature of the state rather than to give up on it.

We need a new theory of democracy that can comprehend the incapacity of existing institutional and ideological models, identify the reasons for this incapacity in a fast-changing global historical setting and provide the framework of active interventions at different levels of world reality to deal with an altogether new human agenda. At present, we have no theory of democracy. The theory that emanated from the west (now defunct) was based on an inordinately atomistic view of both the individual and the state, a disproportionately homogeneous conception of social and cultural reality, and was excessively influenced by the competitive ethos of bourgeois capitalism. Neither the socialist attempt to establish a welfare state nor the communist model of people's democracy have been able to cope with the new consciousness of the rights and dignities of diverse populations that have emerged all around the world, in particular, the Third World. For, the new consciousness cannot find fulfilment by merely focusing on the capture of state power, and the policies and programmes that the state should pursue. We need a democratic theory that accepts the great diversity of human situations and yet provides coherence to them through an active political process, and opens up new and creative spaces within the framework of civil society while simultaneously restructuring the state to realize these ends. The state and civil society have to deal with the issues in the relationship between the state and democratic process in a period of growing social turmoil and global managerial response. We need a theory that seeks to redirect the attention of intellectuals and social and political activists to the institution of the state; a theory that attempts to civilize the state and to make governance more humane than it has been so far.

Such a theoretical state becomes necessary as contemporary India is in a state of turmoil. Whereas there is a widespread commitment to the democratic state in large sections of the society, we have to contend with the profound dislocations in the economic, technological and resource bases of the people, produced by the impact of the modern theory of development in the thinking of the elite. Every society must work on managing the profound consequences of modern science and technology, and the doctrine of development and theory of state that have emerged in their wake. It must deal with the fragmentation and centralization inherent in the modernist world view, and preserve the integrity and inner vitality of its traditions, communities, lifestyles and values, while fully accepting the need for change and developing the capacity to cope with such change.

Reasons for Democracy

Democracy provides the impulse towards change, an impulse that is deeply ingrained in the Indian tradition and provides the leitmotif of its current awakening, engulfing large masses of the people and informing a wide array of social movements. The political process in India is informed by the struggle between the democratic process and the technocratic drives of the elite that militate against such popular aspirations. India is (still) democratic, but for it to stay democratic will depend on the outcome of the struggle being waged not just at the sociopolitical level but also at the intellectual and philosophical levels. The values and aspirations generated by this struggle run into serious obstacles arising not so much from the structural or cultural impediments inherent in traditional society (as was presumed in much of comparative political theory until recently), but rather from the mindless pursuit of the modern developmental paradigm and the usurpation of community resources and lifestyles by the elite. This elite is keen to catch up with other societies than on working to provide equitable and humane conditions for its own people.

With the exception of 1975–76 (the Emergency years), how has India been able to remain democratic? Why, despite massive socioeconomic problems and the prolonged incapacity of governments to resolve them, has democracy not been undermined? How has the democratic polity not given way under increasing onslaughts from ethnic and regional and separatist movements, the rise in religious fundamentalism and the persisting hold of illiteracy and poverty?

These questions are, no doubt, real and genuine. But in part they continue to be posed because of their misplaced theoretical simplicity – that there is an inherent antithesis between democracy and aspects like tradition, economic backwardness, strong parochial identities and low developmental indices of modernization (literacy, urbanization, exposure to mass media, and the spread of rationality and scientific values and temper). If we accept such a standardized conception of the essential 'prerequisites' of democracy, India is bound to be a deviant case, as has been argued from both the right and the left in modern western thought. These arguments ignore the great relevance of tradition and culture to imparting depth and resilience to a democratic polity.

India is a deviant case in a much more fundamental sense – most threats to democracy in India arise from the sector that promotes modernity. The pursuit of state power by this sector crushes traditional pluralities in an effort to turn the country into a modern, united, prosperous and powerful economy and polity. The real threats come from the social strata that are found to be working for this 'modern' enterprise, from those very centres of power and expertise that are destabilizing Indian traditions and the vast populace that is still steeped in those traditions. It is only because of the great appeal for large masses of the people of the very idea of democracy, and of the need to struggle for it, that the country continues to be democratic. Therefore, while India might suffer reverses and occasionally experience widespread civil strife and even an authoritarian backlash, its future as a democracy is assured.

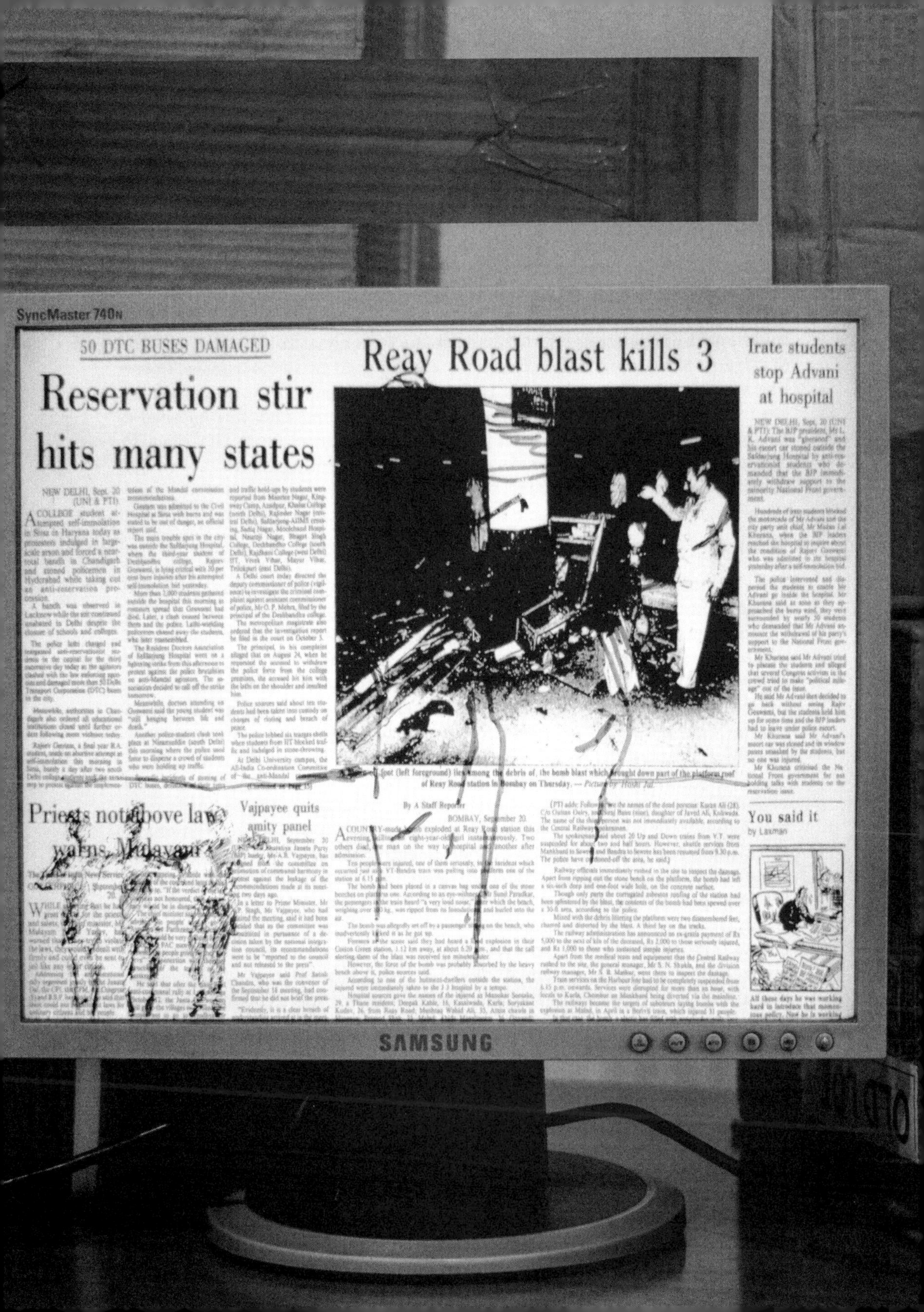
SyncMaster 740N
50 DTC BUSES DAMAGED
Reservation stir hits many states
Reay Road blast kills 3
Irate students stop Advani at hospital
Priests not above law, warns Mulayam
Vajpayee quits amity panel
You said it
by Laxman
By A Staff Reporter
BOMBAY, September 20.
SAMSUNG

THE DEMOCRATIC POLITY: PHILOSOPHICAL AND CULTURAL PERSPECTIVES

India is one of the few countries that has consciously chosen a democratic form of government and followed the choice within a series of progressive measures to empower the people. On examination, it is clear that India has fallen short of realizing what it had set out to achieve. It is the same state of affairs with many other countries claiming to be democracies. There has never been a time when democracy has not been at the crossroads. As we move further into the twenty-first century, democracy has entered a period of prolonged crisis, with growing ambivalence about the specific goals that should be pursued. As a system of conducting human affairs, it is being viewed with increasing uncertainty.

Emerging Threats

The tremendous impact of technological power on the span and size of governmental and corporate organizations has shaken the earlier assumptions on which democratic polity was based. Centralization of initiative, growth in the manipulative component of organizational behaviour at the expense of the participant component, and the growing institutional complexity in the management of power have all led to an increasingly corporate organization of not just the economy but the state as well.

The new economic framework of high capitalism, high technology and high affluence for the elite strata of society is the second major factor taxing the democratic polity. It is a framework in which a growing inflationary spiral has greatly escalated the cost of essential raw materials, agricultural inputs and energy, and consequently the cost of food, shelter and health. Internationally, this framework – whose basic features derive from the Euro-American lifestyle normative even in the vast peripheries of the globe characterized by massive poverty, unemployment and undernourishment – has resulted in growing competition for the distribution of scarce world resources. This problem is further confounded by the growing share of arms production and sale in the economic activity of major industrial nations, militarizing their economy and militarizing nations of the Third World. The acquisition of military hardware exported by the industrialized countries to the Third World spells disaster for the peace in the latter regions. Militarization strains the capacity of the Third-World people to resist the oppression and genocidal acts perpetrated by their governments. The short-term economic revival of industrialized societies identified as democracies may be assisted by arms production on an unprecedented scale, but it can only undermine the fine balance on which their democratic and pluralist polities have all along rested, and at the same time produce an external environment which will destroy the balance of the international order, in particular, Third-World polities and cultures.

Long-Term Trends

Threats to the survival of democratic polity have arisen not only due to the recent developments in the secular arrangements in the domestic and international spheres. They are also the consequence of a basic conflict in the *weltanschauung* of the modern world that can be traced back to the evolution of the west, starting with the Renaissance, crystallizing in the Enlightenment, and flowering in the age of the Industrial Revolution and modern capitalism.

If we examine the malaise that has overtaken humanity in recent times – organized and accelerating violence, decline in human empathy and compassion, growth in exploitation and cruelty, coexistence of corrupting affluence and dehumanizing misery – we are forced to take a hard look at the peculiar world view and philosophy of life, modernity, that first evolved in Western societies and has since spread throughout the world.

In general, the history of western society constitutes the struggle to discover a viable social and political order with a view to minimize the capriciousness of nature, and the solitariness and inherent brutality of man ('man' here represents all that is human). This has been the concern of almost all influential thinkers of the west, despite the Socratic concern with virtue and Pascal's counsel against unlimited rationalism. What has mattered most in western thinking is how to evolve a perfect, good, beneficent and affluent society. As there was inherent evil in man that resulted in strife and wars, it was necessary to not view the great expressions of the human mind as ends in themselves, but as means in the creation of an efficient society free from strife, violence, arbitrariness and unpredictability. Hence the need to not only discover the laws of nature and subject nature to human control but also, as with Hobbes, to discover the laws of human nature and to subject its vagaries to covenants governing all men. Or alternatively, as with Hegel and Marx, to uncover the laws governing history and realize the progressive principles in history that are at once desirable and inevitable.

Such a view of man's place in the universe has generated a powerful sense of man's mastery over nature. Knowledge of the laws of nature has become an important condition of human freedom. The model of scientific cognition and manipulation of the environment has been applied with equal force to human nature and its potentiality, to the building of social and political institutions, and to the conquest of time itself.

In spite of the sense of mastery over nature and the confidence in building an efficient social order, however, modern man's capacity to relate himself to the universe is limited in two major areas. The first involves man and his ability to exercise control over his desires and passions. Although modern biology and psychology have made some spectacular advances in laying bare the process of human evolution, it appears as if the very instruments of domination and control that modern man has perfected vis-à-vis his environment have taken on a Frankensteinian quality and made him the prisoner of his own achievements. Science and industry – the presumed agents of human liberation – have been transformed from being the means of self-realization, to being ends in themselves.

The second limitation of modern man's cognitive capacity involves the very relationship between man and nature that has been the main concern of science. Modern man is in continuous tension with nature. The relationship is based not on an integral view of nature but, rather, on one of manipulation of external objects that become instruments of man's power and righteousness. This is a serious shortcoming in the phenomenological perspective that underlines both modern science and modern philosophy. The divorce between science and morality informs this perspective. The axiology of the latter still falls outside the scope of science. Reason, the principal instrument of scientific method, is limited to the arena of empirical truth in the cognitive sense and has not yet been extended to cover the fields of ethics and aesthetics. Given this limitation, the challenge of evolving an integrated human consciousness remains unresolved. This is the basic weakness of the scientific world view, as it has developed so far.

Immanuel Kant's characterization of western humanism with the belief of each man being an end in himself, led in time to the idea of a free will and to a gradual separation of the world of values from the world of nature. Underlying this schism is the splitting of the human psyche into isolated components of cognition and connation, and, in turn the separation of law from the entities of which it is a law. The concept of free will thrived on such a separation and in secular life gave rise to the meaningless problem, first posed by Plato, of uniting the philosopher and the king.

Such a separation between man and nature, body and mind, intellect and feeling, has produced a mental climate of arrogance. Man in his position of command does not feel the need to view his relationship to the rest of existence as constituting an organic whole. The most striking evidence of this thinking can be seen in the manner in which the findings of Charles Darwin were used for social and philosophical ends. Instead of heeding Darwin's central thesis on the animal origins of man, and his demonstration of the basic unity and continuity in the evolutionary process, his nineteenth-century interpreters were more impressed by the concepts of natural selection and survival-of-the-fittest that appeared to establish man as a superior being. This interpretation has been challenged in recent times but the mindset to which it gave rise continues to persist.

The mindset persists in the Third World too. The gospel of modernization – based on a package of urbanization, achievement motivation, mass media exposure, specialized education, spatial mobility and a rising consumption of finished goods – that has overtaken and intoxicated the westernized middle class in the Third World, has been the principal vehicle of contemporary processes of economic expansion, cultural domination and political hegemony. Its universalizing credo is deeply affecting the autonomy of individual human beings, diverse cultures and most nations as well. It has shaken the self-respect of peoples, made them feel ashamed of their own traditions, and has given rise to a high degree of ambivalence in their relationship to their own societies.

New Class Ethos

It is necessary that we understand the class ethos emerging in modern society all over the world. Capitalism, socialism and social democracy in most countries of the world are being increasingly defined by a middle-class elite that has adopted the model of a technocratic state in which political, industrial and military power are concentrated. It is significant that the economic ethic underlying capitalism has undergone a major shift. Capitalism no longer depends on the habits of thrift and saving that were highlighted in the conception of the Protestant ethic. It now relies on the diametrically opposed economic ethic, the ethic of constant want and waste, that is necessary to keep the industrial machine and its managerial edifice functioning. It is also significant that communism, where it has survived, has also changed its original rationale of freeing human beings from the reified constraints of wage labour, class and the state, to demonstrating technological power and industrial efficiency.

Almost in every part of the globe there has been a growth in the manipulative component of the modern state and its industrial mainstay, both of which are dominated by bureaucrats and professional managers. These groups have firm command in the developing countries too, partly because they are in control in the metropolitan centres. The technocrats of the world operating from command positions operate in a class of their own. In this situation, the role of politics as an exercise of options by ordinary human beings – for freedom, equality and a classless society – is contracted by the concentration of power among a few. This was inherent in the hedonistic world view that assumed charge of modern man and his productive apparatus in the last hundred and fifty years. Therefore, the great advances of modern science and technology have only succeeded in reiterating the elementary problem of human survival – now on a world scale and with the aid of instruments of mass destruction. A war with nuclear weapons or a collapse of the environment may annihilate a large part of the human race.

The Role of Knowledge

Central to the model of life and the class formations it has originated across the world is the role of knowledge in human affairs. Never before had the product of the human mind acquired so dominant a role in the shaping of societies as in modern times. It has changed the world beyond recognition. Its basic contribution has been to give man a tremendous sense of power and the capacity to manipulate. Nothing else could have made man – especially the educated man – so arrogant as this particular role of knowledge. And it has made the purveyors of this knowledge, in collusion with the users of this knowledge, a class in themselves.

It is not that knowledge has by itself brought humanity to grief. The rise of modern science has been a great liberator of man from the horrors of nature and of religious doctrine. But the original promise of the progress of science has been undermined. Because science flourished in a culture (viz. of the west) that looked upon it as an instrument of power and domination rather than as a liberator of the human spirit – knowledge as perceived by the ancient Chinese, the Indians and the Greeks – it soon became an instrument of technology. Not content with overcoming hardships and fulfilling basic needs, technology was used for continuous expansion, competition and domination. It became an instrument of monopoly and inequality with the fruits of technology diffused widely within some societies at the expense of a great many other societies which actually provided the raw materials for the prosperity of the few.

In sum, because of a particular cultural location where modern technology flourished, it has become Frankensteinian in character. The myth that modern technology has given rise to has suddenly exploded – the myth of perpetual progress, of end to scarcity, and of infinite progress accessible and available to all. Today, suddenly, the affluent world faces the consequences of the excesses of modern technology; see, for example, the animated discussion on environmental crises.

However, the environmental crisis is only a symptom of a basic change in relationship – from man's reliance on nature to man's dependence on machines. The domination of man by the machine, and his dependence on it for his sustenance, means not only just the constant and continuous need for energy and raw materials; it also entails less and less need for people. The world now has millions of 'marginal' men and women for whom society has no use. Man has become superfluous and obsolescent; he is being perceived as a burden not just on nature but also on society.

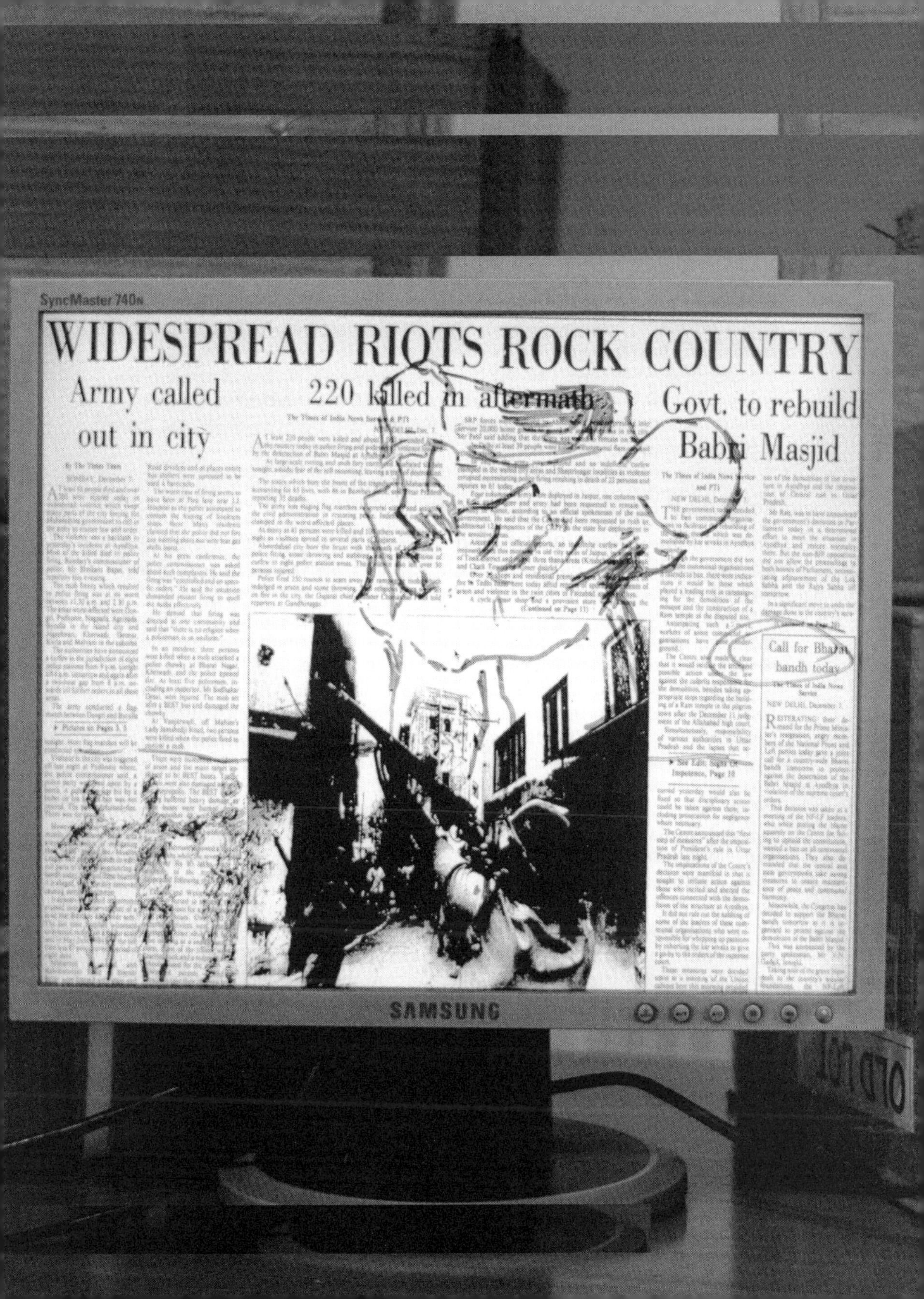
SyncMaster 740N
WIDESPREAD RIOTS ROCK COUNTRY
Army called out in city
220 killed in aftermath
Govt. to rebuild Babri Masjid
Call for Bharat bandh today
SAMSUNG
OLD LOT

Paradoxical though it may sound, man is the most dispensable in a system that modern man has produced.

The crisis faced by modern man has been wrought by a particular direction that science and technology took under the impact of the age of positivism. The full consequences of such a course are seen in our time as it envelops all the crises to which scientists and philosophers have drawn our attention – the threat of total war, of the extreme dualism of a world so divided that its very survival is at stake. It is not certain that such a badly divided species can survive the increasing states of tension and violence that it will have to face. Many other species that have confronted such conditions have perished, and none of them had possessed the man-made instruments of destruction.

Rethinking the Human Enterprise

The need to rethink the general premises of both the liberal state and the democratic polity through which it functions, is now widely recognized. Unless such rethinking takes place in the larger context of the contemporary human condition, it is not likely to succeed in creating a relevant political context in which intellectuals can find their bearings. It is necessary to relate the realm of politics to the realm of science. There is a definite need to critically review the philosophical world view which has made science an instrument of secular power, and in consequence has given rise to a specific class configuration at great variance with the assumptions of both classical liberalism and theoretical Marxism.

There is a need to move beyond both the liberal and Marxist world views, both of which are offshoots of eighteenth-century European Enlightenment and nineteenth-century mechanistic humanism. Those like John Rawls have nobly argued for rescuing the liberal doctrine from hedonistic and positivistic streams of thought; a rescue that is unrealizable. For liberalism contained the seeds of its own demise in being closely intertwined with the theory of infinite progress and the paradigm of science and techno-economic development. Marxism, the principal critique of liberalism, has also suffered from the same basic inadequacies despite the early Marx who was deeply concerned with issues of human alienation and commodity fetishism. These early writings of Marx were resuscitated by Lukacs and his followers in Hungary and elsewhere, and further developed and reformulated by members of the Frankfurt School, like Habermas, and reformers within the Marxist school, like Gramsci – all of which have been since relegated to memory.

All these attempts, as well as the critical writings of thinkers like Marcuse, can provide leads in reconsidering the basic liberal-Marxist framework of modern democracy, but basic work on the whole paradigm of modernity, focusing on issues outlined above is still necessary. Not only do we find the liberal and Marxist frameworks unable to deal with the consequences of the modern industrial state and its international ramifications; we also find that we have, in the last hundred years or so, entered a new phase of politics at both national and global levels which challenge human intelligence afresh. Elsewhere in this book, where the very idea of democracy is critiqued, we will attend to various facets of this larger challenge to human aspirations.

We have looked at the role of knowledge in the arrangement of human affairs and the shaping of societies. In rethinking the democratic model, it becomes obligatory to rethink the paradigm of science, especially that of the social sciences. The close relationship between free scientific inquiry into the structure of reality and the existence of democratic polity does not need to be argued. Social sciences especially, whether in respect to empirical research or normative questioning, cannot thrive except in democratic societies. Thorough investigation of the modes of conducting research, and financial and institutional support for it is likely to sensitize us to the perils that certain types of thinking and research and their utilization pose to democracy. Just as good social sciences can best thrive in an open society and democratic polity, the efficacy of a democratic polity and respect for it in a world at large depends vitally on the quality and integrity of its social sciences.

Social Sciences

It is now well known how certain schools of thought in American social sciences have gravely compromised the autonomy and dignity of the individual, and indeed of entire societies. The overall substantive result of American social scientists' involvement in the conduct of American foreign policy – in South East Asia, Latin America and among the Gulf nations – are not very different from the role of their counterparts in the former Soviet Union. Similar results have been produced by the 'committed intellectuals' of India. In thinking about the future, it is important to consider the ethical dimensions of the involvement of researchers and research institutes in the shaping of public policy and through it, the structure and ideological contours of modern states as well as civil societies.

Apart from such overall considerations of research policy, it is necessary to review certain fields of scholarship in order to arrest the tendency of professional pundits arrogating to themselves the right of being the arbiters of socio-economic, political and administrative systems. Certain branches of the scientific estate – management science, systems research, science policy, certain branches of economics and public administration, foreign policy analysis and area studies – are particularly prone to this type of distortion in the relationship between experts, policymakers and the general citizenry. Many of these branches have lost their moorings in basic disciplines and have established themselves as pseudo-disciplines with claims to special status as applied sciences. Without belittling the importance of certain fields of applied research, it is necessary not to make a fetish of the now-fashionable doctrine of relevance. The doctrine of relevance and these fields of applied research must be prevented from becoming the means to conformity apropos the wishes of governments and transnational corporate entities.

□

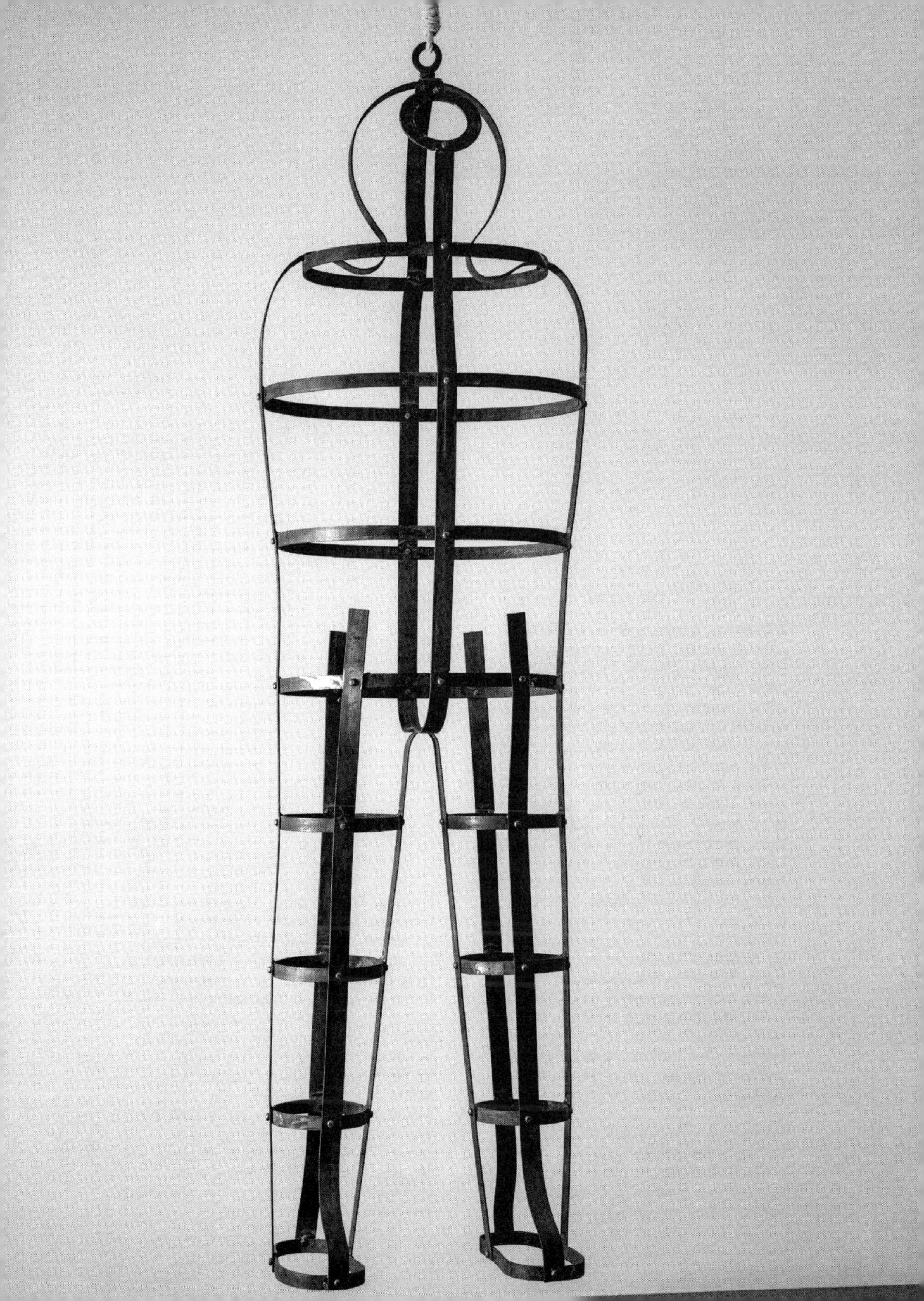

A nation is 'a thing without a past. It is radically modern. It can only look for subterfuges of antiquity. It fears to face and admit its own terrible modernity, because to admit modernity is to make itself vulnerable.' **Sudipta Kaviraj** shows how history-writing in India took on several new responsibilities to assuage the anxieties of modern nation-building, re-presenting complex political events in direct, almost linear fashion through large, general, abstract ideas and a narrative structure 'committed to a telling of a particular kind'. Such a task moves by mobilizing anachronisms, creating communities through creating a 'narrative contract'. This is one of social scientist Kaviraj's best known texts, originally published as the centrepiece of the **Subaltern Studies VII** volume edited by Partha Chatterjee and Gyanendra Pandey (Delhi: Oxford University Press, 1992, pp. 1–39), and later lending the title to the seminal collection of his own essays (**The Imaginary Institution of India: Politics and Ideas,** Ranikhet: Permanent Black, 2009).

Images: Riyas Komu, 'On International Workers' Day, Gandhi From Kochi' (oil on canvas, 2015), and **Dhamma Swaraj** (oil on canvas, 2018) from his exhibition **Holy Shiver** (2018). Frame-grab from Paromita Vohra's film **Partners in Crime** (2011) to make the point about fuzzy and enumerated communities. Deep gratitude to Riyas Komu and Paromita Vohra for permission to re-use. Images from Mehboob Khan's **Mother India** (1955), Krishnan–Panju's **Parasakthi** (1952) and Komu's diptych **Dandi Bridge** (oil on canvas, 2018) to make the point about 'anachronism' and the 'conceit of the present, the precarious ontological privilege that it enjoys over other times'.

2

SUDIPTA KAVIRAJ

1992

THE IMAGINARY INSTITUTION OF INDIA

India, the objective reality of today's history, the objectivity of which is tangible enough for people to try to preserve, to destroy, to uphold, to construct, and dismember, the reality taken for granted in all attempts in favour and against, is not an object of discovery but of invention. It was historically instituted by the nationalist imagination of the nineteenth century. The exact form this reality took was one among many historical possibilities in that situation, though the fact that only this line of possibility came to be realized is so overwhelming that it is now difficult even to conceive of some of the others. To say this is merely to assert that it is a historical object, and it is essential to speak about the contingency of its origins against the enormous and weighty mythology that has accumulated on its name.

To understand nationalism as a historical reality, it is essential to step outside the history that nationalism gives to itself. Undoubtedly, this historical description is not entirely homogeneous, and its axis shifts according to the political demands and exigencies of different periods. Still, there is a clearly identifiable narrative which, despite all its internal variations, can be called the nationalist history of nationalism. This essay does not deal with the complex history of this narrative structure, but only with a brief, comparatively early, stage: the stage at which some decisions were taken that turned out to be crucial for the later development of Indian nationalism. Its analysis might reveal some interesting features in the formation of nationalist discourse and its strategies of self-presentation.

History writing about Indian nationalism meant, for a long time, compiling in increasing detail accounts of those political events which constituted this complex fact. Ideas did of course figure in that account, often in large and dominant ways. But these related to these events in a direct, almost linear, fashion; and in order to relate in such unproblematic ways, these had to be large, general, abstract ideas which were amenable to such causal/quasi-causal attribution. To tell the story of nationalism, these were narratively committed to a telling of a particular kind: an account which separated out of the great chaos of varying ideological events a single thread, and showed nationalism arising and moving to its destiny.

By its nature, this conception of nationalism had to be homogenizing: what I mean by this inelegant term is that although these scholars were often conscious that people opposed the British with ideas that were differently inflected, grounded, expressed, coloured, stylized, motivated, the major purpose of the concept of nationalism was to point to their level of historical similarity. This does not necessarily deny the presence of other strata in these ideas or other possible and appropriate descriptions. But, clearly, what got emphasized (and not unwittingly, because this point was written into the historiographical programme) were the points of similarity, the sense in which all these Indians were doing the same thing with these ideas.

In recent years, historical thinking has tended to turn in some measure away from large, holistic, totalized histories of nationalism. The shift is expressed in several ways and at the risk of excessive simplification we could say that historical attention has tended to turn from political history to cultural history, from events to discourses, and even inside the history of ideas from the content of nationalistic thought to a more sensitive understanding of its forms. This essay focuses on one particular element or figuration of discourse – the narrative.

This figuration, though previously neglected, seems to me of some importance. It is generally conceded that the idea of nationalism stitches together, in ways that are not seriously and minutely analysed, social groups, or communities of people. Formerly, these groups and individuals would not have considered themselves as one single people, having a single political identity. After the emergence of nationalism, they somehow do. It is necessary to investigate this 'somehow', to probe into the various discursive formations within nationalism. This is not to question its consequence, but to enquire into its structure/formation. Indian culture is particularly rich in narrative traditions; and narratives traditionally performed the political function of producing and maintaining cohesion. Religious denominations and sects would maintain their distinctness and internal cohesion by the adroit use of storytelling. Hinduism implicitly recognizes the political character of these stories. It is hardly surprising that in this society, humming with political narratives, the nationalist movement would be quick to see the considerable political possibilities of narrative persuasion.

SELF-DESCRIPTION OF NATIONALISM

Ideologies seem to have a close connection with the narrative function; and this in turn relates to historiography. Indian nationalism is not merely an object of historical enquiry, but a political object – a movement, a force, a party, an establishment, a cultural interest,[1] an ideology and, finally, a state. And it is the nature of all political ideologies to try to coerce enquiry about itself into an agenda constructed by it.[2]

Historically, it is not surprising that this movement had to create a sanctioned, official history of itself. This consists of half-truths favourable to the contingent political configuration within the movement; this history is an intensely political process. But it is important to break down the abstraction of the national movement itself, and of a large formation like the Congress, in order to see the politics that are constantly at play inside historical accounts. Even within a seemingly homogeneous history, it is often essential to ask whose history this is, in the sense of history *for* whom rather than history *of* whom, because there are changes in the telling. Within seemingly homogeneous history there are conflicts between tendencies, the axis and the periphery, the mainstream and the embarrassing fringe, the self and the other. From being the inheritor of one stream, albeit the major one, such a history takes a small, subtle, perhaps historically inevitable step towards claiming to be the inheritor of all.[3]

Clearly, an operation of this kind requires an axis of some sort, a central trend around which the complex and diverse material is organized. Such displacements go on continuously; and there are appropriations within appropriations. In the rewriting . . . of the history of nationalism, this axis has been first the (Indian National) Congress, and more recently, inside the Congress, its Nehruvian stream. By the latter stage, all earlier figures are essentially measured according to their fit with a Nehruvian model of being nationalist. Admitting that those whose mental world was often communal could also be nationalists – indeed sometimes the more hysterical ones – disturbs the harmony of this official universe. This construction underestimates the alarming extent to which the power of Indian nationalism emerged from, or was a merely politically redescribed or redirected form of, the power of violated religious sentiments.

THE QUESTION OF ANACHRONISM AND PERIODIZATION

Anachronism uses the presumption that earlier periods and cultures were structured like our own in their institutions, practices, discourses, meanings, and significations of concepts, etc. Thus the whole universe of significations and causalities of the modern period (however the 'modern period' is identified) are thrown backwards on them. Historians tend sometimes to forget that there is a requirement of minimal distanciation before objects of the past can begin to be properly described. Quite often the worst appropriation occurs not in the process of evaluative judgement but in the apparently innocent act of describing.

The conceit of the present, the precarious ontological privilege that it enjoys over other times, is expressed often in another, subtler, and more fundamental fault of historical vision. This is the temptation to believe that the only function of the past, its only conceivable justification, was to produce the present. According to this procedure, only those aspects of the past are given great descriptive salience that seem to have some causal affiliation with events and structures of the present time.

All nationalist discourse after the coming of Gandhi tries to answer the implicit question: how could Indians best defeat and remove British rule? Arguments about home rule, dominion status, complete independence, for example, are all different answers to the same historical question. They fall . . . within the same horizon of political history, a concept that usefully but undogmatically distinguishes between the possible and the impossible. On closer inspection it appears that, in earlier horizons of anti-colonial discourse, this question is entirely absent. If we turn to the historical horizon inhabited by the Bengali writers such as Bankimchandra (Chattopadhyay) or Bhudev Mukhopadhyay,[4] this question, at least in this form, does not lie within the orbit of possibility of their thinking.[5] *Paradhinata* – subjection to alien rule – is both too fresh and too overwhelming to permit such unfeasible thoughts. Alien rule is a kind of *a priori* of their thinking, a deeply hated limit which they, for all their hatred of it, are not able to transcend. All possible thought operations are consequently carried out taking that condition for granted. These authors remain within these limits not because they like British rule. In some ways their rejection of a colonizing western rationalist civilization often goes deeper and is more fundamental than that of later nationalists; but they simply do not see the end of colonial subjection as a historically feasible project. For them, the epochal historical question around which all social reflection revolved, was: how did a civilization with such varied resources become subject to colonialism? But this was a question very different from the one of how such subjection could be politically ended. It is important to remember, methodologically, that they are not answering

that second and later question in the negative; the question does not get asked within their discourse.

Anachronism distorts our historical judgement by making it appear that the question around which their thinking was structured was also the self-evident one of later, more mature, nationalist thought. What, in this view, can be a more central, a more natural theme of nationalist discourse than the end of imperial subjection? Besides, how can we call a discourse 'nationalist' until it has the courage to pronounce that elemental defiance? Those who argue on these lines make, in my view, an initially correct point, but fail to draw the correct conclusion. They assume that the thinking, or more diffusely the *mentalite*, of these generations was nationalist, but of a weak, hesitant, compromising kind. But this is unconvincing. Indeed, their discourse was not really nationalist in the narrow sense if the internal conceptual condition for use of the adjective is the presence of the idea of a determinate nation with clear boundaries, unambiguous principles of inclusion, established by a clear act of choice. Later, we shall see that there are substantive reasons as well for withholding this common description.

But the argument for homogenizing nationalism is so plausible and forceful that it is difficult to remain unaffected by its seduction. Ironically, historians who strenuously avoid the company of ordinary nationalism for ideological reasons do on occasion fall into its methodological trap. Once, we admit the plausibility of the homogenizing view, we agree to the fundamental mistranslation of the two questions as strict equivalents; then, it is impossible to keep away from standard anachronistic answers and judgements. If the later question resounds everywhere in the history of colonial societies, it would seem that writers of an earlier period were answering it in the negative. In cruder versions of such history writing, the thought of a writer who considered freedom politically impossible but found colonialism so hateful that he could not stop dreaming about it, would be firmly shown to be a collaborator of British rule. This must happen if history is inattentive towards the way in which time and experiential horizons slowly shift and construct a paradigm-like internality of questions, answers, procedures, presuppositions, defiance and conformity. In that case historical horizon is not a metaphor, but a real rigorous historical concept. Otherwise, we slide very often into the notorious difficulties of reading silences.

There is a second form in which the infelicity of anachronism recurs in the analysis of Indian nationalism. An anachronistic view would imply that when we are looking for the history, i.e. the origins, the earlier stages of Indian nationalism, we must encounter it in some suitably smaller, paler, or otherwise immature form – a small-scale version of the later fully-blown nationalism. In early periods, we would thus expect to meet a paler version of patriotism, not the burning enthusiasm for one's country that is felt apparently by later Congressmen or their intellectual representatives. This view finds it much more difficult to acknowledge a patriotism for something else other than an ancestor for Indian nationalism because today those two patriotisms would be politically opposed. Surprisingly, it appears that there is no such necessary connection between being patriotic and being Indian. Indeed, historically speaking, this configuration of consciousness becomes nationalist before it becomes Indian. Happily, Indianness is not entirely an afterthought; but it is certainly a later occurrence. Had it been only an afterthought, this Indianness would have been a mere insubstantial pretence and a large historical movement and a constitutional democratic state after Independence could not be hung on that wispy thread. Because it was an historically available identity, though of later origin, it could perform such historical tasks. Anachronism, by pretending that it was an identity existing from immemorial times, encourages unjustified optimism; an appreciation of its more recent and comparatively precarious historical career would imply the chastening idea that this people have not been used to being Indian for very long, and political policies must take into account its recentness.

THE DISCOVERY OF A NATIONAL COMMUNITY

The intractable modernity of the new identity of a nation, especially a nation mobilized to act for itself, constantly troubles the thinking of early nationalists. They have not yet named a community which would take the responsibility of opposition to colonialism. Curiously, far from there being a united India – an immanent nation, which is repressed, the processes of consciousness themselves show to what extent nationalism is a historical product of colonialism, how, in spite of their fundamental difference, colonialism was a historical precondition for any modern nationalist consciousness. Thus the responsibility, the role, the character of nationalism emerges earlier in history than the community that will perform this responsibility; the responsibility is born before its agent. And contrary to what is said in the common hagiography of the Indian nation, what this community will be is a matter of some confusion and occasionally of dispute. It is possible for early writers to speculate about a Hindu or a Muslim community filling this role, as much as a territorial identity of a radically new order.

Since these writers have still not chosen their nation, it is more appropriate to call the political consciousness of this phase by some other term, for instance *anti-colonialism*. But it is an error to think that until nationalism in the latter-day sense arrives, there is no political consciousness. To equate the political and the nationalist is once more a powerful instrument of nationalist ideological accounts. It disallows any opposition to colonialism other than itself, any dissent organized on other lines the title to oppositional glory. Yet, any involvement with the structure of colonial power – the whole range of political things in the colonial world from its political economy to its world of significations to its politics of language, the battle between the high language of colonialists and the vernacular – must be seen as political.

Anti-colonialism, in the sense in which I am using the term *faute des mieux,* is very different from the usual one in which Marxists commonly use it. This structure of thought is a merely oppositional attitude towards colonialism, and if we gather up all its historical characteristics, it is more a cultural critique, a resentment against ignominy rather than a political–economic rejection of its civilizing pretensions. Its melancholy does not begin to turn into optimism before it changes into nationalism proper. From being a negative reaction to colonial power, it turns positively into a consciousness of a new identity. It must be seen, however, that this something which it supports is not present to it in an objective form. It has got to be constructed, imagined into existence. And the pessimism of anti-colonial consciousness arises partly because of its failure to find easily an adequate social base for its dissatisfaction and its critique. Hostility against colonialism, which is all-conquering, is felt from the ground of older, limited, fragmented identities – of regions, Hindus, Muslims, Bengalis, or rather babus[6] – none of whom in their thinking about history seemed to have much of a chance of success against the colonial machine. For that historical optimism to emerge, they had to find a new identity; although this identity is produced by gerrymandering earlier ones: someone like Bankim could say cleverly that this identity, this new 'we', has never been defeated, because it has never opposed colonialism historically.

But the remarkable thing is that the collective subject is not related to developed nationalism by a relation of standard ontogeny. It is not a smaller, weaker, thinner, earlier form of the same subject that will be called the nation. The nation [is] a thing without a past. It is radically modern. It can only look for subterfuges of antiquity. It fears to face and admit its own terrible modernity, because to admit modernity is to make itself vulnerable. As a proposal for modern living, on a scale quite unprecedented (both in terms of sheer spread and the sheer power of good and evil it can do to itself by establishing a modern state), in a society still knowing only one legitimizing criterion – tradition – it must seek to find past disguises for these wholly modern proposals.[7]

Anti-colonialism is originally pronounced by traditional collective selves, communities which were given in terms of earlier, more segmented, social definitions. At this stage, the community which performs this *enonciation,* or hopefully will in the near future, remains curiously indeterminate. It

SATYA / **PERCEPTION**

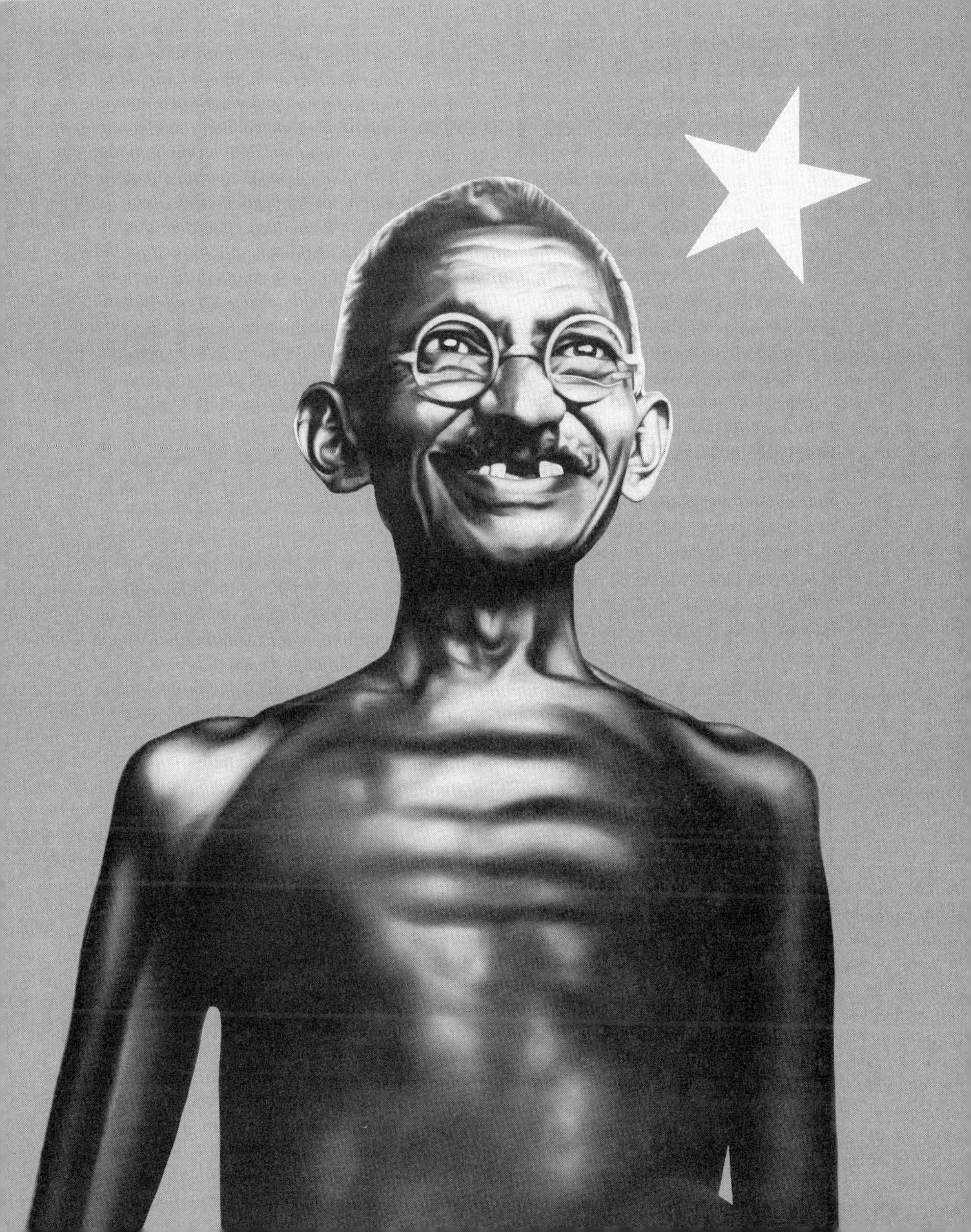

is a rather unclear 'we' who are invited to do this. Indeed, it seems that late-nineteenth-century writers were curiously uninterested in spelling it out, in turning their attention towards an analysis of the strengths and weaknesses of this group, and suggesting a political theory for forming it into an ideal strength adequate to its enormous task. The intellectual process is not directed towards a self-enumeration of the collective subject, still left hazy, immediate, primordial. Arguments are typically concerned with undermining the ideological claims of the colonial administration and its collaborators, that strident claim which particularly irritates Indians that the British were civilizing a savage people. These are concerned with the acceptability of the modernity – truncated, opportunistically edited, and abbreviated – offered historically through colonialism. Often it discusses the comparative principles of organization of the two social orders.[8]

Later, this 'we' becomes coterminous with Indians; but the process through which this happens is instructive. Indianness, along with other attributes and entities of the social world, is also a historical construct. Actually, this India was new, but it required the delusion of an eternal existence. And interestingly, it was European writers writing on India as part of a counter-Enlightenment movement who constructed this India and presented it to Indians looking for an identity.

Whatever its source in western scholarship or Indian publicistic material, this pretence of Indian antiquity was entirely necessary and at the same time largely false. Accordingly, it is impossible to innocently assume the mythology of nationalism that this India was suppressed (i.e. it must exist in order to be suppressed), and gradually won the strength, the cohesion, a god-gifted political organization and leadership, to rise to consciousness and freedom. In fact, this historical process was a less linear, and far more tentative affair.

Interestingly, the British could write 'histories of India' much more unproblematically than their Indian imitators, for they wrote of an India that was externally defined, a territory contingently unified by political expansion. To define the boundaries of British India was a simple operation; this merely required looking at the latest map of British annexations. By contrast, the India that Nehru so painstakingly discovered was an India more difficult to define, for the nationalists he represented sought to demarcate its boundaries by a more elusive internal principle.

To give itself a history is the most fundamental act of self-identification of a community. The naming of the Indian nation, I wish to suggest, happens in part through a narrative contract. To write a history of India beginning with the civilization of the Indus valley is marked by an impropriety. An India internally defined, an India of a national community, simply did not exist before the nineteenth century; there is, therefore, an inevitable element of 'fraudulence', in Gellner's sense,[9] in all such constructions. 'The history of India' is a massively self-evident thing to write about and this powerful transformation of something that is fundamentally insecure into something aggressively self-evident is precisely the mark of an ideological construct. It is ideological because there seems to be no other reasonable way of writing the history of these historical objects.

FUZZY AND ENUMERATED COMMUNITIES

Imagined communities can place their boundaries in time and space anywhere they like. It is not always reasonable to look for the objective criteria for these things. Another way of saying this would be that the objectivity they often display is a historical form of objectivity. It is impossible to justify the objectivity of the entire narrative, but easy to see the difficult objectivity of its consequences. But there is another point to be made about imagined communities. Whether imaginary or real, this way of conceiving a community is a very modern and unprecedented theoretical device. Acquaintance with European history since the Renaissance surely helped intellectuals to use this idea and devise an appropriate form of this for themselves. To understand its implications, let us first try to set out clearly what is involved in this claim. Imaginary or real, these arguments describe and conceive its community in ways that are quite different from earlier, more genuinely communitarian, ways of conceiving one.[10]

Let us call the earlier conceptions of community *fuzzy*. As this is bound to be a contested idea, let me try to be clear about what exactly fuzzy means in this context. Any idea of community is based on an idea of identity, which is predicated in turn on some conception of difference. People who lived in pre-modern social forms had of course a strong sense of community, usually more intense than those of modern societies. They handled their daily experience of social complexity through some system of rules by which people could be classified as similar or different and dealt with accordingly. As contacts with people of other groups were relatively infrequent, it did not require an elaborately developed theory of otherness.

Despite the considerable resources of this distinction, there appears to exist a more complex dialectic between community and nationalist modernity which tends to be underplayed in the use of such a strongly dichotomous model. Modern nationalism commonly arises out of an aspiration to control the forces of modernity, and is therefore affiliated to the rise and growth of *gesellschaft* organizations. If modern nationalism is seen to be affiliated to these processes of transformation of social forms, this produces a paradox. Historically, these organizations tend to erode – either explicitly or by subtler, undeclared processes – the earlier types of smaller, tighter, closer organizational patterns. Yet, in a sense, nationalism tries to steal, to use Marx's phrase, the poetry of primordiality from them, to try to argue about and justify itself through a wholly illegitimate discourse of immemorial aspirations and indissoluble community. Nationalist movements usually try to show the nation, actually a product of a conjuncture of modernity, to be a community which was lost – to be regained. Quite often this regaining requires large-scale political sacrifices which ordinary people are unlikely to accept if they calculate their political actions in a purely rationalistic accounting of individual cost and benefit. The language of monadic individuals and their purely calculating contractual interests does not suit the rhetoric of passion – blood, sacrifice, remembrance – that nationalism as a movement requires.[11] So, although a modern phenomenon, nationalism must speak a 'traditional' language of communities.

Let us now turn to another question: the relation between the nation and those identities which historically precede it, and with which it must be partly at least in competition. In the argument influenced by the modern/traditional opposition, sometimes the relation is seen in excessively dichotomous terms. These arguments ascribe to pre-existing community identities a certain inexplicated 'pregivenness'. Communities (which, it must be seen, refer to a principle of organization, rather than one form of groups) are called primordial, and the way that term is used amounts to an effective denial of history.

Ostensibly, primordiality indicates an organization which is so resistant to change as not to be transformed across historical time. In fact, however, much that is declared primordial and 'historyless' turns out to be historical on closer inspection.[12] Occasionally, these may actually be recent constructions which, like fake antiques, are bestowed an artificially produced look of decay. In pre-modern societies, antiquity is given such high value that constructed things might include in their principle of construction itself a mechanism that seems to erase their historical age. Recently founded dynasties are in particular need of showing their ancestry from the descendants of mythological heroes.

Ironically, if we look at the evidence, it appears that the question – which is prior, the nation or the region? – turns out to be false, or at least not very helpful. Actually, the region, though culturally more homogeneous, is as much a historical construction as the nation. More startlingly, in some cases, the formation of a linguistic region is not of much greater antiquity than the coming of an anti-colonial consciousness, for the rise of a distinct regional language was related to some developments linked to colonialism. This is particularly clear in the case of the Bengali language.

Even Bengal, a most culturally self-conscious region, has difficulties in fitting together a model of a long pre-existing language and a sense of

AHIMSA / **VIOLENCE**

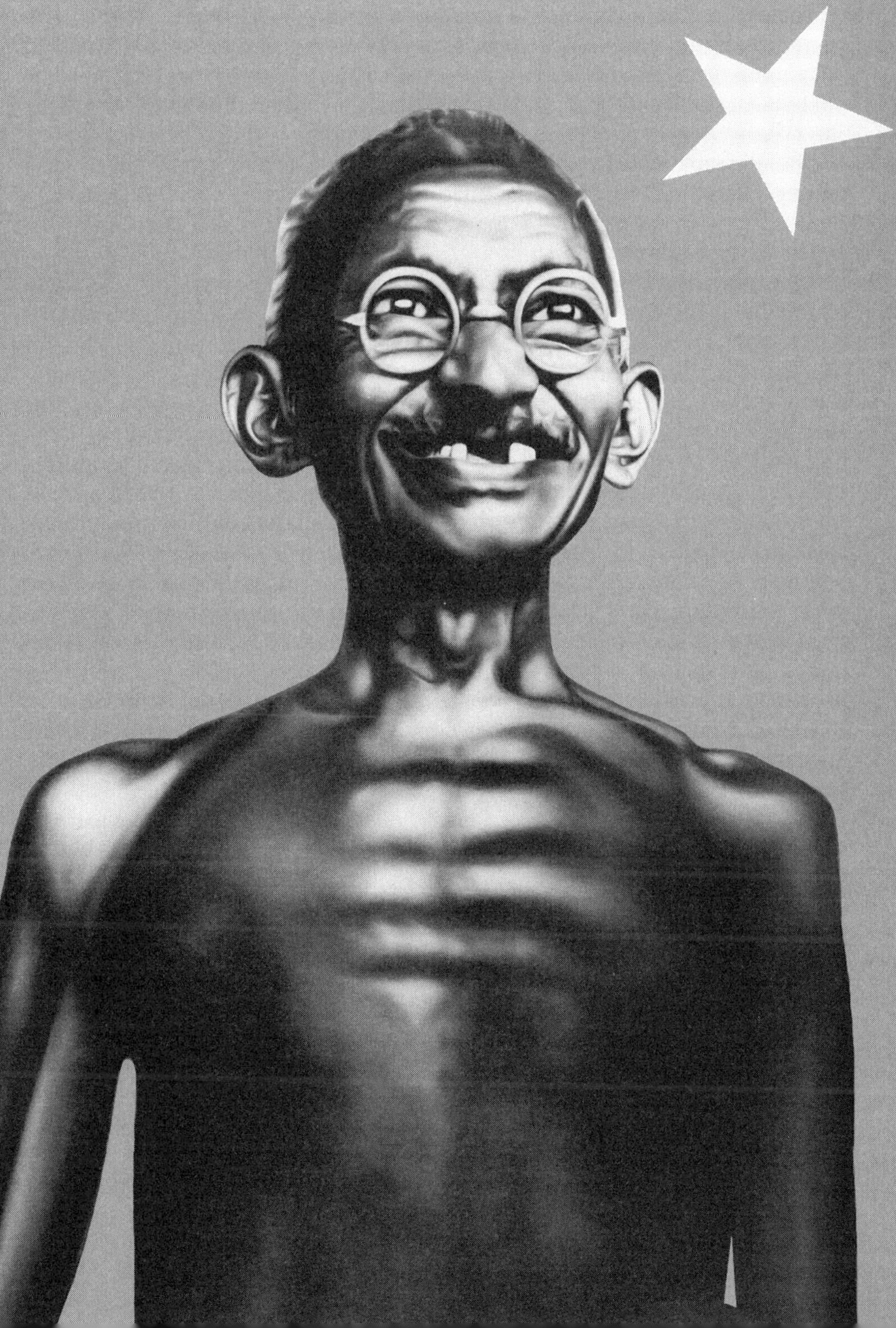

'Indian' nationhood that is relatively recent. In defining regions, language is usually the most significant criterion. But this language – which confers on the region its unity and its name – is not a given.[13] Before the British came, the linguistic map of 'Bengal' would have been quite confused and unfamiliar. The use of language was stratified in several ways. For some purposes, traditionally, Sanskrit served as an inaccessible elite language; for others, Arabic and Persian. The inaccessibility of these languages to ordinary people was complemented on the other side by their universality among the elite. Thus the structure, in linguistic terms, would generally replicate the structure of agrarian societies that Gellner outlines in his *Nations and Nationalism* (1983).

Subsequently, the new literate elite created by western education gradually drop the courtly Arabic/Persian or the priestly Sanskrit as languages of high culture; they try to create a high-culture Bengali via the structural, sometimes even syntactic, imitation of English. Gradually, through the historical selection of the privileged dialect of some area, this elite gives rise to a new norm language. The growth of printing, and the possibilities of standardization it contained, helped this norm language to be consciously adopted by the elites of the subregions; so much so that they become gradually ashamed to utter the dialect which would have been, in an earlier era, the cultural flag of their region. Once such a 'high' language develops, all dialects can now be differentiated from it as lower-order languages. Only now is it possible to draw a linguistic map of a region with some amount of clarity, since what happens in Bengal is repeated in the appropriate regions of Bihar and Orissa by similar norm-setting processes around a similarly constructed Hindi and Oriya language. In less than a hundred years an area which was covered by a mass of small dialects gets restructured linguistically into two or three regions using the highly self-conscious languages of their respective high cultures.

Let us return now to some aspects of what we had earlier called the fuzzy community. In several ways, the communities in which people saw themselves as living were fuzzy compared to the community of the nation that is now proposed. This does not imply that earlier individuals did not know how to handle social complexity in the form of the presence of others in their own life experience. They would meet other individuals routinely inside their villages, or sometimes in non-standard ways, as on pilgrimages. On all such occasions, they would have at their disposal fairly elaborate sets of rules for differentiation by which their responses to others would be determined. If the other person belonged to one level of his community – say, his endogenous caste group – he would know exactly what to do with him. However, such precision did not extend to other aspects of a person's identity or community: it was directed to only certain types of activities and practices.

Thus, earlier communities tend to be fuzzy in two ways in which no nation can afford to be. First, they have fuzzy boundaries, because some collective identities are not territorially based. Religion, caste and endogamous groups are all based on principles that are not primarily territorial. Indeed, there would be a sense that the 'region', the world that is near, is set within a world that is large, far away, vast and limitless, but both the nearness and the vastness would be fuzzy in the same sense. People would be hard put and indeed could not be bothered to tell where the near ended and the far began.

Secondly, part of this fuzziness of social mapping would arise because traditional communities, unlike modern ones, were not enumerated. The most significant implication of this is the following: they did not see historical processes as things which could be bent to their collective will if people acted concertedly on a large-enough scale. Since they did not ask how many of them there were in the world, they could not consider what they could wreak upon the world, for their collective benefit – through collective action. They were thus incapable of a type of large action, with great potential for doing harm as well as good, which is a feature of the modern condition. Living in an unmapped and unenumerated world may have allowed them to live ordinarily in non-aggressive proximity (though one should not underestimate the ability of older societies to do surprisingly large-scale collective harm). Their sense of community being multiple and layered and fuzzy, no single community could make demands of pre-emptive belonging as comprehensive as those made by the modern nation state.[14]

The boundaries of nation states cannot be fuzzy in the same way. Indeed, the territorial attachment of modern states is sometimes so intense as to be rationally incomprehensible, as evident from the cheerful intensity with which modern nations fight wars for control of uninhabitable land. Secondly, a parallel principle, the national community, must be enumerated; nations must know how numerous they are. It is not surprising that in the discourse of Indian nationalism the question of numbers figures so prominently.

If there is an argument which underlies earlier defiance of British rule in India, it is the simple and intuitive one that points to the 'alienness' of the new rulers. It implies the impossibility of a good moral claim of an outsider to rule an alien people. It must be seen that the colonial administration worked in ways which sought to create an ideological justification for itself, and sought to answer such objections. In this justification, utilitarian social theory played an interestingly complex role.[15] Of course, the use of utilitarianism can be explained in a simple historical manner. At the time British colonialism took root in India, and began to see itself as a political rather than a large trading enterprise, the discourse of social theory in England was dominated by the utilitarian debate.

It appears, however, that this was not the only reason for the presence of utilitarianism in the political disputations of the time. Some specific arguments of utilitarian theory made it particularly useful for justifying colonialism. Traditionalist theories of political rule, of the Burkean variety, obviously could not establish a good moral title for the colonial rulers of India. Rights-based theories of the early type would have been equally inadequate: it would have required impossible ingenuity to argue a case in favour of a natural right of the British to rule India. Utilitarian theory was remarkably free of such handicaps. Alien rule could be questioned on moral grounds of a traditionalist type: those who rebelled against British rule in 1857 could be said to have been guided by a theory which could be given a Burkean form. The entry of utilitarianism in Indian political discourse rendered such arguments obsolete. British rule, it was now argued, conferred on its Indian subjects a whole range of new civilized means of life, starting from the railways and scientific education to the most crucial gift of all – a stable political order.

Large numbers of the babus, converted by their education to rationalist thinking, ornamented their collaboration with colonial power by aggressive utilitarian reasoning. Bankim himself asks occasionally about the distinctly ironical joys of being oppressed by an indigenous tyrant, and the defence, on grounds of independence, of a traditional order which involved so much degradation and suffering. The title to rule and the justification of power are not to be decided by prescriptive or traditional principles. These are primarily pragmatic matters. Simple tradition could not justify the existence of governments, and created no valid right to rule, certainly not the flimsy – and to some barbarous – idea that indigenous tyrants are preferable on patriotic grounds to foreign reformers.

Utilitarians among the babus, justifying reformist collaboration with British rule, would have contended that support for traditional Indian society was backward-looking and sentimental. Against this, a new argument advanced by intellectuals of Bankim's generation was that utilitarianism could be faulted on two historical points. First, the claim of the universal validity of the norms of life that enlightenment had set up could be denied. Second, utilitarianism shared with most strands of rationalist thinking on society an untenable belief in an almost total malleability/constructivism of society – going against sociological traditions associated with the names of Montesquieu or Henry Maine which pointed out that the logic of a social order limited very seriously the ability of legislations to construct social action into new forms. Increasingly, the more critical intellectuals of this generation moved towards a view of this kind.

Bankimchandra Chattopadhyay was original in adding a third insight to these. The superiority of the enlightenment ideal depended on the implied premise of re-enactment. Only on the premise that it was possible

SWARAJ / **CONTROL**

to re-enact the history of capitalist modernity in the colonies, and the further supposition that colonial reformists intended precisely that, could the babu rationalist argument be admitted to be serious. Bankim, through travesty in particular, contested these fundamental beliefs. The colonial administration, he argued, was not seeking to recreate an order modelled on after European modernity; and in any case, structurally, colonialism allowed only travesties to be re-enacted.[16] Occasionally, he would also give a more radical twist to the greatest good idea, by asking literally, and subversively, what good this gift of modernity had brought to the greatest number, the peasantry.[17]

As a consequence of these ideas, there is a marked shift in political discourse about colonial rule; for the first time, this discourse qualifies in the narrower sense to be called *nationalism*. If colonial power cannot be justified by rationalist utilitarian arguments, the terrain of political discourse, and consequently of practice, must shift decisively. The central problem now is not why India became colonized, or even whether alien rule could at all be justified. It is already decisively concluded that alien rule cannot have rational justification and must be opposed. Now the concern shifts to whether it is possible to oppose it in practice, and what principles of organization would be most effective in doing so. Moreover, it now becomes essential to ask which collective subject, or on behalf of which collective 'we', the individual subject should begin to oppose British rule. Anti-colonialism becomes modern nationalism only when it is able to make this transition, moving from a discourse on the earlier question to the new one, and *when it has been able to identify a nation*.

By the end of the nineteenth century, this identification becomes possible in several ways; and accordingly the political discourse becomes distinctly less unhappy. When the question of the identification of the nation is asked, the move from a fuzzy to a clear, enumerated community becomes crucial. Enumeration becomes significant for two reasons: first, it is a source of great psychological strength to restate the tremendous numbers included in this 'we', reflected in the fourteen crore (or a hundred and forty million) armed hands that Bankim makes Bengalis raise in defiance, though this involves the unorthodox procedure of equipping each of them with two swords. But this is an evocative slip – its sole purpose is to create a sense of invincibility by this deft, if suspect, multiplication. Second, it is a matter of great political significance to know this collective subject. The appeals that might rouse it to action depend to a large extent on how its boundaries are drawn. This process must be accomplished, at least in principle, before we can talk about a nationalist consciousness in the narrow sense. It is deeply ironic to call those nationalists who have not yet chosen their nation. If they are nationalists, their mode of being so is distinctly different from that of a later age and should not be absent-mindedly assimilated into that.

Finally, there is another fundamental relation at work in this discourse: between nationalist thinking and the rationalist discourse of modernity. By introducing modernity in their intellectual world, doing much institutional change in its name and making modernity the last argument in its own justification, colonial education forced these people to take up considered stances about the whole project of enlightenment modernity. It is its partial acceptance of a modern theoretical view of the world, especially enlightenment's social epistemics, which demarcates this stage of nationalist thought from earlier less historically conscious patriotism against English 'invaders'. One reason why numbers are so important is because of the new view of the social world created by rationalism and urged upon them by colonial education and propaganda.

Obviously, Indians did not become patriotic for the first time in the nineteenth century, but they invented a new way of being patriotic, a new object to be patriotic for. Gellner is right in pointing out that nationalism arises with and within a larger movement and intellectual configuration of modernity in which one of the major regulative ideas is the possibility of pursuit by newcomer peoples of the life, liberty, and ironical happinesses of industrial modernism. Most theories see and abstractly recognize the typical configuration called modernity – industrial technology, capitalist production, a territorial sovereign state, a regime of rationalist cognition, and rational-technical epistemics about the social world – but actual sociological enquiry has given disproportionate attention to one prominent hypothesis about these interconnections. Both Marxist and anti-Marxist theory has put much greater effort into the proof or disproof of capitalism accompanying nationalist aspirations to the exclusion of its other connections.

In Europe, at least there was a clear connection between the nationalist doctrine's urgency of enumeration and the rationalist theoretical view, its attempt to live in a world that is wholly, unsurpassably, classified, enumerated – a world securely distributed into tables. Clearly, this is part of a programme of bringing the world under control by precise cognition, turning every little piece of information into social technology. Nationalism, once it came into its own, through its massive and obedient instrument of the national state, continues to press on with this relentless project of enumeration – the endless counting of its citizens, territories, resources, majorities, minorities, institutions, activities, import, export, incomes, projects, births, deaths, diseases. It counts, it appears, every conceivable quantifiable thing. No doubt this is helped in most cases by the bourgeois character of this nationalism – the easy, intuitive transfer of a language of *possession* from individuals to the more problematic individuality of the nation. But while it happens, it seems self-evidently true that nations possess territories and citizens in the same way as individuals possess their goods.

But this also shows us a paradox in the discourse that this configuration sets in motion. The nation-state is conceived often as part of a modern configuration, as an apparatus that the people need to bring the forces of modernity under control. The language of this kind of society is a deeply individualistic language which speaks of atomistic individuals who enter into relations with each other on the basis of a purely rational calculation of advantages.

On the other hand, the nation is also, invariably, conceived of as a community. This is the point of paradox. National groups, although they are *gesellschaften,* must at least in the romantic period of their rise against foreign control, present themselves to themselves (because usually they are their own primary audience) as a *gemeinschaft*. It is at one level a coalition of group interests which wishes to merge into an overwhelming combination against the ruling power; but apparently it must pretend, because of the newness and unprecedentedness of this sort of collective action, that it is an immemorially ancient community. Actually, it must be a bond of secular interests, but in ideology, it must be represented as a mystic unity of sentiments.

Is the nation, then, it will be objected, unreal? Is it not something 'objective'? The view I put forward does not deny the objectivity of the nation, but displaces its meaning and asks for a softening of the concept of objectivity. Things that exist in history are often objective only in this way, and only to this extent: perhaps to grimly scientific minds an objectivity of a very vulnerable, unsatisfactory kind. Since a primary means of communities reproducing themselves is to tell stories about themselves, it is not surprising that narrative structures predominate in nationalist discourse. But there are limits beyond which a narrative way of thinking cannot extend.

It is remarkable, but hardly surprising, that the narratives of nationalism speak about some things in social destiny and not others. These narratives are explicit and detailed about freedom, sacrifice, glory and such things, and usually very vague about the more concrete and contestable questions of distribution, equality, power, the actual unequal ordering of the past society or of the future one. Narratives here are above all practical things, interpretations of the world and its history which issue in a call to change it. Its pragmatic objectives are incompatible with such fractious stories of production and distribution. After the achievement of independence, these narratives have done their work; if pressed into the service of providing an order to the nation and its state, they begin to falter. Such productive and distributive arrangements can be justified or questioned by a new type of discourse – a discourse of social theory. The new period, to misuse Marx's phrase, 'cannot draw its poetry from the past'.

How important this storytelling form is, for political conviction, is shown by its persistence. Even in people in whom it is least expected, it

tends to reappear. Among the political leaders of Indian nationalism one of the most clear-sighted and convinced about a theoretical orientation was Nehru. Indeed, in his *Autobiography* he laments that Indian nationalism lacks a theoretical view of politics.[18] Yet, when Nehru writes, he provides a complex design of three interconnected narratives – of the world, of the nation, and of the self. Thus the narrative form was impossible to get away from, not because of any intellectual lack in the writers but because collective existence as much as collective actions create their ideological support by great narratives.

ON NARRATIVE CONTRACT

The telling of a story brings into immediate play some strong conventions invoking a narrative community. Ordinarily, these are coincident in terms of their frontiers with social communities of some form: societies, particular groups, sometimes movements aspiring to give themselves a more demarcated and stabler social form. To some extent all such communities, from the stable to the emergent, use narrative as a technique of staying together, redrawing their boundaries or reinforcing them. Participating in a movement quite clearly involves accepting something like contractual obligations, and, I suspect, some of this affiliation of individuals to movements counteracting a monadic individualism is accomplished by narrative contracts.

Narrative does not therefore aspire to be a universal form of discourse. It draws lines, it distributes people, unlike rational theoretical discourse which attempts to unite them in an abstract universe of ideal consensus. Narratives are not for all to hear, for all to participate in to an equal degree. It has a self in which it originates, a self which tells the story. But that self obviously is not soliloquizing or telling the story to itself. It implies an audience, a larger self towards which it is directed, and we can extend the idea to say that the transaction of a narrative creates a kind of narrative contract. For the recipient of narrative cannot be just anybody: it is only some people belonging to particular categories who are privileged by the narration. As P. Acharya has shown, Muslim children could not come easily under the narrative contracts held out by Abanindranath Tagore's wonderfully coloured folktales; there are very real frontiers of indifference and contempt which would keep them out.[19] The nationalist storyteller confers the bounty of the story on the elect, those who are rendered eligible by the conventions of the story. Nationalism clearly uses the contractual character of the narrative to extend its ideological message. Across segments of society, across generations, across all political divides it creates a vast, constantly open, and constantly renewed political contract.

THE NATIONALIST CRITIQUE OF MODERNITY

Historically, the great enterprise called the enlightenment had met three historical frontiers, separated from each other in terms of space and time. It had an internal frontier on the underside of bourgeois society, between the elites and the productive classes within European capitalism. A second frontier lay between its victorious, conquering colonial power and the peoples it subjugated and reduced to political ineffectuality and cultural silence. A final frontier is reached today when that civilization itself feels exhausted and has produced an interesting and complex internal critique.

Capitalism, Marx said, was the first universal social form, at least the first form capable of a possible universality. It imposed, on most people with whom it came in touch, certain peculiar forms of suffering. These several sufferings at the various frontiers of capitalism gave rise to critiques in which those who suffered at its hands tried to make sense of their history. In a sense, each critique analysed and held up for criticism aspects of suffering related to capitalism which were opaque, unperceived and unreported to the others. But as critiques they are potentially connectable; they, as it were, waited to meet each other. It is only now, in the writing of history, that such a meeting is possible. In this, the critique of an aggressive, uncritical, all-conquering rationalist colonialism by the early nationalists is a necessary part. And it is only when these critiques are stitched together that a true map of the unhappy consciousness of humanity, when capitalism reigned, can be put together.

At least three different types of theoretical problems emerge from a study of anti-colonial thought in the nineteenth century. Intellectual responses to colonial rationalism did of course vary widely across the great expanse of the world of European colonies. Every civilization – from tribal societies endowed with tight, highly economical sets of symbolic resources, to ancient cultures reduced to an unaccustomed subalternity – was forced to think of its present as history, and make some sense of what colonial rule did to its society. Until an intellectual history of anti-colonialism is compiled, the history of colonialism will remain unfinished.

Not surprisingly, the history of this third critique is largely unwritten. This is partly due to an absence of the constitution of its object; this third discourse must be first constituted as a historical object before it can be seen to deserve a history. Of course the materials for this history are distributed over several discrete disciplines – the history of nationalism produced by historians, political thought systematized by political scientists, rituals and folk customs reported by anthropologists, myths collected by ethnographers. To have the materials is not to have a history; this is because history is preceded by a theoretical question, it must philosophically constitute and defend the object which it will write the history of.[20]

Unless the people who are subjected to colonialism are seen to engage in such an enterprise which – despite evident internal differences between periods, between high and folk culture, between the great tradition and the small, between the anti-colonialists and the nationalists, between the radicals and the conservatives – is still seen as one, as a single, whole, historical enterprise, its history cannot be written.

The first general point that emerges is to recognize the seriousness of this enterprise, and to respect its authenticity. Serious historical reflection can exist in non-theoretical and non-historical works. What I wish to emphasize is the originality and distinctness of this intellectual enterprise; what was going on inside these intellectual performances was not just an attempt to counter or criticize western theories of social organization by the use of concepts and argumentative structures taken from western theoretical discourse. Its originality lay in the fact that this critique was attempted from outside this orbit or circle of discourse; this originality is essentially an acknowledgement of the distinctness of Indian discourse, the assertion of the abstract possibility of other universes of theoretical reflection.

In modern social theory the point is quite often made that different societies could be said to have different internal standards of rationality.[21] It is also fairly common to speculate about what indigenous traditions, silenced by European colonial power, might have said had they commanded resources of argumentation comparable to European social theory. Sometimes this is artificially arranged by making tribal witchcraft speak the language of modern analytic philosophy in a pretended dialogue with the ideas of modern science. Yet these discussions remain abstract and historically insubstantial; for these depict what discourses could have happened, not what was really said by real people in real historical situations. The discourse of Indian nationalism in its early stages shows that we do not always need such ahistorical constructs in seeking a view of an 'other'. In colonial times there existed not only colonized cultures which spoke limited hermetic languages and which had narrow and undifferentiated horizons of thinking; there were also other cultures, with considerable internal resources of historical self-reflection, which do not require such generosity of external construction of what they may have had to say about colonialism and the imposition of western modernity. Colonial cultures like India carried on much real as opposed to hypothetical reflection about their history, comparative rationality, and the validity of the claims of a universal reason.

If this is so, why does mainstream social theory carry on as if these societies, after their moments of colonization, were entirely divested of discourse? As if, even when there were undeniable episodes of defiance, these were in some sense violently material, unprefaced, unaccompanied

by any discursive negotiation of their world of subalternity?[22] Certainly, in recent years this indifference in western social theoretical discourse has been modified to some extent: relativists in anthropological theory and criticisms of orientalism, particularly Edward Said's influential work,[23] have made some amends for this absence, this erasure of one side from the intellectual history of the colonial world. But these critiques, it must be emphasized, are part of the discourse of western social theory, attempting to restore some balance in its view of the world: they do not provide the necessary representation of the other discourse. These do not write the history of the discourse of the colonized, but point to its existence, and indicate the space where it must be entered in the historical record.

In historical fact, the orient is never reduced to silence: indeed, it constantly gives vent to its resentment against colonialism through an enormous range of expressions from insults, dishonesty, graft, opportunism, gossip, to social reform, political programmes, mass mobilizations, movements, but also serious historical reflection. This is often done in languages, styles, and concepts which would be unrecognizable in terms of western social theory, and are consequently treated as being equivalent to historical silence. Probably, this is not due only to difficulties of language, but to a theoretical difficulty as well. Discourses constitute planes or orbits in which ideas and arguments are made, heard, and contested. But the most significant thing is that there is no single unruptured plane on which all such circles of discourse coexist and can be heard by each other. More often, these are like circles which exist on different geometric planes. Arguments like the anthropologists' or Said's critique of orientalism are oppositional ones within western discourse; however much they abstractly advocate the cause of native rationality, they do not represent or read these discourses.

In writing the history of the discourses of the colonized, we must guard against the mistake of misrecognition, translating its concepts into its nearest European equivalents, like romanticism, socialism, bourgeois theory, etc. It has proved persistently difficult in any case to use evaluative characterizations like 'conservative' and 'radical' when discussing these ideas. They are often articulating positions for which in a strict sense there are no names in western social theory.

The task of the historian is like the work of somebody who partially rebuilds a house (which is an excellent metaphor for history because people do live inside it). He does not put a system in on an empty space brick by brick. There is a structure which already exists, and it cannot be wholly dismantled because he needs to live inside it at least partially; his criticism is to attack it brick by brick, taking a brick away and putting another in its place. After some time, with a large number of bricks changed, this would constitute a structural change in what is called history. Even when the whole structure is replaced (is that possible?) there would still be a memory of the earlier structure precisely through its absence; with the proviso that this is the fate waiting for the new history as well. This is not surprising. It simply confirms the idea that the business of writing history is also a part of history.

□

ग्राम
लौगाँय

Gyanendra Pandey investigates in 1991 what it means to write India's history. The text was written following the author's experience as part of a fact-finding team that published the People's Union of Democratic Rights (PUDR) report of the riots that took place in the town of Bhagalpur in Bihar, in 1989–90. It uses this experience, and its many contradictions, to look afresh at a book by India's leading nationalist historian, Bipan Chandra. The riots, which began in October 1989 in the town and in hundreds of surrounding villages, saw over a thousand people killed, almost all Muslim.

Originally published in **Economic and Political Weekly** (Annual Number, March 1991) and reprinted with permission from the journal. Gyanendra Pandey's support for this project and assistance in helping think it through are gratefully acknowledged.

Images: 'Gram Logain' and 'Kamroz Hodda Khan's house at Timoni which he abandoned in 1989' are photographs taken by an independent photographer who visited several locations in Bhagalpur on the twenty-fifth anniversary of the original atrocity. Images montaged on, atop and around the Samsung 740N Syncmaster monitor are from the 15 April 1990 PUDR report of the riots of 1989–90, as well as PUDR's February 1996 report, **Recalling Bhagalpur: A Report on the Aftermath of the 1989 Riots**. Other images are from Bipan Chandra's **Modern India: A History Textbook for Class XII** (New Delhi: National Council for Educational Research and Training, 1971), which is an abridged version of his **History of Modern India** (1971), and an image from Vivan Sundaram's **Memorial** (1993), a room-size installation drawn from a newspaper photograph of a dead man in Mumbai's streets during the 1992-93 riots that pulverized the city in the wake of the demolition of the Babri mosque in December 1992.

3

GYANENDRA PANDEY

1991

IN DEFENCE OF THE FRAGMENT

Writing about Hindu–Muslim Riots in India

This is not a paper. It is a preliminary statement regarding some of the difficulties of writing the history of violence, more specifically in this instance, the history of sectarian violence in colonial and post-colonial India. The history of violence is written up in the historiography of modern India as aberration and as absence. *Aberration* in the sense that violence is treated as something removed from the general run of Indian history, its distorted form, its exceptional moment: not the 'real' history of India at all.[1] *Absence* – and here the point applies more emphatically to a field wider than Indian history – because historical discourse has experienced very great difficulty in capturing and representing the moment of violence. The 'history' of violence is, therefore, almost always about context – about everything that happens around violence.[2] The violence itself is taken as 'known'. Its contours and character are simply assumed: its forms need no investigation.

The statement that follows is very general, a bare outline as it were of a larger argument about the nature of evidence and the modes of analysis and representation employed in historical discourse. I proffer it in this form in the hope that it will focus some points for consideration in a way that a more detailed statement might not. But I do so with some hesitation.

One reason for hesitation is that the formulations presented here are far from being adequately worked out at this stage: by the nature of things, they may never be adequately worked out.

Another is that I have had to adopt in this piece a more personal tone than is perhaps, as yet, common in social science and history writing. My statement arises in large part out of the experience of the Bhagalpur 'riots' of 1989, which figures in some detail in the latter part of this essay. In writing about this experience, I make considerable use of personal impressions and insights gathered as part of a ten-member team that went out under the aegis of the People's Union for Democratic Rights (PUDR), Delhi,[3] to investigate the situation in Bhagalpur after the violence. The use of the 'personal' is of course now encouraged in both social, scientific and political analyses and writings. However, the important advances occasioned by feminism notwithstanding, its use is something that I feel many of us are still learning to negotiate: and I remain uncomfortable about what may appear as an excessive intrusion of the author's self into what follows.

Finally, and perhaps most importantly, I hesitate because my criticism of some of the most significant writings on contemporary social and political conflict in India may appear ungenerous, especially in respect of scholars and activists who have come out boldly against the sources of oppression and exploitation in our state and our society. I can only say that the kind of criticism (and self-criticism) presented here would have been impossible but for the pioneering investigations and studies of individuals like Asghar Ali Engineer[4] and organizations like the People's Union for Civil Liberties and the People's Union for Democratic Rights.[5] It is possible that my criticism of their writings on contemporary politics and strife will appear academic and of little immediate relevance. I should like to believe, however, that there is some dialogue between the 'academic' and the 'political', and that some of the arguments presented will contribute in a small way to the continuing debates on certain vital political issues of our times.

The present statement deals with the historiography of sectarian strife. This historiography functions, and has long functioned, in a political context where the rhetoric of nationalism is of central importance. In recent times, especially over the last two decades, this rhetoric has taken on a new tone and a different kind of stridency. The highly-centralized state power that now goes by the name of the Indian nation-state has spoken more and more brazenly on behalf of a get-rich-quick, consumerist 'middle class' and its rural rich ('rich peasant') allies. In furthering the ambition of this sectional interest, the state has shown its willingness to mark out all opposition as 'anti-national' – whether this opposition has been located in the industrial working class, among the rural poor, or in other regional and local movements.

MODERN INDIA

A History Textbook for Class XII

The 'fragments' of Indian society – the smaller religious and caste communities, tribal sections, industrial workers, activist women's groups, all of which might be said to represent 'minority' cultures and practices – have been expected to fall in line with the 'mainstream' (Brahmanical Hindu, consumerist) national culture. This 'mainstream', which represents in fact a very small section of the society, has indeed been flaunted as *the* national culture. 'Unity in Diversity' is no longer the rallying cry of Indian nationalism. On the contrary, all that belongs to any minority other than the ruling class, all that is challenging, singular, local – not to say, all difference – appears threatening, intrusive, even 'foreign' to this nationalism.

Writings on Indian politics need to foreground this state-centred drive to homogenize and 'normalize', and to foreground also the deeply contested nature of the territory of nationalism. Part of the importance of the 'fragmentary' point of view lies in this that it resists the drive for a shallow homogenization and struggles for other, potentially richer definitions of the 'nation' and of the future political community.

I do not suggest that resistance by the 'minority' always, or even usually, functions consciously in this way. But the historian, social scientist or political activist who stands back to analyse the conditions of Indian society will perhaps agree that this is an important part of what is happening. There is a historiographical contest involved here too. For the narrow and diminishing view of nationalism described above is bolstered not only by a reference to current world trends in the economic and political practice of states, nor only by those who speak of ancient India as the cradle of civilization and the storehouse of all that is good and valuable in the contemporary world, but also by a 'modern' and avowedly secular nationalist historiography that has reinforced notions of a natural Indian unity and an Indian nationalist essence.

This historiography has elevated the nation-state – indeed, a contingent form of the nation-state as found in India today – to the status of the end of all history: so much so that 'history', throughout schools, colleges and universities in India, still ends for the most part in 1947. It has also crafted for us the neat binary categories with which we have all had to work: secular/communal, national/local (all too often read as 'anti-national'), progressive (='economics')/reactionary (='cultural '), categories that historians have only recently begun seriously to question.[6]

Even today, after decades of powerful and sophisticated history-writing by left-wing as well as nationalist and other liberal scholars, the view from the 'centre' remains the recognized vantage point for a meaningful reconstruction of 'Indian' history, and the 'official' archive (government records or, for an earlier period, court records) the primary source for its construction. This historiographical practice fails, it seems to me, to lay sufficient stress on the provisional and changeable character of the objects of our analysis: 'India' as well as 'Pakistan', 'Awadh' or 'Andhra Pradesh', the Hindu or the Muslim 'community', the 'nation', 'nationalism', 'communalism'.

By attributing a 'natural' quality to a particular unity, such as 'India', and adopting its 'official' archive as the primary source of historical knowledge pertaining to it, the historian adopts the view of the established state. This has surely happened in the historiography of modern India. The inordinate emphasis placed on the (given) unity of India and the unity of the struggle to realize 'her' independence has meant that the history of India since the early nineteenth century has tended to become the biography of the emerging nation-state. It has also become a history in which the story of Partition and the accompanying Hindu–Muslim and Muslim–Sikh riots of 1946–47 are given short shrift.

The history of sectarian strife in general, and of what is called 'communalism' in India, is written up as a secondary story. 'Hindu' politics, 'Muslim' politics and Hindu–Muslim strife appear as a minor element in the main drama of India's struggle for independence from colonial rule; and they are associated usually with the machinations of the colonial ruling class. Histories of Partition too are generally written up as histories of 'communalism'. These are, as one might expect, anything but histories of noble endeavour. They are not even, in any substantial degree, histories of confused struggle and violence, sacrifice and toss, histories of the tentative forging of new identities and loyalties, or of the rise among uprooted and embittered people of new resolutions and new ambitions. They are, in the main, accounts of the 'origins' or 'causes' of Partition, investigations of the chances, the political mistakes or the less amenable social and economic developments that allegedly brought about this tragic event. In this account, moreover, the tragedy appears as one that, for all its consequences, miraculously left the course of Indian history unaltered. In spite of the emergence of two, now three, independent nation-states as a result of this partition, 'India', this historiography would seem to say, stayed firmly – and 'naturally' – on its secular, democratic, non-violent and tolerant path.

Bipan Chandra's *Modern India,*[7] which is perhaps the best textbook on the colonial period available to school-leavers and junior undergraduates, illustrates these points very well indeed. On 15 August 1947, India celebrated with joy its first day of freedom.

> The sacrifices of generations of patriots and the blood of countless martyrs had borne fruit.... But the sense of joy ... was mixed with pain and sadness.... (For) even at the very moment of freedom a communal orgy, accompanied by indescribable brutalities, was consuming thousands of lives in India and Pakistan...[8]

'Pain and sadness': at what can only be read as the hijacking of an enormously powerful and noble struggle. We read on:

> The symbol of this tragedy at the moment of national triumph was the forlorn figure of Gandhiji – the man who had given the message of *non-violence, truth and love and courage and manliness* to the Indian people. . . . In the midst of national rejoicing, he was touring the hate-torn land of Bengal, trying to bring comfort to people who were even then paying, through senseless communal slaughter, the price of freedom.[9]

Who hijacked the movement is not explicitly stated at this point, although other pages make it clear that Hindu and Muslim communalists, political reactionaries and of course the British were to blame.[10] The hijacking leads to senseless slaughter, hundreds of thousands of lives being lost as 'the price of freedom'. Something is elided here, however. Which people pay? For whose freedom? Rather than ask these questions, Bipan Chandra's textbook goes on to record how Gandhi died, assassinated in January 1948, 'a martyr to the cause of unity'; and how the people of India, 'with confidence in their capacity and their will to succeed . . . now [after August 1947] set out to build the just and the good society'.[11]

Here 'Gandhi' and 'the people' become symbols of the nationalist essence, the Indian spirit, and symbols that may easily be substituted for one another. 'Gandhi' clearly stands in for the people in the nationalist account of India's anti-colonial struggle. Similarly, with Gandhi gone, 'the people' apparently take over Gandhi's work and march forward, unaffected by partition, riots, refugees and the like, to build 'the just and the good society'.

Sumit Sarkar's more critical textbook,[12] meant for more advanced undergraduate and graduate students, puts forward a different argument but arrives at the same conclusion about the secular path of the Indian people. Sarkar writes movingly of 'the Mahatma's finest hour', from 1946 until his death in January 1948, when he laboured almost single-handed to try and restrain the passions that were leading to the slaughter of Hindus, Muslims and Sikhs all over northern India. The futility of such 'isolated personal effort' was, however, evident, the historian remarks.

'One might still argue', Sarkar says, 'that the only real alternative lay along the path of united militant mass struggle against imperialism and its Indian allies'.[13] He goes on to describe in fairly optimistic terms the continuing potential for such struggle. Despite the obvious disruption caused by the riots, this possibility was by no means entirely blocked even in the winter of 1946–47. Five months after the August riots (the 'great Calcutta killings' of August 1946), the students of Calcutta were again on the streets on 21 January 1947 in 'Hands Off Vietnam' demonstrations against the use of Dum Dum airport by French planes, and all communal divisions seemed forgotten in the absolutely united and ultimately victorious 85-day tram strike under Communist leadership which began the same day.[14]

The author refers also to the 'strike wave' of January–February 1947 in Calcutta, Kanpur, Karachi, Coimbatore and elsewhere, only to add: 'The strikes . . . were all on purely economic demands; what remained lacking was a sufficiently influential and determined political leadership.'[15]

I have quoted from two of the best general books on the history of colonial India and the Indian national movement, both by scholars writing within the Marxist tradition, to emphasize my point about the quite remarkable dominance of the nationalist paradigm in the writing on Partition and Independence. This history writing is part of a larger nationalist discourse, which finds powerful expression in films, journalism and literature too. Partition was, for the majority of people living in what are now the divided territories of northern and eastern India, Pakistan and Bangladesh, *the* event of the twentieth century – equivalent in terms of trauma and consequence to the First World War (the 'great war') for Britain or the Second World War for France and Japan. The experience of the First and Second World Wars is commemorated in western Europe and Japan through the erection of major national monuments: there is, not surprisingly, no equivalent for Partition in India. However, the erasure of memory goes further in this case.[16]

As in history writing, so in films and fiction, Indian intellectuals have tended to celebrate the story of the independence struggle rather than dwell on the agonies of Partition. This statement requires considerable qualification. There has been a great deal of writing on Partition and the sectarian violence of 1946–47 in Punjabi, Urdu and Hindi. But 'Partition literature' of the early period – of which Sa'adat Hasan Manto's devastating stories are an outstanding example – was largely confined to the strife-torn areas of Punjab and its environs in the decade or so after Partition.[17] Subsequent literary statements on this theme that have come out of northern India fall much more clearly within the secular nationalist problematic, for which Partition was a history gone wrong – a puzzling and in effect, inexplicable failure. The classic in this genre is probably Rahi Masoom Raza's *Aadha Gaon* (1966).

More remarkably still, sectarian violence and its consequences do not figure as a central motif in the Bengali literature of the post-Partition period. A recent study notes that while the famine of 1943 appears to have moved the Bengali litterateur deeply, 'the partition of Bengal [dividing East Bengal, which became part of Pakistan in 1947, from West Bengal which remained part of India] that . . . conclusively changed all erstwhile socio-economic configurations in and after 1947, never became a dominating theme of Bengali fiction even during the 1950s or shortly thereafter'.[18]

In cinema, of course, the great Bengali director, Ritwik Ghatak, produced a series of unparalleled filmic statements about the pain, despair and hopes of those dispossessed and displaced by Partition: *Komal Gandhar* (1959), *Subarnarekha* (1962), *Titash Ekti Nadir Nam* (1973) and, somewhat more indirectly, *Meghe Dhaka Tara* (1960). But Ghatak remains an exception – and not because of his brilliance alone. In Bengali cinema generally, as in the huge Hindi–Urdu film industry centred in Bombay, as also in the large numbers of documentary films produced by the Films Division of India, film-makers have paid relatively little attention to the history and consequences of Partition.

Among Hindi–Urdu films, the example that stands out against this is M.S. Sathyu's *Garam Hawa*, a remarkable statement of the early 1970s which sensitively portrayed the collective insanity, the uprooting, the meaninglessness of existence, and the fear-laden searches for new meaning 'elsewhere' that were the lot of so many people in the aftermath of Partition. The more recent television serial *Tamas*, based on Bhishma Sahni's eponymous novel published in 1972, has acquired a special importance because of the numbers it reached.[19] However, the story marks a return to a less subtle nationalist statement in which *agents-provocateurs* and mysterious evil folk pulling the strings from behind the scenes mislead an innocent and bewildered, but brave people. Partition is represented here, moreover, in the likeness of a natural disaster in which human actions play little part: far removed from the run of daily life. As we have already noted, this is also the line that respectable, academic nationalist historiography has followed.

The reasons for the kind of suppression described above are not far to seek. Difference and strife between Hindus and Muslims persist in India today, and in relating the history of such strife there is the real danger of re-opening old wounds. In addition, there is no consensus amongst us about the nature of Partition. We have no means of representing such tragic loss or of pinning down – or rather, owning – responsibility for it. As a consequence, our nationalist historiography, journalism and film-making have tended to generate something like a collective amnesia. Consciously or otherwise, they have represented Partition and all that went with it as an aberration. 14 August, 1947 (the day of the establishment of Pakistan) becomes 'an accident, a mistake' – and one for which not we but 'others' were responsible.

Although the immediate context for the observations that follow is the experience of recent 'riots', especially the one in Bhagalpur in 1989, I wish to stress that the difficulties of evidence-gathering and representation encountered here point to the folly of our using 'evidence' of, say, 50 or 100 years ago as if it were somehow 'transparent': biased accounts to be

SyncMaster 740N
Recalling
BHAGA
STRUGGLE FOR SWARAJ
277
Khilafat question. After all there was no protest in India when Kamal Pasha abolished the Caliphate in 1924.
It may be noted at this stage that even though the non-cooperation and civil disobedience movement had ended in failure, national movement had been strengthened in more than one way. Nationalist sentiments and the national movement had now reached the remotest corners of the land. The educated Indians had learnt to rely on their own people. The Indian people had lost their sense of fear—the brute strength of British power in India no longer frightened them. They had gained tremendous self-confidence and self-esteem, which no defeats and retreats could shake. This was expressed by Gandhiji when he declared that "the fight that was commenced in 1920 is a fight to the finish, whether it lasts one month or one year or many months or many years."
Gandhiji with the Ali Brothers at the Belgaum session of the Congress
Photo Division, Ministry of Information and Broadcasting
THE SWARAJISTS
STRUGGLE FOR SWARAJ
307
EXERCISES
1. In what ways did the developments during the first World War and in the immediate post-war years favour the resurgence of nationalism in Africa and Asia in general and in India in particular?
2. Trace the early development of Gandhi as a political leader and discuss his basic political ideas.
3. Trace the development of the Non-Cooperation Movement and the Khilafat agitation from 1919 to 1922. How far did these two movements represent a new stage in the growth of the national movement?
4. What were the different aspects of nationalist resurgence in the years 1927 to 1929?
5. Discuss the course of the nationalist movement from the Lahore Session of 1929 to the withdrawal of the Second Civil Disobedience Movement in 1934.
SAMSUNG

sure, but accounts that may be balanced by setting them off one against another, by appropriate additions and subtractions, to give us a more or less adequate reconstruction of 'history'.

II

It has become common in recent writings to describe one instance of strife after another as 'perhaps the worst since 1947', such has been the magnitude and brutality of sectarian violence in the 1980s.[20] Bhagalpur(1989) was one of these devastating outbreaks. This round of violence in Bhagalpur began in the last week of October 1989. Arson, loot and murder spread from the city to the surrounding countryside and raged practically unchecked for several days. The situation was then brought under some sort of control by military and paramilitary forces; but an atmosphere of fear and terror remained for months afterwards.[21]

Given the scale of the 'riots', and the infamous role of the local administration in encouraging the attacks and suppressing evidence, it is impossible to establish the 'facts' of this occurrence – what traditional historians like to call the 'nuts and bolts' of the story. Possibly as many as 1,000 people were killed in the course of the violence, most of them Muslims: but estimates of the casualties still vary enormously.[22] During the first days of the 'riots', trains were stopped repeatedly at different places in Bhagalpur and its neighbouring districts, and from several of these, Muslim travellers were dragged out and lynched: but no one can say for certain how many were killed in this way – not even disturbed Hindu travellers who happened to be caught on one of these trains and saw people being pulled from their particular carriage. In the major attacks, in the rural areas as well as in the city, neither old people nor infants, neither women nor children were spared. There is widespread feeling that women were abducted and raped on a large scale, but none of the surviving victims will talk about rape: the five specific cases recorded by the PUDR team that conducted investigations in Bhagalpur in January 1990 were incidents which the Muslim women informants had themselves heard about.

What is beyond question is that the extent and ferocity of the attacks was quite unprecedented, even for a district which has seen much sectarian strife before, including 'riots' in 1946. At the worst stage of the violence in October–November 1989, some 40,000 people were forced to leave their homes and live in makeshift relief camps. Destruction and looting of property occurred on a massive scale for several weeks. The fears generated among the heavily outnumbered Muslims were such that a great many were unwilling to return to their homes even three months after the initial outbreak of violence: an estimated 10,000 were still in 'relief camps' towards the end of January 1990, apart from those who had moved in with relatives or friends in 'safer' places in or outside Bhagalpur district. At this time, many Muslims were pressing for the permanent retention of military or paramilitary forces in the vicinity of their villages or wards (mohallas) as the only trustworthy means for their protection, and some were demanding that they be given arms by the government for the same purpose. The air was still thick with rumours, and isolated attacks and looting continued to occur: one such incident was reported as late as March 1990.

How do we write the history of such an event? In Bhagalpur, the state's 'archives', those official sources that generations of historians and social scientists have treated as core accounts, more 'reliable' or at least more 'comprehensive' than any other source, are largely missing. Like historians generally, various teams of independent investigators visiting Bhagalpur have been eager to obtain the official account in order to establish 'some overall picture' in the midst of an otherwise confusing investigation.[23] But the view from the centre has largely been destroyed in this instance, at any rate for the first few, absolutely critical days of the 'riots'. A *Sunday Mail* report of 11 February, 1990, made after a fortnight-long investigation into the Bhagalpur carnage and its aftermath, sums up the situation in this regard:

> Crucial records of the period, especially those from the tables of [the] then district magistrate [DM] . . . and superintendent of police [SP] . . . are missing.
>
> Evidence strongly suggests that [the DM] . . . in all probability destroyed the log book of the central control room in which the many SOS received in the fateful week were recorded. The fresh log book that has been placed in the office strangely makes no mention of the incidents.
>
> . . .
>
> . . . [the SP at the time], who has since gained notoriety, too has left his successor. . . without a clue to work [with?]. His records too show a single joint report on the Chanderi massacre (one of the worst incidents in the countryside), just because Patna High Court had issued a notice.

Even the joint report of the DM and the SP on the first incident at Tatarpur Chowk [in Bhagalpur city] on 24 October that had lit the fuse is among the papers not traceable. The fact, incredible as it may sound, is that there is no statement of facts available in either the DM or the SP's office. This kind of destruction or removal of records is of course not unprecedented: the British practised it on a large scale in India after 1937, and no doubt there have been many other instances since Independence. What is less frequently observed, however, is the destruction entailed in the systematic construction of evidence on all sides, official and unofficial, when an event of this kind occurs. Violence produces the necessity of evidence-gathering, of uncovering hidden processes and contradictions that we might normally prefer to ignore; but violence also wipes out 'evidence' and even, to a large extent, the possibility of collecting it in a manner and form that is deemed acceptable by today's social science. Let me illustrate this with reference to the PUDR team's work in Bhagalpur.

In spite of the size of this team[24] and the very long hours it put in during its eight-day visit to the district, we were bound by serious limitations. The majority of the people we spoke to in Bhagalpur were Muslims. They were the primary victims of the 'riots'; they were in the relief camps; they were the people who were willing to, perhaps had need to, talk. Hindus in many of the badly affected areas met us with studied silence, if not hostility.[25] The Hindus we could speak with easily were from a narrow stratum: middle-class intellectuals, political activists, professionals and officials with established opinions (or 'theories') about what had occurred.

In addition, we were confronted with the problem, when we met victims of the violence, or other eye-witnesses, of what questions to ask, and how. The form of a question suggests particular answers, and there were particular answers that we were more ready to hear than others. This is a point to which I shall return. But we faced a further difficulty at the outset: how does one ask the victims of such barbarism – the father and son, or the mother and four little children who survived because they were away or managed somehow to hide in the fields, from where they saw elders and young ones, women and men, every one to be found in the Muslim quarter of their village being slaughtered – how does one ask such victims of terror for details of what they saw?

And yet 'investigators' are bound to ask. And sometimes the victims, survivors and others standing by, begin to talk without even being asked – because they have been asked so many times already, or because there is need for a public narrative of their suffering. However, this narrative too assumes a set form. It appears as a ritualized account, a collective memory or record that has been generated on behalf of the entire community – 'Muslims' or 'Yadavs' or 'Hindus' or whatever. The standard practice in the affected mohallas and villages we visited was for us to be taken to a central spot where many people gathered, and the 'elders' or the 'educated' gave us what might be called the authorized account of local happenings.

The PUDR team went to Bhagalpur three months after the outbreak of this violence, and it is possible to suggest that the ritualized nature of these collective accounts was much more firmly set by then. Yet, I have no doubt that a collective memory, in a set form, will have come into being very soon after the occurrence of the events it describes. This has to do with the living conditions of the local communities, the history of past strife and the difficult relations with the state. But it has to do with another factor as well, that the purpose of the public narrative is at least partly to impress a particular point of view on the state and its agents.

The situation produced by any large-scale outbreak of violence deepens the division that may at any time be seen to exist between privileged people and common folk in India. Such situations also work to level communities and make entire groups that are under suspicion a part of the 'common folk'. At these times, the informant – distant villager, illiterate artisan, faceless member of a makeshift relief camp, and even the elite of a community, such as medical practitioners or university professors, tend to become part of a collective subject that approaches the investigator as 'a person of influence' and appeals to her/him for relief, justice, mercy.

Consequently, much of our conversation with local people in Bhagalpur had to do with minute details of property losses, injuries and deaths which we did not necessarily consider central to our investigation. We were asked repeatedly to go a little further, to this village or the next, to see for ourselves the destruction of this house, to make a note of these names too. We were asked also to record 'First Information Reports' and evidence where the police had allegedly failed or refused to record these, or at least to help in getting them recorded because, as a number of informants said, 'We live under constant threat and may well be killed before anyone bothers to take down our evidence.' We were met in other places with the bare response: 'We don't know anything. We were not here.'

Very often, the accounts we were given partook of the character of pre-emptive narratives. They were constructed, more or less consciously, in order to falsify particular 'theories' or explanations of the course of events. 'Hindus', who were accused of taking out an armed procession and adopting extremely aggressive tactics during its course through the city of Bhagalpur, thus sparking off the violence of 24 October, declared that the procession was an ordinary religious one, like any other on important festive occasions, and that it was accompanied by very large numbers of women and children singing devotional songs and playing on musical instruments as they went along. 'Muslims', who were accused by the local administration and by others of making preparations for a 'riot' from long before 24 October, declared all over the district and almost without exception that they had never had any quarrel with the Hindus and had no reason to fear a riot, that perfect amity had always existed between the Hindus and Muslims of the district, and that 'even in 1946–47' while the rest of northern India burned, there was no (or very little) trouble in Bhagalpur.

Even where the defence of the immediate group or collectivity was not an issue, as when we spoke to urban professionals and intellectuals, the defence of something larger and more intangible was sometimes at stake: the 'good name' of the city (or region), for example, or the very possibility of Hindus and Muslims living together in the future – as of course they must. It was this kind of thinking that led many people to stress the importance of letting bygones be bygones. Some similar reasoning perhaps lay behind the pronounced tendency to lay the blame for the strife on 'outsiders': political leaders in Patna and Delhi, 'criminal gangs', a corrupt and spineless administration. The theory of 'criminal' instigation and conduct of the riots has been especially popular. The argument is that 'criminal castes' from across the river Ganga (which flows west to east through the district just north of the city of Bhagalpur) came into the city and other strife-torn places in large numbers, that these castes (designated 'criminal' by the erstwhile colonial regime) are the cause of much of the lawlessness in Bhagalpur even at other – 'normal' – times, and that criminal gangs making free use of these 'outside' elements were largely responsible for the violence of 1989.

The difficulties of evidence-gathering are, however, only a part of the problem of reconstructing the history of such events. The question of how to write about such experiences, already hinted at, is equally hazardous. For there is the obvious danger of sensationalizing, of over-dramatizing, and thus rendering such strife and its consequences as extraordinary – aberrational. Yet there is, on the other hand, at least an equal danger of surrendering to the demands of an academic discourse, of sanitizing, 'naturalizing' and thereby, making bland and rather more palatable what is intensely ugly and disorienting. Academic discourse too tends to push the moment of violence into the realm of the exceptional and aberrant, as I shall try to show in a moment.

Discussions of sectarian strife in India find it necessary to try and balance an account of 'Hindu' atrocities by some account of 'Muslim' (or 'Sikh') atrocities. So, a few weeks after our visit to Bhagalpur, the chief minister of Bihar spoke, in a public announcement on the steps being taken to restore normalcy, of the numbers of Hindu temples and shrines destroyed in the district along with large numbers of Muslim holy places; against all the evidence, for no investigating team had reported a single Hindu temple or shrine damaged or destroyed on this occasion. So too, a documentary film on the Bhagalpur violence, made by an independent and enterprising film-maker, Nalini Singh, and shown on national television in March 1990, equated Jamalpur (the one Hindu village to be attacked in the course of the 'riots') with Logain (the site of one of the worst massacres of Muslims), implying that the attacks and casualties were of the same order; although the most reliable estimates suggest that seven people were killed and some 70 houses and huts partially burnt and looted in Jamalpur against 115 killed and the entire Muslim *basti* looted, burnt and destroyed in Logain.[26]

This allegedly 'liberal' demand to document and present 'both sides of the case' is frequently accompanied by the social scientists' search for 'outside forces' and 'exceptional circumstances' which are, in this reckoning, very likely to be found behind such acts of extraordinary violence. For Bhagalpur, journalists as well as other investigators have pointed the finger at 'criminal' elements, at the local administration and at the vicious propaganda of the Vishwa Hindu Parishad (VHP)[27] and other militant Hindu organizations. As a newspaper report of 19 November 1989 has it,

> Is it possible that people who live together [have always lived together] and share each other's daily concerns – about food and drink, the marriage of daughters, and electoral politics should become enemies overnight? What have these people to do with the Babri Masjid and Ram Janmabhoomi controversy? But the criminal elements of both communities saw their opportunity and very quickly indeed they filled the minds of the people with a poisonous insanity.

That this task of poisoning the minds of the people could be accomplished so quickly does not seem to raise any problems for the writer: its significance is never discussed. Instead we are told: 'The Bhagalpur riots are not so much the product of sectarian ['communal'] feelings as a calamity brought about by the criminals'.[28]

The moral of the story, which carries over from nationalist accounts of the pre-Independence period, is that 'the people' are essentially secular. The same newspaper report goes on to say: The criminals are armed with rifles, guns, bombs, axes, choppers, spears and the blessings of [powerful] political leaders. What can the people possibly do? *[Becharijantakare to kyakare?].* The members of both [Hindu and Muslim] communities wished to live together in peace and friendship, but the criminals ultimately succeeded in spreading the poison among them.[29]

Explanations of violence in terms of 'larger historical processes' are not so far removed from this kind of analysis as might appear to be the case at first sight. Instead of the activities of VHP propagandists and criminal elements, or dereliction of duty on the part of local officials, these deal in the 'criminalization' of politics; the 'communalization' of Indian public life, not excluding the administration; longer-term economic changes – the rise of the 'backward castes', emergence of new trading groups,

unionization, labour trouble and the like. The PUDR's careful and detailed report on the 'Bhagalpur Riots', for instance, makes an elaborate – if somewhat confusing – statement regarding the complex of circumstances surrounding the outbreak of violence:

> A common simplification of the riots has consisted in placing the responsibility for them on criminals. We feel it may be more accurate to say that it was the sum of relations between criminals, the police, administration, politicians, the dominant elite and the economy which are responsible and, at any given time, one or all of these – along with some local people – were significant factors and agents in the riots.[30]

Too often, however, the statement of complex, long-term historical processes leaves little room for human agency and human responsibility, and becomes a statement about the essential and unchanging ('secular') character of the majority of the people concerned. The 'economic dimension' particularly tends to emerge as the master of all. Two examples from the work of Asghar Ali Engineer, perhaps the most prominent writer on the causes of recent sectarian strife, will serve to illustrate the point:

> *Jabalpur 1961*: The *apparent cause* was the 'elopement' of a Hindu girl with a Muslim boy. However, although it brought the powerful religio-cultural prejudices between the two communities into play . . . it was not the real reason. The *real reason* lay elsewhere. The Muslim boy was the son of a local *bidi* magnate who had gradually succeeded in establishing control over the local bidi industry. His Hindu competitors were very sore over this development. It was not insignificant that the *bidi* industry belonging to the Muslims in Jabalpur suffered heavily during the riots.

> *Bhiwandi 1970:* [Bhiwandi] is a thriving centre of the powerloom industry, with quite a few Muslims owning powerlooms and a large number of Muslim artisans working as weavers on these looms. . . . Also, being on the Bombay–Agra National Highway, Bhiwandi receives a large amount of revenue by way of octroi from the passing trucks. Its municipality thus has a handsome income. Local municipal politics, therefore, assumes [a] great deal of importance. Different parties and political groups vie with each other to wrest control of the municipal council. A section of Muslims with their increased prosperity due to the loom industry developed greater political aspirations challenging the traditional leadership, and this led to communal tension. . . .[31]

In its more extreme versions, this economist's viewpoint tends to reduce all history to a fight for land and profit. Here is a journalist's account of the 'Economy of Communalism' in Bhagalpur:

> It would be simplistic to dismiss the recent Bhagalpur communal riot as a manifestation of the ugly face of our civilisation. Attention must be focused on [the] ruined economy, dying industry and the decadent feudal agrarian structure of the area which provides food [fuel?] to such an event.

Further,

> Religion is no consideration among the buyers and sellers [of firearms]. Profit is the overwhelming motive. They have a vested interest in keeping the communal tension going.... Another factor that keeps it going is [the] profitability of relief camp operations [sic].[32]

Obviously, it is not my submission that economic interests and contradictions are unimportant. However, there is more than a narrowly conceived material interest to the history even of our times. Yet some of the most sophisticated writing in the social sciences continues to reduce the lives of men and women to the play of material interests, or at other times to large impersonal movements in economy and society over which human beings have no control. The thrust of this writing is to suggest that the 'real' battle lies not where it might appear – say, in matters of history or notions of honour, not in the centrality of religion or people's attachment to particular cultural and religious symbols – but in the question of immediate material interests. In the quarrels at this level, furthermore, it is above all the elite groups that count. Let me quote the PUDR report once more: 'The major material long-term benefit the (rural) elite groups are likely to get from the present riots is land.' Or again, regarding continuing tension between Hindus and Muslims in the villages: 'One of the major factors contributing to this state of affairs is property, especially land, of those who left their homes. Threats continue to be made by those who have now set their eyes on either grabbing or buying land cheap.'[33] (By them alone?)

Let me reiterate, at the risk of superfluity, that my point is not that land and property are of no importance in bringing about or perpetuating sectarian conflict. My point is that the emphasis placed upon these factors often leaves little room for the emotions of people, for feelings and perceptions – in a word, insufficient room for agency.

There is one particular aspect of this question of agency that may be spelt out further. The mass of 'the people' appear in a quite passive role in many of our analyses of 'riot' situations. It is economic interests, land struggles, the play of market forces and frequently elite manipulation that make the running. 'The people' find their place, once again, outside history. By that means, perhaps, their pristine qualities (their 'purity') are preserved. For the message of much of the writing on sectarian violence in India in recent times is the same as that found in the nationalist histories of the pre-Independence period. It is to suggest that events like Bhagalpur 1989 do not represent the real flow of Indian history: they are exceptional, the result of unusual conjunctures. It is to pretend that their occurrence on the scale and with the frequency that we have seen in the 1980s still makes no fundamental difference to the essential 'secularism' of the people[34] and to our cherished national traditions: 'secularism', 'non-violence', 'peaceful co-existence'.

III

This is, to my mind, an unacceptable history. It is unacceptable not only because it tends to be reductionist and not only because it continues to ply a tired nationalist rhetoric. It is unacceptable also because, willy-nilly, it essentializes 'communalism' and the 'communal riot', making these out to be transparent and immutable entities, around which only the context changes. In this section, I wish to dwell a little longer on the inadequacies of history writing in this vein.

A point that I have already made but should like to emphasize is that the grand narratives which we produce – and must continue to produce – as historians, political scientists, sociologists or whatever, tend to be about 'context' alone, or at least primarily: the 'larger forces' of history that assemble to produce violent conflicts of the kind discussed above. One advantage, or if you prefer consequence, of this is that we are able to escape the problem of representing pain. This is a sanitized history with which we are relatively comfortable. In it, violence, suffering, and many of the scars left by their history, are suppressed.

It seems to me imperative, however, that historians and social scientists pay closer attention to the moment of violence and try in some way to represent it in their writings. There are at least two reasons for this. First, the moment of violence, and suffering, tells us a great deal about our condition today.[35] Secondly, the experience of violence is in crucial ways constitutive of our 'traditions', our sense of community, our communities and our history.

Many observers have pointed to the new heights reached by Hindu militancy and propaganda over the last few years. This has been orchestrated most visibly by the Vishwa Hindu Parishad (VHP) and plainly had much to do with the increased frequency and scale of Hindu–Muslim strife in the 1980s. The point that is perhaps not sufficiently stressed, however, is that the violent slogans and demands of organizations like the VHP, and the 'riots' they have sparked off, do not poison the minds of 'the people' only for a moment. On the contrary, given our history, the resources available to 'secular' and 'communal' forces in the country, the opportunism of most of our major political parties, and the continued and repeated outbreak of sectarian violence, the most outrageous suggestions about the 'evil', 'dangerous', 'threatening' character of the 'other' community (or communities)[36] come to be widely accepted and to become part of a popular dogma.

Nothing but this acceptance can explain the kinds of atrocities perpetrated in recent instances of sectarian strife: the call to leave not a single Muslim, man, woman or child alive, which was acted upon in several places in Bhagalpur; the massacre of all eighteen Muslim passengers travelling in a tempo-taxi along with the Hindu taxi-driver, when they were stopped on a major country road two-and-a-half weeks after the cessation of general 'rioting', and their burial in a field which was then planted over with garlic; the chopping off of the breasts of women; the spearing of infants and children, the spears with the victims impaled on them being then twirled around in the air to the accompaniment of laughter and shouts of triumph.[37]

What lies behind this insane and incredible brutality, I suggest, is the belief that the victims are real or potential monsters who have done all this and worse to 'us', or will do so if given half a chance. In many cases, the alleged atrocities, for which these actions are supposed to be just recompense, are believed to have occurred 'yesterday' or 'the other day', in 'the town' or a neighbouring district or further away: in Bhagalpur, the rumour that set off the major Hindu attacks in the countryside was that all the Hindu students living in Muslim-owned boarding-houses in a part of the city near the university (many of whom came of course from the villages of Bhagalpur) had been massacred on the first two days of the 'riots'.[38] In other instances, revenge appears to be sought for what 'they' have done to 'us', generally, in the past. The relevant point is this, that what appears to many of us as rabid and senseless Hindu propaganda is widely believed.

In one of its more 'restrained' forms, this leads to the view that all Muslims in India are 'Pakistanis': witness, we are told, their response in the course of any cricket match between India and Pakistan. Following from this is the argument that local Muslims are out to create another Pakistan, in one place after another – Bhagalpur, Moradabad, Meenakshipuram (Tamil Nadu). By this juncture, we are well into that realm where 'Muslims' are represented as being inherently turbulent, fanatical, violent.

Aggression, conversion, unbounded sexuality: these are the themes that make up the history of the spread of Islam, as told by the Hindu historians and propagandists. 'Wherever Muslim communities exist, there will inevitably be a 'dance of annihilation' in the name of Islam.' It is the 'religious duty of every Muslim' to 'kidnap and force into their own religion, non-Muslim women'. Several pamphlets and leaflets distributed by militant Hindu organizations in places where strife has lately occurred set the picture of a 'Hindu' husband and wife with two children (*Ham da hamaare do:* We two, our two) by the side of a 'Muslim' family – a man with four wives and numerous children, accompanied by the self-explanatory slogan, *Ham paanch, hamaare pacchis* (We five, our twenty-five).[39] Thus a whole new 'common sense' develops, relating to the marital and sexual practices of 'the Muslims' (here, as elsewhere referring only to Muslim men), to their perverse character and their violent temperament.

It will perhaps suffice to illustrate the tenor of recent Hindu propaganda and beliefs about the Muslims if I reproduce here the substance of just one leaflet that was distributed in Bhagalpur sometime between the last quarter of 1989 and January 1990. Entitled *Hindu Brothers Consider and Be Warned*,[40] the leaflet asks:

1 Is it not true that the Muslim population is increasing, while that of the Hindus is decreasing [sic]?
2 Is it not true that the Muslims are fully organized [prepared], while the Hindus are fully disorganized [scattered]?
3 Is it not true that the Muslims have an endless supply of weapons while the Hindus are completely unarmed?

. . .

5 Is it not true that the Congress has been elected to power for the last 40 years on a mere 30 per cent of the vote: in other words, that the day the Muslims become 30 per cent of the population, they will gain power?
6 Is it not true that the Muslims will become 30 per cent of the population in 12 to 15 years' time: . . . within 12 to 15 years the Muslims will easily become the rulers of this country?
7 Is it not true that, as soon as they gain power, they will destroy the Hindus root-and-branch, as they have done in Pakistan?
8 Is it not true that, when destroying the Hindus, they will not stop to think which Hindu belongs to the Lok Dal, who is a Socialist and who a Congressman [or woman], who belongs to the 'Forward' castes, who to the 'Backward', or who is a Harijan?

9 Is it not true that the lives and wealth of even those people will be destroyed under Muslim rule, who use today's corrupt politics to make black money and multiply their wealth?

. . .

11 Is it not true that, after the conceding of Pakistan the land mass that remained was manifestly that of the Hindus?

. . .

13 Is it not true that Hindus [sic] are prohibited from buying land or settling in Kashmir, whereas Kashmiri Muslims are free to buy land wherever they want in the country.

. . .

16 Is it not true that Christians [sic) have their own 'homeland'[41] or country, Muslims [sic] also have their own 'homeland' or country, where they feel secure in every way, but Hindus have not been able to retain their country because under the banner of secularism it has been turned into a 'dharmshala' [hospice]?

17 Is it not true that while Hindus are in power, Muslims can live safely, but as soon as the Muslims come to power, life will become difficult for the Hindus – that is, they will be destroyed?

18 Is it not true that all Muslim legislators [Members of Parliament], irrespective of the party to which they belong, spend night and day working to further the interests of Muslims, while there is not a single Hindu legislator in Delhi who sets self-interest aside and devotes himself to the interests of the Hindus.

. . .

21 Is it not true that those Muslim women who have been divorced by their husbands are supported through the Waqf Committee by the government, with funds taken from the government treasury; which means that for the maintenance and joy-(or lust-)filled lives of the Muslims, the majority Hindu community has to bear an additional tax burden?

If these things are true, then Hindu brothers you must immediately awake – awake while there is still time. And vow to sacrifice your wealth, your body, your all for the protection of the Hindu people and nation and for the declaration of this country as a Hindu nation.

What follows from all this is of course a dread of 'the Muslim' and the demand to disarm 'him' – by disenfranchisement and deculturization: adopt 'our' names, 'our' language, 'our' dress. What follows is the demand that if the Muslims wish to stay on in this country, they must learn to live like 'us'. (Who? This is never very clear, but in the circumstances it does not seem to matter):

> *Hindustan mein rahna hai, to hamse milkar rahna hoga* ('If you wish to live in Hindustan, you will have to live like us.') *Hindustan mein rahna hai, to Bande Mataram kahna hoga* ('If you wish to live in Hindustan, you will have to raise the slogan, Bande Mataram — Victory to the Mother.')

Alongside this is sometimes found the paradoxical argument that 'we' shall certainly provide justice to minorities like the Muslims, for, since they are overwhelmingly local converts, it is 'Hindu blood [that] flows in their veins'.[42] But the central message remains: 'Live like us' or — its blood-curdling corollary — face annihilation: *Babar ki santan, Jao Pakistan ya kabristan* ('Descendants of Babar! Pakistan or the grave, take your choice'), a slogan that appears to have been taken literally by large sections of the police and the local Hindu population in Bhagalpur and some other places.

That there is nothing changeless or sacrosanct about all these traditions, value images and self-images associated with particular communities is strikingly demonstrated by the history of the *shuddhi* campaign conducted by the Arya Samaj and other Hindu organizations from the later nineteenth century onwards. Lajpat Rai observed in his *History of the Arya Samaj*, published in 1914, that '*The Arya Samaj, being a Vedic church,* and as such a Hindu organization, engages itself in reclaiming the *wandering sheep who have strayed from the Hindu fold,* and converts anyone prepared to accept its religious teachings.'[43] The *shuddhi* movement was a direct response to Christian missionary attacks on Hinduism and their efforts at converting low- and, to a lesser extent, high-caste Hindus in the nineteenth century: and the Christian inspiration of the Arya organization (into a 'church') and of Lajpat Rai's language ('wandering sheep' . . . brought back by their shepherd) is evident.

Lajpat Rai noted also that while *shuddhi* literally means 'purification', militant Hindu practice of the late nineteenth and early twentieth century had transformed its meaning. It now applied to a range of practices: (i) *conversion* to Hinduism of people belonging to 'foreign' religions; (ii) *reconversion* of those who had at some stage in the near or distant past taken to a 'foreign' religion; (iii) *reclamation*, that is, raising the status of the *antyaj* (depressed) classes and making them fully Hindus.[44]

This redefinition of the Hindu community and of legitimate Hindu practice, and this adoption of 'Christian' tactics like conversion, had something to do with the importance attached to numbers in the political and administrative calculations of the regime in late colonial India.[45] As the assertion of community identity gathered pace at many levels – Hindu, Muslim, Sikh, Ahir, Patidar, Nadar, Bihari, Oriya, Telugu – and economic and political competition took on new dimensions, militant Hindu leaders and organizations called upon Hindus to give up 'perverse' religious notions and practices, the 'silly''anti-national' traditions of caste divisions, the restrictions on inter-dining and on travel overseas, 'fantastic' ideas of pollution and the consequent ban on reconversion which ensured that 'millions of forcibly converted Hindus have remained Muslims even to this day'.[46] In the 1920s, Arya Samajis and more orthodox Hindu leaders 'rediscovered' the 'Devalasmrti', said to have been written a century or more after the Arab raids on Sindh, which prescribed lengthy rules for readmission into Hinduism of Hindus who had been forcibly converted; and in the 1930s, the *vratyastoma* rites (supposedly laid down in the *Atharvaveda* and the *Brahmanas*) for re-admittance of those who were earlier judged to have fallen out of 'Aryan' society.[47] Shastric authority had been marshalled for a new tradition.

If just one or two deaths occur in an incident now, as a local leader of the Communist Party of India (Marxist) observed in Bhagalpur, it is not even considered a riot.[48] Attacks on young and old, the blind and the maimed, women, children and infants; the aim of wiping out the 'enemy' and hence physical destruction (of lives, property, tools for work and standing crops) on a massive scale; the unashamed participation of the police; the lynching of people found on trains or buses passing through the affected area; all these have become standard features of today's 'communal riot'.

When the lynching of railway passengers first occurred on a large scale in 1947, it was remarked that the country had just been divided, two new states were coming into being, they needed time to consolidate their positions, the armed forces and police had also been split: confusion, serious crime and violence was almost inevitable. When such actions were repeated in 1984, it was said that a world leader and enormously popular prime minister had been assassinated, and when a colossus fails some upheaval, some exceptional reaction, is only natural. Now it has become unnecessary to plead exceptional circumstances when people are lynched or burned alive in the course of sectarian strife: newspapers report these occurrences, sometimes on their inner pages, without special comment.[49]

The discourse on violence brands events of this kind as 'extraordinary' but treats them as completely ordinary: inconsequential and unworthy of much attention. It is in this context that I turn, finally, to another 'fragment' from Bhagalpur that provides a somewhat different perspective on violence, a different commentary on the meaning of 'communal riots' today. I present this fragment here not as another piece, or even another kind, of 'evidence'. I propose it, instead, as the articulation of another subject-position arising from a certain experience (and understanding) of sectarian strife, which may say something about the parameters of our own subject-position and understanding. In addition, this articulation provides a commentary on the limits of the form of the historiographical discourse and its search for omniscience.

The fragment in question takes the form of a collection of poems written by a college teacher in Bhagalpur,[50] resident of a mixed Hindu and Muslim, predominantly lower-middle class locality which was not the scene of any of the 'great' killings in 1989, but was nevertheless repeatedly attacked, traumatized and scarred forever. In Manazir Aashiq Harganvi's poems, written for the most part during the first five days of the violence, we get some sense of the terror and desolation that so many people in Bhagalpur experienced at this time. The poems speak of darkness, of long nights, and of those days and nights that seemed to run into each other without meaning and without end. They speak of the hysterical screaming that marked that time, screams for help that were however drowned out by the laughter and shouts of the attackers:

> *Jaan leva hansi/Bhayanak kah kahe/Bachao kia waazen/ Balwaiyon ke beech phansi rah gayeen*
> (Blood-curdling laughter/Terrifying shouts/(Our) cries for help/ Lost among the attackers)

We have pictures here of fields of corpses, and the impossibility of counting them:

> *Ek . . . tin . . . sattar . . . sau . . . do sau . . . dhai sau/Yeh ginti paar nahin lagegi/Inhen ginne se pahle hi/Tum aa jate ho bam aur goli lekar/Ginti ki tadad badhane/Lamhe ki rupah li tasveer koi dekhe aakar!*
> (One . . . three . . . seventy . . . hundred . . . two hundred . . . two hundred and fifty/This counting will never end/For before it has ended/You come again with bombs and bullets/To increase the numbers to be counted/If only someone could come and see the beauty of this moment!)

We have a representation of the 'wake' waiting for the darkness to end and some light to begin to appear, but also – and more dreadfully – waiting simply for the attackers to come again:

Dangai phir aayenge/Aisa hai intezar
(The rioters will come again/We wait expectantly)

Among these poems there are many that talk about rape: a metaphorical statement of the humiliations suffered by a community, or a literal description of events that occurred?

Mar gaye bete mere/Biwi mari/Aur yeh beti jise tum saath mere kankhiyon se dekhte ho/Beshumar haathon ne loota hai ise.
(My sons have been killed/My wife is dead/And this daughter, whom you observe out of the corner of your eyes, sitting by my side/How many have looted her.)

Like the verse just quoted, there are many others that are addressed to neighbours and friends – or people who were once 'neighbours', 'friends'. Neighbours turned killers, people – known and unknown – running away from one another, and people ('all of us') afraid to look in the mirror for fear of what they/we will see. We have in them appeals, and accusations. We have figures of emptiness:

Kuch bhi nahin rah gaya hai kahin
(Nothing is left, anywhere)
Aadmi bahut hi bauna ho chuka hai
Apni lambai ka jhooth aahsas bhi baki nahin dacha
(Man has become a midget, unable any longer even to delude himself about his height)
Ham behad khokhle ho gaye hain
(We have been emptied [of meaning])
Aadhe-adhure log
(Half people, incomplete people)

And the endless search for ourselves, our loved ones, our friends:

Khud apne aap ko dhoondte hue
Ab tum us kinare par khade ho
Jahan se koi nahin lauta
Koi nahin lautta dost
Ab to tum bhi nahin laut paoge
Yaad ki sirf ek shart rahjayegi kijab bhi kahin
Fasad hoga, tum bahut yaad aaoge
(In search of yourself
You have now reached that shore
From where no one has returned

No one ever returns, my friend
Now you too are lost forever
There remains but one condition of memory that whenever, wherever
A riot occurs, I shall remember you.)

It is a fragment that tells us a great deal about the Bhagalpur 'riots' of 1989, and tell us also how much of this history we shall never be able to write.

Standard historiographical procedure since the nineteenth century appears to have required the taking of a prescribed centre (of a state-formation, nation-state) as one's vantage point and the 'official' archive as one's primary source for the construction of an adequate general 'history'. The power of this model can easily be seen in the writing of modern Indian history.

This is a procedure which is not easily discarded, both because states and nations are central organizing principles of human society as we know it, and because the historian must necessarily deal with periods, territories, social groups and political formations constituted into unities or blocs. However, the fact of their constitution – by historical circumstance and by the historian – needs to be borne in mind. The provisionally and contested character of all such unities (the objects of historical analysis) must be underlined.

I should like to suggest, in opposition to the established procedure, that, with all their apparent solidity and comprehensiveness, what the official sources give us is also but a fragment of history.[51] More, that what the historians call a 'fragment' – a weaver's diary, a collection of poems by an unknown poet (and to these we might add all those literatures of India that Macaulay condemned, creation myths and women's songs, family genealogies and local traditions of history) – is of central importance in challenging the state's construction of history, in thinking other histories and marking those contested spaces through which particular unities are sought to be constituted and others broken up.[52]

The PUDR team of which I was a member happened to be in Bhagalpur on the eve of India's Republic Day, January 1990. On the evening of the 25th, we heard extracts from the Indian Constitution being read out on the national television; 'WE, THE PEOPLE OF INDIA, having solemnly resolved to constitute India into a SOVEREIGN, SOCIALIST, SECULAR DEMOCRATIC REPUBLIC and to secure to all its citizens: JUSTICE, social, economic and political; LIBERTY of thought, expression, belief, faith and workship . . .!'[53] The remoteness of Delhi struck us on that occasion in a way that is hard to recapture in writing.

During the days immediately preceding, we had seen men, women and children in many areas, carrying little bundles of their belongings, running away from their villages to 'safer' places for fear of what might happen on 26 January. It was strongly rumoured that on that day of national celebration, Muslims – 'traitors' as always – would hoist black flags (or even the Pakistani flag) on their religious buildings and there would be another 'riot'. We had seen heated altercations among Muslim villagers and townsfolk, between those who said that running away only added to the alarmist rumours and the dangers, and others who accused them of foolhardiness in the light of 'all that has happened'. We had been asked in a relief camp to take down 'First Information Reports' and evidence because the police, who should have done this, were themselves the guilty party and, in many cases, still ensconced in office. The words 'justice' and 'liberty' rather stuck in the throat at this time. The remoteness of Delhi that I have mentioned is not a function of physical distance alone. I have no doubt that many have felt the same remoteness in Kota and Jaipur, in Meham and Maliana (Meerut), in Tilaknagar, across the river Jamuna from the capital of India, and indeed inside the old city of Delhi itself – where too talk of 'justice' and 'liberty' must often appear callous. We must continue to search for ways of representing that remoteness in the histories which we write.

□

A turning point in the modern history of violence against India's Dalit peoples took place in August 1991, in the town of Tsunduru (Chundur) in Andhra Pradesh. While Chundur has seen, over time, a change in the lifestyle of the Scheduled Castes, as 'virtual serfs till a few decades ago' became 'tenant cultivators' or acquired jobs, most of the farmlands continue to belong to upper-caste landlords, even though, unlike in Karamchedu – the site of an even more gruesome attack on Dalits six years earlier – there are few landlords in Chundur who own large tracts of land. The narrowing of educational disparity makes the tension over land more acute.

This iconic report, **The Chundur Carnage August 6, 1991,** by the **Andhra Pradesh Civil Liberties Committee**, is informally attributed to the major human rights theorist K. Balagopal. The support of Ms. V. Vasantha Lakshmi for permission to reprint excerpts is gratefully acknowledged. Also see Balagopal's 'Rich Peasant, Poor Peasant' in this volume.

Images montaged from The Chundur Carnage August 6, 1991, by the Andhra Pradesh Civil Liberties Committee

4

ANDHRA PRADESH CIVIL LIBERTIES COMMITTEE

1991

THE CHUNDUR CARNAGE

The Chundur Massacre has caught the attention of the whole country for, it is an event without parallel in the recent history of Andhra Pradesh. Indeed, after the *Kilvenmani*,[1] this is perhaps the biggest killing of Dalits, at least in south India. A detailed report of the massacre is given below. Here we would like to draw attention to some important diversions of the increasingly common phenomenon of 'atrocities on Dalits'.

The Indian Constitution has formally abolished untouchability in Article 17. Articles 15 and 16 guarantee, as a fundamental right, non-discrimination on caste grounds in certain specific matters such as education, employment and access to natural resources or public facilities. There is perhaps no parallel to these Articles in the Bills of Rights proclaimed by any other country's constitution. But then there is no parallel in the social history of any other country to the abominable caste system that prevails in India.

The protection of the Civil Rights Act later laid down punishments for the specific offences arising from the practice of untouchability. And the commissioner for Scheduled Castes and Scheduled Tribes has been compiling regular reports concerning the practice of untouchability in the country.

However, as time has passed, and as the country was set on the path of a distorted form of development, not only has untouchability not died out, but a new dimension which we today describe as 'atrocities on Dalits' has emerged at the end of the second decade of Independence. It is not that atrocities such as mass assault, arson, murder and rape never took place earlier, but the occurrence of these atrocities on a large and vicious scale is certainly a relatively recent social phenomenon. So that, not satisfied with Articles 15, 16 and 17 and the PCR Act,[2] the Parliament has felt compelled to enact a brand-new legislation aimed specifically at preventing these atrocities, namely The Scheduled Tribes and Scheduled Castes (Prevention of Atrocities) Act, 1989. Reading the provisions of the Act, one gets a clear profile of one major dimension of the recent history of rural India. No legislator would ever dream of the unspeakable offences enumerated in that Act, were it not true that they are perpetrated day in and day out and reported in the press.

It is not necessary to go very deep into the economic and political causes of this phenomenon. It is enough to note what is most important from the human rights point of view. So long as the Dalits were content to bemoan their fate but accept their lot, they were tolerated by the upper castes. They were regarded as lowly degraded creatures, but at least they were not subjected to mass attacks of arson, murder and rape. But once the Dalits started raising their heads and asserting their dignity, they became intolerable to the upper castes. Today a sizeable section has developed among the Dalits which refuses to regard its existence as something decreed by fate, but understands and analyses it as a product of historical injustice. Dalits today are demanding land, economic betterment, education, employment and above all social equality and dignity. It is this assertion that is found intolerable by the upper castes, including those who are themselves not very rich or powerful.

In Andhra Pradesh, the killing of Kotesu, in Kanchikacherla[3] in Krishna district two decades ago is usually regarded as the beginning of this phenomenon. But the recent spate of atrocities against Dalits began with the Karamchedu killing of 17 July 1985. On that day, six Dalit youth were murdered and three girls were raped by an armed gang of youth belonging to the Kamma caste. That caste was disproportionately represented in the Cabinet of N.T. Rama Rao, who was then the Chief Minister, and Karamchedu was actually the village of his daughter-in-law. It is certainly no coincidence that in Chundur it was the Reddys who perpetrated the massacre and that in the present Cabinet of Janardhan Reddy more than 50 per cent of the ministers are Reddys.[4]

We will briefly mention some facts concerning these incidents. One, in almost all the cases, the assailants were not just some persons belonging to upper castes but were persons with close kinship or political ties with those

44 ఏళ్ళ

in power. Two, in almost all the cases, there was prior history of tension between the assailants and the Dalits, and the police were well aware of that fact but failed to prevent the assault. Indeed, as in Chundur, in many cases the police were present at the spot but did nothing to prevent the assault. The Dalits today have reached a stage where they complain that the presence of police in a tension-ridden village is actually bad for them, for while the presence of police is an inhibiting factor for the retaliatory instincts of Dalits, it does not in any way inhibit the upper castes. They feel today that if the police are not present, they can at least have a straight and honest fight. Whenever a village has a long history of tension and conflict, one observes that the police repeatedly arrest and charge the Dalits but take very lenient action against the upper castes, which has a debilitating and demoralizing impact on the spirit of Dalits. Three, subsequent to the assault the action of the police has been equally lethargic. It can be said without any exaggeration that the police have never made any serious attempt to apprehend the principal assailants. Even in Chundur, though more than 70 persons are said to have been arrested till now, the principal assailants are still at large. And this, inspite of the fact that the Superintendent of Police (SP) of Guntur Sri Meena and the Deputy Inspector General of Police (DIG) Guntur Sri Aravinda Rao are persons whose reputation for ruthless policing of naxalite-affected areas where they served earlier is notorious. In all the cases, what has happened is that the assailants themselves surrendered after a month or two of evasion.

Four, the process of justice has been equally tardy. The Karamchedu massacre took place six years ago. It is believed by legal experts who are handling the case that there is enough evidence to convict at least twenty of the accused, and it is evident that if the trial had been completed and the sentence executed by now that would have had an inhibiting effect on the murderers of Chundur. But, after six years, the Karamchedu trial is yet to start. In cases where politically powerful persons are directly involved in the crime, as for instance, Congress (I) strongman Y.S. Rajasekhara Reddy in the Pulivendula arson case, Gorle Sriramulu Naidu in the Jeerupalem arson case, G. Narayana Reddy in the Ambaripet murder case or Telugu Desam Party strongman Karanam Balaramakrishna Murthy in the Timmasamudram arson and assault case, not even the formality of filing a case is observed by the police.

Lastly, we must mention the growing consolidation of upper-caste arrogance that is a distinctly post-Chundur phenomenon. At the time of Karamchedu massacre, there was no attempt by the upper castes to justify the killings. This time round, they are shamelessly and openly defending the Chundur massacre and proclaiming that more Chundurs will take place hereafter. An organization by the name *Sarve Janabyudaya Porata Samithi* (Struggle Committee for the Betterment of All People) has been formed under whose banner the forward castes are rallying their forces and organizing demonstrations, meetings, bandhs, etc. in protest against the self-assertion of the Dalits and what they describe as the partiality of the government. Their slogans are, 'Long live unity of forward castes', 'Those who beg every morsel should not be arrogant', etc. This casteist consolidation is no doubt a fallout of the anti-Mandal agitation wherein, for the first time after Independence, we saw forward castes mobilizing explicitly in the name of caste and being hailed as fighters for justice by the press and intelligentsia. The same faces that were seen in the anti-Mandal rallies are visible in the post-Chundur mobilization of forward castes. It has already resulted in an assault by forward-caste students on a predominantly Scheduled Caste college in Guntur in which they set fire to the books, certificates and clothes of the Dalit students in the presence of the District Superintendent of Police. In REC (former Regional Engineering College), Warangal, the police and the authorities were happy spectators to the bonfire lit by anti-Mandal agitators in the rooms belonging to backward-class students.

SOCIO-ECONOMIC STRUCTURE

What is the socio-economic situation in Chundur, which witnessed the attack by upper castes in which eight Dalits were killed and at least nine others are reported missing?

Chundur, the *mandal* headquarters, is located about 15 kilometres from Tenali town on the Tenali–Madras railway line. With an area of 18 square miles, Chundur has a population of about 5,800 with the Dalits and the upper castes in almost equal numbers.

The most dominant among the upper castes are the Reddys with nearly 800 families, who also own most of the land. There are about 225 Telaga, twenty-five Brahmin and about fifteen Vysya families. Among the Scheduled Castes, the largest group belongs to the Malas with nearly 400 families while there are about 100 Madiga families. There are a little over 100 families of Scheduled Tribes (Erukula and Yanadi).[5]

All was well in Chundur as long as the Dalits observed traditional norms in their relationship with the upper castes. Enlightened by education, the Dalit youth have begun challenging the rights 'attained by birth' of the other castes. This was the cause of the constant friction between the Dalits and the upper castes.

For a village like Chundur, the level of literacy is high. There are three primary schools and a high school in the village. Nearly 3,000 persons in the village know how to read and write, including a good number of women. While nearly fifteen Dalits have done their post-graduation, there are scores of graduates and about 200 matriculates among them. But there are few among the upper castes with such a level of education.

The education naturally helped the Dalits to secure jobs. Nearly 300 of them work in the Railways as fitters and gangmen. Some of them are employed in the telephones department, banks, and a few Dalits have also become Mandal Revenue Officers.[6]

Over a period of time, there has been a change in the lifestyle of the Scheduled Castes. People, who were virtual serfs till a few decades ago have now become tenant cultivators, while the younger generation has acquired decent jobs. This transformation among the Dalits was seen as a threat to their authority by the upper castes. They could no longer address the Dalits in the customary rude manner. Public places like tea shops and cinema halls have come into common use by the upper castes and the Dalits.

Despite their education, the Dalits are economically way behind the upper castes, as most of the farmland belonged to the latter. Of the nearly 2,400 acres of cultivable land in the village, the Reddys own about 1,200 acres and the Telagas, 250 acres. The Dalits own a mere 90 acres. The upper castes of the surrounding villages have about 200 acres in Chundur. The Brahmins own a little over 100 acres and the Vysyas about 65 acres.

Unlike in Karamchedu, there are few landlords in Chundur who own large areas of land. According to the records available with the Mandal Revenue Office, more than 1,100 persons (of whom 68 are Scheduled Castes and twelve are Scheduled Tribes) own less than a hectare of land. About 250 of the villagers own land ranging between one and two hectares while those possessing more than two hectares number around 85.

THE SEQUENCE OF EVENTS

The upper castes gave vent to their seething anger over the self-assertion of Dalits following an incident at the theatre on 7 July (1991). On that day, a Dalit youth, Ravi, a post-graduate student at Nagpur, rested his foot on the seat in front which was occupied by an upper caste boy Kurri Srinivasa Reddy. A minor altercation ensued between Ravi and Srinivasa Reddy when the latter abused the Dalit youth in the name of his caste.

Soon after this incident, Ravi left for Ongole. The next day, Ravi's father Bhaskar Rao, a teacher in Munnangivaripalem hamlet, skirting Chundur, was forcibly taken away by a group of Reddys and subjected to brutal torture forcing him to reveal the whereabouts of his son. The upper castes succeeded in eliciting information from Bhaskar Rao that Ravi would return to Chundur that evening by the Madras–Howrah express.

Ravi was warned by some Dalit youth of the impending attack by the upper castes the moment he alighted from the train. Sensing danger to his

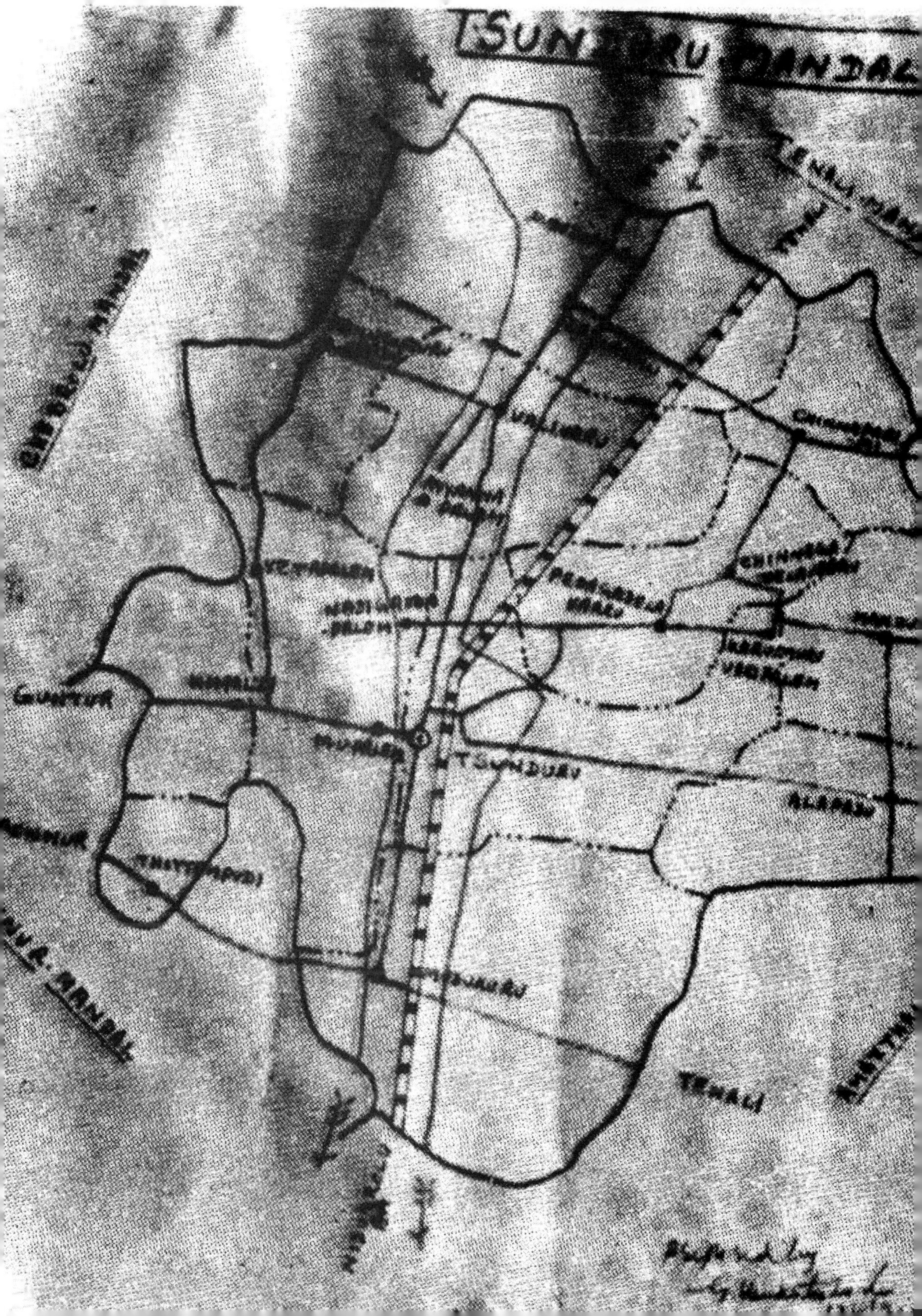
GUNTUR
T SUNDURU
ALAPADU
TENALI

life, Ravi fled to the neighbouring Pedagajulapalii village and took shelter in the house of a Dalit. The upper castes managed to trace him down after falsely alleging that Ravi had fled Chundur after stealing some gold ornaments from a house. Ravi was mercilessly beaten in Pedagajulapalli itself and later brought to Chundur in a tractor. He was kept in the Mandal Revenue Office for a few hours when he was again beaten up and forced to consume liquor. Later, he was admitted to the Government Hospital in Tenali with bleeding injuries. While the police took no action against the upper castes, the latter implicated Ravi in a case of theft. The incident occurred at the instance of the Chundur sarpanch (village leader) Modugula Sambi Reddy, who was also the principal assailant in the subsequent killing of Dalits, on 6 August.

On 9 July, the Reddys and Telagas formed into a committee and decided to enforce a social boycott of the Dalits (Malas). The committee was again headed by the village sarpanch. Since then, the Dalits were not allowed to work in the fields of the upper castes nor were they permitted to enter the upper-caste locality. Land tenancies of the Dalits were cancelled.

The social boycott of the Dalits led to tension and at this stage Section 144[7] was promulgated in the village. While the upper castes engaged outside labour to work in their fields, the Dalits left to places like Tenali and Ponnur in search of work. A 50-strong police picket headed by the Tenali Rural Circle Inspector Saibabu was posted in the village since then.

On the night of 12 July, the upper castes of the village, supported by the Reddys of Modukur, Dindipalem and Valiveru villages, tried to attack the Dalit quarters in Chundur. The Dalits too were prepared to counter any attack. However, the police intervened and lathi-charged both the groups to disperse them. They even opened fire in the air. A constable was reportedly injured when the upper-caste men hurled soda bottles at the police party.

The next day, Circle Inspector Saibabu summoned the Dalits on the pretext of forming a peace committee in the village. The police then arrested eighteen persons from among the upper castes and an equal number of Dalits and registered cases against them. Subsequently, the police arrested eight more Reddys and two Dalits. All of them were released on conditional bail on 16 July. As the village remained incident-free for the next few days, the police lifted the prohibitory orders on 29 July.

Again on 4 August, a Dalit youth, Rajababu, was attacked by the Reddys while he was reading a newspaper in a tea shop. Rajababu suffered a minor injury in the attack. While the police took no action against the culprits, a case was registered against Rajababu following a complaint lodged by the upper castes that he had harassed their girls. The Dalits sought to retaliate but were persuaded against doing so by Chundur Sub-Inspector Srinivas, a person in whom the Dalits had confidence.

The next day, word was sent to Yakob, a Dalit fair-price shop dealer, that the Mandal Revenue Officer (MRO) had summoned him. Even as he was proceeding towards the office of the MRO in the upper-caste locality, he was attacked by the Reddys who stabbed him. The Sub-Inspector came to the rescue of Yakob and took him to hospital immediately. The same night additional forces were rushed to Chundur even as prohibitory orders were re-imposed in the village.

THE FINAL ASSAULT

And then came the final assault on the Dalits on the morning of 6 August. The ghastly incident was pre-planned and well executed by the upper castes with the clear connivance of the police officials present in the village. The complicity of the police is obvious from the fact that the carnage took place when prohibitory orders were in force and the whole village was tense for the past one month.

One version is that a few Dalit youth attacked and inflicted minor injuries on some Reddys who were working in their fields on the morning of 6 August. However, this was blown out of proportion by the upper-caste people who spread the falsity that three Reddy men were hacked to death by the Dalits. The upper castes of Chundur reportedly contacted the Reddys of Modukur over telephone and asked them to be prepared for attacking the Dalits. By then, the upper-caste men of nearby Valiveru, Manchala, Munnangivaripalam and Vellaturu villages were also mobilized for an assault on Dalits.

Around 11 a.m., Saibabu and Vemuru Sub-Inspector Sheik Madarvali came to the Dalit quarters and asked them to flee as CRPF (Central Reserve Police Force) men from Mangalagiri might raid the village anytime to pick them up following a complaint lodged by the upper castes. When the Dalits were hesitant to leave the village, the police virtually chased them away. However, all the Dalit women stayed back.

The Dalits, unaware that they were virtually walking into a death trap began fleeing into the fields only to be chased by the upper-caste men from all corners of the village. The marauders, who came in tractors and scooters and were well armed, first caught the fleeing Dalits, beat them with iron rods and killed them with daggers and axes. They then leisurely packed some of the bodies in gunny bags and dumped them in the river Tungabhadra drain and the irrigation canal. The bodies of three Dalits, who were killed when they were hiding in a jasmine grove abutting the drain, were left there itself.

Several Dalit women pointed out that policemen were present in the tractors which carried the upper-caste men as they went about chasing the Dalits. Scores of policemen, who remained in Dalit quarters after forcing the men to flee remained deaf to the cries of the Dalits being massacred by the upper-caste mob.

As 60-year-old Sampurna recalls, 'On hearing the cries of our menfolk from the nearby jasmine grove, I pleaded with the policemen to protect them from the Reddys. But the police brushed aside my request saying that our men were not being attacked by anyone but were only singing songs while working in the fields.' When the old woman persisted with her plea, a policeman shot back saying, 'What is there with you, except ash. If we support the Reddys, we get bundles.' And as the wife of one of the victims put it later, 'But for the police, our men would have stayed back in the village and resisted any attempt to attack them.' 'It is the police who killed our people,' she said, sobbing.

The brutality of the upper castes is well explained by 18-year-old Dayari Dhanraj, who narrowly escaped death. 'After the police asked us to flee, I and a few others ran towards the railway tracks. We rested there for a few minutes but took to our heels again after we saw the Reddys approaching us. We ran for about 4 kilometres towards the fields belonging to the Reddys of Modukuru. We did not know that the Reddys of Modukur were waiting for us. There, they managed to catch hold of Mandru Ramesh and Devarapalli Jayaraj. Even as I was fleeing, I saw both of them being hacked to death in full public view'.

After he ran for another kilometre, Dhanraj was caught by another group of Reddy men. He was beaten with rods and sticks and his leg was twisted to prevent him from escaping. Dhanraj would have been killed the moment he was caught had he not been kept in a macabre fashion as a 'prey' for a handicapped upper-caste person, Mallikarjuna Reddy, who wanted to have the pleasure of killing at least one Dalit personally. Even as Dhanraj was writhing in pain, the upper-caste mob removed at least a bottle of blood from him with the help of a syringe and left him in the fields. They then left for Chundur by vehicles to bring Mallikarjuna Reddy for carrying out the 'final operation'. Dhanraj, however, managed to jump into the canal and swam towards Alapadu where some Dalit women rescued him. Late in the night, he was dressed up as a female and brought to Chundur railway station. He was later taken to Tenali government hospital and admitted there.

By 7 August itself, most of the Dalits, including women, fled Chundur and took refuge in the salvation army church at Itanagar in Tenali. It was here that 35-year-old Parisudha Rao died of a heart attack after seeing the body of his younger brother, Mandru Ramesh, in the Tenali government hospital.

Four days later, the Dalit victims returned to Chundur after they decided to carry out their struggle by staying on in the village itself.

□

In one of the most poignant and hard-hitting essays signalling the millennial turn, economist **Utsa Patnaik** claims that India is undergoing conditions that must be viewed as famine-like: except that an astonishing combination of policy decisions and economic methodologies are effectively rendering invisible both the famine itself and the people suffering from it. The text resonates with history going back to late colonialism as it explores how people, as human bodies as well as national subjects, are being configured as recipients of 'targeted' benefit.

Originally presented as a public lecture organized by the Safdar Hashmi Memorial Trust (SAHMAT) on 10 April 2004 in New Delhi, on the occasion of the fiftieth birth anniversary of theatre activist Safdar Hashmi, first published in **Social Scientist** (vol. 32, no. 9–10, September–October 2004, pp. 9–35) and reprinted in Utsa Patnaik, **The Republic of Hunger and Other Essays** (Gurgaon: Three Essays Collective, 2007), this is an abridged version created with the support and permission of the author.

Images: Details from Glimpses from the Mukti Morcha (2018) by photographer Anushka Jain, originally published by the **People's Archive of Rural India (PARI)**. Grateful acknowledgement to Anushka Jain and P. Sainath.

5

UTSA PATNAIK

2004

THE REPUBLIC OF HUNGER

In the course of the last five years (1998–2003), the population of the Republic of India has been sliding down towards sharply lowered levels of per capita foodgrains absorption, levels so low in particular years that they have not been seen for the last half century. Between the early 1990s when economic reforms began, and at present, the annual absorption of foodgrains per head has come down from 177 kg to 155 kg. Such low absorption levels were last seen in the initial years of World War II – from where they had fallen further still. Again, after some recovery, the very first few years after Independence half a century ago, and the food crisis of the mid-1960s, are comparable to present average absorption levels.

Over four-fifths of the total fall has taken place in the last five years alone. This steep and unprecedented fall in foodgrains absorption in the last five years has entailed a sharp increase in the numbers of people in hunger, particularly in rural areas, and for very many it has meant starvation. The average downward movement in turn is the outcome of divergent trends – foodgrains absorption is rising fast for the (mainly urban) well-to-do, and is either the same or falling faster than the average for the bulk of the (mainly rural) population.

This phenomenon of increasing numbers in hunger can be established both on the basis of the hardest and most reliable data that we have from official sources, as well as from the ground-level experience of individual researchers and of organizations working in rural areas. The phenomenon is completely independent of the recent drought, and indeed the lowest levels of foodgrains absorption to date has been registered two years *before* the severe drought of 2002–03.

The perception of the government, and of the majority of academics, is however very different from that expressed above: they interpret the development as nothing out of the ordinary, and many indeed even see it as a positive development, indicating a voluntarily chosen, more diversified basket of consumption by all segments of the population including the poor. When as a ground reality, the incidence of hunger rises, a 'denial mode' amongst those who govern and also amongst those who are associated with making or influencing policy during the period concerned is to be expected. But in the present case, the divergence between the reality of increasing hunger, and the prevalent bland justifications of the phenomenon as a positive one, is so stark and so striking, that this divergence itself perhaps requires a theoretical explanation. Never before in the independent history of our country have we seen the kind of wholesale denial of a negative trend, and of its packaging and presentation as a positive development, as we are seeing at present. Moreover, the packaging and the justifications are not being put forward only by the right-wing political class which is responsible for the present debacle. That the present government and ruling class in this country should seek to sanitize, and justify the deeply anti-humanist and negative trend of increasing hunger, is to be expected. What is disturbing is that a large number of hitherto liberal academics are also advancing these justifications on the basis of various theories which are, needless to say, quite fallacious.

THE INTERNATIONAL CONTEXT OF THE DISCUSSION

Before going on to the details of the story in India, let us situate this story within the broader context of the past international approaches to hunger and famine. For this, I will take up two cases – the alleged massive famine in China during the Great Leap, 1958–61, and the internationally unrecognized famine in Russia in the first half of the 1990s. When we look at these cases, it becomes clear that the entire field of discussion of hunger and famine is a highly ideological one, and has been routinely characterized by an abandonment of minimum academic

First, let us consider the allegation that 27 to 30 million people died in China during the 'Great Leap' period. This allegation is contained in the books of two US demographers Ansley J. Coale and Judith Banister.[1] The main popularizer and ardently uncritical supporter of the conclusions of these US demographers has however been Amartya K. Sen, and it is through Sen's writings[2] that the world, and the reading public in this country, has been informed that 'China has had what is almost certainly the largest recorded famine in history (when 30 million people died in the famine that followed the Great Leap Forward in 1958–61) whereas India has not had a famine since independence in 1947'.[3] The figure of 30 million has passed into popular folklore. However, a study of how it has been arrived at shows that this estimate has no scholarly basis whatsoever.

The facts are that there was a run of three bad harvests, and a steep 30 per cent drop in foodgrains output in 1960, while the government's procurement from the villages did not decline, lowering availability per head. The official death rate, which had been falling up to 1958 owing to public health and sanitation measures, registered a rise to 25.4 per thousand in 1960. (This peak 'famine' death rate in China was however little different from India's actual, 'normal' death rate, 24.6, in the same year). The birth rate also fell steeply in 1958, mainly owing to labour mobilization for collective work.

Two alternative routes have been used to estimate 'famine deaths', both of dubious validity. In the first, twenty-seven million in the population pyramid have been identified with 'famine deaths' between 1958 and 1961. The problem with this is that not only were actually living people, who died in excess of normal numbers, included in the missing millions, but hypothetical persons are included who were never born at all and who 'should' have been born if the birth rate had not fallen. This is not a common-sense definition, nor is it logical: for, to 'die' in a famine, a minimum necessary condition is to be born in the first place. The Chinese are a highly talented people but even they cannot achieve the feat of dying without being born. If a person is told that thirty million people died, then quite correctly she would infer that those thirty million were alive and then died. The fact that nineteen million of them never existed because they were never born in the first place, is not conveyed by the formulation. Hence, there is disingenuousness involved in saying that thirty million people 'died'.

The second route followed by Coale and Banister is even more dubious. They take population totals yielded by official 1953 and 1964 censuses in China to be correct, but dispute the official fertility rate, even though it was based on a very large sample of thirty million persons or 5 per cent of the-then population, especially canvassed along with the 1953 census, as Nai-Ruenn Chen had informed us.[4] Instead, they use the much later Census 1982 study to project back very high fertility rates to the past, thus constructing an entirely hypothetical larger total of births between 1953 and 1964.

If more people were born over the inter-censal period 1953 to 1964, correspondingly these extra people must also have died over the same period: for both authors, despite rejecting every official vital rate, display a touching faith in absolute census population totals at these two dates. With this procedure, the official figure of total deaths over the inter-censal period, was raised by a heroic 60 per cent. Both authors then arbitrarily allocated the assumed higher numbers of deaths over the individual inter-censal years, by assuming varying rates by which deaths were allegedly 'under-reported' during each of these years. In short, it was entirely up to the demographer how many extra deaths were assigned to the Great Leap years, and the totally arbitrary nature of the procedure can be gauged by the fact that Coale raised the 1960 death rate to nearly 39 while Banister raised it to 44.6 (compared to the official death rate of 25.4). There is no reasonable basis for either figure.

Nor is this all: a *linear time trend* was then fitted by both, to deaths derived from a variable – the death rate – which always behaves *non-linearly,* and the extent to which the (arbitrarily constructed) death rate was above this declining trend, was then used to derive total 'excess deaths', the figure being 27 million for Coale and 30 million for Banister. We know that deaths in a population can never reach zero, so fitting linear trends makes no sense. The linear trend procedure implies that the Chinese population would have reached zero deaths and attained immortality in a few years – a remarkable achievement indeed, impossible outside the nonsensical procedures followed by the US demographers.

It is a travesty of the norms of academic integrity that grossly exaggerated estimates of 'famine' deaths derived in this arbitrary manner have been uncritically quoted and promoted and that they enjoy so much currency. In my detailed critique,[5] my calculations show that the lowest possible availability figures we can get for China, after taking into account government procurement, is still higher than in India, and it is a puzzle why, given a much more egalitarian distribution, the death rate should have risen even to the officially declared level. Because the internal political developments in China after 1978 were in the direction of attacking Maoist egalitarianism and the commune system, no repudiation from Chinese sources are to be seen.

In sharp contrast to the retrospective, patently ideological, construction of hypothetical large famine deaths in China's Great Leap period and the publicizing of these figures, we find that the demographic collapse in Russia in the first half of the 1990s has been met with a deafening silence from the same academics. The estimation methods which they applied to China are not applied by them to Russia. The facts are that so-called 'shock therapy' to usher in capitalism, under the advice of western experts, led to a catastrophic collapse of Gross Domestic Product (GDP) in the former

लोकजागृति
मध्य प्रदेश

socialist states between 1990 and 1996. The GDP level was half or less in Russia and Ukraine by 1996 compared to a decade earlier, and collapsed to only one-fifth of the mid-eighties level in Georgia, which was the worst affected. Never in peacetime have we ever seen such a comprehensive destruction of productive capacities and outputs, entirely owing to the wrong macroeconomic policies advised by foreign experts and followed by the local policymakers. The human effects have been devastating, with a sharp reversal of the decades of improvement in all human development indicators. The death rate among the able-bodied rose from nearly 49 to 58 (per thousand) comparing 1992 with 1990, and rose further to 84 per thousand by 1994. The male expectation of life declined by nearly six years in Russia. With the steep rise in the death rate, the total population of Russia showed absolute decline – again, an unprecedented situation in peacetime.

Where were those academics who profess to be concerned with hunger and famine, when it came to analysing the economic and demographic collapse in Russia? It can hardly be argued that journalists and the media had no access to the country after 1990. It is not reasonable to count the effects of the decline in the birth rate, if any, to estimate 'famine deaths'. If we apply a reasonable method of simply taking the 1990 death rate in Russia as the benchmark, and calculate extra deaths among the able-bodied by 1996, we get a figure of more than four million excess deaths in Russia alone. In relation to Russia's population, this famine was three times larger than the great Bengal famine in India in 1943–44 and twice as large as the Chinese excess mortality – accepting the official figures – during the Great Leap years. The Russian famine is neither internationally recognized nor publicized, for the very good reason that Russia was making a transition to *capitalism*, and it is *this* process that gave rise to the famine. Those eager to discredit socialism, even at the cost of indefensible statistical procedures, appear to be less than willing to recognize the existence of famine, or to estimate famine deaths, in a 'transitional' society like Russia, even though the case is contemporary and well documented.

THE SIGNIFICANCE OF THE DECLINE IN INDIA'S FOOD ABSORPTION IN THE LIGHT OF HISTORICAL TRENDS

We have not yet reached, in India, the nadir of average foodgrains absorption seen in Sub-Saharan Africa under economic reforms and trade liberalization. The six most populous countries of Sub-Saharan Africa, accounting for 60 per cent of the entire region's population, have seen declining calorie intake per diem, because declining food aid is not compensating for lowered domestic food production.

A large segment of the rural masses in India with a much lower foodgrains absorption than the average, have been already reduced to the nutritional status of Sub-Saharan Africa. On the basis of the NSS (National Sample Survey) data on calorie intake for 1999–2000, I estimate that about 40 per cent of the rural population was at the low absorption level of the Sub-Saharan Africa average. It is not for any lack of effort by the Indian government that the situation is not worse. If the present (incorrect) policies – of official denial of the widening ambit of hunger, the failure to undertake expansionary development policies and the official promotion of export-oriented corporate agriculture – continue to be followed, it may well be a matter of another five years before we see the descent of the whole of rural India to the present average nutritional status of Sub-Saharan Africa.

It is hardly possible to imagine a more drastic reversal of the goal of food security than has been seen in the last five years. The fifty years of a dying colonial rule before Independence had seen annual foodgrains availability per head decline by a quarter (considering five-year averages and leaving aside the individual post-war years). The war years included the terrible Bengal famine with a mortality of at least three million. I have elsewhere argued[6] that, although the proximate cause of the famine was the inflationary burden of financing the war which was unjustly placed on India, the actual toll in the Bengal famine would not have been so large without the preceding three decades of declining nutrition in Bengal, which had seen a larger-than-average drop in per capita foodgrains availability by nearly 40 per cent between 1911 and 1947. Many who had seen the Bengal famine before their eyes had an important role in formulating post-Independence policy: of prioritizing the attainment of food security at least in the limited sense of self-sufficiency. We thus saw a rise, albeit a painfully slow one, in the foodgrains availability per head. While new agricultural strategy and the green revolution no doubt had many drawbacks as regards equity of distribution, the rise in average output and availability was a major achievement, and it should not be underrated.

In contrast, over four-fifths of the loss has taken place in the last five years alone, as we have lost forty years of effort in just the last decade of neoliberal economic reforms. The most remarkable and disastrous feature of the last five years of NDA (National Democratic Alliance) rule in India (i.e. 1998–2004), has been the slide-back to a level not seen for fifty years. Reports of starvation, farmer suicides and deepening hunger should cause little surprise when we consider the recent trends in the official data on foodgrains output and availability.

Even more striking than output decline, however, has been the decline in foodgrains availability, or absorption per capita over the same period. Availability (defined as net output-plus-net imports, and minus-net additions to public stocks) has fallen by four times as much as output. A large gap between per capita output and availability was last seen during the food crisis of the mid-1960s, but in the opposite direction – at that time, since output fell, 19 million tonnes of foodgrains were imported over two years to ensure enough domestic availability, apart from existing stocks being drawn down for the same purpose. By contrast in recent years even though output per head has fallen, both very large additions to stocks as well as massive food exports have taken place, resulting in large availability decline.

Availability is the same as the actual *absorption* of foodgrains, and the two terms will be used interchangeably. There was a slow decline in the absorption of foodgrains per head of the country's population between 1991–92 and 1997–98, after which it has fallen very sharply to abysmally low levels similar to those last seen during the early years of the Second World War which included the terrible Bengal famine. Since the richest one-sixth to one-fifth of the population, mainly urban, has been improving and diversifying diets, the nutritional decline for the poorer three-fifths of the population, mainly rural, has been much greater than the average fall indicates.

Often the argument is heard that, since per capita income is rising, it is to be expected that people should consume less cereals and pulses (which then become inferior goods), and consume more high-value foods: in short, people diversify their diets. A falling share of grains in the consumer budget, as income rises, is known as Engel's Law. It is now argued that, in line with this Law, there is nothing wrong if we see falling availability/ absorption of foodgrains per head. This is a total misconception regarding this Law, one that has contributed to incorrect official explanations of large stocks as arising from 'overproduction'. It is a misconception because Engel was referring to the fall in the share of expenditure for *direct* consumption of grains as income rises, and not to the *total* absorption of grains which include direct as well as indirect use (as feed for livestock to produce milk, eggs, meat and so on, or as industrial raw material). The absorption of foodgrains per capita is always found to rise, not fall, as the consumer's average income rises. The figures of availability, as indeed all official figures of availability, refer to absorption of grain *for all purposes*. (Availability figures do not require consumption data but are calculated directly from output data, which is the hardest data we have, and it is adjusted only for trade and for stocks, so it has by definition to meet all possible final uses).

Availability of foodgrains thus includes not only direct consumption (as roti, boiled rice and so on) but also the part that is converted to animal products, by being used as commercial feedgrains, and that which is at present part of animal products being exported. The availability, or absorption, of foodgrains per head, *because it is for all uses*, always rises as a nation's per capita income rises. This is a very well-known fact, and is supported by an extensive literature on the responsiveness of demand for cereals to rising incomes.

China, with about double India's per capita income, absorbed 325 kg per capita of foodgrains in the mid-1990s compared to India's less than 200 kg at that time. Mexico absorbed 375 kg per capita, high-income Europe absorbed over 650 kg per capita and USA absorbed the maximum, 850 kg per capita, of which less than a quarter was directly consumed and the rest converted to animal products, processed, or put to industrial use.

The recent trend in this country of sharply declining foodgrains absorption per head, while average per capita income has been rising, is thus highly abnormal, not only in the light of international experience but also in comparison with our own past experience – we have always seen rising grain absorption per capita as average incomes rose in the past in India. Between 1950 and 1991, per capita absorption rose slowly from 152 kg to 177 kg as per capita incomes rose. As earlier observed these gains of four decades have been wiped out in a single decade of economic reform, and while availability fell by 3 kg per head in the seven years up to 1998, over eight-tenths of the total fall has taken place in the mere five years of NDA rule.

What lies behind the decline in the absorption of foodgrains? The massive decline at present compared to 1998, is the result of *an unprecedented decline in purchasing power in rural areas* following directly from a number of deflationary policies at the macroeconomic level, combined with international price declines for the larger volumes of export crops produced in India following trade liberalization. Both deflationary policies and opening up to trade are integral to neoliberal economic reforms. This has resulted in a deflation of effective demand as far as the mass of the rural population is concerned.

The continuous decline in purchasing power, hence also decline in foodgrains absorption for direct consumption purposes, resulted in a continuous decline in sales from the PDS (Public Distribution System), which therefore got reflected in the continuous and increasing additions to public food stocks year after year starting from 1998, with the total stocks standing at 63.1 million tonnes by the end of July 2002. This was nearly forty million tonnes in excess of buffer norms – and this, in spite of declining per capita foodgrains output, and two to four million tonnes of grain exports every year up to June 2002, after which exports undertaken by the government have surged to unprecedented levels.

Last year, the worst drought year for two decades, between June 2002 and June 2003, the NDA government exported a record 12 million tonnes of foodgrains out of stocks, and continued to export a million tonnes a month, bringing the declared total exports to over 17 million tonnes by November

2003. Independent India has never before seen such huge exports, only made possible by more and more empty stomachs over the preceding years. It is an utter scandal and a disgrace that, at the same time that millions of the rural poor were going hungry, and those already hungry were being pushed into starvation, rather than undertake widespread food-for-work programmes the government preferred to feed foreigners and their cattle by exporting foodgrains, applying a heavy subsidy to beat low world price. The concerned ministry has had the gall to put full-page advertisements in newspapers in March as part of the government's pre-election 'shining India' campaign, celebrating among other things its export earnings.

Now that the perception of drought has ended, food-for-work projects have been wound up, and the media are full of a good monsoon and record projected grain output in 2003–04, the prognosis for a recovery of absorption levels to anywhere near that of 1998, remain very bleak. Let us remember that millions more than before were going hungry, at only 158 kg average absorption level in the year of the largest harvest seen to date. The difference between output and absorption was going into addition to stocks, held at increasing cost, and into exports.

While the difficult late 1960s and early 1970s also had fairly low availability, only somewhat higher than at present, it has to be recognized that the situation for the rural poor is worse today compared to then, because a larger part of the lowered absorption of today is going into animal products (the consumption of which is highly concentrated with the well-to-do) and into open market sales to processing units.

Thus, no policies were followed of an expansionary nature, to reduce stocks by implementing large-scale food-for-work schemes in all rural areas in order to generate employment and restore purchasing power to earlier levels, as had been widely suggested by progressive movements. All that was done was to allocate larger amounts of foodgrains to relief works in drought-hit areas alone. It is the massive 12 million tonnes of exports plus 6 million tonnes of open-market sales which mainly reduced stocks by July 2003, and these obviously did not benefit the poor. The very fact that 33 million tonnes procurement took place in a severe drought year also indicates distress sales by farmers.

Neither government, nor its policymakers, are prepared to recognize the fact that falling availability reflects a contraction of effective demand. On the contrary, the explanation put forward in official publications of the Finance Ministry and the Reserve Bank of India (RBI), and propagated by most academic economists, is precisely the opposite, namely that there is 'overproduction'. The Economic Survey (2001–02) argued that excess stocks were a surplus over what people voluntarily wish to consume, and represented a 'problem of plenty'. National Sample Survey data on falling share of cereals in the spending on food, were quoted to argue that not

D.J.B

only the well-to-do, but all segments of the population were voluntarily diversifying their diets to high value foods away from cereals. It said that minimum support prices (MSP) to farmers have been 'too high', resulting in excessive output and procurement. The Reserve Bank of India's Annual Report 2001–02 repeated this argument, explaining the alleged mismatch between supply and demand as arising from rising administered acquisition price for rice and wheat, against the global trend of falling market prices, leading to 'wrong' price signals to the farmers, and hence to 'excessive' output and procurement of these crops.

Evidently the authors of these arguments have never heard of the difference between direct consumption of grain and the absorption of grain for all purposes – both direct and indirect – which has been already explained: if they had, they could not have given the above arguments, or talked of overproduction, especially given the fact that the very same reports show massive fall in availability per head. Further, their arguments might have had some little persuasive power if rural growth rates, employment and incomes had been rising. But official data shows precisely the opposite is the case. **For a country which has been seeing sharp deceleration of agricultural growth in the 1990s, falling per capita foodgrains output, and sharply rising rural unemployment, arguments on voluntary dietary diversification for all rural population segments are illogical to the point of being foolish. We now know why the central government undertook massive food exports last year in a situation of steeply falling food availability, and despite a severe drought: it has all been justified and rationalized already, simply by interpreting deepening hunger and starvation as 'voluntary choice,' and way below normal consumption, as overproduction in a grotesque travesty of reality.**

John Maynard Keynes had once remarked that the world moves on little else but ideas: and the socially irrational outcome we see before our eyes, of increasing hunger amidst relative plenty, illustrates starkly the effects that fallacious theories and wrong policies following from them, can have in lowering mass welfare. The fallacy involved in the official view is the *fallacy of composition*, where a statement which is correct for a *part* of the whole, is wrongly inferred to be correct for the whole. With income distribution shifting sharply in their favour, the top one-sixth of the population has certainly been voluntarily diversifying diets, but the poorer majority of the population cannot afford to do so, any more than the hungry poor of Paris, crying for bread, could heed Queen Marie Antoinette's advice to eat cake.

It seems that the question of effective demand and of *demand deflation* is simply not understood by most people. While everyone understands food shortage as in a drought, namely a physical output shortfall which curtails *supply*, it appears to baffle many that even more severe consequences can arise when the *effective demand*, the purchasing power of the masses falls, so that even though the physical supplies of foodgrains are there, people starve or move into hunger, owing to their inability to purchase food or to access food.

The reasons for declining rural mass effective demand, in the 1990s to date, are many and are all connected with deflationary neoliberal reforms combined with trade liberalization. They will be summarized only briefly here. First, public rural development expenditures were reduced to 8 per cent of the GDP by the early nineties. Since 1998, they have been reduced further, averaging less than 6 per cent of the GDP and in some years falling to less than 5 per cent. This means a drop in incomes in agriculture annually. This order of income fall, combined with real income declines owing to other causes detailed below, is broadly consistent with the observed fall in the contribution of agriculture to the GDP during the nineties, from around one-third to just over a quarter at present.

Let us remember that rural development expenditures include all employment generation programmes – special areas programmes, village industry, irrigation and flood control, energy and transport – apart from agriculture and rural development. Further, that public fixed capital formation in agriculture has also continued its decline even more sharply in the 1990s. It is hardly surprising that the rate of agricultural growth has slowed drastically in the 1990s and fallen below population growth for the first time in thirty years, and that the NSS employment surveys show an alarming collapse of rural employment growth. Rural job losses are reflected in a lower participation rate, higher open unemployment, and an absolute decline in the numbers employed in agriculture.

Despite all its recent strident talk of development, and the costly media publicity to every project, the reality is that no government has followed more systematically anti-development policies than has the NDA during the last five years. The decline in rural purchasing power has also contributed substantially to industrial recession: through demand linkages for simple consumer goods and manufactured inputs. The only sector which has grown fast is the services sector which has ballooned, at the expense of the material productive sectors. As income distribution has shifted to the urban elites, a modern version of the medieval Mughal economy is emerging: with dozens of service providers to each individual rich household. Only a small segment of the services sector is highly-paid IT-related services: the major expansion comes from lower-paid service activities.

At the very same time that unemployment was growing and real earnings of the rural masses falling owing to deflationary policies, the government – years before it was required to do so under World Trade Organization (WTO) bending to the pressure of advanced countries – removed all quantitative restrictions on trade by April 2001, and exposed our farmers to unfair trade, global price volatility and recession-hit external markets. It is one thing to open the economy to trade when markets are expanding, and quite another to do so when the world capitalist economy is in recession.

Anyone with a rudimentary knowledge of the past behaviour of global commodity markets should have been able to predict the crashing of prices after the sharp rise of the early 1990s, and also to predict that advanced countries would immediately raise their subsidies as they have always done (this author had warned of both in a 1997 paper). India's policy makers have however been unequal to the task. These free-trade dogmas ensure reduction of protection to their own producers by gullible developing-country governments, at the same time that advanced countries increase their non-tariff barriers and massively raise their subsidies – the greater part of which they have, for their own convenience, already defined as non-trade distorting and placed outside reduction commitments in the (WTO's) Agreement on Agriculture.

While the main prize – for servile implementation of deflationary BWI (Bretton-Woods Institutions) dictates against mass interests – goes to the central government and its policy advisers, the consolation prize for the most adverse state-level policies should go to the Telugu Desam Party government of Andhra Pradesh which, entering into a direct structural adjustment programme with the World Bank, has hiked power tariff on five occasions. This state has seen more than 3,000 recorded farmer suicides in the last five years as well as suicides of entire families of weavers. In 2002 alone, according to police records, as many as 2,580 deeply indebted farmers killed themselves mainly by ingesting pesticides in three districts alone – Warangal, Karimnagar and Nizamabad. We have no record of suicides on this scale in colonial India: our present-day politicians in their servile implementation of imperialist dictates routed through the BWI, have outdone even the colonial masters of the past in their disregard for the welfare of the mass of the people. At least agrarian distress had, at that time, led to some official commissions of inquiry and amendments to laws to restrict land transfer for debt: at present all we see is bad theory and open apologetics.

Advanced countries, as they have always done in the past, have been increasing support to their farmers as global prices fell (the US has legislated subsidies into the future, which will give transfers to its farm sector of $180 billion by 2008 compared to $84 billion in 1998). The majority of our economists, by contrast, are busy attacking the Indian farmer when he is already down, by saying that 'MSP (Minimum Support Price) is too high' and should be cut for these *kulaks*, and by shedding crocodile tears for the poorer farmers and labourers, on the ground that these are net food purchasers and would benefit from lower prices. They are obsessed with the question of support price alone, not the issue price which is the relevant one, and which can in principle be lowered without affecting support price. Further, by focussing on price alone, they implicitly assume that the population is on the same demand curve as before, whereas in fact the demand curve has itself shifted down so drastically for the mass of the rural population that tinkering with the support price is now likely to deepen the crisis.

They seem not to realize that unemployment and income deflation has swamped this sector, that every price is also an income, and cutting MSP today when there is already agrarian crisis, would further deepen income deflation, lead to more indebtedness and more suicides. They forget that for years and decades, India's surplus farmers, the much reviled 'kulaks', sold grain without complaining to the Food Corporation of India at half the global price when global price was high, thus ensuring cheap food for urban areas. Now, when the global price has fallen below the local price, these farmers have a moral right not to be abandoned to unfair competition from heavily subsidized foreign grain and other products, and a right to be given enough price support to prevent their total ruin. If those misguided economists, who put forward unethical arguments about lowering MSP, were seriously interested in the cause of the poorer farmers and labourers, they should be demanding an expansionary fiscal stance, a large hike in public investment and in rural development expenditures, to restore employment and purchasing power.

In 1997, the introduction of Public Distribution System 'targeting' divided the population into 'above poverty line' (APL) and 'below poverty line' (BPL), with lower prices payable by the latter but with a cut in quantity. The problem of wrong exclusion of large numbers of the actually poor from BPL status (which is determined by arbitrary criteria), has been a serious one, and the denial of ration cards has further aided the fall in sales from the PDS that is already taking place owing to decline in purchasing power.

While real disposable incomes for the top segments of the urban population have been rising fast, owing to reform policies of tax cuts and cheapening of primary goods and durable goods, rural mass incomes in terms of command over goods have been, in contrast, falling faster than is evident from consumption data, since higher indebtedness and asset losses have taken place to maintain already low consumption. There is rising absorption of foodgrains for the elites, with a higher proportion going to processed foods and animal products, while the majority in rural areas are plunged into deepening undernutrition, owing to their reduced purchasing power and reduced institutional access to food.

The five-year period of NDA rule has seen the most violent increase in rural-urban income inequalities ever seen since Independence. The urban elites have every reason to feel good as they play with their new toys, in the form of the latest automobiles and consumer durables, enjoy a more diversified diet, eat out more, and reduce their resulting adipose tissue in slimming clinics. But the same neoliberal policies that have benefited them, have also immiserized millions of their fellow country men, women and children, who are getting enmeshed in debt and land loss, and struggling harder merely to survive.

THE IMBROGLIO OF INDIRECT POVERTY ESTIMATES

The NSS Rounds on consumption expenditure collect data not only on the expenditure on food and non-food items, but also on the physical quantities of foods. Since the average calorie equivalent of different foods is known, they also compute and present the calorie equivalent of average diets by expenditure groups. When we directly inspect available NSS data on the calorie intake corresponding to the quantities of foods consumed by persons in the various per capita expenditure groups, we see that by 1999–2000, seven-tenths of the rural population was below the norm of 2,400 calories per day (the norm originally adopted in all poverty studies). About one-tenth had an intake around the norm, and only one-fifth had an intake above the norm. *Thus at least seven-tenths of the rural population was in poverty in 1999–2000.*This method is direct, simple and transparent, and requires no estimation by the reader. Even if a much lower level of 2,100 calories, equal to the lower urban norm, is considered, we see by direct inspection that over half the rural population and about two-fifths of the urban population was below the lower urban norm.

Even though the official and academic estimates of poverty started by using exactly the same poverty norm of 2,400 calories for rural areas, they now arrive at a population in poverty estimate of 27 per cent or less for the same year, 1999–2000, which corresponds to a daily calorie intake of less than 1,900. The very low estimate from the Planning Commission (and the academics today) is because they all now use an *indirect* and non-transparent method of estimation. This indirect method requires some explanation for the lay reader.

The direct inspection of calorie equivalent of quantities consumed by different expenditure classes was carried out by the Planning Commission, using a date which is now thirty years in the past. For later years, no similar direct inspection of the calorie equivalent of changing expenditures was done. *Instead, in order to estimate poverty for later years, it was assumed that the quantities people consumed, hence the pattern of consumer expenditure, remained unchanged from 1973–74,* and a price

index was applied to the old poverty line to update it. The new rounds of consumer expenditure data, entered the picture not for directly revising the poverty line, but only to the extent that they were used to read off what percentage of persons came below the new poverty level, estimated indirectly by applying a price index to the old poverty level.

If the Planning Commission, when it first estimated the poverty line expenditure for 1973–74, had said that it would base its estimate on quantities of foods people consumed thirty years earlier in 1943–44, obviously no one would have taken its estimate seriously. Present-day Planning Commission (and academic estimates) are based precisely on a three-decade old consumption pattern, and they no longer deserve to be taken seriously. In fact, they are no longer worth the paper on which they are written.

There has been no dearth of detailed criticisms of the indirect method, starting from the valid argument that it makes no sense to assume an unchanged consumption pattern: for it has indeed changed considerably over time, and not necessarily owing to voluntary reasons. Labourers are no longer paid wages in the form of grain and meals (not fully valued earlier) and have to purchase food against money wages; common property resources giving free goods have disappeared, so that fuel and fodder have to be purchased, all impacting the quantities of food that can be purchased by the poor out of a given income. As a result, a considerably larger total expenditure is actually required so that its food component can satisfy the calorie norm.

All these criticisms have been completely ignored by both official and academic poverty estimators, who use the indirect method, and who have continued full sail on their unregenerate course: they are rapidly discrediting the entire area of indirect-estimation poverty studies, for their unreal estimates are foundering on the rocks of hard macroeconomic facts that contradict their estimates and cannot be wished away. The fallacious official views on voluntary reduction in foodgrains absorption, and resulting official apathy and callousness towards the reality of increasing hunger, have been reinforced by wrong official estimates showing an actual *reduction* by 1999–2000 of the rural population in poverty of 27 per cent.

Another way of characterizing all the estimates using the indirect method would be: 'Statistical poverty reduction via clandestine reduction of the calorie norm.' The official Planning Commission price-index-updated poverty line, for monthly per capita expenditure for 1999–2000, gives a daily calorie intake which is 1,868 or less – a far cry indeed from the original 2,400 calorie intake norm in the base-year. *To meet the 2,400 calorie norm, a person needed to spend at least Rs 567 per month or Rs.19 daily equivalent to US 44 cents at the then exchange rate of Rs 43.33 to a dollar. This is the realistic poverty line, not the official one of Rs 328.*

The Planning Commission is asking us to believe that people could survive on a mere Rs 11, or US 25 cents daily. This is less than a quarter of the World Bank's own rough and ready dollar-a-day measure. At this rate, poverty can be statistically eliminated completely from India by the indirect method, with just a little more effort by the estimators to get a lower rise in the price index giving, say, Rs 240 per month as the 1999–2000 poverty line. This would reduce the poverty percentage dramatically to only 5, and as these people too would soon be dead, there would be a 'final solution' to all indirect estimation problems.

It is to be noted that none of the quoted papers inform the reader of the implication of their method: that the calorie standard is being drastically diluted, and that the original concept of poverty based on nutritional norm is itself being altered. To present estimates which imply a daily 500 calories, or more cut in the calorie intake, without explicitly informing the reader about it, is not acceptable by any academic standard. Quite apart from the problem of a far distant base year, the indirect method of updating an old poverty level using price indices now, no longer captures even the trend of change correctly, leave alone actual numbers, *because the method can only reflect increase in poverty arising from rise in prices, and cannot capture increase in poverty arising from unemployment and income loss.* This is the final nemesis of the prevalent poverty studies, for in the second half of the 1990s, and especially from 1998, as we have seen, *worsening welfare in rural areas has been caused not by inflation, but by deflation and unemployment.* So pervasive has mass income deflation become that a very bad drought year has seen a historically low inflation rate.

It is to be expected, therefore, that the indirect poverty studies will show, as they indeed do, exactly the *opposite* trend compared to the actual ground reality, namely worsening welfare owing to a higher percentage of persons moving below the calorie norm, and hence a rise in poverty. (The situation now is even worse because daily foodgrains absorption has fallen further by 25 gms by 2003, entailing a loss of another 95 calories daily on this account).

The bizarre element, in all this, arises from the loud celebrations of allegedly declining poverty by the government, and by a number of academics engaged in indirect estimation, whereas the 'decline' is solely owing to gross defects, and the inappropriateness of their own indirect statistical methods. The poverty estimators using the indirect method are doing a grave disservice to the Indian people by continuing with an indefensible methodology, which is by now giving the opposite result to the actual trends on the ground with respect to hunger. While, in the late 1970s, the difference between direct and indirect methods was about 15 per cent of the rural population, and in 1993 the difference was 32 per cent, for 1999–2000 the difference between the direct method (70 per cent in poverty) and the indirect method (27 per cent according to Planning Commission) is 43 per cent of the rural population.

Whether they wish to or not, officials and academics alike using the indirect method and claiming a reduction in poverty in the 1990s, are contributing to the formulation of incorrect policies further lowering mass welfare. If these poverty estimates remained in the ivory towers of academia and of Yojana Bhavan (the offices of the Planning Commission), it would not matter: but now targeted food distribution is being directly linked to poverty estimates. The present government is currently slashing the numbers of people designated as being 'below poverty line', and grain allocations at a low price to the states are sought to be further lowered on the ground that poverty has declined. The failure of prevailing indirect estimates does not lie in the failure to capture ground reality alone: they have become positively dangerous in spreading wrong information and inducing the opposite policy measures to those required. It is high time that academics and administrators working in the area of poverty estimation used direct indicators provided by the NSS consumption data and by per head foodgrains availability, if they are at all concerned about real trends as regards hunger.

In the middle of the Great Depression in 1931, with one-fifth of workers unemployed and factories closed, many economists in advanced countries maintained that economics was about the allocation of 'scarce resources' among competing uses, and that sound finance meant that governments should cut expenditures. They are remembered today for their conceptual blindness, but considerable additional damage was done at that time because they dominated public policy. Today, in India, in the middle of rising rural unemployment, falling per-head grain intake, and a rise in the absolute and relative numbers in nutritional deficit, we find that those who make policy are talking of declining rural poverty on the basis of unreasonable estimation procedures, and by ignoring all other trends. Posterity will remember them too, for their remarkable conceptual blindness. But for now, the prognosis is bleak. Where the diagnosis of the problem of hunger itself is incorrect and a worsening situation is being interpreted as betterment, no remedial measures can be expected of the policy advisers and the rulers of this country which was once a developing economy, but which has been turned into the Republic of Hunger.

□

How'll I not pay, Dora!
When I harvest the crop ...
Think you can cheat
the Nizam Govt!
Do they pay
NO

An iconic essay that effectively inaugurated the celebrated 'Mode of Production' debate in Indian economic theory. Arguing for a mode of capitalist extraction perfected during colonialism, **Hamza Alavi** shows how pre-capitalist class structures get structurally incorporated into colonial–capitalist economic modes without themselves turning capitalist. An imperial apparatus can fabricate a bourgeois state (including bourgeois property, and bourgeois legal and institutional apparatuses) as an integral and necessary complement to its economic domination without endangering its own pre-capitalist character. An Indian agrarian economy can be 'disarticulated and made subsidiary to colonialism', its elements 'no longer integrated internally and directly, but only by virtue of the separate ties of its different segments with the metropolitan economy'. The class of small landholders become suppliers of cheap metropolitan labour. Describing this class as 'pre-capitalist' would do violence to its structural incorporation into the colonial (capitalist) economic structure. Nor is it itself 'capitalist'. Its 'structural characteristics can be defined only within a structural conception precisely of a colonial mode'.

This text is placed alongside K. Balagopal's **Rich Peasant, Poor Peasant,** which proposes, in polemical opposition, an entirely new economic class – that of the rich peasant – which arose after Independence and was enabled by the independent Indian state, notably after the Emergency. The question of whether such developments continue the colonial mode or break away from it remains open. This is an abridged version of Alavi's essay originally published in **Economic and Political Weekly** (vol. 10, no. 33–35, Special Number, August 1975), reprinted and situated within the larger debate in **Agrarian Relations and Accumulation: The 'Mode of Production' Debate in India**, edited by Utsa Patnaik (Bombay: Sameeksha Trust and Oxford University Press, 1990).

Images: In 1979, Gautam Ghose's first film, **Maabhoomi** (Telugu, 1979), set in 'feudal' Telangana and telling the story of the Communist uprising of the early 1940s, also captured the quintessential post-Independence imagination of 'Indian feudalism' that the Nehruvian state promised to eradicate. Telangana would be a frequent setting for evil and unenlightened 'feudalism' in the 1970s–80s' New Indian Cinema. This is a montage of frames from Ghose's influential work of docu-fiction. Grateful acknowledgment to B. Narsing Rao, producer of the film, for permission to reprint, and to Umamaheshwari B. for support.

6

HAMZA ALAVI

1975

INDIA AND THE COLONIAL MODE OF PRODUCTION

Important issues have been raised by Indian Marxist agricultural economists in the debate on the 'Mode of Production in Indian Agriculture'.[1] That debate is taking place in the context of the far-reaching changes which have taken place in Indian agriculture in recent years – changes once celebrated as 'the Green Revolution'. Today, its conservative authors as well as its radical critics are compelled by the force of the surfacing contradictions in rural class relations (as well as in the economy as a whole), to move beyond the limits of justification or condemnation, and to assess the significance of the structural changes that have taken place.

The Indian debate on the mode of production revolves around the question whether, in the last fifteen or twenty years, there has been a decisive movement in Indian agriculture from a feudal mode to a capitalist mode of production.[2] The protagonists in the Indian debate have looked at European (including Russian) historical parallels and at theoretical propositions that have been advanced in those contexts. There is, however, a surprising omission of any reference to the Chinese experience or theoretical contributions.

A more serious criticism could be that, by focusing on the agrarian economy, the debate conceptualizes 'mode of production' too narrowly. We would like to emphasize that both the concept of 'feudalism' in India during the period of direct colonial domination, as well as the contemporary phenomenon of rural 'capitalism', cannot be grasped theoretically in all their implications except, specifically, in the context of the worldwide structure of imperialism into which it is articulated. A consideration of that fact should lead us towards a conception of a colonial mode of production and the structural specificity that distinguishes it from both feudalism and capitalism in the metropolis.

The contemporary changes and the issues in the debate must be looked at in the context of the demands made on the Indian agrarian economy by imperialism and industrial development since Independence, as well as in the context of the successive policies that were instituted to realize the objectives for those purposes. These, in turn, must be situated in the context of the changing framework of class alignments in the Indian political system. For the post-Independence period, this requires an understanding of the complex class basis of the Indian National Congress – the party which has been dominant in the Indian state, at any rate at the level of the central government, since Independence. The class basis of the Congress has not been an unchanging one: and its changes throw much light on the major shifts in agricultural development policy that took place at the end of the fifties.

Before Independence, the Indian National Congress embraced the whole gamut of social classes in India, other than the big landowners, at the time firmly allied to the British Raj (and such other elements as the Muslim middle classes who provided the backbone of the Muslim League which eventually secured the state of Pakistan, the rising elements of the untouchable castes who provided the leadership of the Scheduled Castes' Federation, and other such groups). The Communist Party as well as the Socialists were all in the Congress, together with some extreme right-wing elements.

The leadership of the Congress, however, was firmly in the hands of men who came from a professional middle-class background, and behind whom stood their powerful patrons (the rising Indian bourgeoisie). During the course of the nationalist struggle, the bourgeois and, especially, the petty-bourgeois leadership and cadres of the Congress, by themselves ineffective against the British Raj, began to be more and more involved in mobilizing subordinate classes on behalf of the nationalist cause. The Congress leadership was, for example, prominently involved in the formation of the All India Trade Union Congress[3] in 1920, despite the opposition of Gandhi and others. Jawaharlal Nehru was among the founder members and was later president of the AITUC. Likewise, the Congress leadership is also credited with having mobilized the peasantry. There again, the Congress role was an ambivalent one; for, while calling upon the peasantry to speak for the Congress and the national struggle, they did little to make the Congress speak for the peasant. Gandhi, again, put forward a doctrine of 'trusteeship', advocating class peace, and designating the landlords as 'trustees' for the exploited peasant![4] When Gandhi led peasant 'struggles', they were not directed against the landlords but against the British Raj – in the form, notably, of no-tax campaigns. Nevertheless, that involvement with the peasantry was one which infused many of the Congress leaders and cadres with a populist ideology. Moreover, the Congress could see the landlord class to be the major class force that was aligned against them, in support of the colonial rule. They, thus, developed an anti-landlord rhetoric and were committed to radical policies vis-à-vis rural society, especially to carrying out land reform.

The story of land reform in India is one of a progressive attenuation of radical commitments, embodying the populist ideology then being proclaimed by the Congress, which had demanded the restoration of land to the tiller and the abolition of all intermediaries between the cultivators and the state. While legislation was passed, separately and differently, by different state legislatures, at the state level the power of landowners was greater than at the national level and, invariably, a watered-down version of the initial proposals appeared in the legislation; in turn implemented indifferently by a bureaucracy which was not uninvolved with the interests of landowning classes.[5]

The commitment to rural development however expressed an economic need and, in the light of the disappointing results, there was a willingness to learn. One of the more interesting expressions of that desire to learn was the dispatch of two high-powered delegations sent in July 1956 to China to study agrarian cooperatives and agricultural planning.[6] Their reports, not surprisingly, noted that the remarkable Chinese success derived from their transformation of the rural class structure, and that little could be expected in India without similar change.[7] This view was reiterated by many influential advisers of the government.[8] The limits of gradualism and incremental changes were manifest; progress could not be achieved without a major assault on the classes that dominated the countryside. That realization marked the point of retreat from the radical vision.

It was, however, soon realized that the assumption on which the small peasant strategy was based, did not exist. Although intensive use of family labour resulted in higher productivity per acre in the case of the small peasant, he lacked the resources and capability to make a radical advance in agricultural techniques which might raise productivity. Moreover, the smallholder with his tiny holdings could not market more than a very small proportion of his produce; consequently, a given increase in productivity in his case brought about a comparatively smaller increase in the marketable surplus. The bourgeoisie were not concerned primarily with an increase in productivity (of the small farmer and the consequent improvement in his well-being). Their concern was with increasing the marketable surplus that they required for industrial development.

Chinese land reform, it was realized, had not created a small peasant economy. Rather, the destruction of the power of the landlord class was only a crucial stage in a dynamic revolutionary movement that released new forces and energies in rural society, and made a transition through mutual-aid teams and cooperatives, etc., to a radical reorganization of rural society and economy. It was this reorganization that brought in its wake major leaps in progress and increases in productivity – and it was the increases in the marketable surplus that sustained socialist construction in the towns. It was soon realized that a reversion to a small peasant economy in India, even if it could be achieved, would be a dead-end solution. Nor were the subordinate classes in India to be led to a path of revolutionary transformation of society.

Soon, therefore, there was disenchantment with the small-peasant strategy of agricultural development. Perhaps a most important factor in the ensuing reversal of the populist strategy and, most significantly, in the shaping of the later strategy, was the re-alignment of class forces in the post-colonial state as it crystallized in the fifties. This involved a new relationship between the indigenous bourgeoisie, the imperialist bourgeoisie and the landlords who held sway in the countryside. Before Independence, the indigenous bourgeoisie had lined up with the forces of national liberation and had combated both the imperialist bourgeoisie (though not unequivocally and not without examples of collaboration) as well as the indigenous 'feudal' class which was closely aligned with the colonial regime. That gave rise to a myth – propagated among others by Barrington Moore in his well-known work[9] – that, in India, 'there was an alliance between the bourgeoisie and the peasantry which was the basis of Indian democracy'. The fact of the matter is that the adoption of universal adult franchise in the Indian Constitution of 1951 actually conferred a new political role on the rural power-holders – the landlords – who dominated the factional alignments in the villages.

The Congress leadership, in the context of the electoral contest, forged new links with these local-level power-holders. This too reversed earlier antagonistic relationships, since for them close links with successor regimes were no less valuable than their earlier links with the colonial regime. One liberal academic, an anthropologist, refers to them as 'vote banks';[10] another who has produced a major work on the Congress party refers to the fact that:

> Families which supported the pro-British Justice Party joined the Congress Party after Independence. Many landlord families,

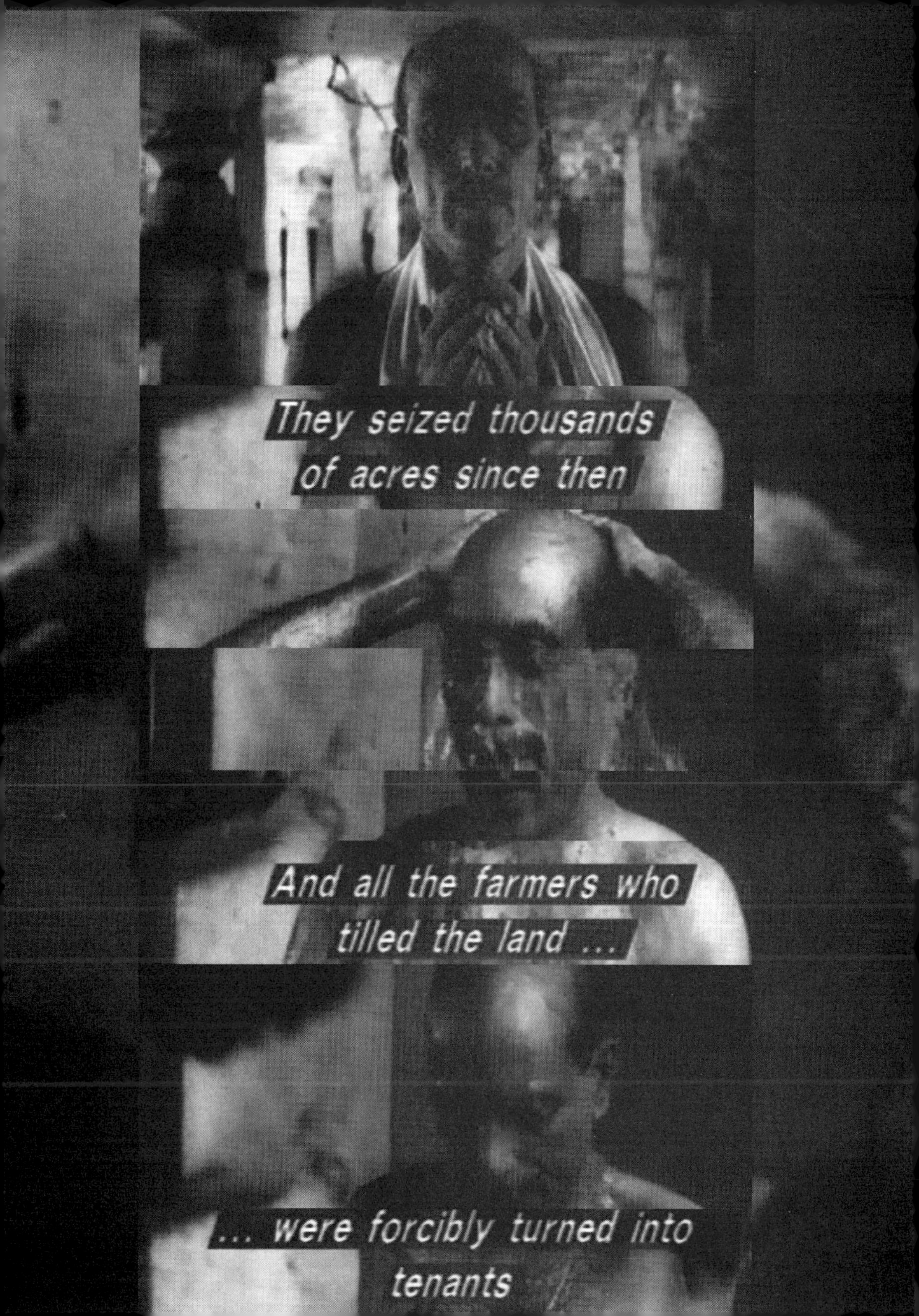
They seized thousands
of acres since then
And all the farmers who
tilled the land ...
... were forcibly turned into
tenants

> eager to protect themselves against the proposed land reform legislation, joined Congress and, in some instances, entered the Legislative Assembly to play an influential role in shaping the character of the legislation. In any event, their influence on the enforcement and interpretation of the legislation by local officials has been greatly enhanced by their participation in the local Congress Party and in local government bodies.[11]

While, at the national level, the indigenous bourgeoisie and the imperialist bourgeoisie influenced the strategic decisions of the government, the main body of the Congress party machine was taken over by the landowning classes. There was a new alliance between the three dominant classes. There was no more any question of the indigenous and foreign bourgeoisie attacking the interests of the landowning classes, who were now their allies.

With the end of the British colonial rule, American influence in India grew steadily — somewhat obscured though it was in the early fifties by the marked contrast provided by Indian professions of international non-alignment against the background of the McCarthyite confrontation with communism. With the crisis of the Indian Second Five Year Plan in 1958, and the heavy dependence of the Indian economy on US aid, American influence became pervasive and manifest. This was countered, though only partly, by the links between the Indian bourgeoisie and the Soviet Union, which had affected the philosophy of 'non-alignment'. American 'advice' began to play an increasingly important role in the shaping of Indian policy in most fields.

The new turn in agricultural development policy was marked by a report[12] by American experts, sponsored by the Ford Foundation, which recommended a major shift in policy – away from populist participatory concepts of community development and towards an emphasis on technological solutions to the problem of agricultural development within the existing class structure. From that new perspective emerged the 'Intensive Agricultural District Programme' or, as it is more commonly referred to, the 'Package Programme'. Its emphasis was on 'measures for immediate increase in agricultural production rather than measures for improving the general context for development or immediate welfare'.[13] The scheme also emphasized the criterion of profitability of the big farm, as an enterprise, as preferable to attempts to sustain the economically bankrupt (even if physically more productive per acre) economy of the small farmers. Finally, in concrete terms, the new policy emphasized the provision of new physical inputs and credit to buy them with to the economically viable cultivators – in effect to the rich farmers and landlords. They were now to have fertilizer, new seed, pump sets for tube wells, and a variety of farm machinery, which the small peasant could not possibly afford for his tiny holding. Above all, large amounts of credit were to be pumped into the willing hands of the rich farmers to enable them to buy new inputs. That was the 'Package Plan'.

It was this transformation of agricultural development strategy that provides the background to the rise of the 'capitalist farmer' in the sixties that the current debate on the 'mode of production in Indian agriculture' is attempting to conceptualize and theorize. This is the 'Green Revolution', once celebrated but soon to be viewed with growing concern.[14] The Green Revolution (and the changes that presaged it) brought about a large-scale eviction of sharecropping tenants and their replacement with American- or Soviet-made tractors, and the complementary employment of a much smaller number of full-time wage labourers or sharecroppers. Many peasants who owned very small holdings, and who were previously able to get by because they were able to lease-in some additional land, were now no longer able to do so, and they were forced to sell the little land they owned. There was a pauperization of large sections of the rural population in the midst of an enormous increase in the prosperity of a few big landholders.

There was, secondly, a contradictory impact on the demand for labour, which probably contributed to generating militancy in the countryside. Large numbers of sharecropping tenants and full-time labourers were displaced. On the other hand, with the large increases in yields in the cropped area (helped by irrigation), the *seasonal* demand for labour multiplied. While there was thus a break in the ties of dependence between landlords and their full-time dependents, landlords and rich peasants were now dependent, more than ever before, on casual labour at harvest time, on men who owed no long-term obligations to landlords.

In the early 1950s, the policy of the state, dominated by a native and imperialist bourgeoisie, was still based on the small farmer strategy and was expressed in the commitments to land reform, community development, etc. The big farmer, however, had taken his future into his own hands, despite the contrary assumptions of public policy. The background to the rise of big farmers was made up, firstly, by the enormous rise in agricultural prices during the war, and after the long depression of the thirties, which had placed large financial resources at their disposal as well as an incentive to invest, and secondly, by the post-war availability of a variety of new inputs which made the investments possible. They prospered within the logic of the capitalist system, rather than through the sponsorship of the bourgeoisie in power. The capitalist class wholeheartedly espoused the new policy, but did so only in the 1960s, by which time the big farmers had already manifested their efficacy and established a firm position in the structure of state power.

To conceptualize the 'colonial mode of production' theoretically, it might be useful to consider first the Marxist conception of the 'feudal' mode of production and, in that light, to look at the pre-capitalist economy in India before the colonial impact and the transformations that were brought about by colonialism.

A mode of production is a complex unity. There has been, all too often, a tendency to reduce that complex, dialectical, unity to a narrow definition of 'relations of production' that focusses on *forms* of relationships between the direct producer, the worker (whether industrial or agricultural), and the class that exploits his labour power. 'Relations of production' cannot be understood, simplistically in terms of dyadic relationships – i.e. apparently one-to-one relationships between the worker and his master. For such relationships exist, and can only exist, by virtue of the totality of the 'structure–superstructure' formation of a society that constitutes a dialectical unity.

The excessive and misleading emphasis on the *form* of the relationship between the producer and his master has bedevilled discussion of the mode of production. In particular, it has obscured fundamental transformations wrought in the nature and the significance of such relationships by virtue of the colonial impact. Although the *form* of such a relationship often remains unchanged, its essential nature and significance undergoes a revolutionary transformation. That is why it is wrong to describe colonial economies as those in which pre-capitalist relationships 'coexist' with 'capitalist' relations. Such relationships, transformed by the colonial impact, are no longer 'pre-capitalist'. In India 'sharecropping' on land has been equated with 'feudal', just as in Latin America the apparently servile relationships of the *hacienda* have also been defined as 'feudal'. But in neither case do they retain, apart from their superficial form, the essential nature of 'feudal' relationships. This is one of the central problems that must be clarified (as also the corresponding problem of the so-called 'coexistence' of the feudal and the capitalist modes of production in a colonial structure). A decisive factor which underlies pre-capitalist modes of production – including the feudal mode of production – is that they are subject to the limitations of exploiting land, and the forces of nature, on a low level of technology without the benefit of the enormous increases in man's power over nature made possible by the embodiment of labour (manual and intellectual) in capital and technology, that made the phenomenal advances in productivity possible under capitalism. The feudal mode of production, therefore, was limited to small commodity-production and to a natural economy in which production and appropriation of the produce as well as the structure of power were essentially localized; long-distance trade was marginal to it, as also the structure of power of feudal kingdoms which was tenuous and fragile.

In view of the limits on capital accumulation, the feudal economy was geared to the conspicuous consumption of feudal lords. It was, therefore, a system of 'simple reproduction', in contrast to the 'expanded reproduction' of capitalism, in which much of the surplus goes into capital accumulation and 'capital intensive' methods of production. In the colonial mode of production, we do not have either of these characteristics. The scale of investments that we have seen in the colonial agrarian economy – especially in very recent years – has been possible only because of the encapsulation of such an economy within the highly industrialized world imperialist economy (and also the subordinated industrial development that has taken place within the colony itself under the aegis of the metropolitan bourgeoisie). In the colonial mode of production we have a system of expanded reproduction instead of simple reproduction, but of a deformed nature. **A substantial part of the surplus generated in the colonial agrarian economy (as well as that generated in colonial industry) is appropriated by the imperialist bourgeoisie and enters into expanded reproduction, not directly within the colonial economy but, rather, at the imperialist centre. Its special characteristic is that the expanded reproduction, and the attendant rise in the organic composition of capital, benefits the imperialist bourgeoisie rather than the colony from which the surplus is extracted.**

Another aspect of a feudal mode of production is the absence of generalized commodity-production. This is a controversial issue. It is well known that, even in the classical feudalism of Western Europe, several different forms of relationships between the direct producer and his master have coexisted – [that] feudalism is not, for example, identical with serfdom. The generalized commodity production in Eastern Europe was possible precisely because of the incorporation of the agrarian economies of those countries within the ambit of the industrializing economies of the west. It was western capitalism rather than eastern serfdom that generated it. I have already suggested, therefore, that we may regard this as a system of *proto-colonial mode of production* rather than as a pure feudal mode of production. In the Third World, generalized commodity production is also precisely created by, and is at the service of, the imperialist economy. The subordination of the agrarian economies of the countries of the Third World to imperialism, as suppliers of food and raw materials, is commonplace. It has also been emphasized by Samir Amin that their economies are *disarticulated internally*[15] so that segments of the colonial economies do not trade with each other; they are articulated only *via* their links with metropolitan economies, and they are subordinated, thereby, to the latter. The concept of *internal disarticulation* of the colonial economy is crucial for an understanding of the colonial mode of production.

The question of the form of the relationship between the direct producer and the exploiting class cannot be understood, except within the framework of the structure of power and the legal and institutional structures in which such relationships are embedded. Laclau, for example, has referred to 'a general ensemble of extra-economic coercions weighing on the peasantry' as a definitive condition to the feudal relationship in Latin America.[16] But we cannot judge the significance and the nature of such 'coercive' relationships, or the nature of 'coercion', without reference to the structure of colonial state power. The difference between the political system of feudalism and the colonial bourgeois state, with its legal and institutional framework, distances the apparently similar forms of relationships in the two cases. This critical condition is all too often dismissed by virtue of a narrow economist reading of Marxism. [Utsa] Patnaik, for example, dismisses the significance of property in land – enforced, somewhat disingenuously, by the British in India – by invoking the concept of 'relative autonomy of the superstructure', suggesting thereby that structural forms and juridical forms were out of alignment with each other. She suggests that there was, therefore, 'necessarily inexact correspondence between production relations on the one hand and juridical forms (as well as other elements of the superstructure) on the other'.[17] But a closer examination of the proposition will show that such a view is self-contradictory, inasmuch as the 'relations of production' are themselves premised here on an aspect of the 'superstructure' – namely the supposedly 'coercive' domination of the peasantry directly by the landlord. It is precisely the nature of that direct 'coercive' relationship that is at issue, which now needs to be examined carefully.

An essential aspect of the feudal mode of production, corresponding to its localized production and localized appropriation, is its localized structure of power. Feudal kingdoms were precarious alliances; their true locus of power was, at the base, in the hands of local lords. The dialectic between the central authority and local power made it a complex polity. [Perry] Anderson speaks of this as the 'parcelisation of sovereignty'.[18] The colonial regime subordinated the power of the local lords under its own structure of institutionalized power within the framework of its *colonial bourgeois state*. It is in the light of that critical and decisive change, that I wrote some time ago that the bourgeois revolution in the colonies was already accomplished by the imperialist bourgeoisie, which created in the colonies a bourgeois state and bourgeois property and a bourgeois legal and institutional apparatus, precisely as an integral and necessary complement to its economic domination.[19] Those who speak of the necessity of a bourgeois democratic revolution in the colonies misconceive the problem by overlooking this: in neither Russia nor China was such a bourgeois state established by the imperialist bourgeoisie.

In the light of that outline of the main criteria of a feudal mode of production, we can turn to the situation in India, and the transformation

You must hound and harrass
them into paying taxes!

that was brought about in the wake of its colonialist subordination. First of all, in pre-British India, *land was a possession* held by virtue of the force at the command of the local lord, rather than *property* held under bourgeois law. However, not unlike the dialectic between central authority and local power in the feudal kingdoms of Europe, the Mughal Emperors made attempts to 'appoint' local lords, who in turn often benefited from the legitimacy thus conferred on their possession, which was an asset for them in their contests with other rival local lords.[20] Land was not yet a commodity which it was to become under the colonial institutional structure.

Land, in fact, was not yet the most valued resource in pre-British India, for there was an abundance of it relative to the number of people available to extract the fruits of the unyielding earth. The truly precious possession was labour. The labourer had, therefore, to be made *unfree* as a necessary condition for his exploitation. He had to be held by coercion. It was only when, under the colonial regime, all land was appropriated and the labourer had no direct access any more to 'waste' land – and had nothing therefore to sell but his labour power – that conditions of his exploitation in freedom arose. Thus, we are told that in pre-colonial India, 'In view of the shortage of cultivators, the *zamindars* (landlords) enjoyed the right to restrain the tenants from leaving the land and to compel them to cultivate all the arable land held by them.'[21] Over the heads of the cultivators stood a hierarchy of parasitic and powerful 'intermediaries' constituting a pyramid that was not unlike European feudalism. They did not *own* the land. They had 'rights' to shares of the produce. The mode of extraction of the surplus was, quite unambiguously, force.

A myth was propagated by the British in the nineteenth century that, in Mughal India, land was the property of the emperor. They quoted, for example, Bernier, that famous traveller who peddled myths that the Mughal emperor himself might have liked to believe: 'The great Mogol is the proprietor of every acre of land in the kingdom'.[22] That view was taken up and widely canvassed by influential men of the colonial regime like James Grant and above all James Mill (who too had entered the service of the East India Company). That, as Eric Stokes has pointed out, had the advantage of legitimizing the claims of the colonial power to a large share of the surplus from Indian agriculture, for it had stepped into the shoes of the Mughal emperor.[23] The colonial regime in India had a big stake in the direct extraction of surplus from agriculture. Indeed, until the extension of the railways in the second half of the nineteenth century, when it became possible to exploit the Indian agrarian economy by way of cultivation of bulky cash crops, which could now be transported economically to the metropolitan cities to provide food and raw materials, the main weight of the colonial regime on Indian agriculture was by way of direct extraction of the surplus in the form of heavy land revenues.

But major changes were already under way. Amongst the most important was the institution of private property in land. The creation of a system of landed property was closely tied up with the system of land revenue 'settlements', beginning with the celebrated Permanent Settlement in Bengal in 1793, by virtue of which the colonial state was to receive 90 per cent of the rental from land. Land which was not in private hands was deemed to be Crown, and appropriated by the state. No longer could the over-exploited peasant even think of escaping from his rapacious lord and hope to settle on 'waste land', because that was now the property of the Crown. The appropriation thus of all land, as well as demographic growth, led to a situation in which the landowner had no longer to exercise 'coercion' over the cultivator as indicated above, for now the poor peasant was 'free' to sell nothing but his labour. He was now free to leave his master – and to starve. Thus, although the form of the relationship between the cultivator and the landlord remained the same, its essential substance was transformed. It was no longer based on direct coercion. It was based on the economic laws of capitalist society and the economic necessities that it imposes upon those who are deprived access to the means of production by the institution of private property.

The colonial regime thus transformed the feudal mode of localized production and localized appropriation, by a complete transformation of the agrarian economy in the second half of the nineteenth century: when railways and steamships were to carry raw materials like cotton, indigo, jute and other commodities, now to be grown by Indian farmers, to England. That was against the background of destruction of Indian industry and the pauperization of the artisans, who went to swell the ranks of the destitute on the land. Instead of a local exchange between Indian artisans and Indian agriculturists, the produce of agriculture was to be carried to distant shores and manufactured items were to be imported. The Indian economy was disarticulated and [made subsidiary] to colonialism. Its elements were no longer integrated internally and directly, but only by virtue of the separate ties of its different segments with the metropolitan economy. It was no longer a feudal mode of production. It had already been transformed into a colonial mode of production. Generalized commodity production in the colony did not have the same character as that in the imperialist centre itself, because of that disarticulation.[24] It was a disarticulated generalized commodity production – precisely, a colonial form of deformed, generalized, commodity production.

Unlike the feudal mode of production that had preceded it, the colonial mode was no longer one of simple reproduction but of extended reproduction. But here, again, we must recognize its deformity, arising precisely from its colonial status. The result of the internal disarticulation of the colonial economy and the extraction of the surplus by the colonial power meant that extended reproduction could not be realized within the economy of the colony, but could be realized only through the imperialist centre. The surplus value extracted from the colony went to support capital accumulation at the centre, and to raise the organic composition of capital at the centre, while destituting the colonial economy. The colonial form was a deformed extended reproduction.

The destitution of the colonial economy and the relative lowering of the organic composition of capital in the colony were reflected in a lower wage-level in the colony. That provided an opportunity for profitable export of capital to the colonies in the case of those industries which are labour-intensive, so that a higher rate of profit could be realized thereby by metropolitan capital. It is in that context that we may consider the special role of the large number of destitute smallholders – 75 per cent of all farms in modern India – in the colonial mode of production. Because such farms are incapable of providing even a bare subsistence to the bulk of the rural families, families are forced to seek supplementary employment, not only in the villages but also in urban industry which was developed under colonial auspices. This enormously lowered the cost of reproduction of labour, thereby making it possible to lower wages even more than they might otherwise have had to be. The small peasant sector of the agrarian economy that produces an insignificant amount of the marketable surplus, and little direct profit for the colonial bourgeoisie through agricultural production, is not therefore just an irrelevance. It is not just a disintegrated element that somehow survives outside the colonial mode of production, besides the rich farmer economy that is directly geared to the production of cash crops and the generation of the surplus for the colonial economy. The smallholder class too is integrated into the colonial mode of production; for, it is a valued supplier of cheap labour. Its existence lowers the cost of reproduction of labour and, therefore, the necessary level of wages in the colonial economy. Here again, a description of this class as 'pre-capitalist' would do violence to its structural incorporation into the colonial (capitalist) economic structure. But nor is it itself 'capitalist'. Again, its structural characteristics can be defined only within a structural conception precisely of a 'colonial mode of production'.

We have identified certain structural characteristics of the colonial mode of production from an examination of developments in the Indian agricultural economy. We might conclude our examination of the Indian developments with some broad observations. First, we encounter, all too often, an *a priori* assumption that there is a conflict of interest between the so-called 'feudal' or 'semi-feudal' class of landlords and the bourgeoisie. Such assumptions are premised on a conception of the coexistence of a 'feudal mode of production' and a 'capitalist mode of production', so that such a class conflict is assumed to exist, *a priori*. Facts are forced into the mould of theoretical assumptions, and examples of political competition that do not necessarily fit with such an explanation are nevertheless 'explained' as examples of conflicts between the 'bourgeois' Congress and opposition parties and groups which, by definition, are designated 'feudal'. Such an integration would violate reality insofar as we find within the Congress party an alliance of the bourgeoisie and the landowner. Nor is there any evidence of conflict between so-called 'capitalist farmers' and 'feudal landowners'. We find instead that the big farmer strategy has served the interests of the bourgeoisie – both Indian and foreign – insofar as it has provided the required increase in the marketed surplus of agricultural commodities. The interests of the foreign imperialist bourgeoisie, the indigenous bourgeoisie, and the landlords and rich peasants coincide, in that respect at least.

Secondly, the contemporary application of the new technology and the corresponding increase in the 'organic composition of capital' in Indian agriculture, carries forward a development that was interrupted by the depression of the thirties and the World War. But it is, nevertheless, a development on a new scale, [made] possible only within the framework of the colonial relationship and a metropolitan industrial production (and a dependent indigenous industrial production) that has made new technological resources available. Here, too, there is a structural correspondence of interests rather than a source of structural conflict.

Thirdly, the development of 'capitalism' in Indian agriculture, wherever it has progressed, has brought about widespread destitution of subordinate classes. It has affected the rural poor directly, by way of displacement of the permanent labour force – for an increase in seasonal demand for labour only partially compensates for the loss of their regular livelihood. This development indirectly affects small peasants, urban lower middle-classes, and urban workers as well as the rural poor, because of the major inflationary impact of an enormously increased expenditure by landowners and rich peasants whose incomes have multiplied, and which have a considerable weight in the total national consumption expenditure. The rapid rise in the prices of commodities has eroded the real incomes of all subordinate classes. Here we have a pattern of development which has created wealth for the few and poverty for the great majority. This has forced smallholders into destitution, so that they sell their land to big farmers and descend into the ranks of the landless poor. The rural poor – both the smallholders as well as the landless workers – have no reserves to carry them through periodic shortages, and a bad harvest is now transformed into a famine in which millions die.

Finally, there is a great increase in peasant militancy. That is not only because of their progressive impoverishment: a factor that is particularly important for the smallholder (middle peasant), but also because, in the case of the poor peasant, the tie of economic dependence – between permanently employed sharecroppers and wage labourers, and their masters – is broken when they are thrown out. On the other hand, the enormous increase in the cropped area as well as in crop yields has greatly increased the seasonal demand for labour at harvest time. This has increased the bargaining power of landless labourers, especially at the time of the harvests.

India is experiencing peasant militancy on an unprecedented scale. The resultant conflict cannot be explained in terms of a contradiction between a 'feudal' mode of production and a 'capitalist' mode. There is no conflict between the urban and rural bourgeoisie on the one hand and the landowners on the other – the indigenous and foreign bourgeoisie too have prospered as a result of rising prices of commodities. Nor is there a conflict in which wage labourers (the 'rural proletariat?) are aligned differently from the other subordinate classes in the countryside, namely, the sharecroppers and the smallholding 'middle peasants'. The alignments are structural alignments and conflicts of the colonial mode of production; not those of the feudal and capitalist modes.

□

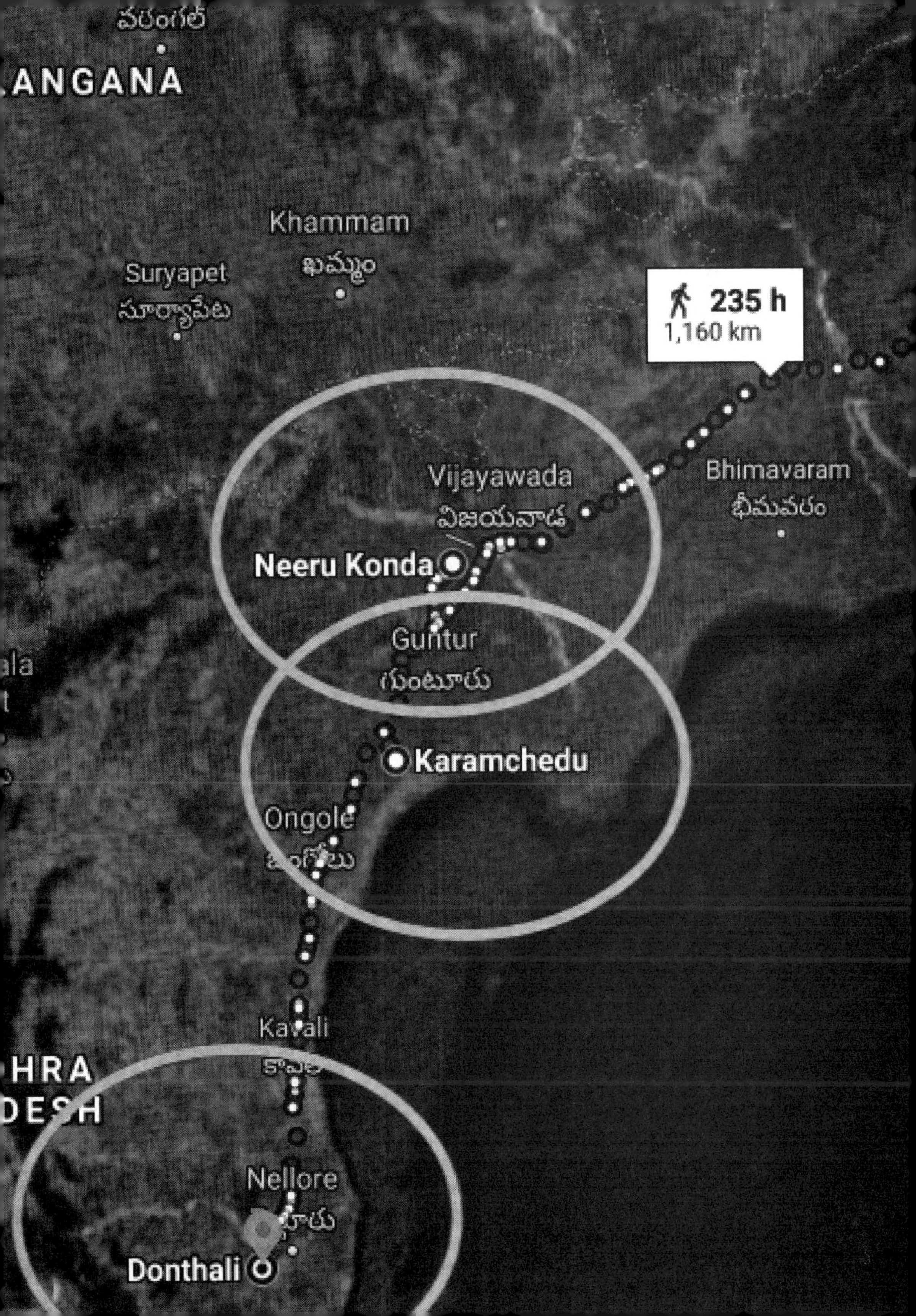
వరంగల్
Khammam
ఖమ్మం
Suryapet
సూర్యాపేట
235 h
1,160 km
Vijayawada
విజయవాడ
Bhimavaram
భీమవరం
Neeru Konda
Guntur
గుంటూరు
Karamchedu
Ongole
Kavali
Nellore
Donthali

Political activist, iconic human rights lawyer and author **K. Balagopal** (1952–2009) wrote numerous texts polemicizing with diverse intellectual, legal and political positions from the viewpoint of his experiences of fighting against Dalit, landless labourer and peasant oppression. Among his influential texts is this response to the 'Mode of Production' debate, where he identifies an economic class that became, he considers, invisible to the theory as it stood: namely, the rural rich peasant. In many ways a product of political independence, this class has, especially since the 1980s, mounted a concerted attack on the Indian state, seeking at the same time growing economic dominance in the countryside.

This text was originally published in **Seminar** (Issue No. 352, **Farmer Power**, December 1988) and later, in another version, in **Ear to the Ground: Selected Writings on Class and Caste** (New Delhi: Navayana, 2011, pp. 224–32). Reprinted here with permission from Seminar. Permission from Ms V. Vasantha Lakshmi to use Balagopal's work is acknowledged with deep gratitude.

Images: Taking from Balagopal's own state and his privileged location of example, these images look at the coastal canal-irrigated Andhra regions where crops like paddy, cotton and tobacco are cultivated, and where the wealth generated by this cultivation 'has taken the form of (and further reproduced itself in) trade, real estate, business, cinemas and lately politics'. The images are from the film **Chanda Sasanudu** (**Dictator**, N.T. Rama Rao, 1983), in which NTR plays a double role, set in this precise history, representing both the old and new feudal elites, in a graphic illustration of Balagopal's central thesis about the rich peasant; images selected by S.V. Srinivas. Google map of the Telangana region showing the villages referred to in the essay.

7

K. BALAGOPAL

1988

RICH PEASANT, POOR PEASANT

The major threat to the Indian state and the social structure supported by it has in recent times come almost exclusively from the villages. It is not that the urban working class is a 'labour aristocracy' and therefore uninterested in or incapable of threatening the structure. A small section of the urban working class has deceptively high wages, but the large majority of them lead lives which are often worse than those of the rural poor. But the urban working class is numerically so small that it has not as yet succeeded in posing a very serious threat to the state. About the only time in recent years (that) the Indian state got a real shock from the urban worker was in 1974 when the railway workers went on a nationwide strike.[1]

There are, on the other hand, two types of pressures from rural India: one, the struggle of the poor peasants and landless labourers, and the other, the struggle of the relatively better-off peasants usually called 'middle peasants' or 'rich peasants'. The two movements differ not only in the classes they fight. The movements of the rural poor fight the rural rich – the landlords and the contractors, for instance – whereas the movements of the 'middle' peasants fight the urban rich and the imperialists.

In the last decade or two, the former type of movements were very much in the news, and it was intellectually fashionable to support them;

now the latter type of movements are rapidly occupying the same position. The shift is sharp, and it is now widely held by one-time radical intellectuals that the fervour of the seventies was a gigantic illusion. The shift is semantically facilitated by the fact that they have supported both types of movements in the name of the same 'peasantry'. The word 'peasant', as used by our intellectuals, means whichever class one sympathizes with among the rural population. It is difficult to arrive at a more precise definition from the intellectual practice of the Indian *buddhijeevi*.[2]

But it is increasingly necessary to realize that there is a third and very strong pressure that works from rural India on the Indian state. This understanding is crucial for a complete comprehension of rural society as well as a proper appreciation of agrarian struggles of both the types mentioned above. The lack of such an appreciation is reflected in the very limited terms on which those struggles are understood. Struggles of the rural poor are analysed in the same terms in which they would have been analysed fifty years ago – land distribution, wages, control of wasteland, bondage, tenancy, unpaid labour, etcetera – whereas agitations of the 'middle' peasants are even more simplistically analysed exclusively in terms of unequal exchange between the primary and secondary sectors of the economy.

The picture of rural India given in the two sets of analyses has nothing whatsoever in common. It is almost as if the rural poor and the 'middle' peasants live in different villages altogether. No wonder that people who are worried about conceptual and analytical coherence have begun to suspect that one of these two must be imaginary, and since the 'middle' peasant world of inflated input costs and unremunerative sale prices appears real – what with the Sharad Joshis and the Tikaits capturing the headlines every second day – the other must be illusory.[3]

To recover our sanity, it is necessary to obtain a total picture that will contain both these movements within a meaningful and internally related whole. The picture is best understood against the backdrop of the wide variety of social disturbances rural India is regularly subject to: struggles of the rural poor for land, wages, and against social oppression; struggles of landed peasants for remunerative prices, cheap inputs and infrastructural facilities; booth capturing, physical assaults and other forms of physical violence at the time of panchayat, assembly or parliament elections; conflicts and power struggles relating to rural cooperatives and government contracts; organized assaults on the rural poor including atrocities on Dalits and other forms of community-based oppression; and so on. It is significant that of all these disturbances, the first two alone occupy the attention of analysts, and are held to be sufficient in themselves for understanding rural society and politics.

This is particularly true of those analysts who are partial to 'middle' peasant agitations, who conceptualize village society in terms of just two classes, labourers and peasants, and analyse the dynamics in terms of the suicidal/treacherous agitations of the labourers against the peasants, and the peasants against the urban capitalists and imperialists. This 'model' would find it impossible to explain much of what goes on in rural India; to take just one instance, the fact that in Andhra Pradesh, nearly 60 to 70 murders have taken place in rural and small town areas during the last year and a half of elections – elections to *panchayat mandals*, agricultural cooperatives, municipalities and *gram panchayats*.[4] In these murders and counter-murders perpetrated by TDP (Telugu Desam Party)[5] and Congress (I) gangs, it was 'peasants' of some variety who killed and got killed on both sides, and we require an analysis that will explain these killings, as well as the struggles of labourers/peasants/farmers, whatever one wants to call them, and the murderous attacks on the rural poor, whether they take place on community or class lines.

Methodologically, the total picture has been missing because rural society is often studied principally on the basis of a single analytical category: the degree of commoditization of the economy. This focus leaves out many things that are essential for understanding the situation in its totality. To achieve a total understanding, we need to focus on not just the degree of commoditization of the economy but on the structure of rural society as it has evolved since 1947. The 'ideological' reason behind this methodological failure is the perception that the Indian state is exclusively an agent of capital, intent on creating a market for goods produced by it and on developing agriculture for the purpose of providing raw material for its consumption and food for its workers' consumption. This understanding, which finds expression in the tendency of economists of the left as well as the right to be preoccupied with matters like the rate of capital formation, has badly distorted our understanding of the role of the state.

The efforts of the Indian state to consciously consolidate and enrich a class of rural rich – not only in the interests of capital but in the interests of the rural rich themselves – has been missed out because of the self-imposed preoccupation of the economists. Since it is assumed that what characterizes the Indian state definitely is its interest – or lack of it – in 'developing' India, and since development means rapid capital formation, and industrial growth requires a certain pattern of trade and a certain transfer of resources between industry and agriculture, this preoccupation is but natural. If we give up this 'problematic' of economic development and take an unimpeded look at what has happened to the rural social structure in the last four decades, we are likely to get a more complete picture. The period of the nationalist movement was also a period of scattered, but frequent and violent, anti-feudal struggles of various sections of the peasantry. These struggles were only selectively integrated into the Congress-led nationalist movement, but the Congress party had no option but to take note of them in devising its policies for post-independent India. Yet that party had so many leaders at the national and provincial levels, who were themselves of the class of rural rich or were politically and communally allied to that class, that it had but to proceed slowly and cautiously. And therefore, immediate action was taken only against the zamindar type of holders of superior revenue rights,[6] and that too only against their revenue rights, and with compensation. Their landholdings, and the wide range of feudal authority the class possessed, were not immediately touched. Nor were the landholdings and feudal authority of the smaller class of landlords – mostly resident landlords whose claim to agrarian surplus was based partly but not principally on revenue rights and mainly on landholding and social authority – touched by the state. But as this small measure did not and could not satisfy the peasantry, further land reforms in the form of tenancy and land-ceiling legislation were enacted, and much rhetoric against feudal oppression was indulged in. This was a much more difficult matter since this class was the mainstay of the Congress party in most parts of the country. And that is why the legislation was not implemented and the rhetoric was not given real content to any greater extent than was necessitated by the agitational strength of the peasantry, which varied from region to region. Today, three decades and more after these enactments, the 'game' of enactment-evasion-pressure-concession has reached a seemingly stable equilibrium.

Government statistics – which are gleefully frank in this matter – say that about one per cent of the total land available for cultivation has been taken over as surplus under land ceiling laws. Miserable as it is, this figure, is still misleading since the land taken over is mostly unsuitable for cultivation. All the cultivatable surplus land was disposed of by the landlords through timely sales and subdivision – some of its *benami*[7] and nominal but some of it real – or by selling it to their own tenants or farm servants, thereby creating for themselves a permanent constituency in the days to come. Tenancy reforms were used by the bigger tenants to liberate themselves and join the class of dominant landholders. As for the smaller tenants, in most parts of the country they got evicted and converted into unrecorded tenants/farm servants/wage labourers, though in some places – depending principally on political factors – they managed to use the reforms to become independent cultivators.

In the process, there has been a gradual consolidation of a class of dominant landholders in villages, who range all the way from old-style landlords holding 100 acres or more, to their modern progeny of ex-tenants holding smaller but usually technologically modernized and highly productive holdings.

However, this landholding pattern does not explain all that is required for understanding rural India. This is another point where accepted

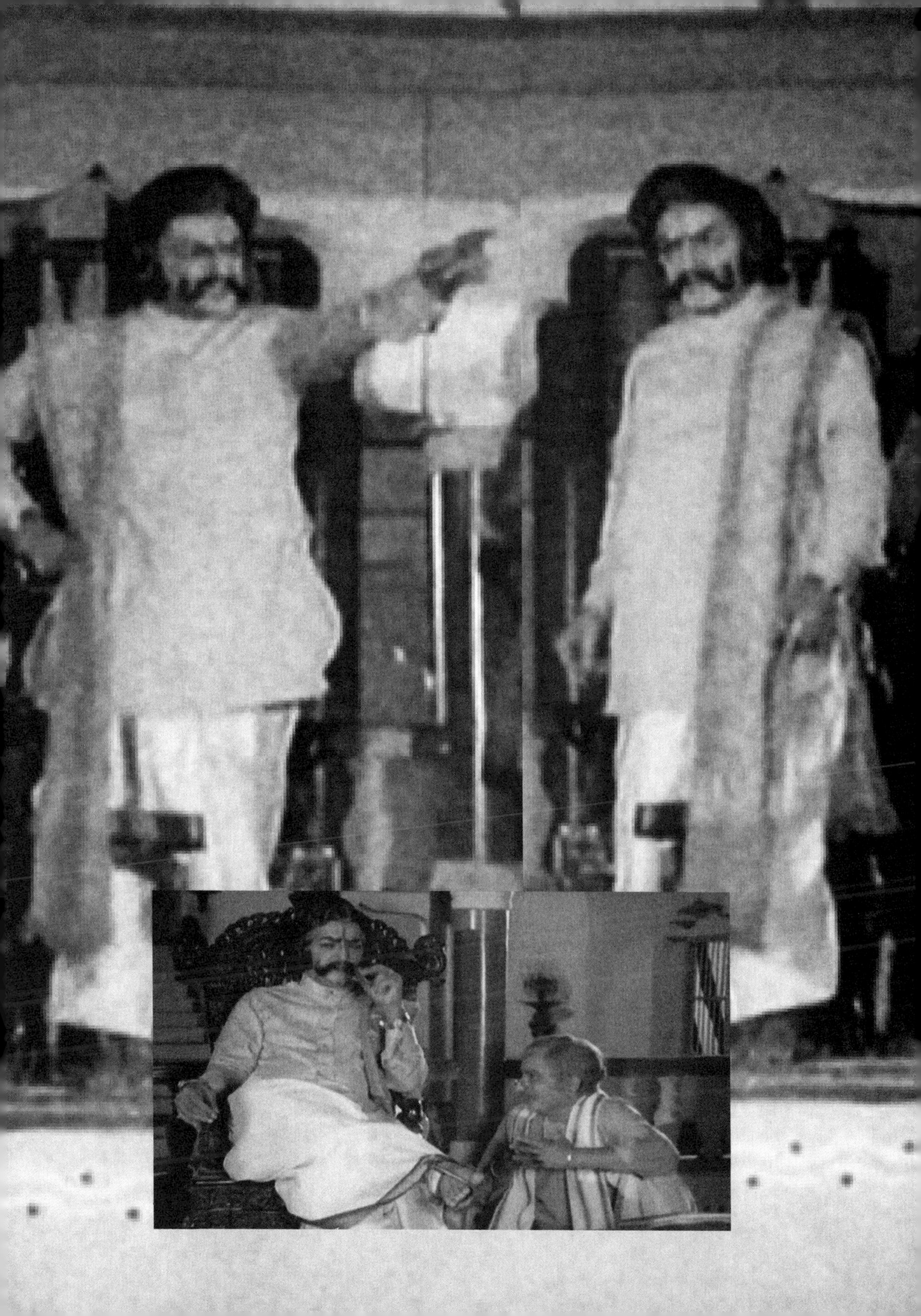

methodologies for analysing rural society are insufficient for our purpose. It is necessary to also see the role played by the state in consolidating and enriching this class, or at least the upper section of this class. As I have said above, the gamut of 'developmental' activities undertaken by the Indian state cannot be and should not be understood exclusively as aimed at creating a pattern of production, exchange and resource mobilization needed for urban-oriented capitalist industrialization.

The technological and infrastructural modernization of rural India – electrification, provision of artificial irrigation, chemical inputs and machinery, setting up agricultural and other rural cooperatives and marketing institutions, extensive development of rural banking in recent years, the widespread habit of giving out most rural works to contractors instead of getting them done departmentally, the ruralization of politics through the panchayat institutions and their linkages with rural developmental works, the extensive infrastructural facilities available for the transfer of rural wealth to urban areas to get invested in real estate, finance, trade, transport, contracts, business, agro-processing industry and the marketable professions like medicine and law – all these must be taken fully into account and seen as aimed at the consolidation of a class of rural-small town rich, the class that has taken the place of the landlords of yesteryears without any rupture or discontinuity.

Taken as a class, it is still land-based to a significant extent and generally village-based. It exercised social domination over the villages through pre-capitalist institutions like caste and through the tradition of domination it has inherited from its forefathers, both of which are neatly integrated with 'modern' institutions like *gram panchayat*s and cooperatives. In the more 'backward' areas, even more primitive pre-capitalist institutions like *begar*,[8] feudal monopoly of political and social opinion and arbitration, and the maintenance of armed gangs for enforcing this monopoly, prevail quite extensively; sometimes many of these institutions recover after a period of apparent demise, in times of drought or political turmoil.

This class, which the Indian state had nurtured as assiduously as it has helped the accumulation of the urban capitalists and imperialists, is completely missed out in the dominant analyses of rural society. The prevalent methodologies are incapable of capturing its existence, and the prevalent conceptualization of social transformation has no place to accommodate it.

And yet, this class is a key reference point for most of the social disturbances that affect the lives of the large majority of the people in India. The CPI-ML (Communist Party of India-Marxist-Leninist) movement, which perceives the agrarian revolution as the axis of the new democratic revolution, has fought this class as the immediate enemy of the rural masses; some of the groups even regard it as the principal enemy. Landlords holding large and prosperous estates of land, those controlling access to common or wasteland and those exercising feudal social domination; corrupt and authoritarian headmen and heads of institutions like *gram panchayats*, cooperatives and marketing societies, oppressive and extortionist and contractors: these oppressors, and the political representatives of these oppressors, constitute the class against which the CPI-ML groups have organized the rural poor. Their agrarian programme has been the distribution of its assets among the rural poor. The issues around which the masses are organized do include agricultural wage rates (and other matters which seemingly pit the landless poor against the middle peasants), but to view it as a 'labourer versus peasant' conflict is to view a political struggle economistically.

The enemies of the movement have themselves never had any doubts about its political content, even when its main demands have been higher wages for transplanting or harvesting paddy. The rural rich – as distinct from the 'middle peasants'– can very well afford to pay the wages demanded, but they have reacted with the correct political instinct and opposed the CPI-ML movement viciously. Where the 'middle peasantry' or a section of it has turned against the CPI-ML movement, it is invariably possible to discern behind this opposition the hand of a landlord, a contractor, a domineering gangster of feudal descent, a corrupt political boss, and suchlike. As the economic, political and political strength of this class increases, the viciousness of these attacks also increases. In recent years, especially after the Telugu Desam Party came to power, the ruthlessness of the repression on the CPI-ML movement has increased manifold, and its class content is clearly revealed in the exchanges in the state's legislative assembly, which is populated by the cream of the absentee landlords, contractors, financiers, businessmen-brokers. Suppression of the rural poor is an important requirement for the strengthening of the hegemony of this class. It is not just that payment of higher wages to them would affect its accumulations, or that the demands for land redistribution would affect its property; it is a political requirement, too.

Contrary to commonly accepted academic opinion that it is the 'green revolution' that is causing the tensions in villages, these atrocities have taken place in all kinds of villages. It is a consequence of the academic's unhappy methodological obsession with capital that the green revolution is isolated from all the fiscal, political, administrative and other measures undertaken by the Indian state to further enrich the rural rich. And these measures have had their impact even in the 'backward' areas. Where a good amount of irrigation is available, the rural rich have been enriched through technological modernization; in other areas, they have found a substitute in government contracts, cooperatives, and the wide variety of administrative and 'developmental' institutions created since Independence.

The major incidents of killing of Harijans have taken place in Karamchedu (Prakasam district), Neerukonda (Guntur district), Dontali (Nellore district), Gudivada (Vizianagaram district) and four or five villages in Chittoor district.[9] Karamchedu is a model 'developed' village in the canal-irrigated part of the old Guntur district. Paddy, cotton and tobacco are cultivated extensively and intensively here, and the wealth generated by this cultivation has taken the form of (and further reproduced itself in) trade, real estate, business, cinemas and lately politics. Neerukonda lies in the unirrigated upland region of interior Guntur district, which has been a centre of commercial cultivation ever since the first *ryotwari* settlement in 1865–66, and especially tobacco cultivation under the aegis of the Indian Leaf Tobacco Development Division (ILTD) in later years.[10]

Dontali in Nellore district and Gudiada in Vizianagaram district are situated in symmetric opposition, outside the reach of the Krishna basin in the south and the Godavari basin in the north; they are the archetypal backward villages in drought-hit regions whose dried-up tanks have rendered paddy more a memory than a foodgrain. Finally, Bandlapalli and other villages in Chittoor district lie in a region that has been agriculturally prosperous in a traditional sense ever since the days of the Vijayanagar empire.[11] The region receives good rains from the north-east monsoon, which drains the Eastern Ghat hills and fills the irrigation tanks and keeps them full all the year round. Paddy, sugarcane and groundnut are grown in plenty here, and the prosperity is symbolized by the temple to Lord Venakateswara built by the Vijayanagar kings in the midst of thick forests on the Eastern Ghat hills.[12]

In all these villages Harijans or other toiling caste people have been killed and their houses set on fire in the last two years. The assailants are mostly ordinary peasants, but invariably they have had the backing and instigation of the class of provincial rich that we have been discussing above. Ministers, MLAs, absentee landholders with trade and business in nearby towns, resident landlords who also indulge in trade and contracts – such individuals have been accused of behind-the-scenes complicity by the Dalits, and claimed as their patrons by the assailants. Caste, of course, works as a cementing factor, but there are many other less visible binding threads. The instigators do not have any insurmountable economic conflict with the Dalits, but they need to suppress the Dalits to consolidate the rural constituency behind them in the struggle with the classes, namely the urban capitalists and imperialists, with whom they *do* have serious conflict over the control and use of the nation's resources. And for ensuring this suppression, they instigate the ordinary peasantry against the labourers by playing upon the insecurity of the former as regards the prevalent agricultural conditions.

Rural electoral violence is another indicator of the nature and the inner contradictions of this class. The culture of gang fights of feudal lords is now carried forward by this seemingly much more modern class. Large parts of Andhra Pradesh – Rayalaseema districts, for instance – are vertically split into factions locally dominated by individuals of the landlord-contractor-quarry owner class owing allegiance to two or three big figures at the district level: usually present ministers of the Telugu Desam government or past ministers of the Congress governments. And yet, as far as their economic activity goes, these overlords are as modern as you could wish to see, complete with Maruti cars and VCRs at home.[13]

During the last year and a half, factional violence during elections to panchayat bodies, cooperatives and municipalities have claimed 60 to 70 lives apart from hundreds of haystacks and houses burnt. The district of Kurnool in Rayalaseema witnessed the remarkable spectacle of 300 villages – about 25 per cent of the total – returning their sarpanches unopposed, a feat for which the villages received handsome grants in cash from the state government, in recognition of the maturity that made them elect their sarpanches by consensus and not wasteful conflict. In point of fact, the successful candidates managed to get elected unanimously because they were sponsored by the factions whose writ runs unquestioned in the respective villages and is questioned only on pain of considerable physical violence. And the writ extends far beyond electoral choices and decides almost everything in the villages.

It is within the matrix of the enrichment and domination of this class that one should make sense of rural struggles – struggles of the poor as well as struggles of the 'middle' peasants. The market orientation of the rural economy is better described as monetization than commoditization, much less capitalist cultivation. The general monetization of the economy forces cultivators to produce marketable crops even when that is not altogether the optimal choice for them. It forces subsistence production into the market without destroying its subsistence character. In severely drought-hit Anantapur district, for instance, peasants who had a choice of wetland crops like ragi and paddy and dryland crops like *jowar*, *bajra* and groundnut, are today growing groundnut almost as an exclusive crop.[14] The unending drought has forced them into dryland farming all over again, and since their credit with the cooperatives has dried up due to repeated defaulting and no moneylender is going to lend money for the cultivation of a non-marketable crop like *jowar* or *bajra*, they are left with groundnut as the only alternative.

This may very well show up in statistical tables as a spurt in commercial cultivation in Anantapur district. Indeed, there is a general tendency on the part of even small peasants to grow cash crops on dryland, not because they are profit-maximizing capitalist cultivators but because any other choice of the crop would leave them starved for credit at one end and cash at the other. For instance, most of the Lambada (Banjara) cultivators in Warangal and Karimnagar districts grow groundnut on their small patches of red soil holdings (*kushki* land), and most of the Gonds of Adilabad grow cotton in their (often illegal) black soil holdings in the forest highlands.[15]

Therefore, remunerative prices for cash crops is a general problem of concern for the peasantry at large and not just the rich peasantry. It will perhaps become a bigger problem as drought conditions increase in extent and intensity. It is not very convincing that the terms of trade are generally in favour of agriculture against industry, as is argued by some people. In any case, the debate is vitiated by the misapprehension that the terms of trade determine the level of prosperity for all classes in villages. However, on the contrary, the prosperity of the rural rich would be affected much more by a drop in government expenditure on rural works, on maintaining and running rural institutions, and a shift in the policy concerning rural contracts, transport and marketing. Yet the rural rich do have a serious stake in the question of 'remunerative' prices.' Partly, of course, it is because they themselves have land and often grow lucrative crops; partly it is because low prices for marketed output affects the savings of the peasantry and thereby the accumulation of the rich since they control and handle the savings through a variety of formal and informal mechanisms; but more than anything else it is because the cause of 'remunerative prices' is the cause of the 'village' and they are and must be seen to be the natural leaders of the village.

There is no other way they can legitimize their claims for a greater share of state-controlled resources, a claim that they frequently assert against urban capital. 'Middle' peasant movements which talk of village vs town, or unorganized sector vs organized sector, play into the hands of this class whether they like it or not. This truth may seem unkind at first, but it becomes evident the moment the rural rich themselves step in to organize the 'peasantry'. Then it will appear in starkest light and thereby reveal the essence of the matter. And here, as in all matters concerning the politics of the rural rich, N.T. Rama Rao's Andhra Pradesh is already taking the lead.[16] Recently the state government has constituted a body called the *Karshaka Parishad*.[17] It is funded by the government and is supposed to look after the interests of the farmers. Members are enrolled at the village level and office bearers are elected. Its president is, of course, the chief minister's younger son-in-law, Chandrababu Naidu, who was born in a poor peasant family but owns more than a hundred acres of land and palatial house in Hyderabad. The *Karshaka Parishad*, of course, talks the language of 'Bharat', and indeed a delegation is reported to have gone to the different states to study the farmers' movements of those states.

It is necessary to realize the potential, if not actually present, domination of all the farmers' movements by the same class. It is not a matter of the subjective honesty and Gandhian simplicity of the leaders, whether real or put-on. So long as the matter is analysed in terms of the conflict between capital and peasant production, between organized industry and unorganized primary production, between capital-intensive production and labour-intensive production, the danger will remain inherent. The only way the farmers' movements can avoid cooptation by the rural rich is to recognize class as an oppressor on par with urban capital.

Very few peasants need to be told this, since they suffer the oppression, exploitation and swindling of this class in their day-to-day lives, but it needs to be recognized conceptually and integrated into a political line of struggle. It is much more difficult to fight this class than it is to indulge in rhetoric – or even *rasta roko* (roadblock) agitations – against urban capital, but there is no other way one can organize a genuine peasant struggle for better farm prices. And this is where it also becomes possible to unite the struggles of the landless for wages and land, and against social oppression of the rural rich, with the struggles for better prices for agricultural produce. For the oppression of the rural is a fact of life for the mass of the peasantry as much as for the poor. In any real-life village, it is truly impossible to separate the problems and the rural poor. Indeed, it takes a shoddy methodology and political sleight of hand to achieve the miracle!

□

This influential essay restates the key categories of tradition and contemporaneity to identify a specific problem being posed by modernism in India and, more generally, in the non-west. Given that modernism as a cultural term is squarely situated at a particular point of western history – from where it can take off both into an imperialist character as well as a potentially revolutionary one – the problem that many non-western nations face as they struggle with the processes of modern*ization* is that they find themselves excluded from (or, more likely, rendered incidental to) modern*ism* per se. Modernism must, **Geeta Kapur** argues, confront the 'thorny face of the modern', that of its bourgeois ideology which can simultaneously possess a noble universality alongside Eurocentric imperialist criteria for the rest of the world.

This argument was, it is important to note, first presented at the Third Havana Biennale (**Tradition and Modernity in Third World Fine Arts** conference, Cuba, 1989). The essay was first published in **Social Scientist** (vol. 18, no. 3, March 1990) and later in **Third Text** (vol. 4, no. 11, 1990). A more elaborate version, 'Detours from the Contemporary', in the book **When Was Modernism: Essays on Contemporary Cultural Practice in India** (New Delhi: Tulika Books, 2000, pp. 267–82), would become the launchpad for Kapur's further extension to argue for a non-western avant-garde.

Images: From Moinak Biswas's two-channel video installation, **Across the Burning Track** (2016), and Bhupen Khakhar's painting, **Seva** (oil on canvas, 1986). The installation uses Ritwik Ghatak's last film, the monumental **Jukti Takko aar Gappo** (**Reason, Debate and a Story**, Bengali, 1977), which is projected atop a truck that passes through contemporary Kolkata. It includes an animated drawing of the falling over of Neelkantha Bagchi (played by Ghatak), the 'failed' drunken teacher-intellectual who dies in a crossfire between student guerrillas and the police.

Neelkantha/Ghatak is placed here alongside Khakhar's self-image as the old man who does *seva* to his male partner. *Seva*, literally translating as selfless service, whose representational leitmotif is 'pressing another's feet or legs to relieve suffering' writes R. Srivatsan,[1] has a long political history, used especially by M.K. Gandhi to turn its ritual service expiation into a constructive, organized, non-violent war. The 'untouchable', says Srivatsan, 'had no right to do what he thought was right for himself; he had to submit to the painfully masochistic ministrations of the sevak'. The pain would extend into the nationalist subject as it translated from strife and disagreement into 'consensus and coercion'. The autobiographical artist-self, volunteering to enter conflict zones and to literally perform with his body the act of sacrifice, donation, expiation, self-abnegation, comes into India's 1990s wearing, to use Geeta Kapur's phrase, the 'double mantle of contemporaneity'.

Grateful acknowledgment to Moinak Biswas for permission to reproduce and for images from **Across the Burning Track**, and to Dhaval Khakhar for permission to reproduce **Seva.**

8

GEETA KAPUR

1989

CONTEMPORARY CULTURAL PRACTICE

Some Polemical Categories

The persistence of the terms *tradition* and *contemporaneity*, as they figure in Third-World debates, are best appreciated if we see them as notations within the cultural polemic of decolonization. They may be used in all earnestness as essential categories and real options, but in fact, they are largely pragmatic features of nation building. Indeed, the terms function in a hyphenated form and mark the double (or multiple) register of a persuasive nationalist discourse. Sufficiently historicized, either tradition or contemporaneity can notate a 'radical' purpose in the cultural politics of the Third World.

TRADITION WITHIN QUOTATION MARKS

Certainly, the term as we use it in the present equation is not what is given or received as a disinterested civilizational legacy, if ever there should be such a thing. This tradition is what is invented by a society's cultural vanguard in the course of a struggle. It marks off territories/ identities of a named people, as for example Indians. In that sense it is a loaded signifier, drawing energy from an imaginary resource (the ideal tradition), but always remaining by virtue of its strongly ideological import an ambivalent, often culpable, sign in need of constant historical interpretation, so that we know which way it is pointing.

What in India we call tradition today was put in the fray by nineteenth-century nationalists. The manifestos of swadeshi (political and cultural self-reliance) in the first decades of this century produced, in conjunction with the ideal tradition, a kind of aesthetic at once didactic and contemplative. This is best exemplified by the great scholar A.K. Coomaraswamy and followed by Bengali artists and intelligentsia with arguable success.[2]

Since tradition, even in its conservative allegiances, emerged in the decolonizing process as an oppositional category, it has the power of resistance, as we know very well from Gandhi.[3] The power to transform routinely transmitted materials from the past into discursive forms, that merit, in consequence, to be called contemporary, even radical. If the *savants* of this century, among them Coomaraswamy, have excavated the past to provide the present (in their opinion, errant and impoverished) century with perennial life-symbols, the exercise has rather special significance when this is contextualized within an anti-imperialist struggle. Coomaraswamy (in the context provided by Gandhi), even when he addresses national cultural issues from a conservative position, produces an interventionist discourse opening up new and numerous other issues besides 'Indianness' – issues about the function of art in society and about the advanced role of artists in the formation of a more universal world culture. These are the issues Rabindranath Tagore takes up in virtual opposition to the more severe injunctions of swadeshi.[4]

Let us look at this a little further. With Coomaraswamy, tradition, besides its metaphysical status, is the code derived from and applied to actual/ideal iconography forms. Being also a set of working canons, it can include, in an intricately worked hierarchy, high art with everyday objects. For, canonical rigour, despite the transcendent meanings to which it refers, is based on the form and function of idols and objects. But it is precisely Coomaraswamy's contemporary, Rabindranath Tagore, who handles tradition in a way so as to dismantle the code. Tradition with him is a notional category allowing an infinite extension of its own nurturing body through poetic allusion and metaphor. The Tagorean way is, as we know, the romantic way and it deals with immanent energies that are inexhaustible in the mythical fashion, and encourage continual transfigurement of material resources within and beyond a given culture. This includes the anthropological evidence and spiritual experience of extant forms. It includes the emotional resonance of the *rasa* theory, for example; or an encounter with the numen which irradiates from the heart of iconic forms. It includes the linguistic particularities of folk objects that are seen to provide the infrastructure of the civilizational process.

Rather than the canonical, it is the 'romantic' designation of culture that gains ground in India. It is in a sense the more protective, Utopian dimension. It is the line with the modern – the romantic tradition is the direct antecedent of the modern in Europe. And it allows non-systematic, or intuitive, interpretation of traditions with two quite opposite options. The option of finding elective affinities at the level of feeling and also more anarchic disjunctions, of loosening and then upturning the forms of tradition. The two filmmakers, Satyajit Ray and Ritwik Ghatak, both heirs of Tagore,[5] reflect the one and the other option within the broadly romantic view of tradition.

But even the very act of handling the tradition is in a sense political; it involves personification/meditation/representation of material that is seen to have been hitherto buried. Received like a patrimony, tradition has a heroic and authoritarian aspect. Is the code for Coomaraswamy like the Law of the Father (or like the Canon of the Master-Craftsman?) On the other hand, are the affiliations to tradition understood as a nurturing body, or as the matrix embedded in the unconscious more difficult to wean off, leading to softer options in aesthetics and art practice? These personifications themselves are tricky, and it becomes necessary to demystify the sustaining figures of Father (law) and Mother (womb)[6] through less tenacious symbols that stress the engendering *function* at once masculine and feminine. We can, for example, take tradition as an androgynous figure and empower it the more; but also, by this hypothetical entity, subvert the very knowledge of it. Part of the politics in the handling of tradition is to play both with its fantastic figures and its actual functions.

When I use the word function, I mean the study of genres, conventions, rhetorical devices, symbologies and other linguistic features. If tradition is functional, it will also contribute to cultural praxis: there is a kind of plunder involved, and continual replenishment of desacralized resources.

This has further implications. That we work less with seamless systems like myths and more with constructed forms like epic and allegory. Remember Brecht. Or, we subject myths to allegorical readings, turning them inside-out and placing them as open secrets within larger epic structures that give myths transcendent purpose, and an existential exit into new meanings. Ritwik Ghatak achieves precisely this in his six films. It also means that we work less with spiritual consensus on life-symbols, and more with morphologies of art objects; more with formal analyses of given imageries where the signs float up, so to say, each with its memory-cell intact, but each fixed with a flick-tail that allows it to manoeuvre itself into new formal configurations. Into elaborate montage. I am thinking of the films of Mani Kaul.[7] Is such functionality a reductive process, giving us only the mechanics of traditional forms? There is a function beyond functionalism that can point to the sensuous efficacy of

images acted out in iconographical elaboration, that can push towards more reflexive structures, towards further narratives. I am referring to the cinema of Kumar Shahani.[8] But this functionality is nothing without wit, or what I called play, which displaces the relationship between canon and craft, between metaphor and structure, A wit that uses dissembling devices that are both naive and irreverent. The work of two artists, K.G. Subramanyan and Bhupen Khakhar,[9] shows this to marvellous effect.

There are other, broadly sociological, ways of looking at the Indian tradition as it has come to us since the nineteenth century. The social matrix yields at least two distinct aspects, the aristocratic and the middle-class, each with its own way of interpreting cultural nationalism. The princely attribute of Raja Ravi Varma of the House of Travancore[10] makes up one part of the lineage, a quasi-classical art aspiring to restore a civilizational poise to its people. On the other hand, the ambience of the landed gentry of nineteenth-century Bengal inclines them, as for example the Tagore family, towards a pastoral nostalgia for a people of the land. Against the courtly (and sometimes kitsch) pictures of Ravi Varma, the Tagore legacy includes poetic references to Upanishadic hymns[11] as also to peasant songs. We know that the aristocratic tradition may be, on the whole, conservative. But we must also acknowledge that even the quasi- (or neo-) classical mode can attempt an allegorical/heroic model that provides valour and rationality to a contemporary society, and plays in that sense a progressive role. As for the romantic view, the Tagore family, for instance, combines noble learning with dilettante experimentalism within the framework of the new national enlightenment called the Indian renaissance, and brings into this frame of reference the *art of the folk*. There is a strongly pedagogical aspect to this project particularly as it is carried out in Tagore's university at Santiniketan.

It also points to a larger sociological context, the aristocrats' alliance with the folk in matters of culture, a principle on which romanticism in Europe and realism in Russia develop. In this lineage as well there is then a definite democratic urge.

Indeed, it is this aspect which combines in the first half of this century with the artisanal basis of Gandhian ideology and the craftsman's canonical aesthetic of Coomaraswamy, to give us the threefold composition of nationalist culture in the area of arts and crafts. In the actual practice of artists such as K.G. Subramanyan and his pupils, heirs of this nationalist culture, the aristocratic mentality vanishes completely to arrive, after a series of modernist mediations, at a strategic notion of the *contemporary*

The other aspect of this invented tradition is less indigenist (less connected with ancient India or the Indian soil), more bourgeois/ metropolitan. It is most clearly attributable to the Indo-Hungarian artist, Amrita Sher-Gil, who is trained in Paris in the 1930s, and it develops in the late 1940s in Bombay, as also in Calcutta and Madras during the 1940s–50s. One need hardly reiterate the progressive elements in bourgeois consciousness as such, or its initial engendering and later appropriation of a further, more revolutionary, consciousness.

In India, the progressive element in the programme of metropolitan (or simply urban) artists is once again mediated via nationalist aspirations, or the promise in existential and political terms for self-determination. Taken in the direction of modernization, this leads the cultural aspirations of what now comes to be called, in liberationist terminology, a Third-World polity towards a more comprehensive, more radical, more sympathetic *international* formation. Calling themselves progressives, several generation of Indian artists, including writers, seek to represent the peoples' voice – even if this be a rhetorical (or perhaps more correctly, emblematic) stand. At any rate the progressives among the painters, as for example F.N. Souza, M.F. Husain, S.H. Raza and Ara in Bombay, Ram Kumar and Satish Gujral in Delhi,[12] can be seen to be fellow-travellers, in what is still believed through the fifties to be a transitive society – a newly-independent people transiting towards socialism.

The paradigm I have proposed, for this invented Indian tradition, is of course extremely schematic. It sees the folk as appropriated by the aristocratic elite; and progressive (socialist) ideologies as appropriated by the metropolitan intelligentsia. Even if such a scheme works, its truth is of the most general kind. There are several cross-references involved:

(i) The appropriation of the folk by the elite could be a way, for example, of correcting a too-easy coincidence between the norms of progressivism with those of imperialism; it is a way of deferring the question of modernism until it can be handled with a more independent intelligentsia with a more questioning mentality.

(ii) Not only that, it is precisely folk traditions (rather than an indeterminate proletarian culture) that is taken up by the Indian communists. The Indian Peoples' Theatre Association (IPTA)[13] experiment in the 1940s–50s mediates folk traditions, especially in the area of performance, to progressive, clearly socialist, ends.

(iii) There is another kind of mediation towards an indigenous variant of socialism – the Gandhian framework – where peasant communities are seen as the self-complete prototypes for a new and Utopian social structure.

Nor is the matter so simple in the other part of the equation. The artists and intelligentsia put in the bourgeois/metropolitan category, in this simple paradigm, also show strong nationalistic sentiments, and their modernism can be seen to be not only mediated but, in fact, fashioned to serve the cultural self-image of a nation declaring its resistance towards imperialist nations of the first world. In India, one might say, the inhibiting, the camouflaging, as well as the liberating, aspects of modernism are held at bay by a fairly independent bourgeoisie and a fairly self-conscious intelligentsia, who are able to pose the issues of their own identity even when they cannot so easily resolve the problematic that fetters the process of their own liberation.

CONTEMPORANEITY AND ITS DOUBLE MANTLE

Though obviously a temporal category, the term *contemporary* assumes a kind of neutrality, and stands in an asymmetrical relationship to the value-loaded term, *tradition*. We can, if we want, 'correct' the situation by giving contemporaniety the ideological mantle of the term modernity. Immediately, of course, an agitation begins but that is perhaps the point, to include the turmoil and give a definitional ambiguity to the present, so that the future is predicated at a higher level of consciousness.

But 'modernity', a common affective in India, stands in a relatively undefined relationship to its two other companion terms – modernization and modernism. Modernization is a social and economic process now applicable mostly to the underdeveloped/developing societies (of the Third World). It is a term full of ideological import, even over-determined, one might say, by sociological theory and usage. Modernism is, on the other hand, a cultural term now seen to be squarely situated at a particular point of western history – the nineteenth century. It can take on an imperialist character, but it has *also* the potential to evolve into a revolutionary culture. In envisaging socialist internationalism, modernism plays a vanguard role.

Non-western nations, though struggling with the processes of modernization, are excluded from modernism per se. Or they are seen to be incidental to it. They stay, therefore, quavering a little, with a neutral term like contemporaneity. Yet so far as they undertake to modernize, the thorny face of the modern must be examined, even as the aura that surrounds it must be seen to be what it is: a signalling device for the future. On the one hand, then, there is the specifically bourgeois ideology of the modern that makes it assume for itself a noble universality, while obviously imposing a Eurocentric (imperialist) set of cultural criteria on the rest of the world. By the same token, a unitary logic of advancement, as this was conceived of in nineteenth-century Europe, continues to be imposed: so that someone or the other among the peoples of the world are always seen to be out of step. Further, the same linear model assumes, in the metropolitan concentration of culture, other geometrical figures: like centre and periphery. This camouflages the crude progressivism of the linear model. Backwardness is not spelt out as such, but questions of marginality (minor groups/minorities) come up in its stead.

In view of the critique mounted from all parts of the world on the euphemistic projection of bourgeois culture as the 'universal modern', there is an attempt by western ideologists to change tactics. A good deal is now said about the abandonment of the linear model, and of the model of the centre and the periphery as well. The new system for perceiving *difference,* the key word, is to project cultural phenomena into an infinite series. A problematic universe is mapped out into a differential system that is, as system, considered neutral. There is, in consequence, the reduction of the world into sameness. It looks like we in the Third World can hardly gain from one or the other model.

THE THIRD WORLD

The term 'Third World', full of problems, comes in handy for primarily ideological reasons. In a sense, it supercedes, or even denies, historical sense in order to be polemically effective. The Third world is a new world, emerging to chastise the first and the second worlds. By definition volatile, it is possible that the Third World wedges itself in the global bind established between the first and the second worlds. But issues are confounded when the term is used not as a simple lever but substantively, as a concept.

When it attempts to condense past struggles and present crises of a medley of post-colonial societies telescoped in history, the Third World becomes the symbolic option, and the polemic enters an entirely hypothetical area.

The political truth of colonial experience, and of the anti-imperialist struggle, is evident but its logic excludes several other political truths. Even fundamental categories like production systems and class relations are bracketed. Nor do the Third World countries yield comparative cultural formations. Historically, invented in the process of decolonization, tradition, governed in each case by a national ideology which emphasizes difference, becomes a sufficiently variegated sign to merit close and special attention.

Matters are altogether far from simple in societies designated as post-colonial. Here, if anywhere, capitalism and socialism are contested. Here is the world arena for ideological battle. This generates deeply vexed identities in terms of class and language, race and gender. Individual destinies are at stake as much as new collectivities. Indeed, the profoundly paradoxical nature of existence in the societies newly inducted into world history offers less, rather than more, possibilities of generalization. If we

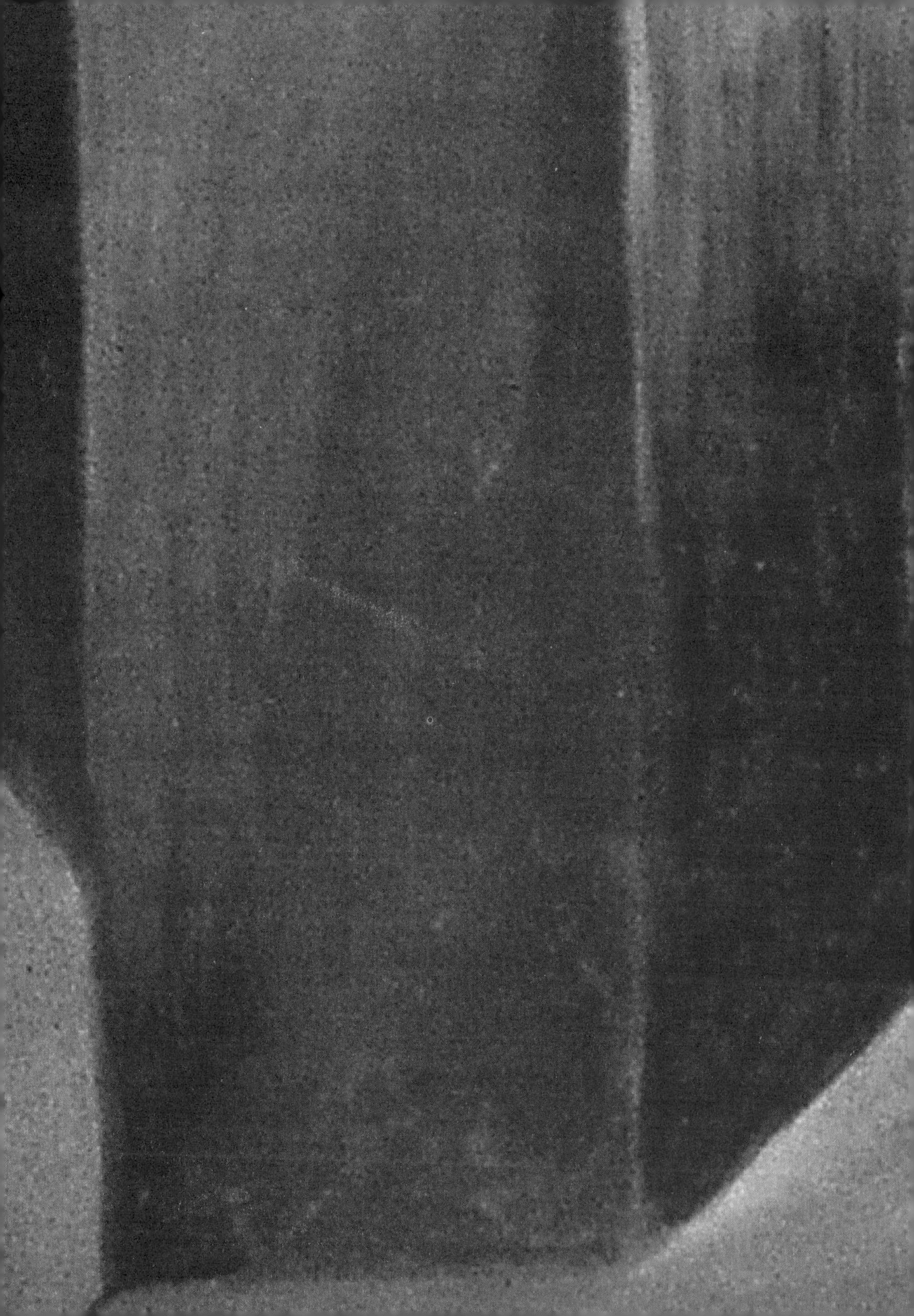

must in any case undertake to bring the anarchy of differential practices (including custom, knowledge, art) into some kind of recognizable order, one frame for which is the Third World, it also means that the theorizing must need to be so much more complex. Once independence has been gained, nationalism itself poses ontological questions – what is at stake in being Indian? And though the question may easily devolve into rhetoric, there is a burden of it that rests on a particularly fraught class and its individuals. This is the urban middle-class intelligentsia, including the artists.

This cultural elite rests most uneasily on its privileges. Even after a century of self-identification within the nationalist paradigm, it is seen to stand accused among its people. Even those among them who opt for the Left find that the status of fellow-traveller is ambiguous even as the goal of socialism remains unfinished. Moreover, when nationalist truth and unrealized socialism no longer suffice, this class must cope with the further states of social entropy. The responsibility of reckoning with that falls neither on the state nor on the national bourgeoisie (nor on the peasant or proletarian classes), because none of these are so far evolved in their consciousness of identity and role. It falls on the middle-class intelligentsia. This is the sort of burden, perhaps unreal and pretentious, that Tagore envisaged for the individual intellectual and artist in India. The responsibility to evolve his or her own subjectivity into an exemplary selfhood that indirectly but surely fulfils the demands of an exemplary nationhood. This burden assumes, by proxy, the ideal of a collective identity that may moreover come to resemble socialism, as Nehru hoped. Certainly, the Left constituency of the intelligentsia can envisage totalities of another, more egalitarian, order. The imagination turns these expectations into allegorical accounts: all Third-World narratives are national allegories, Frederic Jameson says.[14]

What is to be remembered in the Indian (and presumably the Third World) context is that contradictions are rife, and you have to put up all the fights at once. If the primary fight is against the imperialism of the first world, you have equally to fight the anti-democratic forces of local dynasties and dictators. The fight is also against reactionary forces, especially aggressive in traditional societies like ours; indeed, against the anti-modern forces that use tradition, which served a useful function in the national struggle, as a ruse to regress into communal and religious fundamentalisms.

In view of this, definitions of tradition and modernity are constantly being repositioned in the discourses of the Third World. What is more, the relationship between the two at a substantive level has to be thought through at every point so as to avoid replicating the exploitative relationship the west has established towards traditional societies in the non-western world. From the over-determined nationalist bind in which tradition and modernity have hitherto coexisted, we have to bring them into a larger, more universal, discourse.

The point is to tackle the very problems western cultural hegemony suppresses or neglects. This requires above all that the two concepts, tradition and modernity, be disengaged from the abstracting ideology of capitalism – restoring to one a self-reflexive mechanism, and to the other the Utopian dimension. We have to bring to the term tradition, for example, the concreteness of extant practice, and to make the genuine extension of small particularities into new and contemporary configurations. Also, at the same time, we have to bring to the term a less monolithic, a less formalistic, indeed a less institutional, status so as to at least make it what it was once: a vanguard notion leading to a variety of experimental moves. Only with such initiatives can Third-World cultures begin to justify their worth as alternative cultures.

Nor is this an entirely hypothetical proposition. Already, in the nationalist phase, the colonial intelligentsia contextualize the terms tradition and modernity via patriotic norms. Tradition is not simply an anthropological phenomenon, as it was conceived of by western modernists when they discovered primitive cultures. Even though nationalism-as-ideology introduces its own measure of abstraction into the concept of tradition, it also, in the very moment of inventing it, poses the problematic in contemporary terms and thereby sees it as *process*. A tradition-to-use, shall we say – rather than producing, as in the case of the west, a discourse *about* the oriental (including primitive) cultures, rather than distancing alternative civilizations into objects to be processed by western subjectivity – the nationalists make at least some genuinely anxious, and possibly responsible, approximations within their own societies. If all Third-World texts are national allegories, all national allegories are attempts to restore conceptual wholeness to lost communities.

Appropriated tradition in the nationalist phase may, in fact, resemble that endemic form of eclecticism the modern imagination encourages, but without the extremity of otherness which produces forms alienated from function and meaning. At the same time, this eclecticism can yield, as with the moderns, *acts of transgression* which lead to cultural radicalism. Thus, positing a tradition-in-use in Third-World societies encourages an effective method of politicizing culture. It must, in addition, find a way to resist the business of *reification* to which the artefacts of 'other' civilizations succumb, in the wake of western modernism. It is true, of course, that capitalism anywhere produces reifications and correctives are not easily at hand. In societies like India, modernization after the capitalist mode has produced a commodification of traditions as such, and of traditional forms and artefacts, to serve both the state and the market. One might also add that today the political mode of aesthetic transgression followed by the moderns is considered ineffectual in the contest of multinational capitalism and its appropriating (devouring) techniques. The post-modern vanguard proposes other means of politicizing cultural practice – by a more strategic form of minority (class/race/gender) *resistance*. And the question arises whether postmodernist strategies are especially useful to us as well?[15]

Post-modernism, while it seems to accommodate otherness as never before in the history of capitalist culture, does so (as I said before) through a process of such infinite differentiation that all questions of identity are destroyed in any case, along with the normative function of culture and even the necessity of choice. This makes us more captive within the capitalist art market. We, who still must speak in favour of subjective identity at the individual level and living collectivities at the social level, have to learn to question the tendency towards formalism within the modern. But we must equally question the careless and aggressive laissez-faire of the post-modern which is hitched to the merry-go-round of multinational capitalism and throws entire cultures to the gambler's wheel, treating cultural artefacts like so many fetishist pawns in the game as it were.

Although the Indian intelligentsia must engage in transnational discourse on the question of Third World and alternative identities, Indian artists must derive the norms of their actual practice from the very specific aesthetic and ideological issues that they find pressing in their own (geographical/national) environment. That is to say, we have to beware a little of a Third-Worldist mentality. There is now a Third-World rhetoric surpassing the Third-World solidarity and over-determining the representations of radical issues for us. The first world (if not the second) continues to use the principle of primacy quite literally to subsume the polemic into a larger appropriate project – sometimes through theory, sometimes through consumer tactics. And sometimes through radicalism-by-proxy that pre-empts praxis on sites where it matters, and makes it, as if, redundant.

It may also help to resist letting the post-modern categories of discourse coincide entirely with the political entities that arise in consequence of decolonization. Third-World people must not simply lend body to the stripped phantoms of the deconstructionists' art. By not allowing too neat a fit between the dilemmas of decolonized cultures and post-modern theorizing, one may safeguard the material and political struggle, save it from appearing subordinate to categories within western academic discourse. It is however in our interest to recognize one thing. The sea-change created by the emergence of other cultures, that is our cultures, in the role of historical protagonists, has required western intellectuals to fashion different perceptual modes (and theoretical models). The post-modern phenomenon may be the consequence, not a description, of a universe realigned by social praxis within hitherto displaced societies, necessitating in its turn a theory of displacement.

Even as to the discourse set up by expatriate blacks, this tends for our purposes to become too much the privileged voice of the diaspora whose members are themselves positioned in the western academic world. They are inclined to establish canons for radical discourse for the rest of blacks everywhere in the world. It is true that there is a certain urgency in their task, since the enemy is large and clear, but there is also this tendency to establish a hierarchical superiority for a black-culture-in-exile which declares itself more militant. It should be recognized as what it is – a mode of operation suitable precisely to the mentality of the diaspora in the heart of the white world. Theirs is not the only call for militancy though we should hark at it all the same.

We have, in other words, to look at the peculiarly structured inter-referentiality of Indian national culture as a continuous formation: to look at ourselves aspiring to enrich the neutral ground of our contemporaniety with a crop transplanted from a unique tradition, as also with the universal maker of the age that is modernism. And then to look at ourselves, again, in the form of a post-colonial nation-state coalesced into the Third World to gain political solidarity. And, finally, rather than allowing ourselves to be theorized into political homogeneity we must engage in a dialectic that takes into account the material factors within our own traditions but in terms of our projected history that can no longer be less than a universal project.

The artists, in the meanwhile, are in any case engaged in the less ideological, more concrete, task of making a tradition-in-use that nurtures contemporary existence. If the Third World is a political entity, an oppositional discourse and a compendium of cultural practices, then it is the last that requires our sustained attention.

If the Third-World intelligentsia, among them artists, perform a task, it is to bring existential urgency to questions of contemporaniety. And as with all existential expressions, it is split into two aspects. Tradition is turned into a critique and culture into a matter of practice, and both together into a civilization's discourse that goes beyond nation-state and Third-Worldist dogmas, beyond also the dividing bigotries of the present world. In this respect, the artist and intellectual of India and the Third World are not different from their counterparts in the first and the second worlds. It is important to remember this, too, so that we are not simply overtaken by ideologies and left with polemical rather than life-sustaining forms of cultural practice.

SECTION II

DISAPPEARANCES

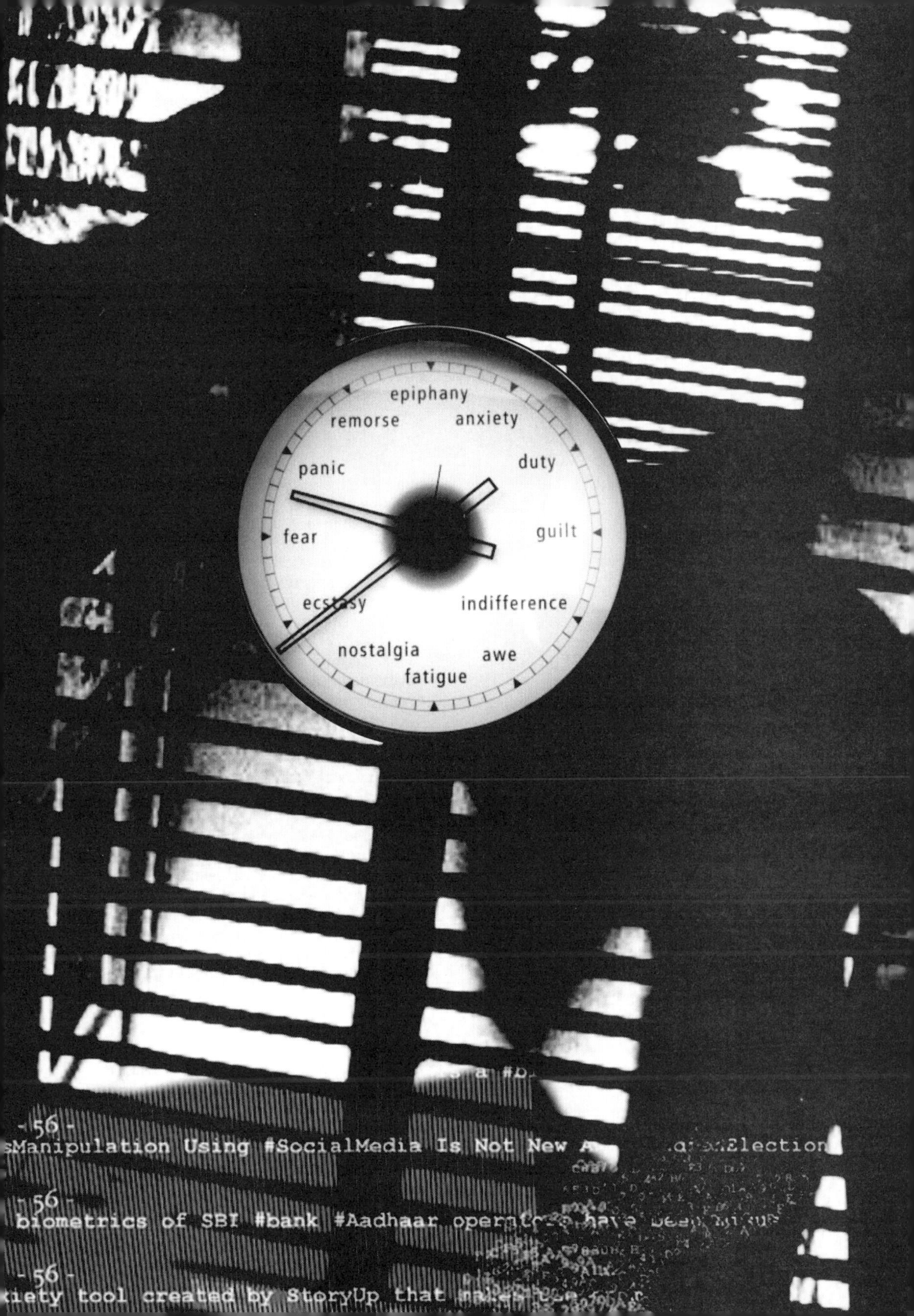
epiphany
remorse
anxiety
panic
duty
fear
guilt
ecstasy
indifference
nostalgia
awe
fatigue
- 56 -
Manipulation Using #SocialMedia Is Not New
Election
- 56 -
biometrics of SBI #bank #Aadhaar
- 56 -
tool created by StoryUp that

Ravi Sundaram's text was written in the era of bulletin boards and dial-up internet links that lasted twenty minutes. And yet there is an extraordinary prescience to the 'nationalist panopticon' that leads to the digital dystopias of the present period (at the time of this anthology), starting with the massive Aadhaar project of giving all Indian residents a unique identity, and culminating in the deeply controversial National Population Register and the Citizenship (Amendment) Act.

This is an abridged reprint of a paper first presented at the 5th International Conference on Cyberspace, Telefonica, Madrid, 5–6 June 1996, and later published in John Caldwell, ed., **Electronic Media and Technoculture** (New Brunswick: Rutgers University Press, 2000, pp. 270–94). Grateful acknowledgment to the author for permission to reprint.

Images: From Sarai in the early 1990s: the Cybermohalla project, images of Nehru Place and map of the mediascape of Madipur Colony, from the **Publics and Practices in the History of the Present (PPHP)** project; in **Raqs Media Collective**, 'The Street is the Carrier and the Sign', **The Cities of Everyday Life: Sarai Reader II** (Delhi: Sarai, The New Media Initiative, 2002, p 101).

From **Karthick K.G.**'s interactive installation, **Datamugshot.** In the installation, as the viewer's data profile is created through live interaction with a sensor, an algorithm crawls over the internet and feeds on the stream of tweet messages with #uidai #aadhaar #biometric, and visualizes them as grids of scrolling headlines. The two combine to produce what the artist calls a 'pseudo-identity' that is uploaded to the @datamugshot Twitter handle. The installation comprises a projector, a desktop monitor, a Kinect motion sensor, a Mac Mini, speakers, a script for the visuals, the data for sound and the Twitter feed harvesting. It was shown as **Mold to Modulation: Dusting the Fingerprints** (14 July–12 August 2017, Vadehra Art Gallery, Delhi). Grateful acknowledgment to the artist and to FICA, New Delhi.

The clock, from **Escapement** by Raqs Media Collective (2002), first installed at Sarai, the basement, CSDS, Delhi. Permission to use from the artists is gratefully acknowledged.

Horizontal silhouette: first appearance of meme adapting the 'spirit' figure from K.P. Reji's **Thumbingal Chathan** (oil on canvas, 2012).

9

RAVI SUNDARAM

1996

BEYOND THE NATIONALIST PANOPTICON

The Experience of Cyberpublics in India

Writing from a country that is located firmly within the periphery of late capitalism, there are many senses in which the old ideologies of nineteenth-century modernity are in deep crisis – the great *promesse de bonheur* of nationalism and Marxism has failed to materialize in South Asia. What we are instead witnessing is a dramatic and simultaneous process of both de-territorialization as well as territorialization, where received notions of order, based on historical associations of citizenship, borders, time and history are being actively re-worked.

At first glance, there seems cause for celebration. But the world as we see it does not present a pretty sight – particularly at the margins of the metropolis. To take recourse to a Hegelianism, it is as if the World-Spirit, defeated at the final moment of self-consciousness, has enacted a terrible revenge for sacrificing its grand vision. In particular, for the Third-World citizen, searching for identity among the ruins of the now-decaying artefacts of nationalism, it seems more and more clear that the storm of progress has passed on, with no promise of returning.

However, here lies the paradox. At the very moment that modernity could free itself from its nineteenth-century variant, the power of the west, which was *the* imaginative embodiment of the modern, seems more fragile than ever. For the first time since the sixteenth century, there seems to be a secular shift in the centres of wealth from the west to Asia's eastern frontier, and possibly China. The old state-system of modernity based on secure borders and sovereignty has collapsed; in the west itself, canonical notions of subjectivity, representation and freedom have taken a battering from which one suspects they will never fully recover. The great western millennium, beginning with the violence of the crusades and culminating in European power may end with the very idea of modernity seriously compromised.

What has this to do with the engagement with virtual spaces in a country like India? In the first place, the dynamics of India's movement into electronic spaces have occurred within the backdrop of the crisis of western modernity and its product: the territorial state based on a particular concept of sovereignty. Further, it seems to me that it is the very *fragility* of the 'west' that gives cyberspace a particular attractiveness for the Third-World users, at least in the case of India. This fragility of the eastern imaginary in the real world contrasts with a certain efflorescence in virtual spaces. It is this disjunction that informs new modes of travel by the Third-World elites to the west, through virtual space. These are modes that need to be addressed as occupying a distinct space, departing from the old borders that defined the Third World's relationship to the west.

It is here that the old Third Worldist/classical Marxist critique of 'cyberspace' seems limited. Such critiques have focused on the museumization of the Third-World cultures in the space of the Web, or the domination of multinational capital in the political economy of the information superhighway. There is a strong element of truth in both positions, but neither can explain the complex implication of virtual spaces in local/regional strategies for re-mapping *national* identity. In the event, while the relationship to an imaginary west is important to cyberpractices in India, this relationship by no means exhausts the complexity and local interconnectedness of such practices. What is needed when looking at cyberpractices in India is what Ernesto Laclau has called a 'radical contextualization', where the violent abstractions of 'west', 'capital and 'nation' do not erase the richness and contradictions of initiatives into virtual space.

INDIA, CYBERSPACE AND THE PUBLICS

If one were to adopt a certain diffusionary model of the spread of cyberpractices in India, we would have to consider the following:

SyncMaster 740N
SAMSUNG

a) The simple fact of India being a peripheral society in the capitalist world-economy: with one of the lowest saturation rate of telephones in the world; only a small minority of the population has electricity.

b) India has no tradition of cyberpunk; in fact there is no indigenous science fiction tradition. Most existing cultural communities have remained ambivalent about technology. Historically, representations of science and technology have been state-sponsored and social-realist in form.

Despite this, a significant number of people are linked to electronic networks in India, and the number is fast growing. For a Third-World country with inequalities like India, this is quite remarkable. 'Cyberspace' has emerged as a significant term in public discourse in India, becoming the focal point of much coverage and speculation in the media. Behind all of this is the growing community of users. Till date anonymous, and lacking the 'heroic' qualities of the old nationalist scientist, the contemporary user lacks any visible representation of his or her agency.

I have tried to map the 'user' into three, overlapping cyberpublics. 'Public' is used here very loosely, indicating a cybercommunity in the making, where mutual rituals of initiation and excursion are only now being invented. The three cyberpublics are those of the nationalist state, the transnational elite, and that of the space between the market and the state occupied by various bulletin boards, and social movement networks. While the boundaries of all the three publics are fuzzy, they are also uneven in internal differentiation and modes of address. Cyberpublics are a relatively new phenomenon in India. What is attempted here is a very preliminary examination of these communities-in-formation, by mapping certain practices of the nationalist organization of space, and its consequences for agency and movement.

Nationalist policies employed a certain social cartography which attempted to organize space, representation and identity. Maps generated 'borders', which in turn sought to institutionalize identity, frame representations of citizenship, and mediate the relationship with the west and modernity.[1] Mapping activities which were backed by the state's monopoly of legitimate violence were also implicated in a particular version of post-war modernism. The metaphor of the map is also useful to highlight different strategies which emerged in the post-national period, which sought to re-organize space by dislocating it from territory, and posit new forms of identity.

CYBERPUBLIC 1: NATIONALISM

There is a general consensus among writers that the anti-colonial struggle in India produced a rich constellation of overlapping, contested visions of nation and nationalism. Given the wide range of social mobilization, this was to some extent inevitable. For a long time, competing discourses within the anti-colonial movement on issues of identity, modernity and 'building the nation' remained dormant; it was only after the experience of development following Independence that some of the older questions and dissenting views, notably those raised by Gandhi's practice, assumed greater significance.

The post-colonial period after 1947, under the leadership of Jawaharlal Nehru, affirmed an accelerated transition to modernity through building rational institutions of state order, which would functionally reorganize national space for the purposes of accumulation and industrialization. The Gandhian cultural constellation was seen as dysfunctional, and what emerged is what Lefebvre has called the construction of an 'abstract space', not accessible through ordinary experience, and the preserve of purposive-rational modernizers.[2]

Gandhi's discourse had included a reassertion of 'place' as a site of genuine experience and action – consider his symbolic evocation of the village as a site of anti-colonial politics.[3] This was in contrast to the abstract temporal cartography of colonialism, which held out the developmental possibility of the railway imaginary to overcome the 'village society'. Colonial ideology further stressed the use of English as a passport to the cultural world-system and the virtues of colonial law as a *sui generis* means towards order and non-revolutionary evolution. Gandhi's evocation of the everyday and a new aestheticized anti-colonial strategy[4] (the innovative use of counter-commodities like *khadi* or homespun cloth) was viewed with skepticism by the Nehruvian inheritors of post-Independence India – Gandhi was accorded a hagiographic status in official histories, and marginalized.

While post-Independence nationalists like Nehru excluded Gandhian economics from state-building strategies, they were quick to incorporate the growing discourse of *development* and make it an instrument of state policy. Right from the 1950s, the conquest of national space was seen as a necessary precondition to incorporation into the world economy. The 'national economy' became a shorthand representational device for the nation itself,[5] accessible only to a privileged and 'enlightened' class of modernizers.

What thus obtained was a *legislative* modernity where *soi-disant* intellectuals/modernizers saw 'society' as a *tabula rasa*. The modernist grid of the Plan (borrowed from Soviet experiences) was invested with phantasmagoric qualities: *plan=development=order*. Here *development/*

order went hand in hand with what David Harvey has called the logic of space-time compression.[6] The annihilation of space by time, following the expansion of global capital, led to the 'disembedding of social relations' and thence to homogenization. *Temporal acceleration* was a significant part of the imaginary of developmentalism – inherent in the logic of 'catching up' with core areas of the world economy by privileging a strategy of growth that actively delegitimized local and 'traditional' practices.

What obtained was an imaginary with similarities to Bentham's Panopticon. Here, the residents of the Panopticon live an ordered, supervised environment committed to an abstract ideal of freedom. In the eyes of its innovators, the political technology of the Panopticon had the great merit of imposing order while simultaneously preventing the oppressed from visualizing power. As Zizek points out,[7] the great 'dark spot' at the centre gave the Panopticon its greatest use. It was this abstract centre, that space of anonymity from the nation and the everyday, that gave the Nehruvian developmental bureaucracy its greatest relief. Meritocratic, upper-caste and English-speaking, the state-managers of post-Independence India cultivated an anonymity that was seen as necessary for a legislative modernity – an abstract vision that would transcend sectional, regional and religious claims.

Temporal acceleration, development and 'order', were the *focus imaginarius* of Nehruvian nationalism's struggle for modernity. In terms of *historical* practice, such an imaginary had to be mediated through a republican democratic politics. The remapping of political/social space by political actors/movements through political representation, meant that the claims of panoptical political technology were *continuously* contested. New social movements of oppressed castes by the late 1980s threatened the exclusivist vision of the Panopticon and compromised Nehruvianism's old 'map'.

BUILDING THE NETWORK

All of twentieth century's movements have their iconography. As opposed to the Gandhian evocation of the village, Nehruvian nationalism privileged the dam. The dam was the 'temple of modernity'; it evoked the power of secular labour over nature. It was Nehruvian nationalism's great dream of controlling and disciplining energy. In newsreels and in print, Indians were exhorted to 'visit' Bhakra Nangal, the first major post-Independence dam site through a pre-virtual tour.[8] As Deshpande points out, the identification of the dam (along with sites that produced steel and electricity) as a site of post-Independence nationalist 'journeys' was based on privileging the 'economy' and production as markers of patriotism and national

SyncMaster 740N
SAMSUNG

development. This privileging of the 'economic' was, by the 1970s, grafted to a highly centralized and repressive state whose self-representation was dynastic rule by the Nehru-Gandhi family. 'Development' was paralleled by state-sponsored compulsory sterilization drives aimed at the poor.[9] This project ended in political defeat for Indira Gandhi and the Congress party. In the 1980s, the Congress was back in power – but the old nationalist architecture was in considerable crisis. A new approach was put into place in the early 1980s, actively encouraged by Rajiv Gandhi (Nehru's grandson) who later became prime minister in 1984. This new constellation had two main components.

The first was to ensure temporal acceleration while at the same time performing the task of emancipating the state-managers from the everyday. In other words, the annihilation of space through time would obtain without the messy political problems that spatiality and its associated politics produced.[10] What was needed was a solution that would shift from old-style nationalist policies, seen by the elite as restricting initiative and growth. This was resolved, by the late 1980s and the early 1990s, by evacuation of 'national' space ('globalization'). Under pressure from the IMF (the International Monetary Fund) and the World Bank, the old import substitution regime was gradually dismantled.

The end-result of all these moves was a decisive reconstruction of the old nationalist imaginary in ways that would dissolve it to the point of no recognition. 'Development' remained an issue, but was reconstituted as a problem of *communication*. The computer soon became the iconic space around which almost all representation, both state and commercial cohered – the effect on nationalist discourse was incredible.[11] As opposed to the Nehruvian focus on nineteenth-century *physical* instruments of accumulation (steel, energy, coal), state discourse after 1984 posed a *virtual* space where issues of development would be resolved. Through public lectures, television programmes and press campaigns, state managers simulated this new space, which though unseen was seen as transcending the lack inherent in Nehruvian controls.[12]

This new image of the computer was akin to reification – as the old critical theorists like Lukacs had described in *History and Class Consciousness*. Except this largely unseen object[13] was also a simulation machine, generating a new form of abstract space (the network) which would accelerate the transition to modernity and the 'west'. The 'national' was re-affirmed, but through a new discourse which complicated the notion of borders and sovereignty that were so central to the old visual regime.

By the mid-1980s, the state promoted a national network to process information relating to development and administration. This was the development of NIC (National Infomatics Centre), set up in the mid-1970s to promote computerization in administration, which in the 1980s became a satellite-linked network, NICNET, easily the largest network in the country.[14] It links up all district, state and national centres, runs large databases on social science, medicine and law; it works all state research institutes in the country (1994). Apart from putting all these centres on the NICNET e-mail network, NIC provides users with web and internet access. Internally, large research projects on artificial intelligence and CAD (computer-aided design) are being undertaken. Today NICNET has easily eclipsed India's other state network ERNET (Educational and Research Communication Network) to become a visible *public* presence.

NICNET was not just about more computers in administration and education – it intended to change the very technics of power. Hence its aggressive 'public' profile. Very simply, NICNET sought to mould a new state cyberpublic from the late 1980s onwards. It was unusual for a state organization in India to adopt such an aggressive public profile and it brought NICNET in conflict with institutions that argued for an older and more centralized bureaucratic form of control.[15]

NICNET understood the new panoptics of state power where older methods of surveillance would not work.[16] While privately, NICNET administrators pooh-pooh any efforts to censor networks, they have campaigned publicly for opening up the airways to 'ordinary citizens'. NICNET opened some of its airways for public access to put forth its case for ending old-style state restrictions on communication.

The NICNET eχperiment attempted to rework the old modernist grid of Nehruvianism that had been based on representational realism, identity based on Westphalia-style national borders and development which privileged the 'economy' as a site of national renewal and transition to modernity. The networks that NIC put into place did not *directly* confront the old model but instead sublated it, retaining elements of the old imaginary (development, a new 'nation', temporal acceleration). The crucial innovation was to introduce a simulated space which would *accelerate* that which was lacking in the old.

NICNET's new grid for the network was in effect a simulation of earlier panoptics: each district connected to state capital and in turn to the national capital. District-level campaigns retained Nehruvianism's old crusading vision. Reporting on the effort to set up a district infomatics centre in the Gurdaspur district in the state of Punjab in 1989, the NIC wrote:

> The NIC Gurdaspur Centre first became operational in 1989. In the beginning was the toughest part. A new technology, a new way of doing things, a new way was being advocated. The people of Gurdaspur had to be made aware of the utility of informatics, government personnel had to be trained in computers. Gaining acceptance was no easy task, but help was always at hand. Thanks

> to the support and co-operation of the district administration and the unstinted efforts of the NIC officials the Gurdaspur District Centre got off to a flying start. . . . Deemed to be an underdeveloped district, today Gurdaspur is well on its way to development.[17]

This language continues to play on 'development', but adds the new simulated space of connectivity which would guarantee the unity of the national – the space of which is constantly threatened by internal strife and global incorporation. This phantasmic neo-national space is complicated by two factors: the simple brutal fact of *peripheralization* – constant *network breakdown* which militates against a seamless web of communication[18] – and the *multiplication of networks* that cancel the monopolistic legitimacy of panoptic power.

THE TROPE OF JOURNEY

In many ways, cybertime in a peripheral society like India can be seen as radically revising the idea of the *journey*. Travelling was the basis of knowledge about others in pre-colonial civilizations – including that in South Asia. The great temporal community of the traveller was largely oral, and based on sustained interaction with other communities. In the world of the *Dar-ul-Islam*, which dominated the pre-modern world, travelling was the duty of every Muslim, either on the Haj to Mecca at least once a lifetime, or to learn about other Islamicate states in the realm. These were not the journeys of the Creole intelligentsia in the period of print-capitalism – a premium was placed on *oral* interaction with fellow Muslims. This was a journey without frontiers – the traveller was constrained only by physical limitations. Time operated through different registers – there was no temporal compulsion on the travellers' return: travellers came back after many years.

The *nationalist journey* was the great invention of Gandhi. The Gandhian journey began with a paradox: it used the railway network – one Gandhi had denounced as having destroyed the pre-colonial narratives and experiences of the Journey.

The railways disrupted the Indian body politic, which Gandhi saw as a huge body digesting and assimilating different cultural elements. He then showed how the two technologies, reflected in pilgrimage on foot by rail, represented memory and erasure respectively. The pilgrim's progress was an act of faith. The arduous act of pilgrimage to different corners of India gave the pilgrim a sense of both neighbourhood and nationhood, helping him to internalize both similarities and differences.

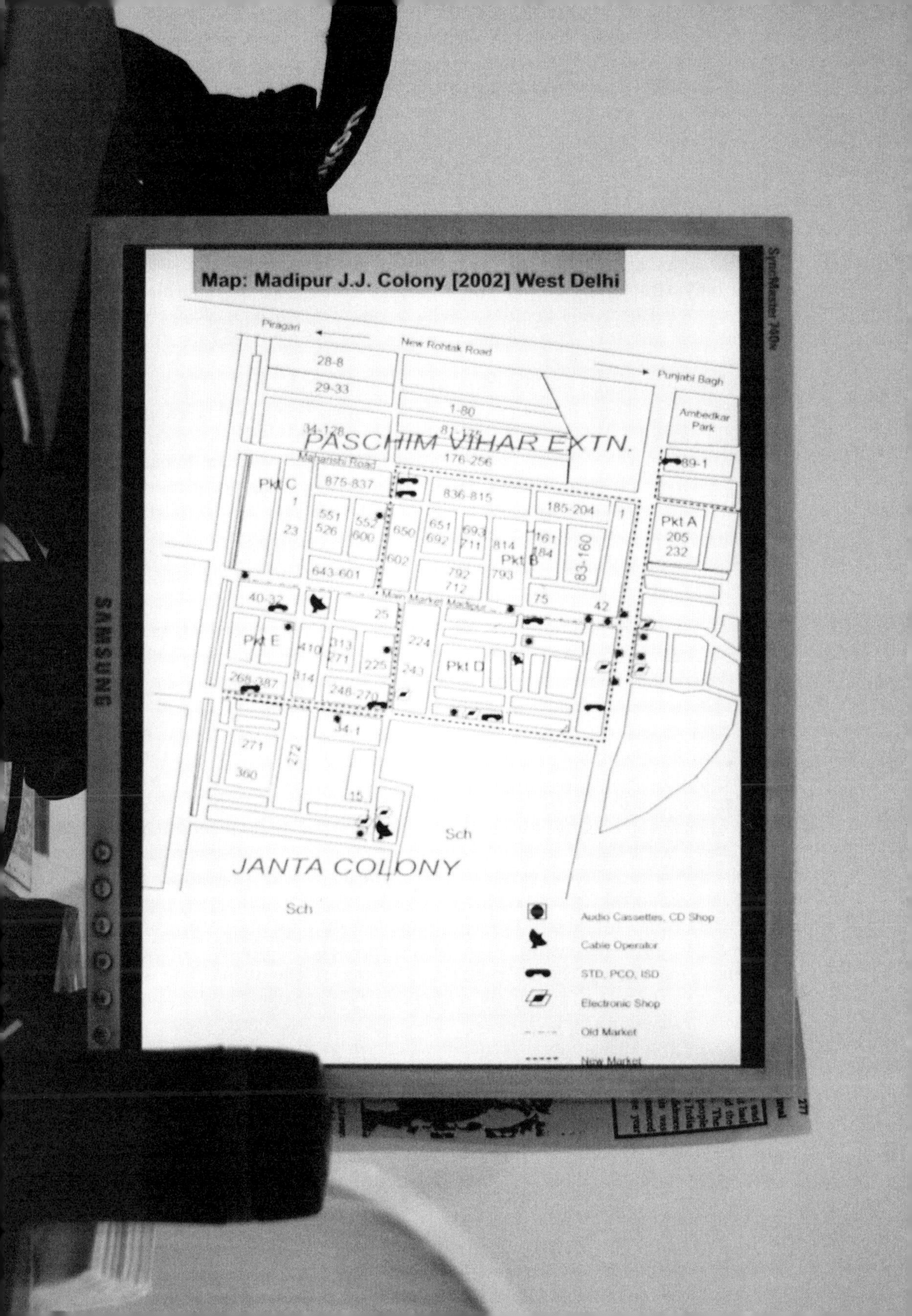
Map: Madipur J.J. Colony [2002] West Delhi
Piragari
New Rohtak Road
Punjabi Bagh
Ambedkar Park
PASCHIM VIHAR EXTN.
Maharishi Road
Pkt C
Pkt B
Pkt A
Pkt E
Pkt D
Main Market Madipur
JANTA COLONY
Sch
Sch
Audio Cassettes, CD Shop
Cable Operator
STD, PCO, ISD
Electronic Shop
Old Market
New Market
SAMSUNG

The mechanical negotiation or 'ingestion' of territory through rail travel erased the sanctity of places and turned them into physical spaces.[19]

In fact, Gandhi's privileged journey was foot-travel. The practice of walking meant a different language of interaction, of knowledge. It was only through walking that humans came into interaction with different cultures and peoples – which abstract motions of locomotion could not provide. The allusion to the pre-modern traveller/pilgrim could not be more direct.

However, Gandhi *did* use the railway eytensively during anti-colonial agitation. To counter his own ambivalence vis-à-vis the industrial capitalism, Gandhi carved out an area *within* the train – the third-class compartment – a *simulated* space where people 'entered' the train with the humility of the pre-modern pilgrim. Gandhi's innovation was to transform the Journey as a vehicle to politically remap the nation. This was also a journey-as-dialogue, with conventions of public interaction, anti-colonial agitation and spectacle. In a typically Gandhian way, the railway grid (colonialism's most ambitious disciplinary structure) was subjected to a series of inversions. This was despite Gandhi's own ambivalence vis-à-vis modern technology.[20] The Gandhian journey was also a public journey, with the attendant modes of representation constructing an imaginary community of nationalism.[21]

Colonialism introduced the political technology of the modern state, with the attendant modes of political control. Frontiers became Borders, and modern citizens in post-colonial India were subject to new mechanisms of political identity. The Journey was governed by clear notions of sovereignty; passports became a necessary precondition for travel abroad. Indian nationalism was always suffused with cartographic anxiety[22] – a phenomenon made worse by the partition of the subcontinent and the wars with Pakistan and China. State-sponsored import-substitution industrialization drives regulated the import of foreign consumer items, and so what obtained was a kind of physical separation of the 'everyday' from the west for about twenty years. Filiality to the border became a marker for citizenship with state campaigns against smuggling intensifying during the authoritarian period of the 1970s. The state's claim was that of a monopoly over identity formation, citizenship and national representation.

From the 1950s onwards, popular cinema generated a series of films where a large part of the narrative unfolded in the west with Indian characters. While the melodramatic structure of the films was based on a final resolution at the point of origin (India), what is interesting is the visual mapping of the 'west' simulating a virtual tour of that geographic space for millions who had been denied that chance. This substitute travelogue, though mediated through the foundational myth of nationalism, nevertheless speculated on the space 'outside' the border.[23]

James Clifford has written that 'a journey makes sense as a "coming to consciousness" its story hardens around your identity. (*Tell us about your trip*)'.[24] Journeys into virtual space allowed for the de-stabilizing of this 'hardening' of identity – it has generated new 'boundary stories' about virtual cultures in India. For one, the idea of the Border, so central to state-nationalism is transcended. The new experience of cyberspace that allows the citizen to 'arrive without having set out' disrupts the old realist confines of the Journey: for the first time in the history of the visual regimes set in motion by the west, the Third World is allowed entry into hitherto prohibited spaces.

This journey is nevertheless embedded in new networks of power: the ethnoscapes of post-nationalism:[25] a de-territorialization of the old nationalist space, confined by the Border and a transnational territorialization where India was being invented in virtual space by sections of non-resident Indians. The state actively pushed a new category of identity in cultural/political discourse – the figure of the diasporic citizen, also known as the NRI or non-resident Indian.

With the NRI, the border was extended to those spaces outside national sovereignty where the diaspora lived. In the old nationalist imaginary, people left the home of the nation only to return – sometime. The discourse of the 1980s restated the idea of the emigrant's 'return' – only to make it temporally indeterminate. The NRI was now part of a 'national' community – yet emancipated from the 'place' of the nation. As the NRI had a natural affinity for Home, any capital he/she brought in to the country would be motivated by patriotic feelings in contrast to say, multinational capital. In the 1990s however, as national development receded, the NRI began to play a prominent role in new virtual spaces. The idea of the Return now became less relevant – it was achieved in pure space.

CYBERPUBLIC II: THE NEW ELITES AND THE DIASPORA

By 1995, both state and private networks had spread to connect around 1,20,000 users in India.[26] Though small in comparison with the west, it represents one of the largest figures for a Third-World country. ERNET, the main state network after NICNET, plans to network around 8,000 colleges – in addition to the 6,000 institutions it already connects.[27] Various problems dog existing networks. While the networking market has been seeing a steady 100 per cent yearly growth, Wide Area Networking (WAN) suffers from poor infrastructure inadequate for high-speed connectivity.

While individual users who use dial-up connections from home are growing with the expansion of private networks, large numbers still work from offices, research institutions and from public terminals. As expected, most users are male and come from the middle and upper strata both in economic and social terms of community and caste. A large proportion of them are from research institutions and universities – though private networks may soon equal the share of the state networks once the telecommunication policy is liberalized.

What has the rapid spread of virtual space through the networks meant in terms of *public* discourse? The coming of the Web and discussions on the information superhighway in the US have reached India with such a force that it is difficult to pick up a newspaper without reading an average of two stories a day on 'cyberspace'. The term, coming in the context of the dismantling of the old nationalist regime, posits a new virtual landscape at a complex intersection of practices that map new borders of identity-formation, rewritten through new Journeys.

In the first instance, discourses on the Web seem to reproduce old nationalist tropes. Most commercial providers have sought to pose their web strategy as providing a window for 'Indian' capital to the 'world'. In this reading, Indian company sites on the web have the best possible chance for 'national' development. It is in virtual space, emancipated from the territorial limits of old-style capitalism (inherently biased in favour of the west), that Indian capital could take its message. '(Here) even smaller players get world-wide publicity.'[28] To be a genuine 'national' capitalist, you must transcend the Border and enter virtual space.

Behind the impetus towards virtual space is the retreat of large sections of the old upper-caste, anglicized elite from the political sphere. Since the 1980s, the cartography of the political public is being actively rewritten with the emergence of new social movements of oppressed castes challenging old panoptics of the state predicated on a homogenizing legislative modernity, and led by an enlightened elite of modernizers. For the old elite, the state is no longer the *secure* kingdom of cultural hegemony and identitarian certainty.[29] Metropolitan centres are being reconfigured to accommodate a reinvented suburbia free from subaltern intrusions: simulated landscapes of designer villages, transplanted American post-modern designs and private security. But what of the nationalist journey? New practices have emerged to overcome the corporeality of the nationalist border while, at the same time, attempting new 'nationalist' electronic communities conforming to a 'Hindu' imaginary. The second cyberpublic is *doubly* coded: by practices that map out a space beyond the nation, while attempting at the same time to inscribe a new Hindu nationalist community in virtual space.

At the centre of this new landscape have been technologies of representation that disrupt old tropes of both anti-colonialism and Nehruvian nationalism. If the village and the 'economy' functioned as representational shorthand for the Gandhian and Nehruvian imaginary respectively, the cultural landscapes in the 1990s saw a complex of initiatives, centred

@datamugshot
#startup_states

****
#bank #Aadhaar operators

- 56 -

ety tool created by StoryUp that makes use of

- 56 -

ections And #2019Elections Would Also Face It

- 56 -

e u…by @rrajeshbardeRT @privacyvakil: #Data o

- 56 -

to f…by @tifosi392 RT @RoblemVR: #Healium is

- 56 -

#ElectionsManipulation Using #SocialMedia Is

- 56 -

Logins and biometrics of SBI #bank #Aadhaar o

- 56 -

nd anti-anxiety tool created by StoryUp that

- 56 -

9Elections Would Also Face It. Spam Ac…by @

- 56 -

to generate u…by @rrajeshbardeRT @privacyvakil

- 56 -

are in order to f…by @tifosi392 RT @R

[*_+]I
01|0

k*a*r*t*h*i*k*k*g********

around consumption and desire, that resist easy historicist classification. These practices are centred around television, video, music and one of the world's largest film industries. Foreign satellites now beam images to India, effectively breaking the state's monopoly over television. India now has among the world's largest video- and audio-cassette industries.

The space is criss-crossed by a fluidity of national/regional/global cultural styles mediated by the recognition of a new agent – the 'consumer-subject'. Old moral codes regulating desire are being reconstituted, and a Hindu nationalist imaginary cannibalizes the new practices for its political project. For the time-being at least, the claims of a legislative modernity are suspect. The panoptic vision of a regulated cultural practice, while voiced periodically, lacks the authority and legitimacy of the past.[30]

In this context, the Web offers the phantasmic possibility of playing with an identity that recognizes displacement. The Journey into virtual space is the journey beyond the nation. For the web traveller, a typical member of the displaced elite public in India, the west is recreated/simulated as a *simultaneous* presence. There is a certain experience of web travel when logging on from the Third World, that almost evokes Benjamin's analysis of Baudelaire's *flâneur*, or the stroller in Second Empire Paris. The web traveller seeks out the virtual space of the Web to experience the 'shock of the new', which Benjamin calls the distinctive feature of modernity. The city for the *flâneur* has a labyrinthine character, with secret passages, a web of experiences and unknown dreams which is sought out by the stroller.

Web-strolling from India enhances the feeling of being in the 'west'. Like Baudelaire's *flâneur* who sought out the crowd in his search for 'ever-new', the web traveller journeys on the highway to look for the new. The websites constitute a simulated exhibition ('places of pilgrimage to the fetish commodity' – Benjamin) where the traveller-consumer, like the visitor to the nineteenth-century site, is asked, 'look at everything, touch nothing'.[31] These pilgrimages have the effect of an experience of modernity (shock, ecstasy, entry into power–knowledge spaces) hitherto unknown in the periphery – even for the elite. Yet, they are fleeting experiences – burdened by real-time constraints.[32]

Web journeys, then, are informed by a double-coding: one side is the elite cyberpublic's emancipation from the old nationalist grid and the other the creation of a naturalized space of 'India' on the web. Dominated by expatriate Indians sympathetic to Hindu nationalism, these websites[33] pose Hindu identity as isomorphic with India: purged of ambivalence.[34] The old legislative modernity of the Nehru period has been transplanted to virtual space, purged of its democratic political sphere.[35] In the virtual space of 'India' on these websites, 'Hindu' identity becomes an *artefact* – a contestable process is replaced by a reified boundary. For the NRI, the virtual space of India finally replaces the actual pressure of the Return. The Journey is now sanitized. Here websites act as markers of homogenized spiritual space, with rigid cultural borders, where 'India' functions as a virtual museum for those for whom Hinduism can fulfill the great unfulfilled dream of legislative reason, a world without ambivalence.

CYBERPUBLIC III: BULLETIN BOARDS, ACTIVISTS AND THE SEARCH FOR ALTERNATIVES

The third cyberpublic remains the most ambiguous of the three domains of cyberdiscourse in India. Existing in a fluid space, between that of the state cyberpublic and the elite domains of the web, it contains a wide range of actors seemingly unconstrained by either state or transnational market. The map of this cyberpublic is typically rhizomic, a constantly shifting zone of activist networks, small bulletin boards and dissident scientists. Its borders are, once again, fuzzy. Less hybrid than experimental, this public speaks to the possibility of radical reconstitution of electronic space as one which touches real time through its myriad surfaces.

In the opening up of electronic space beyond the frontiers of the state–market dichotomy, bulletin boards (BBS) have played a crucial role. Numbering just a few score until last year,[36] BBSs have mushroomed not only in all the major metros but also in small towns all over India. Led by a combination of small business persons and computer/telecom graduates, BBSs cater to a population that finds both the web and the state networks inaccessible: either due to prohibitive costs or lack of an imaginative space.

Initial BBS discussions concentrated largely on the computer trade. Recent discussions have been broader, concentrating on politics and sexuality. The latter is a topic that most system operators tend to be wary of (most discussions are not yet online), but this has not prevented frank discussions of issues hitherto invisible to the public sphere. BBSs walk a fine line, with recent media stories about sites offering explicit pictures for free downloading. State regulation is also a threat, with recent legislation threatening to tax BBSs heavily (this threat seems to have receded, for the moment).

BBSs are a recent phenomenon in India, and one is yet to see the kind of experiments that the CommuniTree group initiated in the United States in the 1970s. However, any comparison, or even the suggestion of 'fitting' India in an evolutionary schema based on the development of virtual systems in the west, would be wrong. For a very, very, long time to come, electronic space will be out of the reach of the majority of the urban population, let alone those who live in the villages. The importance of BBSs remains elsewhere.

Existing between state control and the power of global capital, BBSs offer a novel form of agency *within* the discourses on virtuality, the possibility of a new performative space. It is the very novelty of the BBS, along with its semi-underground status, which opens up the possibility of experimentation – a process which has just begun. As sites proliferate, so will the variety of experiences. Women, hitherto a marginal voice in the BBS community, are slowly making their appearance. Strategies of self-representation remain dominantly realist, with users only using different 'faces' when discussing explicit issues. The historical identity of realism and scientific practices was hammered into the popular space by nationalism – hence the tendency to stick to a realist mode during the *initial* moment of initiation into technoculture by most novices. It seems to me that the time for a genuine *aufhebung* to a new non-realist mode of representation is already on the agenda of the BBS community.

SOCIAL MOVEMENTS, NATIONALISM AND TECHNOCULTURE

Most social movements in India have as their point of departure the cartography of the post-Independence nationalist state. As pointed out earlier, the state privileged a model of development, iconized the dam and the steel mill as the imaginative reference points of development. Here, science and technology were opposed to culture, abstracted from notions of play, creative tradition and aesthetic experiment. The new social movements after the 1970s generated a critique of the technological/developmental imaginary of nationalism, stressing a range of alternative practices. The various movements (those of women, untouchables, anti-dam) did not pose a cohesive alternative: their opposition to state-sponsored technological practices was generally uniform.

When the computer was initially introduced in the 1980s as the neo-modernist successor to the dam, the hostility of both new social movements and the old Left was total. They parodied the utility of the computer in a peripheral society like India, a critique that generally echoed then-prevalent notions of utility, sustainability and concerns about workforce cutbacks.[37]

Today in the 1990s, social movements accept both the computer and the creative possibility of networking. This is a dramatic change. Old movements are in a crisis: many have either disintegrated or entered the NGO sector. The crisis of old-style nationalism and Marxism has reshaped the old reference points for the movements. The fast-growing NGO sector is linked to global donors and this sector's incorporation into global electronic space is only a matter of time. While these factors are a necessary explanation, they are not sufficient to explain the widespread

**********************c*s*d*s**s*a*r*a*

misused to generate u…by @rrajeshbardeRT @pr

- 139 -

hardware in order to f…by @tifosi392 RT @Rob

- 139 -

c…by @_PTLB RT @_FairElection: #ElectionsManip

- 139 -

has been misused. Logins and biometrics of

- 139 -

axation and anti-anxiety tool create

- 139 -

And Elections And #2019Elections Woul

- 139 -

have been misused to generate u…by @rrajeshba

- 139 -

er to f…by @tifosi

- 139 -

nipulation Using #

- 139 -

of #UIDAI has been misused. Logins and biom

- 139 -

232 088 098

c relaxation and anti-anxiety

18:43:27

- 139 -

*****d*a*t*a*m*u*g*s*h*

acceptance of electronic networks among the movement-community. At the heart of the transition are also hidden issues of desire and identity.

The old sites (of the large dam and the steel mill) were enlarged symbols of the nationalist will-to-power, generating the violence of displacement and the destruction of local communities. As violent symbols, they are still the focus of large movements. On the other hand, the world of virtual space that exists 'behind' the computer lacks the corporeal violence associated with developmentalism. Virtual spaces evoke a world of pleasure and initiation for individual activists without the violence of developmental modernism. An aesthetics of experimentation had already been experienced by activists, in their search for alternatives to developmentalist disasters. With e-mail, the internet and then bulletin boards, a liminal space emerged, where utopian desires for modernity, the possibility of experimentation 'without destruction', overlapped with the pleasures of initiation rituals into technoculture. Further, there is the possibility of a dialogue with the self: more rounded forms of identity that the nationalist period had mistrusted as an ambivalence.

To be sure, only a very small minority of activists are 'connected': either urban, relatively affluent, or with access to global funds. What is remarkable is the widespread legitimacy of electronic space among dissenters and activists who would have been equally critical of the technological monuments of nationalism. It could be argued that the entry of virtual spaces posed technology as a cultural practice in a way that the developmental modernism[38] of the Nehruvian period (with the singular emphasis on *monuments*) could not have done. This anticipates a new situated technosocial space, perhaps a 'cyborgness' for the periphery. Following Donna Haraway's call for 'situated knowledges', we can argue that new practices could emerge in India, marking the transition from the binary spaces of developmental modernism.

Developmental modernism has operated within a Third-World version of what Foucault called the blackmail of the Enlightenment. Foucault uses this formulation in his famous essay on Kant's 'What is Enlightenment' to refer to the violence of philosophical choices: 'you either accept the Enlightenment and remain within the tradition of its rationalism . . . ; or else you criticize the Enlightenment and then try to escape from its principles of rationality . . .'.[39] There is, says Foucault, simply no other choice: *no tertium datur*. In the Indian case, the canvas was less Olympian: it operated within the rather simplistic oppositions of development/science/progress versus tradition/reaction/stasis. For many decades, the first triad was overwhelmingly hegemonic, based on the state's monopoly of power and violence and even extending to old-Left oppositional movements. It is only in the recent decades with the rise of the new social movements, that elements of a genuine *aufhebung* have emerged.[40]

The current generation of activists have been reared on this new diet, where opposition to large dams and displacement could go hand in hand (wherever possible) with ventures into virtual space. This transition is so significant that it is remarkable that it has gone unnoticed.[41]

Nevertheless, despite the richness and potentials of the third cyberpublic in negotiating a space between the market and the state, the access to virtual space still remains a *privilege*. The plans of the state network ERNET to connect 8,000 colleges and schools will undoubtedly expand this public. The current neoliberal mood of the ruling elite is hostile to any public space in the electronic media, a long battle is ahead for activists.[42]

CONCLUSION: ARTIFICIALITY, MODERNITY AND ALTERNATIVE FEATURES IN THE PERIPHERY

It may be important, at such a moment, to listen to Nietzsche's savage warning: 'The destruction of an illusion does not produce truth but only one more piece of ignorance, an extension of our "empty space", an increase of our "desert".'[43] Living in a country at the periphery of the great centres of capital accumulation, it may be useful to point out that **an unmediated celebration of the 'new' is not just not feasible, but also not very interesting. Every historical appearance of 'newness' in South Asia, right from colonialism to developmental modernism has been embedded in violence and domination.**

At the same time it is not necessary to adopt the position of a nineteenth-century *Kulturkritik* in denouncing the cultural social landscape of our time, or to deny that fundamental re-orgnizations in the terms of representation, subjectivity, and the old boundaries of western modernity are taking place. For India, cyberspace arrived as a representation of the 'new', in ways that were complexly coded.[44] A number of loose cyberpublics emerged, reflecting diverse state, neo-elite and popular strategies to negotiate the crisis of the old Panoptical grid of nationalism and the supremacy of the Border.

Cyberculture came within the framework of a new package of globalization which contained a potent mixture of pleasure and danger. **If globalization unsettled the old nationalist/Marxist denial of the consuming public, the 'global' also came on the backs of transnational corporations with their power and contempt for popular participation.** To be sure, the inherent feature of 'newness' is contingency which may contain the possibilities of its demise. The problem is that the 'new' does not reproduce itself globally in fundamentally similar ways. Despite all the fantasies of virtuality, 'newness' is inscribed in a different set of overlapping imaginaries when it reaches a 'Third World' country like India.

What is needed is an approach that is sensitive to the situated character of knowledge formations and cyberpractices in the Third World, where narratives of critique and fluidity in the west may have entirely different consequences when represented in a country like India. Consider, for example, the emergence of new techno-practices in the west which have led to the blurring of the historical distinctions between nature and culture, between the body and the machine. As a number of writers have pointed out, the overlap of technology, biology and culture have led to a situation where the old distinctions between organicity and technology, between culture, experience and science, have lost their old categorical fixity.[45] This involves a crucial transition from the old Enlightenment oppositions of nature and culture from which flowed the representations of human praxis and subject formation.

What happens to this transition when it reaches the periphery of world-capitalism? A new biosociality is implicated in the plunder of plant species from the Third World and their relocation to the west. Technoculture is, likewise, a clear part of new expansion strategies of multinational companies into the periphery. And while Technosociality speaks to elite strategies of withdrawal and re-occupation of the national, it is also implicated in a culture of distinction and distance from the lives of the underprivileged.

My point is not to score old-Left polemical points against the new cultural constellations emerging in the west. These constellations are part of a new flexible system of accumulation on a world-scale, where 'a dizzying sense of bodily freedom'[46] for one may mean displacement and loss in another part of the world. To neglect this would not just be unreflexive: for those of us who 'live' and enjoy the pleasures of virtual space, it would be connivance with the new grammar of power emerging on a world scale.

However, boundary stories do matter, even on the periphery: the stories have been less about the individual body-space of the citizen as about rewriting new maps of the national wherever cyberjourneys have punctured the old Panoptic Border. From the point of view of situating knowledge, we can rewrite Haraway's brilliant statement on the idea of 'nature': 'The certainty of what constitutes the *nation* – (that is, as) a source of insight, a subject for knowledge, and a promise for innocence – is undermined, perhaps fatally.'[47]

CONSTITUTION
OF
INDIA

'Language', writes Madhava Prasad, 'will cease to matter only when language is assumed to matter, when it is treated not as an ethnic particularity but a basis of a living community'. While language may on occasion be the basis of national identity, it also has another role: 'it is in language that the universalism implicit in the nation-state manifests itself as concrete reality'. This landmark essay explores how a reconfigured and politically informed language can play a new role for community. To do so, it should also re-invigorate the role of the state, and its capacity to reconfigure the community. 'The present order must be described not as some elusive reality which escapes the normative demands of nation-state discourse, but as one which is inescapably determined by the mutually impacting co-existence of the norm and the reality', 'a state of in-betweenness that must be taken to constitute a state in itself for purposes of description'.

This is an abridged version of the essay first published in Anjan Ghosh, Tapati Guha-Thakurta and Janaki Nair, eds, **Theorizing the Present: Essays for Partha Chatterjee** (New Delhi: Oxford University Press, 2011). Reproduced with permission of Oxford University Press India. Grateful acknowledgment to the author for permission to use this version.

Images: Details from Riyas Komu's work, Fear II (2018, wood, metal and archival prints). The work uses the Eighth Schedule of the Constitution of India, which originally recognized twenty-two languages, under Articles 344(1) and 352, as possessing the right to official representation. The image that deals with Citizenship (Part II, Article 5) has been montaged on K.P. Reji's monumental **Thumbingal Chathan** figure. Grateful acknowledgment to Riyas Komu and K.P. Reji for permission and support.

10

M. MADHAVA PRASAD

2011

THE REPUBLIC OF BABEL

Language and Political Subjectivity in Free India

Linguistic nationalities in India are today increasingly vociferous in their self-assertion. The problem posed by this development could be treated as a question of what philosopher Charles Taylor has named as 'politics of recognition'.[1] Taylor argues for the right of a minority identity to be recognized and protected by the state, not only in the present but in its continued survival. But, as Anthony Appiah has pointed out in an illuminating discussion of the problem, the situation is complicated by the demands of democratic political existence: 'Though the desire that an identity shall be maintained is not a negligible one, it has to be conditioned and contoured by other considerations, including the requirement of participation in a larger polity. A politics of recognition, in short, must be buffered by a recognition of politics'.[2]

The problem, needless to say, hinges around citizenship. Appiah adds, 'The exercise of citizenship requires the capacity to participate in the public discussion of the polity, and so there needs to be a language that is one of the instruments of citizenship. We can call this the political language.' All citizens, it follows, must be educated in the political language, and must at the same time be given the option of learning their 'own' language in addition. In effect, there are two ways in which you can deal with a minority language within the framework of identity-plus-citizenship that Appiah employs, where the issue is formulated as 'bring[ing] full citizenship to minority-language communities'. One, the language in question can be made one of the political languages, and two, they (the people of that community) must be taught the political language 'while allowing them . . . to maintain their own, which is the route that has been followed in India, and the multilingual countries of Africa'.

To Taylor's insufficient way of posing the problem of minority languages/cultures, Appiah counterposes a more complex argument which rightly insists that the problem cannot be tackled outside the specific political context. Modern nation-states require one or more political languages. By their very nature, these units of modern political morphology tend to include peoples who do not speak them, and their ability to participate in the political life of the nation requires them to learn them. The question of their own cultural identity in so far as it is tied to language is then, according to Appiah, to be treated as an additional requirement of provision of cultural rights.

Appiah includes India under the second of his two ways of guaranteeing full citizenship. In a technical sense, he is of course right. Hindi (and English) are the political languages of the republic and languages like Assamese, Bengali, Oriya, Telugu, Kannada etc. are minority languages. While we are all required to learn Hindi (and we all want to learn English), we are free, if we wish, to learn our 'own' languages. I think that we can at once recognize both the 'official' correctness of this description and the actual inaccuracy of it. Theoretically, we might say that while Appiah brings a necessary political perspective to bear on Taylor's narrowly ethical treatment, there is a historical singularity to the actual state of affairs that, as philosophers, neither of them has bothered to engage with.

THE PLACE OF LANGUAGE

The place of language, or the (natural) languages that we speak, in the social life of human groups, and especially in modern societies, has not been given much attention by those who study sociopolitical formations and processes. The historical rupture which separates pre-modern communities from the modern is also the line of demarcation of two spontaneous theories of language that feature in social theory whenever the question of language is discussed. The first of these theories states that language, like race or religion, is one of the attributes of community which is liable to become the basis of identity for groups seeking political

THE CONSTITUTION OF INDIA

WE, THE PEOPLE OF INDIA, having solemnly resolved to constitute India into a SOVEREIGN DEMOCRATIC REPUBLIC and to secure to all its citizens:

JUSTICE, social, economic and political;

LIBERTY of thought, expression, belief, faith and worship;

EQUALITY of status and of opportunity;

and to promote among them all

FRATERNITY assuring the dignity of the individual and the unity of the Nation;

IN OUR CONSTITUENT ASSEMBLY this twenty-sixth day of November, 1949, do HEREBY ADOPT, ENACT AND GIVE TO OURSELVES THIS CONSTITUTION.

autonomy. As such, it is one of those primordial properties that groups use to win legitimacy for nationalist aspirations. This approach is reflected in innumerable references to language as among the 'divisive factors' that threaten the unity of the Indian nation. Such a characterization of language-identities depends upon a second theory, that of the purely instrumental role of language in human affairs, reflected in the popular description of language as a 'medium of communication'. Thus the chairman of the Official Languages Commission, set up by the Government of India in the 1950s begins his report by noting his basic assumption that language is important 'only at the level of instrumentality' and is of no 'intrinsic consequence'.[3] In a similar vein, social scientists writing on language as a political issue warn us against treating the problems posed by linguistic diversity 'as though they were *in themselves* fundamental to the survival of the polity as a nation'.[4] T.V. Satyamurthy, quoted here, is criticizing a tendency he observes among western scholars writing about the Indian sub-continent, recommending instead a new approach where 'Language and religion are no longer linked in an abstract framework or scheme with nationhood, but consciously related to the concrete conditions under which they emerge as potent factors in politics'. This approach is

> the result of scholars undertaking, to an increasing degree, research of an empirical nature relating to specific areas of policy, interest formation, movements of a political character, etc., involving an interplay of language and/or religion and social, economic and political as well as administrative aspects of a given phase of development of a specific region or country.[5]

Thus language ('and/or religion'!) only features in the political domain in the service of interests that are at play in politics. Although 'movements of a political character' are mentioned here, it would appear that there can be no political question of language as such. This approach can be described as a pragmatic one which evacuates linguistic (along with religious) questions of all symbolic, ideological, universalist content and treats them as elements that are mobilized in a political game tied to a 'given phase of development' of a society. Any integral relation between democracy and language is flatly denied.

But democracy is not just a matter of transferring a conflict of interests from one kind of political arena into another (parliamentary) one. The advent of parliamentary-democratic politics is also to be understood as the advent of the people in the political arena. The field of democratic politics is not a clash of interests in a state of nature but in a political order, whose fundamentals are set in such a way that they constitute the common idiom in which these conflicts will be played out.

One of these fundamentals of the parliamentary–democratic order is 'the people itself', the fictive community of the nation which subsists under the conflicts. This entity must be called into being, it must be interpellated. It cannot just be herded into the polling booths periodically, it must subsist, at all times, as a mobilized polity. It must be addressable as one. And this oneness must have a basis.

THE PRIMORDIAL, THE PARTICULAR, THE UNIVERSAL

There are two ways that this oneness can be established in the address. First, one can explicitly invoke the foundational fiction, the primordial racial, religious or linguistic identity which unites the nation (and thus automatically excludes those who lack this attribute, pushing them into a secondary status of anxious onlookers at the mercy of the primordial group); or, secondly, one can delegate to the common language itself, and the mere fact of its intelligibility, the burden of securing identity. While the former approach turns the present into a fantasmatic replication of a fictional past, the latter secures the autonomy of the present by instituting, not a linguistic community but a community of *speakers of a language*. The community of speakers of a language is an open community. While this may not be the ultimate open community that can be imagined, it is the only kind that parliamentary democracy is capable of guaranteeing.

Language will cease to matter only when language is assumed to matter, when it is treated not as an ethnic particularity but a basis of a living community. In practice, however, the question of language is reduced to a question of ethnicity/religion/race, as if it were just one more claim to particularism that militates against the universalism of modern life. The success or failure of such a strategy depends on practical considerations: speakers of a relatively minor language will find themselves accommodating to the unfolding situation by learning the 'political language', whereas if a linguistic community is of a considerable size, it tends to wriggle and squirm uncomfortably under such an imposition, leading to the tensions and conflicts we are all familiar with.

The three bases of national identity that we know of are not identical in their effects and consequences. Race is strictly non-negotiable, religion is not an immutable basis of identity to the extent that conversion is possible; language is the most open of all identities. While language may be invoked for purposes of determination of ethnicity, it is not amenable to the sorts of policing procedures or procedures of verification that are used to determine race or religion. The other important aspect of language, which is so obvious that it often goes unnoticed, is that while a nation-state can, at least theoretically speaking, function without any racial or religious discourse, it cannot function without language. Language is universal in this precise sense. The question that remains is whether the language(s) that will be used will be chosen from among those that are already spoken by the people, or whether a different one, which is alien to all language communities within the nation, will take its place. The nation-state ideal has always been associated with the language of the people, but in many post-colonial states the decision in this regard has been influenced by historical factors. Thus the continuation of English as official language in India has been importantly influenced by the fact that it is the language of no particular community in India. Its neutrality has been its strongest point. In many such instances, there is little possibility of replacing the language of the colonizer with an indigenous language. In Pakistan, the choice of Urdu was problematic in a different way: it is an indigenous language, but it is not the language of any of the nationalities that make up Pakistan. This practical difficulty is reflected in political scientists' refusal to deal with the question of the political salience of language as such, in spite of the fact that in many such states, language has become a contentious issue. Since religion and ethnicity are equally contentious issues all over the globe, the quite different place of language has gotten buried, even as the dominant binary – of 'primordial passions' versus secular democratic rationality – prevails in thought.

Language is the only concrete universal that can bridge the gap between the ethnic particularity of a group and the featureless abstraction of the citizen. Language can never be fully reduced to the property of a definite community; it is not figurable as a bounded entity except in the moment of its decline and disappearance.[6] Language can be learnt, it can be acquired after birth, and the 'mother' is not the indispensable facilitator of such acquisition, notwithstanding the ideology of the 'mother tongue'. The linguistic group can never be made to perfectly coincide with the group defined by racial/religious or other attributes. In language, there are always extra spaces for unexpected guests to occupy: speaking positions are not pre-assigned, they are potentially infinite.

But this potentiality is only realizable on two sites: the market and the modern nation-state. In the market, the pressures of communication in actual dealings will determine what language will prevail. And what prevails is often an inter-language of sorts, not inhibited by political standardization efforts, but nevertheless susceptible to the pressures of the moment of exchange. In the nation-state, the choice is determined by reference to the majority population. This choice is always motivated by at least two considerations: one, the dominance of the majority, its will to impose its own language on the territory bounded by the state, and two, the practical consideration of universal communicability of laws. There has been altogether too much emphasis upon the former aspect in considering

Part XVII

Official Language

Chapter I—Language of the Union

Official language of the Union.

343. (1) The official language of the Union shall be Hindi in Devanagari script.

The form of numerals to be used for the official purposes of the Union shall be the international form of Indian numerals.

(2) Notwithstanding anything in clause (1), for a period of fifteen years from the commencement of this Constitution, the English language shall continue to be used for all the official purposes of the Union for which it was being used immediately before such commencement:

Provided that the President may, during the said period, by order authorise the use of the Hindi language in addition to the English language and of the Devanagari form of numerals in addition to the international form of Indian numerals for any of the official purposes of the Union.

(3) Notwithstanding anything in this article, Parliament may by law

the language question in India, which has led to the equation of language with ethnicity or region. There is a certain disavowal in operation here, as if our experts would rather not deal with the normative dimensions of the question.

Language is already the cross-over universal in which every particular human being dwells, the unconscious universal of the tribe, beyond its control, controlling it. To be such a universal is to be open to the pathways of alienation, to always be subject to the dimension of the unknown.

Language is the first universal, the organically generated inorganic element in which humanity inscribes itself and sets off on a journey that will henceforth unfold, not according to natural cycles, seasons and seasonal urges, but along the inorganic pathways of history, community and communication. It is the reserve of human alienation, the distraction of natural being into the treacherous but seductive embrace of history. In real political situations, where the formation of complex social orders such as the nation-state is involved, a sacrifice is necessarily demanded of the speakers of a minor language (keep it for your private needs, but forego the universal dimension, alienate it into the majority language: in other words, learn the latter for political purposes).

But we have also seen language being proclaimed as the property of the people who speak it. If so, it is an elusive possession – you cannot point it out to visitors, nor can you have your picture taken beside it. It does not have discernible boundaries. If you keep walking, you will soon reach the limits of the Kannada-speaking territory, but even if you keep talking your whole life long, you will not reach the limits of Kannada. Still, if people persist in this impossible endeavour to possess language, to clasp it to their bosom and hold fast, a situation arises in which such a disposition is possible and pleasurable, tempting and frustrating at the same time.

We must understand this situation, which appears new to us, even if it should later turn out to have been not so new after all. It seems new to us because it seems to affect us with an intensity our ancestors have not reported experiencing, vis-à-vis language.

MODERNITY'S LIMITS

It seems that in what is called modernity, the relations between languages have undergone a complete transformation. Some linguists adhere to the normative principle that all languages are 'equal', that each is complete in itself and capable of containing within itself all that needs to be contained or expressed. A language is in this sense a universe all on its own. But this theory was itself forged just at that moment when this putative equality was being irrevocably undermined by political developments. It was almost like a compensatory theoretical gesture for the transformations wrought by modernity and development. While it remains trivially true that a language is just as good as it needs to be for those who speak it, it is also the case that the speakers of certain languages have begun to discern the limits of their language as their worlds become embedded in other encompassing worlds. *The experience of the pressure of these limits is arguably one of the defining experiences of modernity.* To this corresponds the historical experience of language – the English language in particular – as a concrete universal from whose point of view the perishability of the other languages must seem inevitable. In any case, it is certain that modernity fundamentally altered, or at any rate introduced an altogether new element into, the relation between human beings and the language(s) they speak.

What did happen? First of all, the idea gained ground that modernity – political modernity or democracy in particular – was necessarily tied to a nation, which in turn was associated with a language. The nation-state came into being as a new mode of social existence, a new community replacing pre-modern ones that were based on various forms of social stratification. Whether this was the fulfilment of an economic necessity, or a pure beginning which brought something new into the world, it is clear that the nation-state reconstituted the social order thoroughly and brought a new kind of subject into being. In establishing this larger entity in reality, one of the requisite features that had to be developed was a national (standard) language. Political theorists sometimes say that claims to national identity are based upon three different bases: race, religion or language. This may be true, but these terms are not equal. Language is different from the others in the sense that no matter whether the basis claimed is race, religion or language, the last one will remain indispensable. It is not as if a religious basis for nationalism will make the official language/ standard language question superfluous.

Thus language has played a dual role in the history of political modernity. It may function on occasion as the basis of national identity but it also has another indispensable role. It is in language that the universalism implicit in the nation-state manifests itself as concrete reality. Every nation-state has to address this question of the language, in which the new community has its concrete identity inscribed. Sometimes the matter is treated as if it were of merely secondary importance: as if the nation-state were complete in itself already without a universal language (which is what the national/official/standard language effectively is), and providing for the latter is a matter of administrative convenience and efficiency.

A familiar idea in social theory is that the advent of modernity marks a shift from community to society; where modernity's work is first of all to dissolve the communal bonds that were sustained by kinship and other pre-modern relations. But the dissolution of older communities does not mean the disappearance of community altogether. Nor is community confined to the imaginary domain of nationalism. Indeed, it would be more accurate to say that while the nation, by itself, offers only an imaginary or fantasmatic image of community, the state is the real community in the new situation, and the state's communal function (one of) of substituting for all those networks of relations through which traditional communities were sustained, the unitary anchoring point of the Law. Henceforth, instead of direct relations between individuals as the concrete medium of community formation, individuals will relate to each other indirectly through the mediation of the Law. Conformity to Law is the form in which allegiance to community manifests itself in modern societies. This story could equally well be told in reverse, without fundamentally altering its historical significance. In other words, we can see the nation as the fantasmatic image of primordial belonging that is produced as the discourse of a state, as it undertakes to reconstitute community through the impersonal medium of the Law.

It is in language that this new relation achieves the status of an immediate and absolute fact. It is by analogy with the interchangeable and universally employable personal pronouns of language that the citizen position is constructed. Indeed, pre-modern languages do not always permit universal exchangeability of pronouns in practice.[7] In that sense, the modern revolution subjects language to many modifications and transformations. Language alone links the particularities at the ground level – the individuals defined by their pre-modern social positions – to the promise of the Law to overhaul these positions and reground the subjects. Capable of this dual determination, the universal language is the indispensable middle without which the two ends, of nation and state, would be unable to sustain their two-in-oneness.

In spite of the existence of the usual exceptions – Canada, Switzerland, Belgium – the nations of the first world may be said to function according to a principle that makes national identity reliant upon a universal language. The exceptions themselves can be shown, by contrast to the more numerous exceptions that we encounter outside the first world, to be effectively operating under the same principle and therefore not entirely exceptional. Thus the difference between English and French in Canada on the one hand, and say, English and Kannada in India on the other, is that in Canada both English and French are universal or are, as Appiah terms them, political languages. It does not occupy a secondary status, as a language that may or may not receive all the messages put out by the state. French speakers do not have to eavesdrop upon the conversations of an Anglophone national community in order to figure out their own status. If there is a message from the state, it will be relayed in both languages. And when we examine the issue in depth it is clear that what matters to

Part II

Citizenship

Citizenship at the commencement of the Constitution.

5. At the commence... who has his domicil...

any language that seeks to define itself as the basis of a nationality is this status of universal language.

What bothers the speakers of a language in a situation where their language is deprived of this status, is the particularizing – the culturalism, into which this deprivation pushes them. Either a community has other traditional means of sustaining itself or, once it is deprived of that basis, it must seek a new guarantee of community in language and Law. Language cannot be the basis of a traditional community: it is by definition a *new* kind of community, and it is not achieved until the language in question achieves universality.[8] In language, the universal is given practical effectivity in the here and now. This is important because democracy is a politics of the here and now: there is no such thing as a state which is not democratic now but will become so slowly.

The territorial connection between nation and state is based on the territorial claims of the nation. Absolute monarchy had, of course, an insatiable appetite for territory, but here in the encounter between the state and the nation, whose territorial claims are self-restrictive rather than expansionist, the state comes up against a claim to concreteness that is uncongenial to its way of doing things. Thus the old (the sovereign state) encounters the new (the nation coming into being through the efforts of the population), and a compromise structure is devised. In this nation-state, we sometimes think that we see the triumph of, say, the French nation, composed of its entire people, against the sovereign state. While there is no doubt that the French nation effected an irreversible historic transformation, the final result was not an elimination of the sovereign state, but rather an adoption of its non-organic principles of inclusion to the purposes of the nation-state. The nation has no theory of rule of its own. The state kept alive a principle of virtual belonging (through citizenship and of course, through learning the language!) as effective and real belonging, as a counterpoint to the nation's assumption of organic and originary belonging. The imperial powers' ability to instrumentalize the nation in the quest for colonies is related to this essential duality.

In contrast to this scenario of nation-states that came into being through a long process of conflict, struggle and gradual transformation culminating in revolution, we have nation-states like India, which seem to be caught in a linguistic trap of some kind. But in fact India is hardly an exceptional case. As Coulmas points out, most of the countries that came into existence out of colonial rule are multilingual.[9] In these countries, there has been a sort of crystallization of cultural identities around language, which renders the processes of linguistic change, interaction, adaptation etc. highly visible and contestable. Moreover, the presence of the colonial master-language in the position of the neutral external agency to which disputes are habitually referred creates a situation where the immanent domain of cultural co-existence is systematically submitted to the arbitration of the colonial language, and through it, history, the world, etc.

The responses to this predicament have been several: in parts of Africa, the adoption of French as the language of the universal in order to overcome the debilities of colonial subjugation and the intractable complexity of the linguistic (dis)order, has been proposed and implemented. In other places, efforts have been made to adapt the local languages, to render them modern and 'equal', in a new measurable way, to the dominant languages of the world. This can in turn take two forms: either a self-sufficiency approach, a conscious effort to develop alternatives to the terms of the dominant languages using the resources of the receiving language (Chinese and Tamil have taken this route), or a sort of market-economy approach involving absorbing the terms of the dominant languages into the receiving language, and expanding it thereby (Malay, Japanese; in Kannada and Telugu, as in many other Indian languages, both these methods are adopted).

Coulmas' exploration of the various linkages between language and economy shows the way in which the capitalist market transforms languages internally, as well as changing the relations between languages internationally. In countries with a colonial past, a bilingual order instituted by the imperial power with the language of the rulers (English) and one or more local languages enmeshed in relations of hierarchy, complementarity or dependency, often adds a further level of complexity to this scenario.[10] Indeed, it is at this level that the cultural dimension of language, more specifically the question of the 'subject in language', which is intimately tied up with that of citizenship and democracy, is manifested in its most intractable aspects.

Two interdependent dynamics, which formed a part of the overall social transformation wrought across the globe by the bourgeois revolution, have diverged to such an extent that the efforts of many new post-colonial societies aimed at reintegrating them seem doomed to fail. The imperial powers were each a nation-state, which came into being during and through the industrial revolution and colonization of the world. The internal homogeneity that they manifest, especially linguistic homogeneity, is the result of centuries of political and economic overhauling. But at the heart of this entire process, which was played out as a global drama of masters and slaves, conquerors and conquered, colonizer and colonized, was also the democratic revolution, which instituted the figure of the citizen as the sign of a new kind of freedom that was defined as *universal*. The French Revolution marks the advent of this figure of the citizen in all its glory. This freedom seemed, in spite of the difficulties attending its institution and elaboration, to be a natural attribute of the nations of the west, to the spokesmen of the west as much as to the leaders of the national movements among the colonized. The citizen figure may well be one of the products of the processes of commodification and the new turns in the process of social abstraction induced by the rise of capitalism. Nation and state were the collectivities that corresponded to the two individual entities that emerged in the process: national subject and sovereign citizen. These interlocking figures, whose separate definition is still a matter of dispute among political theorists and the collectivities they corresponded to, became the desirable political goals around which the national movements in the colonies were mounted.

LANGUAGE IN INDIA

In accordance with the logic of the appropriation of these political forms as the means of self-reconstitution, the nation-states that emerged out of colonialism had to deal with the question of language. And the solutions they resorted to were dictated by the nature of the linguistic reality that they inherited, which determined the field of possibilities for achieving the linguistic homogeneity that was felt to be the *sine qua non* of nation-state functioning. As in most cases, the countries that emerged out of the colonial experience were unified by no organic criterion, but merely by the exigencies of colonial administration, and so the resolution was not easy. In Francophone Africa, for instance, many leaders of independent states advocated the adoption of French as the *lingua franca*, in the face of a linguistic diversity that was further complicated by the absence of scripts and traditions of education in the languages.[11]

In India, the nationalist leadership was more ambitious in its vision for a unified modern nation-state. It sought to eliminate English altogether from its position of command in the colonial bilingual order, to replace it with Hindi as the national language, and to allow the provinces, where several major languages with long histories of literary and political development existed, to function in their respective languages. While retaining the term 'nation' for India as a whole, this was effectively a proposal for a multinational federation. It was a bid to achieve political self-sufficiency to complement the Nehruvian state's programme for economic self-sufficiency.

But, from the beginning, the tension around the question of which of these entities was the real nation remained. While after Independence, the central government showed an inclination to deny the existence of linguistic nationalities within its territory, these latter were not inclined to let the matter rest, since the legitimacy of the internal linguistic concentrations had always been acknowledged in the Congress, ever since Gandhi introduced it as a principle of organization on assumption

CONSTITUTION OF INDIA
सत्यमेव जयते

of leadership of the party in 1920.[12] The recognition of the nations of India, indirectly through the recognition of the mediation of Congress activists from these language regions as a necessity for the party to succeed in mobilizing the masses, was a turning point in the history of the national movement. And yet it is possible that in the minds of the Central leadership, this amounted not to recognition of national identity but merely a strategic necessity.

At Independence, however, as in other fields (notably culture), the Indian state found it expedient to adopt the same consensual conservative policies that the British, in collusion with the communal elites and feudal powers local and European, had put in place (which during British rule, the Congress nationalists had opposed as being against the spirit of nationalism). Abandoning the constructive, forward-looking elements of a nationalist vision, the Congress fell back upon the sanctity of the given and increasingly endorsed a civilizational image of India consonant with the fantasies of eighteenth-century Europe. This approach also proved useful insofar as it engendered a picture of the masses as belonging to an altogether different temporal-cultural order than the one the leadership had promised to bring into being, and therefore assured the leadership that its essentially social-engineering approach to change was appropriate to the situation. The leadership in Delhi needed very much to believe in the complete malleability of the Indian masses. In Lacanian terms, the (nationalist) desire for India was the desire of the (European) Other, a fantasy difficult to dislodge. And in this game of intercivilizational love-hate, the aspirations of the linguistic provinces began to seem like 'provincialism' to the central leadership. Another factor that contributed to this diminution of the importance of immediate steps to further democracy was the greater importance that the central government obviously gave to the Hindu–Muslim question, which had resulted in the holocaust of Partition.

But for all that, the whole process of eventual reorganization of states along linguistic lines happened relatively smoothly, as essentially an intra-Congress affair.[13] It was an internal quarrel and it was finally resolved, little by little, beginning in 1953 with the creation of Andhra Pradesh and carried further by the 1956 States Reorganization, over the next ten years.

The situation of linguistic diversity within a subcontinent-sized will-to-nation that India effectively is, poses a problem that can be understood by reference to the Hegelian problem of *redintegration*. This can be treated also as a problem of the molecular structure of political compounds, where it would have to be acknowledged that the linguistic component resists molecular restructuring, just as say, caste does. The difference is, however, that the latter is universally acknowledged as an obstacle, whereas with the former, there is an equally universal disavowal. Caste is seen as a social residue susceptible to the corrosive power of development, whereas language, even though some would like to treat it that way, cannot be reduced to the social: its foundational importance to political existence being beyond dispute. Thus, while social scientists can pretend to have reduced intra-national linguistic conflicts to ethnic (or other) types of divisive identity, they cannot deny the necessity for a nation-state of a common language as such. Since most of political science is of the conflict-studies type, the theoretical question of the constitutive relation between language and modern state does not ever feature in their horizon and has, as such, been conveniently neglected – or explained away by recourse to the positivism of language as means of communication. Of course, the primacy of development (christened 'socialism' by the government of free India) to the new nation may have rendered the language problem less urgent, since in a state with an illiterate majority, the existence of a common language may not have mattered much. But we have yet to assess the successes and failures of socialism/development by reference to the linguistic factor, a problem which is by definition invisible to the social sciences as they exist in India, where we see much evidence of impatience or indifference to language questions, except in their reduced form as sources of conflict.

LANGUAGE AND PROVINCIAL ELITES

This narrative might give the impression that the regions were eager to embrace their national identities through achieving a linguistic state, while the centre stood in their way by pitting national unity against regional assertion of identity. But it was not always and everywhere so. There was a determined section of the Congress leadership which desired such unification, and the demand found endorsement among the intellectuals, especially the poets and writers who, under the influence of English literature, had begun to elaborate a modern literature for their languages. But the picture is far from one of general enthusiasm. In the first place, the majority of the people, being unlettered and only included in the fight for Independence or linguistic national identity as spectators, were not in the picture. It was the literate middle classes who were most keen on the idea. Secondly, at the time of unification of the different parts of the linguistic province into one unit, there was in some cases (as in Karnataka)[14] and Andhra Pradesh[15] a distinct lack of enthusiasm, if not open opposition to the idea. This had a lot to do with the fact that the erstwhile princely state of Mysore was, for instance, not keen on diluting its power structure to incorporate the former regions of Madras and Bombay presidencies and Hyderabad state. Similarly, there was reluctance to merge the Andhra region and Hyderabad into one, out of fear of the consequences of such a merger for the political bargaining strength of the regions vis-à-vis each other. Another interesting part of the story is that, in deference to the Central leadership's fight with the Muslim League on various issues, the provincial literary intelligentsia silently endorsed the primacy of Hindi and put the claims for their own languages on hold (out of barely-concealed Hindu solidarity), in order to defeat the plan to give equal status to Urdu.[16]

Thus while the new states (here I am talking about the southern Indian states in particular) came into being with a flurry of song-writing and celebration, they were not exactly a picture of popular enthusiasm. This is the interesting part: where were the people in all this? And what kind of participation can we expect from them when the leadership was so divided? This is where the role of cinema becomes central and, in an interesting development following the linguistic re-organization of states in 1956, functions as the site for the consolidation of linguistic identity among the masses, contributing to a tendency to political delinking (to use Samir Amin's term) from the national party structure in certain states. This is a story I have elaborated elsewhere. Suffice it to note here that linguistic nationalism was content to play second fiddle to religious nationalism as long as it was confined to the literate civil society, and that it was only with the entry of the masses, via the mediation of cinema, that it acquired a potentially universalist character, while at the same time being vulnerable to an ethnicist reduction.

At present, the language question in India has come to seem intractable and a nuisance, thanks to the priority of development over democracy characteristic of poor nations across the world in this moment of globalization. The question of language and nation is not foreign to the national movement, nor was the movement unaware of the link between language and democracy. All the moves to introduce Hindi as the national language bear witness to the recognition that the nation-state needs a common language. The manner in which this question then evolved to yield the present stalemate, is an instructive index of the fact that the historical emergence of development, as an idiom of global interdependence, overruns the process of resolution of the question of language, or of any number of other questions that might have seemed indispensable for democracy. The future wins over the present. The familial rationale, of economic prosperity within the existing state of affairs (or range of opportunities) takes precedence over the community rationale of forging a people with a common identity.

We can state the linguistic conundrum in the following terms. We know (or rather we knew) that a common language is essential to democratic functioning. Hindi was chosen as the language that would serve this purpose. This was opposed by the linguistic regions. In deference to their wishes and to the groundswell of popular resentment, the implementation of Hindi as sole national language was indefinitely put off, and it was agreed between the centre and the states that English would continue to be an official language alongside Hindi. This is a peculiar solution to the perceived problem. It prevents the imposition of one alien language (Hindi) upon a large segment of the Indian population, by imposing an even more alien language (English) upon the *entire population, including the Hindi speaking part*. This substitution, or superimposition, in no way contributes to achieving the democratic goal of developing the universal resources of the state languages. It persists with English as a way of appeasing the linguistic regions, rather than as a positive policy. What is done with English is not a *substitution* of it for Hindi, but a co-existence of the two. The regional languages are not brought into the national mainstream, Hindi is pushed back into its regional base, without any corresponding attempt to develop the universalist resources of the regional languages. English is retained for its economic benefits and for its arbitrator's role between nationalities.[17] The needs of the present, which are communal needs, are sacrificed for the needs of the future, which are the needs of individual economic agents. The question of the relation between language and democracy is permanently pushed onto the backburner.

Meanwhile, within the borders of linguistic states, governments try to promote the illusion of cultural continuity by constituting 'language development' authorities and making appointments to these positions from among the vociferous nationalist elites, while continuing with educational practices suited to the needs of global capital. New organizations emerge, representing the ethnic anxieties of the neo-literate and prone-to-violent means of asserting national identity in quasi-religious terms (e.g., the Karnataka Rakshana Samithi, which increasingly resembles the Shiv Sena).[18] But at the same time, the new economic climate and developments in the media have led to a new consolidation of linguistic economies, and autonomizing tendencies, as yet not publicly acknowledged. Today, the economy is the site where 'the languages of the people' have acquired the kind of importance that they have been denied by the political apparatus over the last six decades.

What is the way forward? Are we stuck with a normative model of one-nation-one-language, which may be just an accidental feature of some states, as the impossible ideal we struggle in vain to achieve? Is there some way in which a democratic polity can be conceived without this requirement? Or do we need to re-describe our own political existence in other terms than that of nation-state? Are we then dealing with an older state form, or some as-yet unrecognized new one? The answer to such questions is a long way off, since we have hardly begun the task of analysing the present linguistic order. However, there is one fact that we can take as given: the present order must be described not as some elusive reality which escapes the normative demands of nation-state discourse, but as one which is inescapably determined by the mutually impacting co-existence of the norm and the reality. It is a state of in-betweenness that must be taken to constitute a state in itself for purposes of description. When we consider the issues that constantly come up for debate and sometimes violent agitation in the regions, we will scarcely appreciate their true import if we fail to take this state of affairs into account.

□

The social scientist M.S.S. Pandian (1958–2014) is best known for his extensive work on Dravidian politics, less so for his work in urban studies – e.g., the project **Museum. Exhibition. Backyard. Chennai** (2008). This short essay, one of the few that brings both disciplines together, explores the concept of a political 'void' – the symbolic domain in Indian politics that would become increasingly significant in the 1990s – as a vacuous, empty signifier within which diverse political meanings jostle with each other as they try to enter into and appropriate it. In an astonishing story of a public statue that disappeared overnight, Pandian reads a blank space in which 'traces of the past and submerged memories, as if a palimpsest, flood the public domain'. The essay is set within a history of popular politics in Tamil Nadu, its key dramatis personae producing a ghostly public presence as they weave through history, print journalism, cinema and literature.

Originally presented at the **2004 Inter-Asia Cultural Studies** conference at the Centre for the Study of Culture and Society, Bangalore. Conference paper reproduced here with grateful acknowledgment to S. Anandhi. A different version of this paper was published in **Inter-Asia Cultural Studies** (vol. 6, no. 3, 2005).

Images: In 1968, ten statues of important figures from Tamil history were unveiled on the Marina beach in Chennai. Only one of these was of a fictional character – a figure from literature, but perhaps more famously, from the cinema. Images taken from the finale of R.S. Mani's epic **Kannagi** (Tamil, 1942), alongside editorials and newspaper clippings of the disappearing statue montage on the Samsung 740N Syncmaster.

11

M.S.S. PANDIAN

2004

VOID AND MEMORY: STORY OF A STATUE

The Temporal status of any act of memory is always the present.
– Andreas Huyssen[1]

On the night of 6 December 2001, the Public Works Department of Tamil Nadu and the Chennai City Police, in a swift and secretive operation, removed a statue from a Chennai beachfront.[2] The ten-feet tall bronze statue, which had been standing on the Marina Beach (Marina) for thirty-three years, is that of the legendary Kannagi, the female protagonist of the well-known Tamil epic *Silappathikaram*.[3] The statue captured a dramatic moment in the epic in which a fiery Kannagi, holding an anklet in her right hand, seeks justice at the Pandya king's court for the unfair death of her husband Kovalan. After the removal of the statue, the public was kept for days in a state of guessing as to where it had disappeared. And finally, it had resurfaced in the Madras Museum. It was locked away in one of the storage rooms away from public gaze.

The statue of Kannagi – along with the statues of nine writers and scholars who contributed to Tamil language and literature – was installed on the beachfront on 2 January 1968 as part of the Second International Tamil Conference.[4] The conference was sponsored by the state government led by the Dravida Munnetra Kazhagam (DMK), a Tamil nationalist party which espoused its own version of rationalism.[5] The DMK came to power for the first time in 1967 on the wave of an anti-Hindi agitation, which opposed the introduction of Hindi as the sole national language of multilingual India. The statues formed part of the move by the DMK to infuse the spaces of Chennai city with a Tamil identity. Renaming streets after Tamil nationalists and construction of monuments to celebrate Tamil literary figures formed part of this effort. Being a colonial port city with a multi-ethnic population, Chennai never carried the regional Tamil identity. In fact, when the states of India were reorganized in the 1950s on the basis of language, Telugu speakers made an unsuccessful claim on the city.[6]

The Kannagi statue, when it stood on the Marina, never acquired the auratic presence that the Tamil nationalist DMK hoped for. It was instead engaged in distraction by the city dwellers.[7] At most, it served the purpose of pointing to a bus stop on the Marina. Perhaps the only occasion when the statue enjoyed an aura was during its unveiling in 1968. Although the unveiling of the statue was part of the scholarly International Tamil Conference, the DMK separated the academic sessions from the event. The statues of Kannagi and others were unveiled in a colourful carnival-like public function in which tens of thousands of people participated. Interestingly, the money for the Kannagi statue was raised entirely from the student population of the state.

Valorized as the epitome of chastity and Tamil female valour, the disappearance of Kannagi from the beachfront rendered it in a state of new visibility, i.e. it once again acquired a temporary aura. The public arena of Chennai city proliferated with newer images to substitute for the missing statue. In protest meetings organized by the DMK, young girls dressed up as Kannagi attempted their skill at political speech; large cutouts were displayed prominently at such meetings; Tamil scholars attempted to install a new statue made of Plaster of Paris in its original location, only to be prevented by the police; and both print and electronic media carried numerous photographs of the statue from its past. The *Tamil Sanror Peravai* (a Tamil cultural organization) declared that it would construct five temples for Kannagi.[8]

This new visibility of the icon was accompanied by a series of competing public utterances about the statue and its significance. In important ways, these utterances disclosed the multiple meanings that the statue had generated, both in its presence and absence, in excess of the original nationalist intent of the DMK. And traces of the past and submerged memories, as if a palimpsest, flooded the public domain. After all, ruins and memory are intimately connected. As Georg Simmel perceptively noted, 'The ruin creates the present form of a past life, not according to the

Karunanidhi fails to garner support on Kannagi statue
By Swati Das
Times News Network
CHENNAI: Last month, when the statue of Kannagi, the ancient angry woman, on Marina beach was removed, it raked up a political furore led by former state chief minister and DMK president M. Karunanidhi.
The government maintained that the statue was knocked down by a lorry and it was removed as per the advice of the former city police commissioner as it hindered traffic.
However, Mr Karunanidhi said the government got rid of the statue because of astrological reasons and as per instructions from his bete noire, former state CM and AIADMK chief J. Jayalalithaa.
Mr Karunanidhi had alleged that the statue's removal was an insult to Tamil literature. His campaign was supported by a few political parties. Mr Karunanidhi tried to make it into a major issue. But his efforts seem to have been wasted as it has failed to become a mass movement.
Then, can we celebrate all the spirits
physical fitness examination in Baira

content or remnants of that life, but according to its past as such.' Here is a case not exactly of a ruin but of a void – a void that was being filled with memories of the past.

The reason offered by the state government for the removal of the statue was rather functional, one of traffic management in the city. It was claimed that an erring truck had hit the pedestal of the statue and, being located at a T-junction, it was a distraction to motorists. But the sheer secrecy that veiled the removal of the statue gave rise to a volley of rumours. One set of rumours claimed that the statue was considered, by the weight of opinions of astrologers, as inauspicious both to the city and her political future by the chief minister of Tamil Nadu, J. Jayalalithaa.[9] The rumour carried a certain credibility given Jayalalithaa's well-known belief in astrology. She has sponsored several special pujas in temples in the course of the past few years to enhance her political fortunes. Another set of rumours claimed that the statue was removed because of Jayalalithaa's open animosity towards M. Karunanidhi, the leader of the DMK.[10] Jayalalithaa heads the All India Anna Dravida Munnetra Kazhagam (AIADMK), the main rival of the DMK in state politics. It was pointed out that the Kannagi statue was the only statue on the Marina to carry Karunanidhi's name on its pedestal, as he presided over the function in 1968 to unveil the statue. The rumour claimed that Jayalalithaa did not want his name on display. These rumours found their way into the print media and circulated widely.

The first public response against the removal of the statue came from expected quarters, on expected lines. The DMK and its allies claimed that the removal of the statue was an assault on the heritage of the Tamils, and demanded its reinstallation. Thus, the void provided an occasion to the DMK to affirm its Tamil nationalist credentials. Karunanidhi described the removal as a 'challenge to the Tamil pride' and called on 'self-respecting' Tamils to protest. He further declared, 'This is a fight to save Tamil culture, dignity and tradition.'[11]A large number of Tamil scholars and writers endorsed this culturist rhetoric and a series of public meetings protested the statue's removal.

There were other voices that spoke a different language. Even before the removal of the Kannagi statue, some considered the fiery statue as not auguring good to the city. In 1999, writing about the statues in the city, a journalist quoted an old-time beach-walker thus: 'Have you noticed? Ever since the Kannagi statue was installed, we have never had a day of peace. I think we should persuade the authorities to turn her around, so that she can curse the sea [and not the city].'[12] After the removal of the statue, similar sentiments were aired. A letter-writer pointed out in the Tamil daily *Dinamalar* that a section of the residents of Triplicane, a city neighbourhood towards which the statue's outstretched hand pointed, thought that the statue had affected its prosperity.[13] If the DMK wished the statue to be a sign of Tamil-ness, it could not control the production of other meanings around it.

Similarly, others used the context to critique the rationalist DMK's secularization of Kannagi, who is deified and worshipped, mostly by women, in temples in some parts of Tamil Nadu. The installation of the statue was claimed to be an act of dispossessing Kannagi of her divinity. Bird droppings that defiled the statue every day and the milling crowd spitting in its vicinity were cited as evidence of her de-sacralization. Some argued that the removal of the statue was an occasion to relocate Kannagi in a temple so that she could be worshipped.[14]

The disappearance of the Kannagi statue also brought back memories of pan-Indian nationalism from a distant past – a nationalism that has a discounted presence in the state's politics. After the Indian-nationalist Congress Party lost power to the regionalist DMK in 1967, it was reduced to a minor player in the state's politics. A stretch of the beach close to the Kannagi statue was once known as Tilakar Tidal or Tilakar grounds. Named after a nationalist of the extremist faction, B.G. Tilak, it was a place where political meetings were often held. In the late 1960s, a volunteer corps organized by the first DMK government built a permanent podium known as Seerani Arangam, which became the new identification for the pre-existing Tilakar Tidal. The Executive Director of Gandhi Darshan Kendra (Centre for Viewing Gandhi), a nationalist Gandhian organization, recalled, 'It was there from which Lokamanya Bal Gangadhar Tilak called upon the people to liberate our country from the British. The name [Tilakar Ghat] was conceived by "Mahakavi" Bharathi and its formal naming was done by Subramania Siva, both great nationalists.'[15] He went on to accuse the Tamil nationalists of the DMK for their antipathy towards memories of pan-Indian nationalism: 'As part of obliterating the memory of freedom struggle, the Dravidian party that formed government constructed an auditorium and named it "Seerani Arangam".'[16] The demand for the reinstallation of the Kannagi statue became an occasion to plead for the beachfront's Indian nationalist past.

This avalanche of different memories and claims disrupted the Tamil nationalist connotation of Kannagi and rendered unavailable their dream of a singular vision for the city. It also affirmed the different ways of being in and belonging to the city. What the DMK had achieved was an overwriting of Tamil nationalist imagination on past memories, and not their erasure. Those past memories, at the moment of the statue's removal, bled into the public to interrogate DMK's vision of culture. Perhaps it would be instructive here to remember Michel de Certeu's description of habitable places: 'There is no place that is not haunted by many different spirits hidden there in silence, spirits one can "invoke" or not. Haunted places are the only ones people can live in – and this inverts the scheme of the *panopticon*.'[17] In the specific context of the Kannagi statue, we need to substitute the singular vision of culture promoted by the DMK's regional nationalism for De Certeu's panopticon.

Then, can we celebrate all the spirits from the past, for they make the city a mosaic of different visions? We cannot. At least one strand of opposition to the Kannagi statue produced a more acute exclusivist imagination than the DMK's nationalism, which in its secularism accommodated adherents of different religions under an encompassing Tamil identity. Sections of the Hindu right chose the occasion to question DMK's secularized notion of culture. For instance, *Thuglak*, a popular right-wing Tamil magazine, in a virulent editorial on the statue controversy, characterized the DMK men as '[those] who derided [Hindu] religious devotion which is intertwined with Tamil culture, reviled sages who spread religious devotion, and mocked devotional literature' and ridiculed the DMK's version of Tamil culture.[18] It was indeed true that DMK's rationalism in the past questioned, *but did not deny the space for*, Hindu religious practices. But by aligning culture and Hindu-ness, what the Hindu right sought to exclude was other religious communities' claim over versions of Tamil culture and its inscription in the city spaces. Tellingly, the public interest litigation petition filed in the Madras High Court seeking to restore the Kannagi statue to its original position was by a Muslim, Hasan Mohamed Jinnah. He claimed that his effort was to undo the damage caused to the 'collective Tamil psyche by the removal of the Kannagi statue'.[19] The Hindu right's vision of Tamil culture will not have space for Hasan Mohamed Jinnah to speak as a Tamil – a space that has been offered by the secularized version of Tamil culture that the DMK has spawned.

Memories indeed pluralize. All remembrances need not produce a future city wherein competing claims on the city could be accommodated and negotiated. Some remembrances desire exclusion and dream revenge. What spirits from the past are resurrected, what memories are invoked, are as important to the future of the city as the fact that memories contest singular visions for the city.

□

Media practitioner Shuddhabrata Sengupta analyses the highly mediatized legal evidence that followed the 13 December 2001 attack on Parliament, in which armed 'terrorists' entered the Parliament House in a car with official stickers, got out and began shooting. Delhi Police officials claimed that the gunmen received instructions from Pakistan and the operation was carried out under the guidance of Pakistan's Inter-Services Intelligence (ISI) agency. Four persons – Mohammad Afzal Guru, Shaukat Hussain Guru (cousin of Afzal Guru), university lecturer S.A.R. Geelani and Shaukat's wife Afsan Guru – were accused. The trial ran over six months. Afzal, Shaukat Hussain and Geelani were at first convicted, but on appeal, Geelani and Afsan were acquitted while Shaukat and Afzal were given the death sentence. Sengupta shows how diverse fantasies of mediatized technology played a central role in the reconstruction of the event itself. As several films dealt both directly and indirectly with this incident, and mobilized popular images of 'terrorists' and their so-called modus operandi, their forms began to overlap with police investigations and news media coverage to create a 'metaphorical identikit photograph of the terrorist in our heads' and thence a new genre of mediatized legal process.

Earlier versions of this essay were published on Sarai reader lists, in the **Journal of the Moving Image** (2005), and in the book **13 December, a Reader: The Strange Case of the Attack on the Indian Parliament** (New Delhi: Penguin Books, 2006). Grateful acknowledgment to the author for permission to reprint.

Images: From Sanjay Kak's documentary, Jashn-e-Azadi: How We Celebrate Freedom (2007), alongside the kitsch displays of military-digital tech in the film **16 December** (Mani Shankar, 2002), a lowbrow fictional re-enactment of the 13 December attack.

12

SHUDDHABRATA SENGUPTA

2005

MEDIA TRIALS AND COURTROOM TRIBULATIONS

The Battle of Images, Words and Shadows in the 13 December Case

> The acquittal of an innocent man is not an occasion for celebration, but a cause for reflection.
>
> – Syed Abdul Rehman Geelani, on his being acquitted by the Supreme Court on charges of conspiracy in the 13 December 2001 'Attack on Parliament' case, 4 August 2005

On 4 August 2005, the Supreme Court of India gave its verdict on the 13 December 2001 'Attack on Parliament' case, acquitting two of the original accused, S.A.R. Geelani, lecturer in Arabic at Zakir Husain College, Delhi and Afsan Guru (aka Navjot Sidhu), wife of one of the other accused – Shaukat Husain Guru, and upholding the death sentence pronounced by the Delhi High Court and the special POTA (Prevention of Terrorism Act)[1] court on Mohammad Afzal. The High Court's pronouncement of a death sentence on Shaukat Husain Guru was commuted to ten years imprisonment. In announcing this verdict, the Supreme Court of India upheld the Delhi High Court's acquittal of S.A.R. Geelani and Afsan Guru. Geelani had been sentenced to death and Afsan

Guru awarded five years of rigorous imprisonment by the judge of the special POTA court, S.N. Dhingra, on 18th December 2002.

The Justices P.V. Reddy and P.P. Naolekar, while acquitting S.A.R. Geelani on the grounds that the prosecution was not able to present adequate evidence against the accused, maintained that there was still a 'needle of suspicion' against S.A.R. Geelani, but that suspicion alone could not form the basis of a sentence in the absence of robust evidence.

With the pronouncement of this verdict by the highest judicial authority of the Republic of India, a sordid chapter in the history of this republic has come to a provisional and uncertain conclusion. One hesitates to use the term 'end' because the unpredictable nature of events as they unfold, perhaps in the immediate future, perhaps due to a random discovery in the archives many decades hence, may yet deliver us another 'turn' in the unravelling of this story which might still give cause to startle us all.

Or it might not, as in what befalls many unexplained twists and turns in the script of our times. We may learn to become inured to the tug of an uncomfortable and persistent memory of things and people that went amiss. Like the 'out-takes' in footage that never quite made it into a film, about which we can say that we have a memory of being present as witnesses at the shooting but little or no recall of ever having seen them on screen, like papers, documents, transcripts, bodies and memories that turn to dust and are scattered, the history of the attack on the Parliament of India too will in all likelihood become a hazy recollection, with only the words and images of 'terrorists' and 'martyrs' and 'threat to national security' thrown up in bold relief, and with all else obscured within a labyrinth of shadows.

Some people call this forgetting, others call it history. The history of the Republic of India could fill an archive of lost memories. Perhaps there needs to be, somewhere near India Gate, not far from the present 'National Archives' and the Parliament, a site earmarked for a building to house a 'National Archive of Forgetting'. A building – part Lutyens, part Le Corbusier, part Raj Rewal,[2] part Kafka and part Borges – that, in its architectural imagination, would do true justice to the delicate combination of pomp, paranoia and amnesia that buttresses the foundations of the republic.

While there may be widespread relief in the knowledge that S.A.R. Geelani and Afsan Guru are now acquitted (if not unconditionally exonerated) by the judicial apparatus, the turn of events does not give anyone any cause for celebration – neither the Delhi Police nor the prosecution, who have seen their arguments fall like so many dead birds from the judicial sky. Those who have stood by Geelani and sought to defend him can breathe easier, but there is little cause to rejoice. As Geelani himself said in a press conference immediately after the pronouncement of the verdict: 'The acquittal of an innocent man is not an occasion for celebration, but a cause for reflection.' Why, after all, did the police and concerned security agencies, and large sections of the 'independent' media, have to go to such lengths to frame a man against whom they could not provide a shred of quality evidence in the special POTA court, in the High Court and in the Supreme Court? Now that at least two of the accused can walk free, and one other can live (albeit in prison), we need to begin to ask what really happened. Some others may have to do whatever is necessary and permissible under the law to ensure that Shaukat Husain too is able to leave prison sooner and that Mohammad Afzal does not take the final walk to the gallows.[3]

If Mohammad Afzal is indeed executed, then some of the truths that he alone (barring some of his handlers and interrogators) has access to will follow him to his grave. In the event that the spin doctors of the media continue to play the role that they have played so honourably in the duration of this entire set of trials, it is unlikely that anything approximating the truth will ever be made available to the public in India, or indeed anywhere in the world. For an alternative version of the events to eventually emerge, it is crucial that Mohammad Afzal's death sentence be challenged, and that S.A.R. Geelani stay alive. Let us recall that there have been two extra-judicial attempts on Geelani's life, once while he was in prison and again outside his advocate Nandita Haksar's[4] residence by an as yet unidentified assailant in February this year. Both Geelani and Afzal need to live if we are to get any closer to the truth of what happened on 13 December 2001, and why Geelani was framed. It is vital to understand that the 'climate of suspicion' that has led to Afzal's conviction, and to the Supreme Court's unwarranted remark that a 'needle of suspicion' still points at Geelani, are a product of more than four years of consistent information management and production of images. My hunch is that the critical media literacy of the highest judiciary of the Republic of India is not so immaculate at present as to render it immune to prejudice. The role played by the production of moving images, in film and video, in cinema and on television, is particularly pertinent here, and I will attend to this in some greater detail later in this essay.

As of now, barring a presidential pardon, or the unlikely re-opening of the case, Afzal will hang. One hopes, for all our sakes, that it is otherwise, and that the circumstances that led to the alleged 'terrorist' attack on the Parliament of what is sometimes loosely called the 'largest democracy in the world', to the passing of the most draconian preventive detention law by the legislature of the same 'largest democracy' (the thankfully now-repealed POTA), and to the situation of near war that lasted for more than a year between two nuclear-weapons states that are also neighbours, will one day become available in the public domain. Until then, the delicate combination of secrecy and hyperbole, of understatement and exaggeration, of straight lies and half-cooked truths, of skulduggery and sentimentality, will continue to taint the history of communication practices in our republic of forgotten truths and remembered illusions, where (as elsewhere) the 'media', the 'television and film industries' and the 'intelligence community' dance an elegant tango in which it sometimes becomes difficult to discern who leads whom on the dance floor.

This text is only a call for a sustained meditation on this condition. And an attempt to account for and ask some questions about the overproduction of images and the aporiae within them that surround the representations of what is called 'terrorism', the events of 13 December and the trials that followed. I do not pretend to give a comprehensive account of what happened, because I do not possess the necessary critical forensic–legal apparatus by way of training, nor am I an expert media 'analyst'. I am a media practitioner, and I write this from the standpoint of someone who practises media and who observes what others practise. I do hope, however, that reading this might prompt those who have the necessary legal–forensic apparatus, or who may lay claim to being expert media analysts, to ask some hard questions on the role that the media have played in this case and with regard to the representation of 'terrorism and counter-terrorism' in general, and provoke some reason for introspection within the community of media practitioners.

This text is culled from preliminary notes towards such an exercise, but even in making these notes, I have become aware of the fact that the task of reflection on the media requires us to consider media materials, not as isolates but as elements in a networked reality, where cinema, television, newspaper reportage and even public service messages enter into elaborate interweaving feedback loops that reinforce and sustain each other, either through direct quotation or through narrative 'enhancements' that create a situation where each message enhances its claim to credibility by relying on the credentials of the other. Events and processes such as the 'reading' of 13 December and its aftermath take place at the intersections of a densely networked media space where messages, memories, events and mediums relay and overlay each other. These realities make the task of sophisticated and sensitive readings of media not an academic exercise but an urgent political task, that has bearings not only on the destinies of our polity but also, as in the 13 December case, on the life and death of individuals. The galling neglect, incapacity or unwillingness on the part of a vast majority of media scholars and critics in India to undertake this exercise, and the lax ethical standards of many media practitioners, has, in the final analysis, to be read against what happens to us as a polity, and what happens to the lives of individuals and to those close to them.

It is important to remember that on seeing the pictures of the bodies of the slain alleged 'terrorists' who entered the precincts of the Parliament building on the morning of 13 December, the then home minister, Lal Krishna Advani,[5] is said to have remarked that the assailants 'looked like Pakistani terrorists'. Advani must have known what he was talking about (at least the part about their looking like 'Pakistanis') since he looks a lot like a Pakistani himself (as do many north Indians and migrants to India like Advani from the provinces of British India that became West Pakistan in 1947). But more importantly, he was able to assert the fact that they looked 'like terrorists'. It is important to pause and consider how exactly we know that someone looks like a 'terrorist'. The Delhi Police, which has had considerable experience in handling 'terrorists' and 'terrorism' over the years, has reminded us in a series of thoughtful public service advertisements that 'terrorists' are suspicious because they stand out by virtue of their somewhat unusual appearance and behaviour (they wear clothing unsuited to the weather, etc.), and that simultaneously they are suspicious precisely because they blend in so easily with the general population. It is this combination of 'standing out' and 'blending in' at the same time that causes alarm. But to this, like Advani, we know that we can respond with certainty, because we feel we know that when we see a 'terrorist' we will be able to recognize one. We have seen the face of the terrorist so often and so intimately as a moving image that in a sense, the terrorist actually lives in our own heads, and were we to ever come across his body, living or dead, or his image, we would be immediately in a position to cross-check his features against the indelible impress of those features in our nervous system.

The production of terrorism is not something that happens *sui generis*. The production of terrorism is almost always, in every society, also a production of images of terror. In fact, the fear that terrorism induces in general terms is not so much by way of the actual impact of explosives, gun shots and incendiary or lethal materials, but by way of a circulation and amplification of images and their effects. We know this from every instance of spectacular terrorism that we have witnessed in the last hundred or so years. So much so that even more or less arbitrary calendrical notations like 9/11, 12/13 or now, more recently, 7/7, become indexical images of terror. If the production of terrorism is so interlaced with the production of images, we can also say that the production of certain images is also linked to a climate that gives credibility to the production of a certain set of seemingly self-evident truths about terrorism.

The tried and tested tactics of infiltration into existing terror cells or political groups, or the creation of such cells where none exists, or when those that exist are too weak to perform a spectacular act of terror, are well documented in the extant literature on the work and function of intelligence agencies of various states. The MI6's murky relationships to the IRA (Irish Republican Army), and later, the provisional IRA, Mossad's successful infiltration of the Palestinian Abu Nidal group, and the Italian and Belgian intelligence agencies' dealings with the mafia, ex-Nazis, far-right militias, fascists and secret societies in setting off a chain of spectacular terrorist incidents in the 1980s (including the Bologna train station bombing of 1974 and 1980 that killed 113 people and wounded 180) that could later be attributed to 'left-wing' terrorists is very well documented, as is the history of the infiltration of the 'Naxalite' movement in India in the 1970s by India's Intelligence Bureau and special police operatives. The picture of a shadowy dalliance between 'terrorism' and 'counter-terrorism', between 'militants' and 'surrendered militants', between people in and out of different kinds of uniform, is also beginning to emerge from the battlegrounds of Kashmir, Assam and the North East. Military intelligence officers, 'special task force' personnel, intelligence bureau operatives and a host of 'freelance' professionals (including 'surrendered militants') occasionally masquerading as 'militants' and performing violent acts in order to create the necessary climate for stringent 'counter-terrorism' measures is a well-established pattern.

There is no reason to suppose that the tacticians and strategists of the 'intelligence community' that owes its fealty to the Indian state do not, from time to time, have to consider it necessary to 'create' or manufacture instances of terrorism, when it suits the purposes of the state to do so. This is standard practice worldwide, especially under the conditions of the 'global war against terror', and there is no reason to suppose that Indian intelligence professionals are anything but abreast of key global trends in this regard.

This 'creation' of terrorism is something that generally requires a calibrated media strategy and information management, such that the bodies and actions that characterize a particular operation can be 'rendered' in a manner that is convincing and useful. Television channels and newspapers routinely projected the accused and the arrested as 'terrorist masterminds and co-conspirators' without even the caveat that this was as alleged by their captors.

The enthusiastic reportage of the 'arrest' of the prime accused Afzal, Shaukat Husain and Geelani, which in some instances bordered on the hysterical, particularly in the week following 14th December (when Geelani was detained under POTA), is particularly noteworthy. In the stories that began to make their appearance, the swoops were a result of brilliant investigations carried out by the police on the mobile phone records of the phones and sim cards found on the bodies of the alleged slain terrorists. Not one newspaper or television channel paused to ask why a group of terrorists going on what could clearly be a 'suicide mission' or one in which the chances of their being captured was very high, should carry identity cards, diaries detailing their actions and plans, and mobile phones that could be made to yield entire directories of their contacts. Court records show that the phone records relevant to the conversations between Afsan Guru and Shaukat, or to certain conversations that Geelani is said to have had that were produced by the police as evidence (after much dithering), are actually of the days 'after' they were detained. These inconsistencies in the record were then sought to be explained away as 'typographical errors'. Not a single newspaper or television news programme in those days, or in the early days of the trial in the special POTA court, could exhibit the necessary degree of reticence or patience required in the handling of a case as sensitive as this one.

The fact that the death sentences handed out by the POTA court were on the basis of false, forged, or inadmissible or absent evidence was not remarked upon by any news channel. A notable exception, however, which should not go unremarked, is the reportage of the case in *The Hindu*, which, barring a stray story in the early days, was marked by balanced and fair reporting, especially the reports filed from the court by Anjali Mody and which even subjected other media reports of the case to some degree of critical scrutiny.

Finally, when the defence asked for the phone records to be produced and examined by independent and knowledgeable witnesses, what came to light were discrepancies in translation and transcription. The fact that the translated sentence 'It becomes necessary sometimes' (*'Yeh kabhi kabhi zaroori hota hai'*), apparently said in response to a question about 'what has happened in Delhi', which Geelani said referred to a domestic dispute and which the prosecution claimed was about the attack on Parliament, and on which hinged the entire structure of the case against S.A.R. Geelani, was not found to be audible in the tape of the phone intercept when it was played repeatedly for the benefit of the two independent defence witnesses – a documentary filmmaker, Sanjay Kak, and a trade-union activist, Sampat Prakash, both native Kashmiri speakers.[6]

It needs to be mentioned that while the media attention on S.A.R. Geelani as the 'intellectual preceptor' of the terrorists was particularly intense, it was less so with regard to Mohammad Afzal, the man whose 'confession' in detention, an instrument inadmissible in ordinary law as evidence (although permitted in POTA), escaped much by way of scrutiny. The media nailed Geelani on the basis of this confession.

But the media did more. Newspapers detailed property Geelani is said to have amassed as rewards for his labours, as well as the minutiae of his contacts with a student of 'West Asian' origin who must have been an 'Arab terrorist'. But no newspaper or television channel ever mentioned that Afzal, identified as a former JKLF militant and fruit merchant, was in fact a 'surrendered militant', and that he had for seven years been harassed by, and on occasion worked for, the 'Special Task Force (STF)' – a shadowy counter-terrorism outfit that operates with impunity in Kashmir. The fact remains that, in his statement to the court, Afzal said unequivocally that he met one Tariq, a trusted lieutenant of the arch-terrorist 'Ghazi Baba' who is said to have motivated him to return to the ways of the 'jihad for *azaadi*' in an STF training camp in Dral in south Kashmir, and his wife's statement that Afzal was instructed to bring two of the men later identified as the 'slain terrorists' in the Parliament attack to Delhi and provide them with shelter while they were in 'transit' by none other than his STF handlers, went unremarked, with one significant exception, to which we will refer later.

It is interesting to speculate as to how some stories made their way into the media, and how some stories remained virtually 'out of bounds' even if they made their appearance sometimes in court documents. It is also interesting to consider whether this pattern of omission and insertion or fabrication pointed to the collaborative authorship (between the police, the intelligence community, and the media professionals and channels/ newspapers) of these media materials. One thing is certain, the efficient public relations and media exercises carried out (whether through fear or favour, or simply, access) by the 'Special Cell' of the Delhi Police in order to make the journalists community simply reproduce what was fed to them in routine press briefings seems to have worked well. The operation worked particularly well with television, with several channels broadcasting 'exclusive' interviews with what seemed to be an affable and loquacious prime accused Mohammad Afzal on 20th December.

If media professionals highlighted elements from Afzal's first 'confessions' in custody to substantiate their allegations against Geelani, they also obscured the fact that later, during the filming of the 'broadcast confession' of 18th December, Afzal explicitly denied the fact that Geelani had anything to do with the conspiracy. It was only when footage from this 'interview' was reproduced in a special *Aaj Tak* programme ('100 Days after the Attack') that it came to light that Afzal had actually explicitly exonerated Geelani. When S.A.R. Geelani's defence lawyers called upon the *Aaj Tak* reporter who took that interview as a witness, it became clear from his deposition that journalists had in fact been instructed, indeed threatened, by the much decorated Delhi Police 'Special Cell' officer and 'Encounter' specialist, ACP Rajbir Singh, that airing the latter part of Afzal's 'confession' would invite dire consequences on any journalist present who chose to do so.

These developments did not deter Zee News, one of the most zealous extra judicial prosecutors of the 13 December case, from producing an extensive 'docu-drama' on 13 December, which it aired on more than one occasion even as the trial progressed.

This television programme has an interesting and chequered history. Its premiere screening took place in the august presence of the then home minister and 'dead Pakistani identification expert', L.K. Advani. Advani praised the film as an excellent example of investigative journalism and in fact (on a later occasion) even compared it favourably to a subsequent Zee TV expose (on the attack on 'Akshardham' in Gujarat[7]), saying that the former was much more meticulous and thoroughly produced. The film, with a stentorian commentary by the Bollywood 'B'-movie star Raza Murad, featured a troupe of actors enacting the 'conspiracy'. The script of this television programme, as stated in a text insert at the beginning of the programme, is based on the charge sheet of the Delhi Police in the case. What is particularly interesting are the many parallels, in plot, *mise-en-scene* and narrative detail, between the charge sheet, the Zee TV film and the Shah Rukh Khan–Manisha Koirala-starring film by Mani Ratnam, *Dil Se* (1998). We see the same procedures: procurement and manufacture of identity cards, reconnaissance of the landmarks of Lutyens Delhi on winter days, listening to Hindi film music as terrorists work (on radio in the film, downloaded from computers in the TV programme), the hint of romance, the presence of a hard-line intellectual ideologue, the same locale – the alleyways of Old Delhi, around Karim's – and the same method of masquerade as security 'personnel'.

There is an uncanny similarity between the plots of large parts of these two audio-visual documents (one a fiction film and the other a docu-drama), almost as if the 'terrorists', the police investigators and the producers of the docu-drama had seen the film (*Dil Se*) together and discussed its merits in a film analysis class before going their separate ways to give form and shape to their different agendas. Or, could it be that the police genre of literature and filmmaking, which often shapes the trajectories of alleged 'terrorist' incidents, found in '*Dil Se* – 13 December' a suitable vehicle for the execution of one of their most complex plots? It is self-evident that a private news network gaining access to the highest echelons of the home ministry in order to be able to re-enact and shoot on the grounds of the Parliament, with the extensive operational cooperation of police and security personnel, points to a close embrace between the security apparatus and the same media agency. And just as the Justices of the Supreme Court may well have their reasons to continue to point their 'needles of suspicions', we too will have reason to begin looking for, and pointing, our needles of suspicion in the directions that they lead us. We will have to continue to ask why the prosecution's case in the 13 December case had to be argued, not only in the court, but also on air, in living rooms, between commercial breaks.

The dense tangle between film and reality in the 13 December case does not begin and end with *Dil Se*; there are two other films that bear looking at

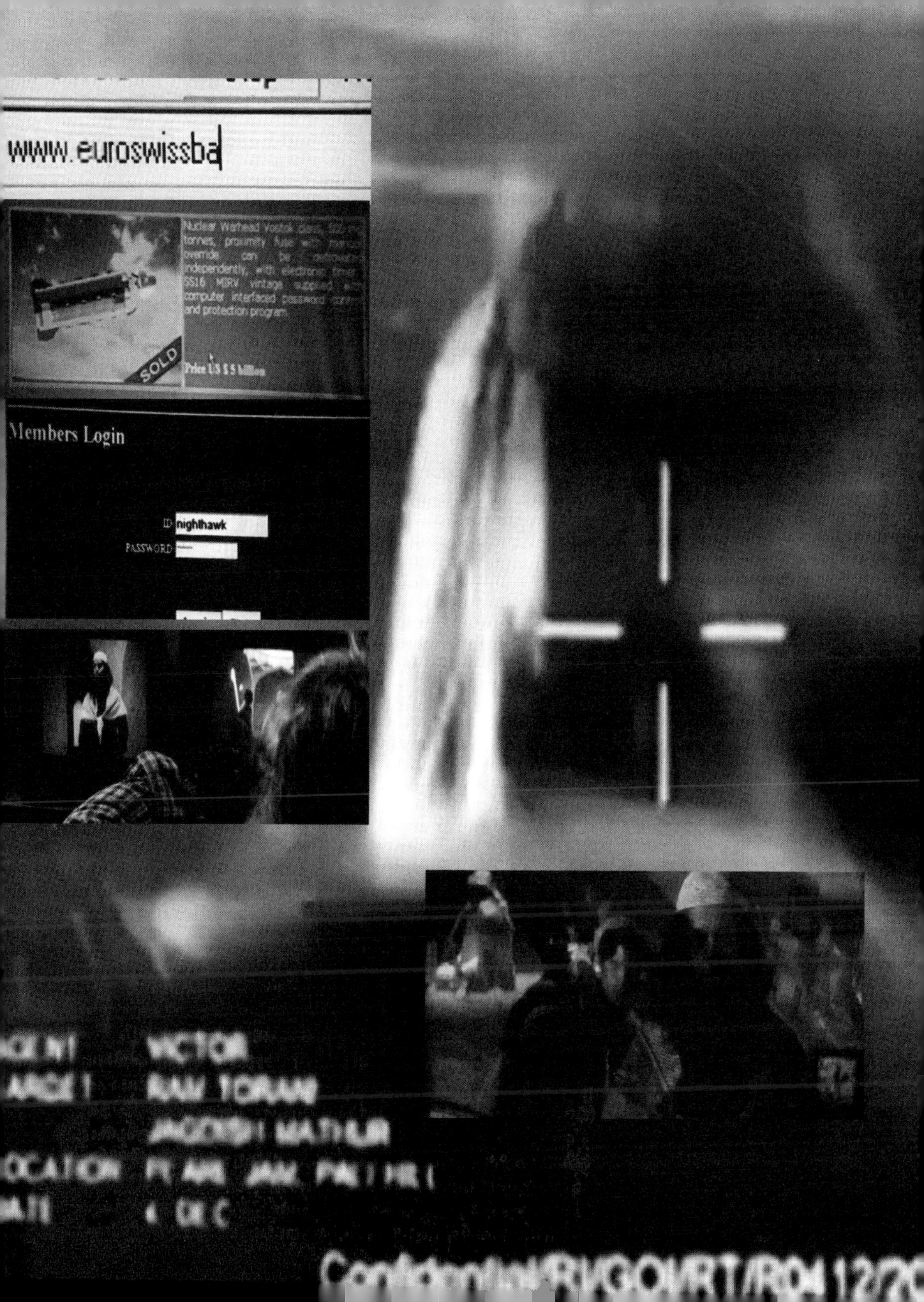
www.euroswissba
SOLD
Members Login
ID nighthawk
PASSWORD
VICTOR

as well, one being *16 December* (Mani Shankar, 2002), and the other *Khakee* (Raj Kumar Santoshi, 2003). *16 December* is titled so because it happens to be the date on which India won the 1971 war against Pakistan, and so is the date when, in the film, a Pakistani soldier-turned-terrorist wants to unleash a nuclear attack on Delhi as an act of vengeance. As can be expected, the film features a dedicated bunch of Indian intelligence operatives (including the model-turned-actor Milind Soman who portrays a surveillance expert with a special fondness for mobile phones) who foil the plot and save Delhi, India and the world from nuclear Armageddon. What is interesting about *16 December* is the way in which it 'naturalizes' surveillance technologies (CCTV cameras, satellite-based video surveillance, human surveillance through street-based 'agents' who happen to be an army of blind beggars with sharp ears, and mobile-phone interception) to produce a seamless evidentiary narrative. Mobile phones are high technology, the capacity to tap mobile phones is still higher technology, and truth flows out of higher technology. What is even more interesting is a remarkable sequence in the film when the entire intelligence apparatus connives to create a 'simulation', an image of a location in faraway Afghanistan on the floor of a 'film studio' so as to hoodwink a drugged and captured 'terrorist' into talking. This tacit admission of the practice by intelligence agencies of 'staging' incidents relating to 'terrorism' as a measure necessary in order to combat terrorists is almost like a sudden revelation of the 'repressed' narrative of how intelligence agencies actually create the realities that we think they are combating.

One might recall also the climactic revelation in the Sanjay Dutt–Jackie Shroff–Hrithik Roshan starrer *Mission Kashmir* (Vidhu Vinod Chopra, 2002) (with its own oblique references to the enigmatic figure of 'Ghazi Baba') of how a 'video simulation' of 'terrorists in Indian-army uniforms' (found during the course of a raid by Indian military personnel dressed as 'terrorists' on a 'terrorist hideout') blowing up a Muslim holy shrine in Srinagar in Kashmir is yet another instance of the way in which the 'production of images' is seen as key to the 'production of terror'. The deliberate confusion in the appearance of combatants in and out of uniform, of masked men who appear in the middle of the night and wreak devastating violence, in the pursuit of an 'image', who could be 'militants' or 'soldiers' or 'both', is a reflection of the shadowy realities that have overtaken Jammu and Kashmir. It is as if the apparatus of illusion that is the cinema had taught many lessons to the secondary art of the moving image of statecraft, at least in its 'terror/counter-terror' avatar.

Seen in the light of the extraordinary 'entente cordiale' between security and intelligence agencies and the image-producing agencies of the media in India, the film *16 December* becomes an interesting if unwitting source for the making of an oblique comment on the reality of '13 December'.

In a similar, though perhaps more conscious vein, the film *Khakee* (starring Amitabh Bachchan, Akshay Kumar, Ajay Devgan and Aishwarya Rai) actually invoked the figure of a 'rogue security agent' acting to protect what he thinks are the interests of the nation-state, by seeking to eliminate what we are at first led to believe is a 'suspected terrorist mastermind', a Dr. Ansari, whose appearance, demeanour and dignified silence, particularly in the first half of the film, cannot but fail to bring to mind what we know of S.A.R. Geelani. Ansari is later revealed to be someone who knows 'vital information' about the engineering of a communal riot by corrupt politicians (shades of 'Gujarat 2002 here) and his silence is an effort to protect what he knows so that he can reveal it at the most appropriate moment. Although the film follows the formula of good cops versus 'rogue' cops, it again points out the macabrely pantomimic character of 'war against terror'.

What do *Dil Se*, *Mission Kashmir*, *16 December* and the Zee TV docu-dramas add up to? They add up to the metaphorical identikit photograph of the terrorist in our heads whom we can recognize when we look at almost anyone's face, regardless of whether they 'stand out', or 'blend in'. This is the terrorist writ large as 'everyman' so much so that Zee News can use the footage from the 're-enacted' scenes of the 13 December film even in another programme, an 'Inside Story' special broadcast barely on 'the Al Qaeda Terror Manual' on the evening of 24 July 2005, in the wake of the London bombings of 7 July and barely days before the final Supreme Court verdict on the 13 December case on 4 August. This programme, which can be seen as a sort of do-it-yourself – 'how to become a terrorist even if you never thought of becoming one' – with details of how to obtain and mix chemicals to make bombs, the details of poisoning drinking water systems, how to form cells and conduct communications using codes, etc. (in a classic example of the 'system' actually egging people on to become the 'terrorists' that it can then frighten the rest of us with) again used the same scenes of the actors playing Geelani, Shaukat, Afzal and the five dead men. Though this time it did not name them. But anyone who had seen the earlier '13 December' film would immediately recognize once again the fictionalized S.A.R. Geelani hectoring his cell comrades in the sequence on 'organization of terrorist cells'. Just as anyone who had seen the '13 December' film would have seen the gratuitous and grainy images of 'terrorists' training under pine trees and of a televised 'encounter' with the late and larger than life 'Ghazi Baba' caressing a strangely shaped 'Scorpion' pistol in what was marked 'file footage'. Like a nightmare or a bad B-movie that condemns its audience to constant re-runs, the 'images' of the Zee TV-Special Cell collaborative genre of 'terrorism' refuses to give up its ghost. It returns to haunt our television screens, back to back with 'Crime Reporter' and a host of other sensational programmes that can only be described as a sad case of police-porn-snuff movies on late night but prime time television.

It returned to our screens momentarily when Geelani was shot by an unidentified gunman in Delhi on 9 February 2005: earnest reporters and television news anchors across channels, for several days following the incident, instead of asking why the police were constantly shadowing Geelani, his brother, his friends, asked why his advocate had thought it wise to save his life by taking him immediately to hospital and not wait for him to succumb to his injuries as she went through the process of filing, first and foremost, a 'proper FIR (first information report) as per procedure, with the Delhi Police'.

The night of 4 August 2005 was occasion for broadcasts on the final Supreme Court judgement on the 13 December case. Zee News produced yet another 'special', dovetailed into its prime time news show at 9 p.m. This time it was titled *13 December: Ek Saazish* ('13 December: A Conspiracy') broadcast on 24 July 2005. The news report had shown a high ranking Delhi Police 'Special Cell' officer Ashok Chand (in a split screen with the first ever viewing of surveillance camera footage from the Parliament on 13 December) offer an explanation of the splendid conduct of the Delhi Police in the case – after all, Afzal had been convicted as a result of the investigation. The others could not be convicted, because, as the reporter explained to the anchor in the studio, the terrorists had used 'high technology' – mobile phones and laptops. And what this implied was that we need better and stricter laws to deal with such 'high-tech terrorists', so that no one would be able to get away. There is some irony in the fact that the 'very high technology' which had helped the police write their chargesheets in the first instance, was now being blamed for their inability to fix the blame on, say, a Geelani, on whom, the report continued to assert, the 'needle of suspicion' stayed firm and unwavering, though somewhat unsubstantially. So, mobile phones help catch 'terrorists', mobile phones are also so high-tech that they can be used by those 'terrorists' and their advocates to subvert the commendable work done by hard-working police officers. Therefore, bring back laws, or make new laws that can make the task of using evidence from mobile phones and other high-tech devices 'easier' for the prosecution. In other words, bring back or make laws that enable phone tapping and surveillance on a generalized scale, that facilitate the faulty transcription and translation of taped conversations, that enable the manipulation or obfuscation of phone records, and that do not have to produce the taped evidence in court in order to obtain a necessary conviction, and that enable the airing and unofficial pre-censoring of 'interviews' of the accused in detention in the media while a trial is in process, so that television network news executives can have an easier night's sleep and count their takings.

In a remarkable admission, while playing once again the 'dramatization' of Afzal's indoctrination (once again from the '13 December' film) the Zee News broadcast commentator said: 'Afzal was a surrendered militant, he had worked off and on for the STF for seven years, and he had met Tariq in an STF camp in Dral.' Why was this piece of information which had been available in the court records, like everything else in this case, since 21 September, 2002, not made public knowledge either in the previous Zee News programmes, or in any programmes thereafter to inform the public? Any reasonable person would surmise that a person (in this case Afzal) who has been in regular contact with intelligence operatives of the Indian state, who has been harassed by them, who has had money extorted by them (as per his wife's statement made to a newspaper) must also be asked what relationships these operatives had to the sequence of events leading up to 13 December. If one needle of suspicion points at 'militants' and their handlers, whether local or across the border, then, clearly, another 'needle of suspicion' (which looks stronger, at least, circumstantially) also points to the activities and personnel of the shadowy agency or cluster of agencies called the 'Special Task Force'. Until these details are investigated, we cannot come to any certain conclusion about who Afzal is, what role he played, and why he has to die.

Why, also, were the surveillance camera footage of the vehicle seen proceeding towards the Parliament building about as far as the 'Red Cross Road–Sansad Marg' roundabout not ever made public before? Was it because the channel had to 'wait' until the case was satisfactorily 'closed'? Surely, any journalist or television producer would know that the vicinity of the Parliament and other sensitive government buildings have been photographed on CCTV cameras for a long time. Could it be that the white ambassador car we see in the surveillance footage had prior clearance to approach the Parliament, at least till a sufficient distance, before all hell could break loose?

In the end, more questions than ever remain unanswered. About the conduct of the intelligence and security agencies, about the conduct of the media and about our gullibility as citizens to be quick to condemn, first S.A.R. Geelani, and now Mohammad Afzal. Questions remain about the fact that news channels and papers can see it fit never to apologize either to S.A.R. Geelani and Afsan Guru for the deliberate distortions of the truth that these organs of the media were party to, throughout the course of the trials. Not once, did Zee News or any other news channel offer an apology to any of the accused, or to the public for the emotional stress that their broadcasts may have caused, even as they continued to highlight the 'plight' of the families of the 'martyred' security and other personnel who fell in the line of duty on 13 December 2001. Even in the telecast of 4 August 2005, Zee News considered it necessary to provoke the family members of one of the 'martyred' security personnel into an outburst demanding death for all the accused. It did not however deem it necessary to reflect on the fact that the families of S.A.R. Geelani, Afsan Guru, Shaukat Husain or Mohammad Afzal too had to suffer, first knowing that their loved ones were in prison, that they were brutally tortured, and that they had to go through the trauma of hearing that they had been awarded death sentences. The events of 13 December and their aftermath, along with the sad episode of the Kargil War, are probably the nadir as far as a deviation from media ethics and professional standards are concerned for a vast swathe of the 'free and independent media' in India.

In the end, the truth, or the truths (there may be many and conflicting truths) may yet turn out to be more complex and disturbing than either Zee News or the Supreme Court of India can permit themselves to imagine or ask. Zee News, or 'any other alphabet TV' is not asking, at least not yet, any of those slightly difficult questions. And if the Supreme Court of India is to have its way, Afzal is going to hang some day. Some of the answers will die with him. S.A.R. Geelani remains alive, and we hope he lives long, but as he has himself said, 'let us not celebrate the acquittal of the innocent, let us instead pause to reflect on where we are and how we got here.' Geelani has reminded us that his fate is not special, that there are many in his generation, in Kashmir and elsewhere, who have had to go through things that are as bad, or worse. And few have had the good fortune that he has had, to come out of it all, alive and sane. For their sake, and for Geelani's quiet and dignified fight for justice – for those still in prison, or for those who are facing the gallows, or have 'disappeared', or have turned up with bullets in their heads – we must all continue to ask some very hard questions, for a very long time. It is possible that the mainstream media will be a weapon in the process of silencing such questions. It is also possible that professionals in the mainstream media will become more aware and sensitive to the ethical and professional demands associated with their practice, and will occasionally refuse to toe the lines dictated in smoke-filled back rooms where channel executives, editors, senior correspondents and intelligence agents gather for quiet chats. I hope for the latter. The demands of justice and freedom in South Asia will depend on such acts of refusal to 'spin' stories out of blood and smoke.

□

cello: Ah, I see you have a splendid Morandi.
ner: Yes, I love it very much. The objects seem to be bathed in the light of memory
hey're painted with such solidity and real feeling that you can almost touch them—
might say that art has left nothing to chance. There is a calm that weighs on me. It
ace that makes me afraid. . . . Perhaps because I distrust it above everything. I feel that
nly an appearance, that it hides a danger. . . . They say that the world of the future
be wonderful. But what does that mean? It needs only the gesture of a madman to
roy everything.
rico Fellini, La Dolce Vita, 196

Framed photographs of two anonymous people in a frame-maker's shop wend their way through a street, a home and a stage, as communal riots rage. Ordinary people fake ordinariness to imagine a condition of normalcy. Kannada author **Jayant Kaikini's** famous story, **Amritaballi Kashaya** (1993), written just after the destruction of the Babri Masjid, forms part of the volume **No Presents Please: Mumbai Stories** (New Delhi: Harper Perennial, 2017).

Reprinted here with permission of author and translator, whose support is gratefully acknowledged.

Images: Atul Dodiya's Bako Exists. Imagine (2011, wooden cabinets with archival prints, paintings, sculptures and found objects), dedicated to Gujarati author Labhshanker Thaker, reconstructs the classic museum–drawing room–global exposition that brought the world into the middle-class home, as portraits of people, known and unknown, share space with objects of art, devotion and everyday use.

Insertion of detail of reclining man on p. 253, second appearance of meme adapting the 'spirit' figure in K.P. Reji's **Thumbingal Chathan** (oil on canvas, 2012).

Grateful acknowledgment to Atul Dodiya for the images, and the generous permission for the form in which they have been used.

13

JAYANT KAIKINI

Translated from Kannada by Tejaswini Niranjana

1993

UNFRAMED

Gangadhar of Golden Frame Works was busy with his annual ritual of removing all the objects in his shop and washing the floors with phenyl. He would dust and wipe the frames, the glass panes and the sheets of plywood and put them back neatly in the shop. His assistant, Vicky, was throwing away all the rusted nails and filling the box with shiny new ones. The shop had been around since Gangadhar's father's time. Frames for women's embroidery, for actors and actresses, for Gandhi–Nehru, for school group photos, for couples from long ago who stood on either side of a plastic flowerpot with folded arms – this narrow shop, where there was always sawdust underfoot, existed to frame them all.

In his father's time, there were only wooden frames. But now there were aluminium and plastic ones too, and coloured frames and glass. Among the pictures hung up to attract the attention of passers-by – pictures of landscapes, gods and goddesses, President Radhakrishnan, Tirupati Venkateshwara[1] – hung the photograph of Gangadhar's father lit by a red zero-watt bulb burning like a small piece of coal. For them, it was as though one day, after years of framing and hanging pictures, he had suddenly stopped his work and climbed into the frame above.

Gangadhar began to hurry. He wanted all the frames and the glass sheets back in the shop before the sun rose higher in the sky. One by one, Vicky picked up all the framed pictures ready for delivery. Gangadhar separated them into lots and arranged them. The embroidery, 'Welcome', button ducks, peacocks made from coins – these on one side; wedding photos in one pile; gods and goddesses in another; and individual portraits that had been blown up on yet another side. Gangadhar was always very careful about the last category. These portraits were usually of people over fifty, and were often brought to the shop by youngsters. Gangadhar could tell at one glance that these were mostly photos selected for framing after the person's death. Some would bring pictures cropped and enlarged from wedding photographs, or from other group pictures. These photos had a funereal look to them. Sometimes such pictures would be of very young boys and girls, or someone in NCC (National Cadet Corps) uniform, and the parents who came to fetch them would have trembling hands when paying their bill.

When the cleaning was almost over, Vicky placed before Gangadhar some pictures tied in cloth, and asked, 'What should we do with these?' These were the pictures left undelivered every year. Perhaps customers got transferred, or forgot, or had money troubles. Most of the uncollected frames contained embroidery, landscapes and gods, with a few being those of actors and actresses. As was his habit, Gangadhar started sticking slips on these, saying 'For Sale'. Since these pictures cost just the price of the frame, people who had acquired a new *kholi* (room) in a chawl (tenement), or moved up from a hutment to a chawl, often bought them. And this lessened Gangadhar's burden too.

But this year, as he was pasting the 'For Sale' slips, Gangadhar sat up in shock. In the midst of these pictures were three portraits – that of a woman past fifty, that of an old man, and that of a middle-aged man. The three did not seem related to one another. Different people must have given the photographs in at different times for framing. But those who brought them had not come back. And the pictures stayed here, like prisoners no one comes to visit. Gangadhar looked at them again. The woman's photo had been extensively touched up. A brush had been taken to the flowers in her hair, her *bindi* (forehead makeup), the flowery prints on her sari. The two men's pictures seem to have been blown up. Even though the pictures had been wrapped in paper all year long, the eyes hadn't closed, thought Gangadhar, feeling a strange fear. The woman's photo had an expensive frame. Then why hadn't the customer come back? Vicky laughed mischievously and asked, 'Shall we put stickers on these too?'

'Cheh, cheh,' said Gangadhar sombrely. Hesitantly, he looked up at his father's portrait. The ash from the incense stick had fallen here and there on the garland around the frame.

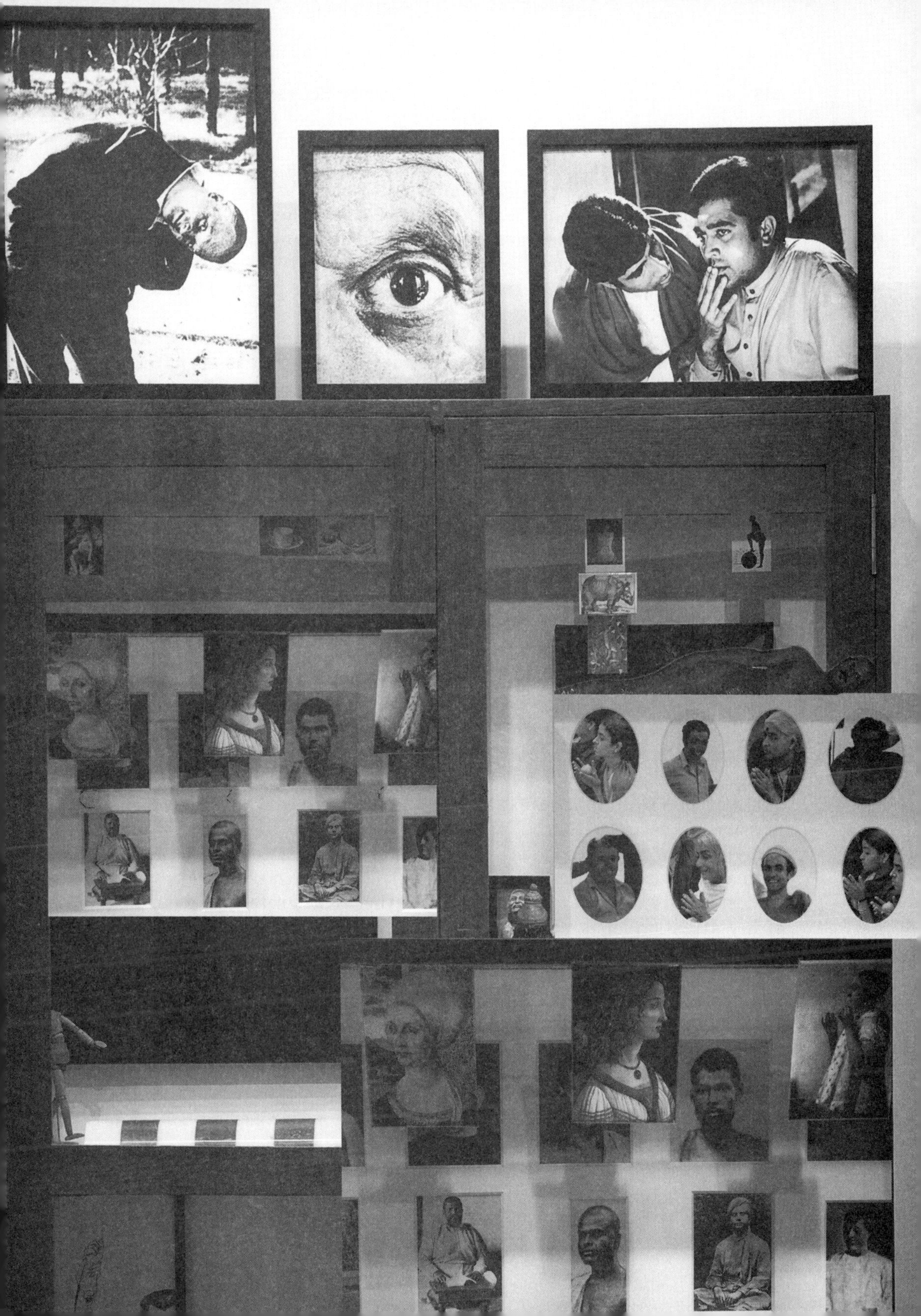

The entire afternoon Gangadhar worried about who might have left those pictures. Did they not feel the need to collect them, or had they also left this life behind, or did the urgency with which they had handed in the picture diminish with time?

'Let's re-use the frames and the glass, and tear up the photos,' said Vicky.

'Why are you in such a hurry?' asked Gangadhar. He would speak to Maayi when he went home that night, and ask her what to do. After his father died, Gangadhar would not take a step without consulting Maayi. Except for his father, everyone in the *chawl* and the locality, including her son Gangadhar, called her Maayi. She was hardly ever at home, but this was not a new thing. Since Gangadhar's childhood, she spent more time outside the house than in. When Gangadhar was born, her milk was sufficient for a number of infants born at the same time in the hospital. It was said that even after she returned home, she would go regularly to the hospital to feed the babies whose mothers did not have enough milk. Gangadhar's father was irritated by what he saw as her crazy behaviour.

Having fed so many infants, Maayi used to wonder how many of the young people she saw in the bazaar or the fair she had suckled. With Maayi usually looking after a boy in the neighbourhood who had jaundice, or nursing some young girl with a fractured leg in plaster because there was no space in her house, Gangadhar never felt that he was an only child. He seemed to be part of a large undivided family. And the fame of Maayi's *amritaballi* (medicinal herbs) decoction was another thing altogether. No one knew how and from where she managed to get hold of the herb. She used to dry *punarnava* and *amritaballi* and prepare a *kashaaya* (herbal decoction). Everyone with a fever wanted Maayi's *amritaballi* decoction. Those who liked the taste would come up with any excuse, like a fake back pain, to be able to drink some *kashaaya*. Amidst all this flurry, Gangadhar and his father were grateful to get a little of her attention and a morsel to eat. In later years, Maayi had developed another habit. She would go to the city's hospitals, seek out those who did not have any friends or family, and feed them gruel. The city's loom which wove lakhs of helpless breaths came as a boon to Maayi. Whenever she had some free time, she would carry gruel and pickle to the municipal hospital wards. She did this even on the day after her husband died.

At night, Gangadhar brought up the topic of his abandoned photographs.

'You have lots of space in your shop to hang up all those useless pictures of fruits and flowers and gods. And you don't have any room for these three poor memories?' said Maayi. 'If you don't want them in the shop, bring them home,' she added.

When Gangadhar's father died, Maayi had virulently opposed the garlanding of his picture. All this framing business seemed to Maayi like part of the funeral rites. 'Why put a frame around memories,' she argued. But it was not that she was stubborn about it for long. One year after her husband died, she said, 'Let's have one photo of his in the house. Is it enough just to keep him in our minds? Shouldn't we look at him from the outside too?'

Gangadhar thought he would display his abandoned portraits in the shop front. 'Why should you think they're dead?' said Maayi. 'Maybe they will come themselves to pick up the pictures.'

The next day, Gangadhar wiped the portraits clean, changed the rusted nails, and hung them up among the samples. Surely someone amongst the millions of people who walked by would be drawn by them, surely there would be some relative who would see them. Maybe at least one of them would reach its proper home. Vicky did not like this idea.

'Why put dead people's pictures in the display?' he wanted to know.

Gangadhar answered with ease, 'Why do you imagine they're dead? They might come in person to collect their picture.' Vicky laughed.

Soon, these three people who hung there disregarding the dust, the heat and the wind began to seem to Gangadhar like people he knew well. It also seemed as though there was some connection between those three – an old husband, a housewife, and her younger brother perhaps. Gangadhar went on stringing these wires as he worked. Customers who came to order frames looked blankly at the three portraits. What feelings they must have invoked in them!

One man asked: 'Are they your relatives? These pictures have been here for a long time, haven't they?'

'No, no,' said Gangadhar vehemently. He wondered later why he had denied the suggestion with such force.

One day a friend of Vicky's, a young stage actor called Bandya, was standing around the shops, chatting. '*Arre*,' said Bandya. 'This photo is so large, so clear. One can see it from the balcony seats too. It would be first class to have this on stage.' And he went on: 'The drama companies of this town need pictures like these. You know, when we have to show the dear departed parents in a social play? Can I have them?'

Since they had featured in his display for a long time now, Gangadhar didn't feel as strongly as before about them. 'All right, let them find a new use,' he said, agreeing to let Bandya take them. When Bandya offered to pay for them, he said: 'No, no money. But only one condition – if someone comes looking for the pictures, you have to return them.'

'Certainly,' said Bandya cheerily, wrapping the portraits face to face in newspaper.

As he prepared to leave, Gangadhar felt odd, and called out: 'One minute.' And immediately he added, 'Nothing. Carry on,' and sat down quietly in the shop.

I assumed that everything
would lead to complete failure,
but I decided that it didn't matter
- that would be my life.

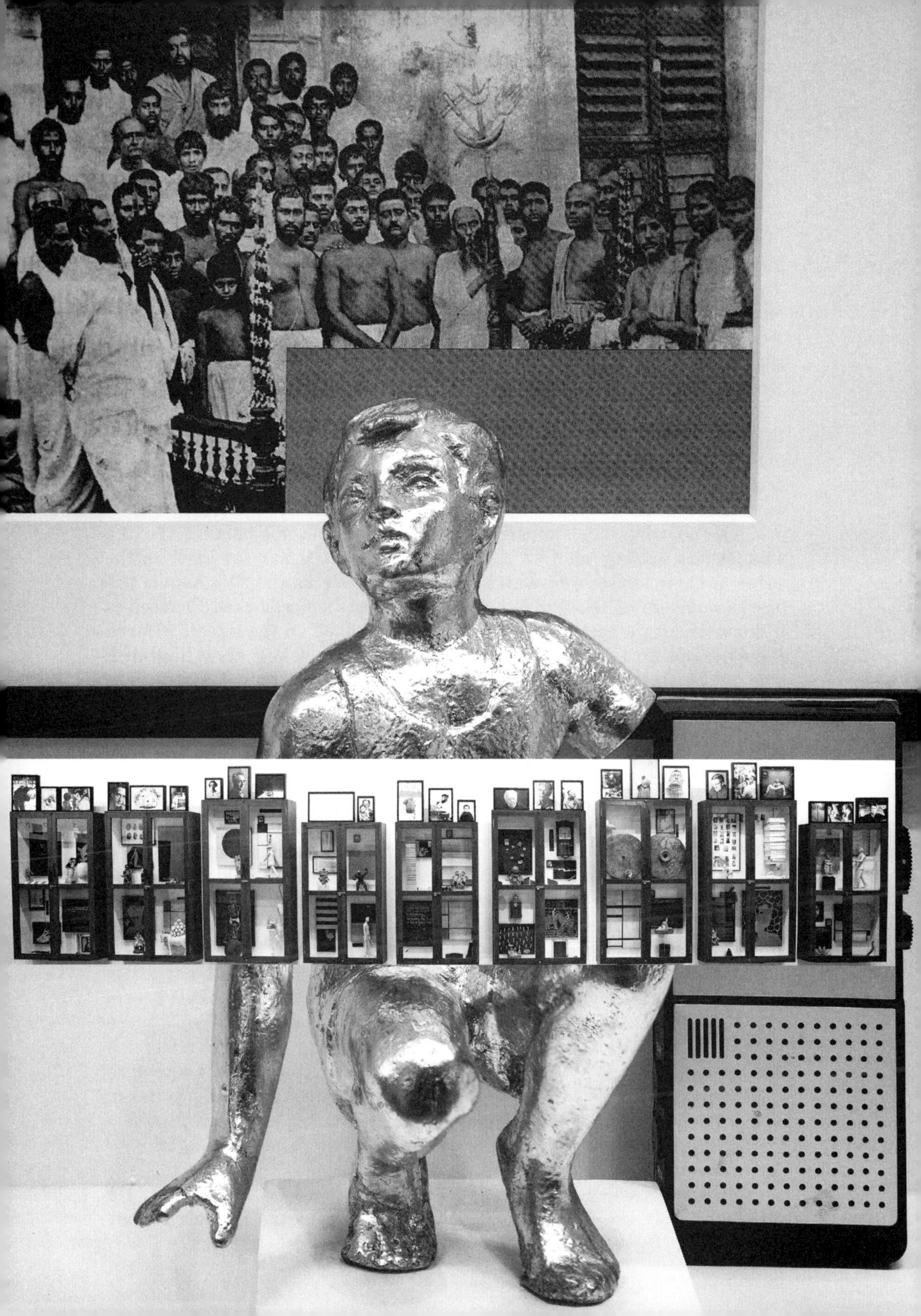

At night, he summoned up courage to tell Maayi what he had done.

'Son, what would have happened if they had remained in your shop is exactly what could happen on stage. There's no connection between those poor creatures and your frame business. Is yours the only shop in town? There are probably thousands. That means abandoned photos in every shop. Think how many there might be. If you all took an advance, this wouldn't happen at all,' said Maayi, laughing strangely. It was a laugh that put paid to Gangadhar's curiosity about which stage the photos would appear on, or whose parents they would represent.

In his nightmare he saw thousands of photographs being burnt in the city square. The housewife's touched-up sari, the veins on the old man's forehead – the fire did not affect them. Gangadhar sat up in fright, sweating. The light was still on. Maayi was putting dried pieces of *amritaballi* into a pot of boiling water on the stove.

The following day, communal riots broke out in some parts of the city. The leaders, having set two communities on each other, sat back on the sofas in their houses and watched appreciatively as the TV channel put up the numbers of those killed. Those who had homes, locked themselves inside without going to work, and those who lived on the streets offered their bosoms up to the knives. When names were asked, they hesitated. The art of stabbing where one plunge took the gut out of a man was perfected. In the hospitals, barbers smelling of spirit waited to shave those who would be operated on. No one came to claim the bodies lying in the morgue, or the people suffering in the hospital beds. Because there too one had to provide a name, and an address, and thus reveal one's religion. Once again a bosom bared, once again a stabbing. Respectable citizens phoned each other to find out if all was well, while labourers on the footpath stayed under the sky with their eyes open, spending the night like ghosts. Laughter was banned on the streets. Looking someone in the eye was banned. Schools wore the silence of hospitals. Ambulances shrieked through the night streets, requesting relatives to take away the wounded since the wards were overflowing.

Stealthily the shops began to open again. Gangadhar did not know what to do. Outside the suburban train station, there were pasted sheets showing the names of those admitted in the city hospitals. People were jostling to read them as though they were looking for their children's SSC (Secondary School Certificate) results. Who knows what they were looking for? Maayi, however, wandered from ward to ward with her flasks of gruel and *kashaaya*, not listening to anybody.

During this terrifying time of curfews, a boy came to Gangadhar's shop. 'Greetings, I need some help,' he said.

Gangadhar asked him to sit down and listened to his request. He speculated that the boy had lost something or someone in the riot, but that turned out not to be true. The boy's story was this: he was an orphan who had grown up in the city's armpits without a mother or a father. He had caught the pulse of the city, and shaped his life according to the clock tower's hands. Now he drove an autorickshaw. He had fallen in love with a beautiful girl. He would do anything for her. He wanted to marry her – had already bought a real gold *mangalsutra* (marital necklace). He had purchased a *jhopdi* (hut) with a running water tap in Subhash Nagar. The girl knew he had no family, but had told his parents that his father and mother were dead. If they learned he was an orphan, they would not agree to the marriage. So when her parents came to visit him in the *jhopdi*, he wanted to display the photos of an old man and woman. He was even prepared to keep the photos with him forever. Gangadhar was shocked. He didn't expect this turn of events. The boy seemed honest and helpless. 'If you had come one week ago, your problem would have been solved. *Cheh*,' said Gangadhar, wringing his hands. He asked Vicky about Bandya.

'How can you think you'll get those photos back?' said Vicky. 'Who knows which drama company they've gone to? Why don't you ask the owner of the frame shop on the western side of the station?'

Gangadhar took the boy and crossed the bridge to the west. 'No, sir,' said the owner. 'We shouldn't get caught up in this kind of mess. Above all, there's a riot going on. A time of death. Lots of work for us. In the next two months, we'll have to make a lot of frames. So why get involved in this kind of *lafda* (scandal)?'

Gangadhar regretted that he had given the photos to the drama company when they could have gone to as good a place as the young man's hut. 'Don't worry, your marriage will definitely take place,' he said to the young man.

'I'd look after the photos carefully. Our marriage will take place in front of the photos. We'd give them all due respect during the ceremonies,' the boy said pleadingly. Gangadhar thought of another idea, and went looking for the photo studio on the upper floor of the market on the eastern side. The studio owner did not listen to Gangadhar's request.

'What if tomorrow the photo owners come and raise a fuss about loss of reputation?' he said reasonably.

'Look here, sir, we're using them for an auspicious ceremony. No one can object to that,' cajoled Gangadhar, but the studio owner would not budge. Gangadhar returned to his shop with the young man. 'Come back tomorrow,' he said. 'We'll think of something.' The boy put out both his hands and shook Gangadhar's before leaving. When he closed the shop before dusk to go home, the neighbouring shop owners were reading aloud the news of the riot casualties from the evening newspaper.

When Gangadhar reached home, Maayi was filling gruel in two large flasks. She had put her *kashaaya* into a thermos flask. 'I won't be coming back tonight. I'm going to J.J. Hospital. There's a young man there, the same age as you. Patient Number 2132. The nurse was saying that he had been admitted a week ago with thirteen stab wounds. He has three fractures, including one in his skull. After he bled in the street for two hours, someone brought him to hospital. He's lucky – they saved his life after a number of operations. But he's lost his memory. Can't remember his name, his family, his age, his address – nothing. He's like a newborn infant. If I stroke his back and look into his eyes, it looks as though he's smiling,' said Maayi, as she put a pair of Gangadhar's pyjamas and a shirt into her bag. 'If I hadn't been there today, they might have discharged him saying there's no space for new admissions. Where will the child go in this tomb-like city?'

Maayi continued: 'If needy people come asking for clothes, don't hesitate, And don't give them torn clothes. See, there's your father's wedding coat. It's quite sturdy. Give that away too. It will come in handy against the cold. And my saris are here.' Saying this, she went away.

Maayi did not come back that night. Gangadhar took out clothes to give away. As he pulled out his father's coat, he thought how all the clothes would acquire a new life. As he lay down to sleep, Patient Number 2132 appeared before his eyes.

Having lost his religion, address, age, name and surname, and become a human infant, this 2132 is being fed by Maayi as he lies on the bed. Unprotestingly he is swallowing the gruel in small gulps. At the corner of his mouth, a sliver of a smile is slipping out. He is wearing Gangadhar's blue shirt.

When would the sun rise, when would he open his shop, and when would the young man in need of photos appear? Gangadhar waited anxiously. In the morning, he put the bundle of clothes in the neighbour's house and strode rapidly to his shop. The boy was there, as if he had been there all night. Opening the door hastily, Gangadhar climbed up on a stool. He removed the garlands from his father's portrait, unhooked the picture, wrapped it in newspaper and handed it to the young man.

As though he had found a hidden treasure, the boy stammered: 'This is enough for me, sir. Anyone would understand that the mother is anyway there . . .'. He shook Gangadhar's hand and sped away like an arrow.

□

Death, as ceremony and as mourning, as pleasure in this life and as the promise of eternal bliss in the hereafter, takes a specific turn as caste inequalities define both the Dalitbahujan norm and the Hindu exception. A pivotal chapter from Ilaiah's well-known *Why I Am Not a Hindu: A Sudra Critique of Hindutva Philosophy, Culture and Political Economy* (1996). Reproduced with the permission of the copyright holder and the publishers, SAGE Publications India Pvt Ltd, New Delhi, and SAMYA, an imprint of Bhatkal and Sen, Kolkata. Grateful acknowledgment to the author and to Mandira Sen for support.

Images: K.P. Reji's monumental triptych Thumbigal Chathan ('The Spirit of Thumbigal': oil on canvas, 2012), depicting the legend of how a Dalit used his body as a *bund* to protect the paddy field from the flood. The body has been used through Section II of this book as an enduring meme, appearing at different points as a 'data shadow' and as a museum object.

Thumbigal Chathan is a name, a title, as well as an ascription. Its contextual reference derives from the lore of subaltern resistances as a figure of heroic deeds, often physically challenging the upper caste domination. The figure of *Chathan* was eventually transposed into spirit worship as a deity who is both benevolent and malevolent, with immense power over the life of people, thereby complicating categories of the historical and mythical - Santhosh S.

Satish Poduval writes: Reji's masterwork is about Dalit 'sur-vival' or 'living-on': between mythic memory and historical time, between death-in-life and afterlife. Dalit kids with cutting tools dawdle across a habitat teeming with animal life, *en route* to Gandhi Jayanti festivities at school where they clean premises and overgrown grass. A ship floats by – originally the **HMS Hermes** during the Falklands takeover in 1982, then **INS Viraat** purchased by India in 1986, and finally in 2012 (just before Reji began his painting) in Kochi for its last patch-up. Against historical time is framed an undead past *(bhootham)*: green trees bracket leafless branches teeming with crows *(bali-kaaka)* betokening spirits of martyred ancestor-heroes. Past noisy ducks is the legendary figure of the *chathan* (spirit) of Thumbigal, a Dalit peasant believed to have been lynched for loving an upper-caste woman, his corpse dumped in a paddy field as a warning to others. An individual protects a breached *bund* by sacrificing himself to save his community. The Spirit of Thumbigal confronts us in a specific mode: with open eyes that lock with the viewer's gaze, and in a reclining pose reminiscent of the Buddha before attaining *nirvana,* the brutalized Dalit corpse and evil/troublesome spirit *(chathan)* doubles up as a wise and divine guide *(shastha)* for his community today.

What drives the boy's gaze as he stares at the ship with a hidden sickle in hand, what insight might emerge when the *chathan* interposes to look at us staring at that boy behind him? What ought schooling to entail? Is open defecation 'polluting', or 'natural' but also 'deprived'? What disavowals meet the stare of a sacrificial goat? What instruments of labour might double as weapons?

In the masterful stories of Dalit writer C. Ayyappan, ghosts both physically and metaphorically 'evicted' from history provide a calm but disconcerting testimony. Spectral speech insists that casteism, hidden-from-plain-sight, requires a new lens. 'The field of visibility that constitutes the grid of our mutual exposure and thus our identities is the domain of the social, constructed through rituals of mutual exhibition and recognition,' notes literary scholar Udaya Kumar[1]. 'This field is destabilized in the experience of forced, improper exposure'. Ayyappan's 'ghost narrators interrupt the enchantment of foundational idioms of the modern social domain (as their) ghost-speech, the litany of rage and lament with its unflinching grip on time, (becomes) the letter that Ayyappan insistently brings before contemporary Kerala'.

14

KANCHA ILAIAH SHEPHERD

1996

HINDU DEATH AND OUR DEATH

The way human beings are born is the same, except for the fact that the mother who gives birth suffers less or more according to her caste/class background. Our birth into a particular caste is accidental. We may have little control over our upbringing in caste-culture. After a certain age, however, we continue to live in the culture of our own caste through a conscious decision. Having been born into a caste, very few – we can count them on our fingers – consciously move out of their caste-culture.

Though it is not in our hands to decide where we should be born, it is certainly in our hands to decide how we should die. It is a fact that death is inevitable, but it is also a fact that such death can be moulded into a death according to our own ideas and beliefs. In the concept of death, and the experience of death, Dalitbahujans and Hindus differ in a big way. In our country there is Dalitbahujan death and there is Hindu – Brahmin, Baniya, Kshatriya and neo-Kshatriya – death. The notion of death here differs more than it might between people who belong to two different religions, say, Islam and Christianity.

HINDU BRAHMINICAL DEATH

The difference lies in the very concept of death itself. A Brahmin believes that life must be lived for the sake of death, which will make him eternal. *To live this way is to live a life that constantly thinks about death* for life in this universe must ensure a perennial life in the other world, that is, in heaven. The gods are being propitiated, time and again, to provide two things. One, a happy life here on this earth, which in philosophical terms is a *kshanabhanguram* (a life that survives only a minute). At the same time, however, this short span on this earth must also be made to ensure a permanent life of privilege and pleasure. So, for a Hindu, death is a transition from this *kshanabhanguram* to eternity. But how does one spend this very short life here? One should eat in the name of that god who guarantees a permanent happy life. One should eat all the best things available on this earth to please the god who bestows the life of permanence. Though this body merely awaits day in and day out the transitory death that will carry it from the *kshanabhanguram* to eternity, it must eat rice, dal, milk, vegetables, ghee, fruit and nuts in various forms. It must eat all this in the form of *daddoojanam, pulihoora, perugannam* (different varieties of rice foods), *pappukuuralu,* and other curries, in several flavours. Some curries must be sour; some must be sweet; *ghee* plays an important role in the cuisine. The vessel holding ghee (clarified butter) has a special place in this impermanent life. All this must be followed by sweets – *laddus, jileebis,* fruit salad, and so on. In the sweets too, those made of *ghee* occupy the highest place. In other words the *kshanabhanguram* body ought to be as fat as possible, with a rounded belly and unexercised muscles.

In this impermanent life, sex also plays an important role. To the gods, who enjoy the pleasures of the other world, the most beautiful women like Ramba, Urvashi, Tilothama and Menaka[2] were available. In order to facilitate this life of *kshanabhanguram,* of few pleasures, and to ensure a permanent life where more and more pleasures will be available, a son is indispensable. Since it is essential to ensure that the son is his and his alone, he needs a wife who enters his life when she is a child who has not yet attained puberty, and who will later produce a son. When a Brahmin died, if not now, in the past, to ensure his permanent pleasure in heaven, his wife must also die along with him and make herself into a sati (ritual self-immolation).

In the process of working for this most-needed death, two things are necessary: (i) leisure and (ii) prayer. Leisure in this context is a divine leisure. It must keep the mind focused on acquiring the permanent life and partaking the pleasures thereof. However, this leisure is also used to develop skills that negate the Others (who are sinners because they produce the

goods and commodities that prolong the life of *kshanabhanguram* that a Brahmin would like to end as soon as possible). Why should he eat the products produced by the labour power of Dalitbahujan castes which will prolong his life on this earth? He believes he is eating, not for his own sake, but eating for god who alone can ensure him *moksha* (enlightenment) or release from worldly life. Why should he indulge in sex which only results in another life, like his own, which he himself wants to end? Even this he does for the sake of god's eternity, which in turn becomes his own eternity. As I said earlier, a son is essential if he is to enter heaven, and this son is a gift of god, who is also eager to take this *punyaatma* (one who has done only good by not working at all) back to his kingdom. Why is the Brahmin a *punyaatma*? Because he has eaten all that is produced by the Dalitbahujans and also treated all of them as untouchable rascals. Thus, for a Brahmin, that is, for a Hindu, food and sex are two prerequisites of death.

The life of leisure, when supplied with food and sex, automatically ensures two things. One, it ensures that the *kshanabhanguram* is longer than the unsanctified life of the Dalitbahujans because it gets the best of foods. The emphasis on sex ensures the continuance of this life in his progeny. But this truth is systematically glossed over with the second instrument – prayer. Prayer provides legitimacy for all this drama. Prayer is a weapon in the hands of a Brahmin. It sets him apart from the rest of the masses. It is through this prayer that he establishes his hold over the rest of society. In a fit of madness, which might be a result of their lifetime alienation from work, life itself begins to look meaningless to them. They call this madness the life of penance.

However, when a Brahmin, who does penance throughout his life and who fathers a son to ensure a place in heaven, dies, according to the Brahminical notion, it is the day when god's call comes. This death appears very different from the death of a Dalitbahujan. A Brahmin's death is adjusted with the movement of stars, *grahas* (planets) and so on. Death is not supposed to be mourned. Immediately after the death of a person, the Brahmins around pour into the house. Some begin pujas (prayer), some begin *prardhanas* (recitations), some begin bhajans (devotional songs). The people around are not allowed to weep loudly; they can only do so quietly. After the dead body is carried out, only men follow the funeral procession. Women are not allowed to take part.

From the day a Brahmin dies till the twelfth day, instead of mourning, feasting takes place. While alive the Brahmin's body is sacred (this is the reason why others must not touch him except when doing *paadapuja* (that is, touching the feet and asking for his blessing). After death, that sacred soul begins its voyage to *swarga* (heaven) and the body becomes untouchable (this notion got extended to Dalitbahujans also). The priests pray for their fellow priest's soul to be given a permanent seat in the other world. Even the death of a Brahmin is a tax on the already burdened Dalitbahujans. The living Brahmins will have more feasts, which in turn will result in further extraction from the Dalitbahujan masses. In the beginning, there is a *shraaddha* (ritual of homage to ancestors) every day, gradually it becomes a month-wise *shraaddha*, and afterwards every year at the death anniversary a *shraaddha* takes place. Even after death, the soul does not merge into collectivity.

Is there any change in these notions of life and death among modern Brahmins? Not qualitatively. There are perhaps some quantitative changes, but the essence remains the same. Even today, an average urban Brahmin does not think differently from his ancestors. In post-colonial India, the Brahmins have urbanized themselves in a big way. The notion of *swarga* may not dominate their day-to-day life. There might be slight reversals in their notions of this life and life after death. Because of fast growing technology, an average Brahmin or Baniya publicly confesses that the life here should be lived with all the luxuries, but this does not mean that he or she reduces the emphasis on the permanent life in *swarga*. To achieve this, the discourse has been changed from *dharma* to merit. The state and the civil society are moulded to suit 'merit' in modern times just as it was moulded to suit dharma in ancient times.

Earlier, the life of *kshanabhanguram* involved only eating without producing the food that was eaten. Modern Brahmins and Baniyas not only eat the best and most modern food available in India, but also have the best houses. Their styles of living have been modernized. They now have cushioned double beds, air-conditioned houses, air-cooled bedrooms (depending of course on the climate). They have the most decorated houses. Even here, modernity has been cleverly Brahminized. The centrepiece in a well-decorated room is, not uncommonly, a painting of a Hindu god or goddess. A picture that is commonly found in the homes of Brahminical families is that of Krishna's *radhasaaradhyam* (as charioteer); another is of Krishna preaching the Gita to Arjuna. All this is now couched as art and stamped with the stamp of modernity. The largest number of colour TVs are possessed by Brahmin and Baniya families. The largest number of private cars (perhaps about 70 per cent) belong to Brahmins and Baniyas. The largest number of people who travel by air in India are Brahmins and Baniyas. The highest number of people who travel in air-conditioned trains and luxury buses are again Brahmins and Baniyas. Today, they do all this in the name of service to the 'masses'. They did the same thing in ancient India, calling it the service of god, done in the interest of *lokakalyaanam* (betterment of the people). Nationalism reformulated Brahminical philosophy, replacing the divine with the 'masses', as this was essential at a time when adult-franchise was on the global agenda. The change from 'god' to 'masses' is a trick of the trade. Expanding the scope of the pleasures to be enjoyed in this world, pleasures that are increasingly on sale in a capitalist market, is an essential prerequisite, and hence the restructuring of Brahminism is the need of the day. During the post-1947 period, enjoying political power became one of the pleasures of life.

This did not diminish, however, the Hindu ambition for the permanency of life in the other world. As Brahmins and the Baniyas exploit the Dalitbahujans from positions of political and bureaucratic power, and industrial and capital markets, there is a growing sense of sin which, in their view, may bring early death. There is a danger that after death, sin may haunt them in the other world too. This is sought to be overcome by constructing posh temples and establishing puja rooms in their modern houses. Both in the temples and in the puja rooms of posh houses, Brahminical gods – Rama, Krishna, Shiva, Ganapathi, Lakshmi, Parvathi, and so on, are depicted in modern forms. All this is to facilitate exploitation and also to prolong life here and in the other world.

Even in modern times, death is mourned with feasting and feeding people from their own castes. After death, third-day celebrations, eleventh-day celebrations, month celebrations, anniversary celebrations, all are occasions for feasting. Those who have done little except cheating and eating in their lifetimes, are made to be historically important persons. Their biographies are written, their photographs are publicized and their names appear in the media. Newspaper advertisements have become modern methods of 'upper-caste' celebrations of a person's death, and of the perpetuation of the dead man's memory. They have acquired crores to spend in this way. Even after a Hindu dies, living Hindus go on wasting social wealth on him. Obviously, they think this social wealth is their (Hindu) wealth.

THE DALITBAHUJAN DEATH

For Dalitbahujans, life now and life after death has a different meaning from that of the Hindus. For them, life is a one-time affair. This philosophy is expressed in the proverb, *puttindokasaaresachindokasaare* ('we are born only once and die only once'). A dead man/woman in a Dalitbahujan family is a loss in terms of productive work. Each person would have developed several productive skills of his/her own. Each person would have added some instruments for enhancing production. A Kurumaa[3] man would have discovered new areas of sheep-breeding. He would have improved the skills of cutting wool. A Kurumaa woman would have added to the skills of spinning wool. Several women spun wool, rolling the spinning stick on their thigh muscles. If a woman who discovered the technique of wool spinning, died in the process of discovery and in the process of putting it to

use, sometimes the process stopped for generations. In the death of such a woman the development of technology stagnated for quite some time.

In this philosophy there is no concept of heaven or *swarga*. All the descriptions of *swarga* that are part of the day-to-day discourses of Hindu families do not exist in Dalitbahujan families. In a Dalitbahujan view, life here must be lived for life's sake. Further, life here is related to work. The more it works, the more sacred that life becomes. The proverbs, *paneepraardhana* ('work is worship'), *panileenipaapi* ('one who does not work is a sinner') demonstrate that work alone makes life meaningful. In contrast to Brahminical notions of eating, Dalitbahujans consider eating as a part of life on earth itself. Dalitbahujan women demonstrate this philosophy in which eating is considered as a part of work. They say*annipanulutiirinaayi, okkatineepanitappa* ('all my work is done; the only job left is to eat'). The routine process of eating has no relationship with god or the sacred. Both cooking and eating are done at a secular and mundane level.

Among the Dalitbahujans, quite a considerable debate takes place about whether human beings have to eat to live or whether they should live to eat. In their discourses, they normally come to the conclusion that they have to eat to live. As work is central to their lives, every discourse relates to work. The context itself provides answers to philosophical questions. The life of the Dalitbahujans starts with work, but does not start with bed-coffee or bed-tea. It starts with cleaning: sweeping the surroundings, washing, taking the cattle to the field, tilling the land, and so on. In their everyday lives, the question of eating comes much later. A Kurumaa's life starts straightaway, attending to the herd of sheep or entering into the field, a Goudaa (caste of toddy-tappers) starts his day by reaching the toddy tree, a Maadigaa (artisanal caste, commonly working with leather) starts his day by taking his *aare* (an instrument that cuts skin) into his hands, working at his household industry of shoe-making. Usually they do not wash their faces in the morning. Face-washing and cleaning the teeth takes place at *buvvayalla* (eating time, around 10 a.m.). The conclusion that they have to 'eat to live' is based on their daily experience: they work first, eat later.

The act of eating is very simple. A woman quickly swallows some rice from the *buvvakunda* (rice pot) and some curry from the *kuurakanchudu* (curry bowl). She also feeds her children with the same food and carries some to her husband. The husband stops his work for a few minutes, eats his food and resumes work. This philosophy of eating to live is exactly the opposite of the Brahminical notion of living to eat. The gods and the goddesses whom they worship occasionally – Pochamma, Maisamma, Potaraju – do not appear to be gods or goddesses who order them to make obeisance in daily puja; they do not demand divine feasting. Even on festive occasions, eating does not involve even one-tenth of the ritual that the Hindu Brahminical gods and goddesses require. So, the number of items of food that appear in the ritual only indicate the desire of human beings to eat those things.

At a festival, the Dalitbahujans will kill a lamb, a goat or a hen and give a small amount (*padi*, ritual offering) to the goddess or the god once in a while, but life (in terms of prosperity) or death (in terms of eternity) do not figure in their relationship with that goddess or god. Fear is not totally absent, but fear is not given a philosophical justification. Further, 'freedom from fear' does not require the eternal protection of the goddess or the god. In other words, the notion of prayer as investment in eternal life is not the basis of the relationship between the goddesses or gods and the human beings. One reason for this could be that among the Dalitbahujans, of the two things that a Hindu expects as a matter of right – leisure and prayer – are absent.

The interaction of Dalitbahujans with land, water, forests, animals and reptiles, is in order to get something new out of these things. It is a scientific interaction and a creative one. This is the reason why in their day-to-day lives the earth is referred to as Mother Earth (*tallibhoodeevi*), the forest is referred to as Mother Forest (*adavitalli*), water is referred to as Mother Ganga (*Gangammatalli*). None of these forces demand prayer; they are forces that the Dalitbahujans constantly interact with. If any of these notions exists among Hindus, it is because of the influence of Dalitization. It is through the interaction with natural forces that the new emerges, and this newness through the addition of labour (not leisure) changes into a socially useful product. A Hindu uses every one of these socially useful products, but does not know how, or by which process, it is produced. He or she thinks that it is a product of prayer. The Dalitbahujans know that it is a product of labour. Therefore, here labour is valued and leisure is condemned.

Since this labour is combined with constant interaction with other social beings, it produces a language, a grammar and a literature: for example, a song is an integral part of labour. If any Dalitbahujan is not involved in work, such a person is known as *paniipaataleenoodu* (a person without work or song). The parallel proverb of Brahminical Hindus is *chaduvusandhyaleenoodu* (a person without education or prayer). In the Dalitbahujan notion of *paniipaata*, we find creativity and science; in the Brahminical notion of *chaduvusandhya*, education has degenerated into a non-labouring leisure activity, which causes human beings to degenerate. Dalitbahujan philosophy is not linked to the sacred. The reason for the degeneration of Hindu society, even in the modern period, lies here. Leisure and prayer are concepts that not only have different connotations in Dalitbahujan lives, they have a very marginal role in their socio-political formation.

What does sex mean to Dalitbahujans? Sex in these lives is not an activity of leisure-based pleasure but an essential social function. This does not mean pleasure is seen as antithetical, but the Brahminical leisure-based pleasure does not find any justification. A people who developed so many arts, never thought of developing, as Vatsyayana did, the arts of sexuality. For them, such sexuality has leisure-based vulgarity and it had no scope of acquiring a social base. That is the reason why the Vatsyayana type of exercise is absent even in the oral tradition of Dalitbahujans. For example, while the Brahminical temples are full of sculptures based on Vatsyayana's 64 arts, no Dalitbahujan temple – no shrine of Pochamma, Maisamma, Kaatamaraju, Beerappa – bears such decorations.

As against a Brahminical notion of sex, Dalitbahujans perceive the man-woman pairing as a social combination of collective production and collective procreation. Procreating children is a social function, and also adds hands to the labouring process. It is not that a son does not get better treatment than a daughter, and not that a son does not play a ritual role when the father or the mother dies. *Talagooru,* a water pot carried in front of a dead body, does play a role at the time of death. But a son is essentially seen as the caretaker of old parents, not as one who ensures a place in heaven. As the notion of *swarga* is not central, life after death is not important. If a person lives a socially useful life, it acquires meaning. Death is an end in itself. If someone plays a socially negative role, after death such a person becomes a devil and keeps hanging around troubling others. Thus the difference between *punyam* (virtue) and *paapam* (sin) is that *punyam* ends life forever, while *paapam* turns a person into a devil. Dalitbahujan castes perform third-day and eleventh-day ceremonies, but after that the dead people lose their identity. Anniversaries are not celebrated and the identity of the dead person is not retained. All the dead become part of the *peddalu* (elders who have passed away). The priest, though he comes and performs the *shraaddha*, never – even notionally – concedes an equal place for Dalitbahujans. No priest proclaims that in performing the *shraaddha* for the Dalitbahujan, his or her right to enter *swarga* is recognized. In fact, even the death of a Dalitbahujan is a means used by the priests to make money. In modern urban areas, Dalitbahujans do not touch a dead body. This is because their reference point has become the Brahmin family. They have internalized Brahminism.

Hindu and Dalitbahujan concepts of the death of women also differ. A Hindu woman does not find any important place in Hindu ritual hierarchy. A woman's death is mourned, but not eloquently. Among 'upper' castes, when a woman dies, if a man weeps loudly he is said to be unmanly. But among the Dalitbahujans, weeping aloud is possible. People gather around the dead body, and generally women outnumber men. I remember when my mother died, my father wept. The men around began to say, 'You are a man, how can you cry like that?' But the women intervened and said, 'Let him cry, if he does not cry now when will he cry?'

It is this autonomous space and public role of women that sets the norm for man-woman relations among the Dalitbahujan castes on a different footing even at the time of death. They provide a different social space for the death of Dalitbahujan women.

After death, in the case of women too, the third day, eleventh day and the completion of one month, are observed as *maashikam* (death ritual). After that, the dead person is only another of the dead elders. Among Dalitbahujans, the bodies of married men and women are burnt down to ashes. Children and unmarried women or single men of whatever age are buried. This practice is an extension of Brahmin practice. Cremation is an unscientific method of dealing with dead bodies because it leaves no history in the form of fossils. If the whole world had done what the Brahmin rituals require, the whole fossil history of human bodies would not have been available. Quite a lot of ancient and medieval history was reconstructed based on skeletons of human bodies that could be studied even after centuries. Burning of human bodies burns every evidence. I wish Dalitbahujans could have developed a different practice even in this respect by giving up the practice of burning dead bodies. Today, the practice of burning dead bodies is used by state agencies like the police and the army, to destroy the evidence of torture and murder. Brahminism must have evolved this practice in ancient India as Hindus killed several Dalitbahujans who had revolted against them to destroy evidence of torture and murder.

Dalitbahujans are not used to being photographed: the old especially offer resistance. This is because Brahmins did not allow them to maintain any history. Though architecture, painting and sculpture were Dalitbahujan occupations, a painter or an artist never left a history or a picture of his or her family. Ironically, it was Dalitbahujans who painted and sculpted the family histories of Brahmins and the Kshatriyas. But they were not allowed to retain a sense of their past in any visible form. This is another reason why the death of a Dalitbahujan means that he or she dies forever. But now we must change this situation. We must see that the dead Dalitbahujans would live in the form of history; that they live in art, in paintings, in sculpture and in literature.

Hinduism left no stone unturned to destroy the wisdom, the faith, the feelings, and the images of Dalitbahujans while they were living and also after their death. In this respect Hindu Brahminism is unparalled. Its inhumanity is unequalled. As I have shown, when alive, Dalitbahujans share nothing with Hindus, and even after death they share nothing with them.

□

SECTION III

SURFACE/DEPTH

Meanings of the Heroic and the Ordinary

Veena Das turns to the 'Bhopal incident' – the gas leak at the Union Carbide plant in December 1984, widely seen as the world's deadliest industrial disaster – and to its legal, political and eventually ethical implications. Her concern is to explore the category of the 'suffering individual', as the capacity of the individual to suffer came to be intertwined with, and used for, an astonishing variety of disciplinary, political and economic ends: as beneficiary of state action, as target of modern medicine, as legal petitioner.

This is a version of the text originally published in Das's celebrated anthology, **Critical Events: An Anthropological Perspective on Contemporary India** (New Delhi: Oxford University Press, 1995, pp. 137–74). Reproduced with permission of Oxford University Press India. © Oxford University Press 1995. The author's support and encouragement in producing this version is acknowledged with deep gratitude.

Images: Images from the Union Carbide plant after the gas leak, from Julian Nyca. Some of the images have been montaged together with newspaper reports on the Samsung 740N Syncmaster, against the silhouette of the 1984 sculpture **Memorial** (1984) by Ruth Kupferschmidt that still exists outside the Union Carbide plant. Other found images include the chemical spraying of migrants caught in the government lockdown in April 2020. The photograph **Tank 610 in 2010** (during decontamination, Tank 610 was removed from its foundation and left aside) montaged with an ink drawing references K.P. Krishnakumar's sculpture, **The Thief** (1985). Grateful acknowledgment to Wikimedia Commons.

15

VEENA DAS

1995

SUFFERING, LEGITIMACY AND HEALING

Can one analyse discourses produced by different agencies of the state to see whether there is in these an underlying theodicy, comparable to that of a religion, which protects the legitimacy of the state in the face of suffering and evil? Do individual members of society carry the marks of pain as the price of belonging to a society? The industrial disaster at Bhopal in December 1985, and the intervention of the state to provide redress to victims, provide the ethnographic focus here.[1] But first we need to ask what suffering means in this context.

In his classic essay on theodicy, Max Weber contended that suffering poses an existential and cognitive problem of loss of meaning to the individual. Religious cosmologies which claim that the world is meaningful and ruled by divine justice are threatened by the doubts that suffering generates in the individual, and such cosmologies must seek to answer these doubts. Theories of *karma* and divine grace are examples of such theodicies, in which religious beliefs are systematized to provide these answers.

Pain and suffering however, are not simply *individual* experiences which arise out of the contingency of life and threaten to disrupt a known world. They may also be experiences which are actively created and distributed by the social order itself. Thus, we need to examine the social mechanisms by which the manufacture of pain on the one hand, and the theologies of suffering on the other, become the means of legitimating the social order rather than being threats to this order. It is precisely their location in these domains which invites us to examine modern institutions with the same sorts of questions that have traditionally been asked only of religion, namely, how do these institutions maintain and signal their legitimacy in the face of massive human suffering?

TWO ORIENTATIONS TO SUFFERING

I will begin by making a distinction between two important formulations of the place of suffering in human life, and then illustrate how these orientations can give different directions to the meaning of suffering. I shall call the first orientation an *internal* orientation. This creates an elaborate discourse on the meaning of suffering, essentially in order to legitimize the producer of the discourse rather than the victim. I shall call the second an *external* orientation. This holds suffering to be accidental. It acknowledges frankly the inability of any theodicy to adequately explain why people suffer and, paradoxically, allows the emergence of novelty and the creation of a healing discourse. In the case of the Bhopal disaster, we shall see how the first orientation was embodied in the judicial and medical discourse, thereby providing legitimacy to the producers of the discourse (the scientific profession, the law court), while the second orientation was subtly repressed. The first orientation to suffering, the internal orientation, creates a movement out of two distinct but related moments. In the first moment, the injustice of a life in which meaningless suffering occurs, is recognized; in the second moment, suffering is converted into an accusation against life, thus making life itself something which must be justified. This orientation, embodied in the discourse of power, insists that responsibility for suffering must be accepted by the sufferer herself. This masks from the powerless the manner in which their suffering may have been manufactured and distributed by an unjust society, and further, by holding that they are personally responsible for what has befallen them, disallows the powerless to exorcise their suffering. Cosmologies of the powerless hold the capriciousness of gods and the sheer contingency of events responsible for the disorder of their lives; this, at the very least, has the potential of freeing those who suffer from having to take personal responsibility for their fate, even as it masks the real sources of their oppression from them. But in the cosmologies of the powerful, conversely, there is no place for chaos. For, if the contingent and chaotic nature of the world were acknowledged in these, it would have the potential to dismantle the structures of legitimacy through which suffering is

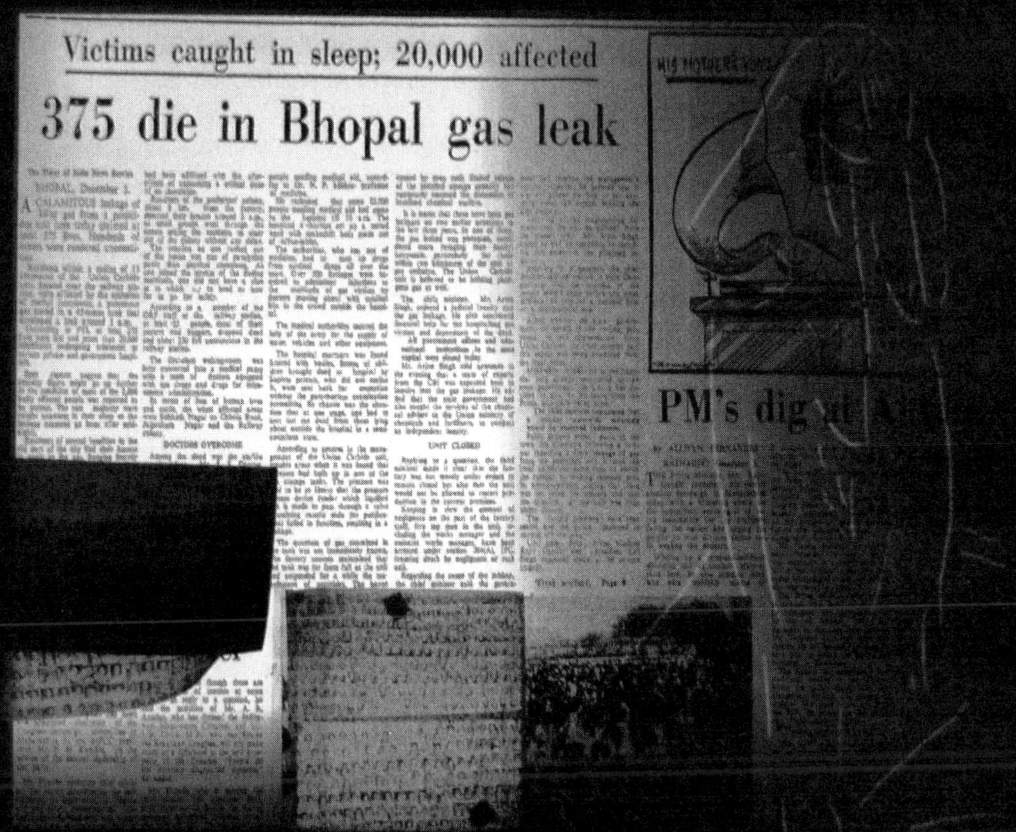
Victims caught in sleep; 20,000 affected
375 die in Bhopal gas leak
PM's dig

imposed upon the powerless. Clothed in the language of responsibility, the discourse of power ends up with the equation that pain is equal to punishment, and that the injustice of life, testified by debilitating illnesses which they believed were caused by their suffering, can only be redeemed by further suffering.

The second orientation to suffering, the external orientation, holds existence to be blameworthy but points to the capriciousness of gods, the inexplicability of the world, and the contingency of life as the reason for suffering. It does not make the sufferer internalize her suffering, nor does it posit a meaningful world or a just god or a comprehensive, scientific discourse within which suffering can be made comprehensible. Dare one say that it gives irresponsibility a positive sense? By renouncing a search for meaning, it paradoxically affirms existence.[2]

THE BUREAUCRATIC, SCIENTIFIC AND JUDICIAL APPROPRIATION OF SUFFERING

The industrial disaster in Bhopal was acknowledged all over the world as the worst such event in history. Unlike the crises created by the large-scale abduction of women or the occurrence of *sati* (which could be contributed to the ills of Hindu society needing correction by a progressive and civilizing state), the magnitude of the gas leak in Bhopal directly involved scientific, legal and administrative structures of modern society.

One of the best-known studies of the legal and moral issues arising out of chemical disasters was made by Schuck in the Agent Orange case.[3] This case represents the attempts of millions of Vietnam veterans to seek legal redress for grievous and debilitating illness which they believed were caused by their exposure to Agent Orange, a herbicide used by the United States Army to defoliate Vietnam's jungle cover. This herbicide was initially considered harmless to animals and human beings. Yet, as veterans spread over different parts of the United States began to experience similar symptoms, including delayed onset of cancer, a pattern began to emerge in which it seemed probable that the impact of Agent Orange on human health had been severely underestimated.

Schuck argued that Agent Orange represented a new kind of case which required judges to incorporate vastly altered quantitative dimensions in their understanding of tort. There were 1,500 networks of law firms representing the plaintiffs. The costs of litigation and administrative machinery were staggering enough, but the issue also called for a new kind of jurisprudence. Whereas traditionally the tort of personal injury cases 'were essentially isolated disputes in which law's role was simply to allocate losses between putative injurers and victims according to a moral conception that Aristotle called corrective justice',[4] in the new cases of mass toxic tort there were large-scale economic and social interests involved. A relatively simple and comprehensible body of evidence was simply not available in this case, and courts found themselves weighing risks and benefits for which individual tort-oriented jurisprudence – which depends upon mechanical notions of causality – seemed to be ill suited. In the Agent Orange case, for example, courts became sites on which the Vietnam War and its hardships were symbolically re-enacted. The same lawsuit could also be seen as a cathartic drama in which war veterans gave public expression to annoyance at their dismal treatment at the hands of their society: the court case became an occasion to comment upon the moral problems of contemporary society.

Other observers have similarly argued that chemical disasters and public response to them provide an opportunity to understand the construction of normality in a society. Reich observes: 'Chemical disasters appear by surprise. They represent an extraordinary event that disrupts the normal flow of social life. But paradoxically such crises in society create windows on normality. Through the windows of a chemical disaster, one can peer at political and social processes not usually accessible or visible.'[5]

One of the most important aspects of these political and social processes is that despite the pervasive uncertainty which surrounds such disasters – an uncertainty arising from the fact that the impact of toxic chemicals in the environment on human beings cannot be described in mechanistic terms – bureaucratic decisions are presented as if they were grounded in certainty. Toxic victims and their representatives often contest these bureaucratic definitions of illness and safety, and also try to expand the scope of the event from private suffering to the political issue of public policy. In the nature of the chemical disasters Reich analyses (contamination of cooking oil in Japan and animal feed in the USA), his emphasis is on understanding the transformation of private trouble into public issue. He also shows how bureaucratic rationality resists this transformation.

In the Bhopal case, however, the disaster was experienced right from the start as a collective disaster. Yet the inherent legal complexities of mass toxic tort cases, the power of the organized chemical industry (especially a multinational), the financial and organizational difficulties faced by victim groups, and the application of bureaucratic expert norms to the definition of disease, all came together in such a manner that the victims were denied their suffering. This denial did not occur through repression and censorship alone, but rather by talking about suffering in such a way that it came to be constituted purely as something verbal. Language came to be deployed as an end in itself, creating a discourse of which the function was to dissolve the concrete and existential reality of suffering victims.

THE EVENT

Sometime at night on 2–3 December 1984, between 30 and 40 tonnes of methyl isocyanate (MIC), stored in a huge tank, escaped from the Union Carbide (Union Carbide Corporation or Carbide) factory located in Bhopal, the industrial capital of Madhya Pradesh. The earliest descriptions of the gas were of a creeping, deadly, yellow, choking vapour which was intensely irritating to the eyes and lungs. Between 3 and 6 December about 2,500 people died as a result of inhaling this deadly vapour.[6]

Within a month of this tragedy, suits were filed by many American lawyers in US courts on behalf of several victims. Earlier, several American lawyers had flown into Bhopal and obtained powers of attorney from victims in order to pursue cases against the Union Carbide Corporation (UCC) and its Indian subsidiary. In view of the difficulties of pursuing the case by such a large number of poor victims against a most powerful multinational, the Government of India passed the Bhopal Gas Leak Disaster (Processing of Claims) Act (henceforth the Bhopal Act) in March 1985. With this Act the Government of India, in accordance of its *parens patriae* function, took upon itself responsibility for the conduct of the case, as well as for the provision of welfare to the victims.

The legal and litigational issues arising out of this case are important[7] and they will surely become part of the ongoing debates on toxic torts.[8] Here, I shall extract two kinds of texts from this complex web. The first is the medical discourse as presented in the courts; the second is the judicial discourse as embodied in two judicial texts, i.e. the judgement of the Supreme Court of India delivered on 22 December 1989 and 16 February 1991, on the constitutional validity of the Bhopal Act. These are texts in which we can see clearly the professional transformation of the suffering of the victims of Bhopal and the window it opens towards the understanding of how suffering of victims can become an occasion for the legitimation of power, exercised in this case through the mediums of science and state in contemporary India.

THE LITIGATIONAL HISTORY

The major events in the litigational history of this episode which need to be kept in mind are the following:

1. The Bhopal Act was passed by the Government of India in March 1985, consolidating all claims arising out of the Bhopal disaster and making the government the only competent authority, on the basis of the *parens patriae* function of the state, to represent the victims.

2. The case was initially pursued in 1985 in a New York district court, in which the Government of India represented that its judicial system was not competent to deal with the complex legal issues arising out of this disaster. The Government of India's strategy was to either force Carbide to submit to US laws on environmental protection, safety regulations and liability of hazardous industry, and thereby secure compensation for the victims in accordance with law and standards of compensation in the USA (which Union Carbide seemed anxious to avoid); or to ensure that Carbide, as a multinational entity, was brought under the jurisdiction of the Indian courts. This was important, since Carbide's strategy was to deny that any entity other than its Indian subsidiary, with far lower assets, was liable. Judge Keenan, in whose court this was adjudicated, declared faith in the Indian judiciary and bound Carbide to the jurisdiction of Indian courts.[9]

3. Hearings of the case began in 1986, in the district court of Bhopal. An application for interim relief was filed on behalf of several victim organizations in 1987, and the judge ruled that Carbide should pay Rs 350 crores as interim relief, which would be adjusted against the final settlement. Carbide appealed against this ruling in the High Court of Madhya Pradesh, where the quantum of interim relief was reduced to Rs 250 crores.

4. Carbide appealed to the Supreme Court against the Madhya Pradesh High Court order. It was while hearing the petition for interim relief that the Supreme Court, to the surprise and dismay of victims, made a judicial order on 15 February 1988 asking the Government of India and Carbide to settle at 470 million dollars. Part of the settlement deal fashioned by the court was immunity granted to Carbide and its subsidiaries against any criminal or civil liability arising from the Bhopal disaster at present and in the future.

5. There were widespread protests against the settlement, although it received the support of some important jurists.[10] It was believed by many that the courts had been pressurized or influenced by the Congress government, which was then in power, to issue the order, and that the government had made a private deal with Carbide. Regardless of the truth or otherwise of these allegations, the order was challenged on several legal grounds. One of these was a challenge to the constitutional validity of the Bhopal Act, since it took away from victims the right to be heard.[11]

6. The court gave its judgement on the Bhopal Act, holding it to be constitutionally valid, on 22 December 1989. The court was not required to pronounce on the settlement since that was to be heard by another bench; nevertheless, the court made several pronouncements defending the settlement.

7. Review petitions were filed in the Supreme Court, challenging the settlement on behalf of some victim groups. The Janata government, which came into power in January 1990, supported the review petitioners. The Supreme Court, in a judgement delivered in October 1991, upheld the settlement which it had itself fashioned. But it struck off the criminal immunities granted to Union Carbide, instructed the government to provide insurance cover to victims, and recognized the right of unborn children to reopen litigation in case further proof of the mutagenic impact of MIC on human organism became available at a later time.

THE VICTIM'S BODY AS CONTESTED SITE

There are certain similarities, as I said, between the Agent Orange and Bhopal cases. In the first, the judge had fashioned an overall settlement because he felt that, despite the moving evidence of human suffering, legal uncertainties would create further hardship for the veterans and would be risky for the chemical companies. There were severe criticisms on the amount of this umbrella settlement, reliably learnt to be lower than the chemical companies had been willing to pay. This aspect of the case concerns us less at the moment than the anger felt by several veterans, not only at the amount of the settlement but also at the refusal of the chemical companies to admit guilt, of the government to admit its responsibilities, and at the fact that certain damning documents had been returned to the defendants without even unsealing them. The words of the judge, as quoted in Schuck,[12] acknowledged this suffering:

> Broken-hearted young widows who have seen their strapping young husbands die of cancer, wives who must live with husbands wrecked with pain and in deep depression, mothers whose children suffer from multiple birth defects and require almost saint-like daily care, the strong men who have tears welling up in their eyes as they tell of fear that their families will be left without support because of their imminent death, the man whose mind is so clouded he must be prompted by his wife standing by with his defective child in her arms to go on with his speech, the veterans trying to control the rage that wells up within them, the crippled and diseased with running sores and green fungus growths, and the women who volunteered for field or Red Cross duty and now feel themselves rejected and sick with what they believe are Agent Orange related diseases.

But having acknowledged the reality of this suffering, the judge nevertheless felt the court was not the right place to pronounce in a decisive way on whether guilt could be unambiguously laid at the door of the chemical industry or the government. As he remarked, he expected at least the lawyers to understand and acknowledge the limited power of the court in the matter of establishing proof: 'It is likely that even if plaintiffs as a class could prove that they were injured by Agent Orange, no individual class member would be able to prove that his or her injuries were caused by Agent Orange.'

What interests me here is the question of whether we are witnessing two alternative visions of a court of law in relation to the sufferings of the victims. One view constructs the court of law as a public space in which a dramatic expression can be given to the suffering imposed upon vulnerable people. The public and dramatic re-enactment of private sufferings, in this view, would impose upon a whole society the necessity to recognize mutilated bodies and damaged minds of veterans and families, rather than hide these from public view, and to think seriously about the question of guilt.

The second view was that pronounced by the judge on the strictly limited nature of modern courts of law. In this view, scientific innovations of the kind on which the prosperity of industrial society depends involve some risk-taking.[13] While the suffering of the Vietnamese veterans was real, it could not be decisively proved that it was caused by Agent Orange. Hence, chemical companies should respond to the suffering, but they could not be held guilty for it. In fact, in an extremely ambiguous statement, Judge Weinstein asserted that the public could assume for the first time that there was some merit to the claims of those exposed to Agent Orange 'that they are suffering because of their war and post-war experiences'. The suffering was real, but the cause of suffering was diffused and spread over a range of war and post-war experiences. Guilt could not be pronounced on any one party.

At first reading, it seems that the Vietnam veterans were operating within a cosmology in which suffering, expiation and guilt were interlinked. They were formulating a theodicy in which they had suffered because of the wilful actions of giant profit-making corporations which callously exposed human beings to health risks for the sake of financial gain. In contrast, the chemical companies and the judge who fashioned the settlement worked with a view of the world that was contingent, the argument here being that the very process of creating a prosperous society exposes some people to risks; chemical disasters were part of the risk of living in a modern world. Questions of guilt were irrelevant in such a world. What was necessary was 'risk regulation'. Underlying these two views is a certain similarity: it is assumed by both sides to the dispute that courts of law are spaces in which a victim becomes a plaintiff by acquiring the means of proving that damage had been done to him.[14] But the very certainty demanded by the judges, within a context where the toxic hazards of chemicals were either not known or not revealed by the chemical industry, robbed the victims of the means by which the damage done to them could be *proved.* Victims were in effect being told to learn how to transform their suffering into the language of science in order for it to be judicially recognized. But if both plaintiffs and defendants were obliged to speak *only* in the language of science, then surely it has to be conceded that the proceedings in the court were being conducted on two different registers: one, the register of scientific speech; the other, the anguished expression of victims in a case-by-case enumeration. If the second kind of evidence was finally to turn out not to be evidence at all, then why was this suffering exhibited as display?

THE CONSTRUCTION OF MEDICAL KNOWLEDGE

Recall here that, at the time of the leak, very little was known about methyl isocyanate. Diseases caused by a single inhalation of methyl isocyanate in dose-concentrations as high as this were simply unknown to medical science. During the earliest stages of the tragedy, Union Carbide officials repeatedly claimed that MIC was not more potent than tear gas, and that it caused only surface damage.[15] The large number of deaths within a few hours of the leak were attributed to the behaviour of the victims. Dr Peter Halberg, one of the three doctors flown in by UCC as part of its relief operations within the first few days of the leak, stated that MIC created a heavy cloud which settled very close to the earth, killing children because of their immature lungs, the elderly because of their diminished lung capacity and those who ran because their lungs expanded too rapidly. The survivors, said this report included those who stood still and covered their faces with handkerchiefs.[16] While it is true that any activity which lead to increased inhalation of the poisonous gas would have led to greater damage, what is striking in the report is that it is not the character of methyl isocyanate that seems to be at issue but the behaviour of the people who tried to run when faced with this inexplicable phenomenon.

Between the period of the gas leak and 1989, several studies were conducted on methyl isocyanate. These were experimental studies conducted on animals, clinical studies on survivors, epidemiological surveys and autopsy reports. The production of this knowledge was primarily through three sources. The first was the large number of animal experiments conducted by Carbide scientists. The second were clinical studies under the guidance of the Indian Council of Medical Research

(ICMR), a body entrusted with sole responsibility for providing medical evidence to the Government of India (which was representing the victims). The third source was the experimental studies and small surveys on health, reproductive disorders, etc. conducted by certain independent doctors in pursuit of scientific interest and a concern for the victims. The victim groups were not in a position to generate scientific knowledge themselves. The ICMR scientists, whose work was simply not unavailable to the victim groups until 1990 – it was treated as confidential by administrative order – did not appear to be taking the suffering of the victims seriously. The reasons for this are complex and varied, but one of them is that the very process by which doctors become transformed from healers into certifying agencies seems to contribute to this desensitizing process.[17]

The first assumption in mass toxic tort cases, which is that objective scientific knowledge on the impact of toxic chemicals would be available to the judge, was therefore belied by the facts. Hazardous chemicals continue to be used by the chemical industry, and an assessment of their impact on human health only begins after an accident has occurred or after a pattern of disease establishes itself in repeated low-exposure cases. Victims are nevertheless expected to provide proof, linking exposure to the chemical with their disease pattern through a straightforward chain of cause and effect. Let us see how victim groups fared in this process.

First, on the basis of experimental studies conducted after the Bhopal disaster, it had been established that, of all the known industrial isocyanates, MIC is the most potent pulmonary irritant and the second most potent sensory irritant. Its toxic hazard is related to the fact that the vapour pressure of MIC is exceedingly high: hence even a short duration of exposure is likely to result in severe effects.[18] At higher dose levels, there were life-threatening manifestations of pulmonary damage among the survivors, reflected by clinical conditions of bronchi-constriction, pulmonary oedema, etc. At intermediate levels of exposure there was eye damage, including corneal opacity, and high risks of cataract. At relatively low doses, sensory and neurological responses were found.[19]

Second, although Carbide scientists tried to maintain that MIC had no long-term effects, other research showed chronic respiratory conditions, corneal opacity and an involvement of the immune system.[20] Third, review petitioners stated that while initially scientists had assumed that most symptoms caused by MIC exposure were reversible, epidemiological surveys concluded that symptoms in exposed populations had increased; that populations initially asymptomatic were now showing signs of lung and eye disorder, besides chronic fatigue; that period-prevalence surveys of morbidity revealed that exposed populations were ill for longer periods of time in the year than unexposed populations; and that children's health had deteriorated.

Union Carbide contended on the other hand that the medical categorization done by the Madhya Pradesh government had shown that, out of the 3,59,793 claimants who appeared for medical examination, only 2,574 suffered serious injury, only 40 suffered permanent disability, and only 10,534 suffered temporary disabilities. It was also alleged that many people had put in false claims. The petitioners on behalf of Union Carbide quoted from the first ICMR manual, which had stated that the symptoms reported by victims in 50 per cent of the cases for certain disorders were out of proportion to the clinical, radiological and pathophysiological features of the patients.[21]

The power of the medical profession to pronounce people as malingerers became starkly evident during the hearings. To take a few random examples, Union Carbide arranged the visit of one Dr H. Weill in a consultative capacity one week after the disaster. After a week's stay Dr Weill said that while he had not had an opportunity to examine injured persons, nor had direct access to lung function or pathological data, the anecdotal information collected by him enabled him to make an informed speculation: the symptoms reported by patients were highly exaggerated.

The most offensive biological argument was perhaps the one which said that most of the victims were suffering from malnutrition or a previous disease, such as tuberculosis; hence it was not possible to distinguish between a disease caused by the inhalation of MIC from that which may have resulted from a combination of factors, such as a history of lung disease. This was like saying that, because human beings were not like laboratory animals, the toxic insult to their bodies by the inhalation of methyl isocyanate – about which science did not possess definite knowledge – could not be decisively linked to the diseases encountered. One might even rephrase this to mean that those whose lives were already wasted by poverty and disease could scarcely claim just compensation merely on account of this further exposure to industrial disaster.

The population of more than 3,00,000 which resided in the thirty-six wards near the factory, went through total and abject suffering. Yet, they did not possess the language now required to transform their horror into the legal, technical and scientific forms that were being demanded as making sense in the political domain within which their grievances had to be addressed. In the medical text, the causation by which links could be established between the inhalation of methyl isocyanate and the disease pattern of survivors was only possible through a slow and laborious process. Even then, the links were likely to look only probable, given the complexity of the human organism and the fact that carcinogenic and mutagenic effects can take anything up to thirty years (or one generation) to manifest themselves. Meanwhile, the necessity to speak definitively in court probably led doctors to speak of survivors as malingerers – people who were filing false claims, exaggerating their illnesses, feigning symptoms. Even allowing for the fact that there is likely to have been a small percentage of false claims (given the strained economic circumstances of the affected populace), the callousness of this discourse is overwhelming.

THE JUDICIAL DISCOURSE

Under the Bhopal Act, the government used its *parens patriae* functions to represent the victims. Evoking this particular power of the state was an important judicial innovation since the costs of pursuing the case would have been too staggering for the victims. But we need to enquire a little more closely how the state constructed itself as a surrogate victim.

In normal circumstances, *parens patriae* refers to the inherent power and authority of a legislature to provide protection to the person, and property of persons, who are *non sui juris* – such as minors, the insane and the incompetent. The victims of the Bhopal disaster had been assimilated into this category of *non sui juris*. The circumstances were compelling enough to regard their lack of resources to pursue the case themselves as equivalent to their being judicially incompetent. The Bhopal Act was challenged on the grounds that, by its enactment, the government had constituted itself as a surrogate of the victims and taken away their right to be heard. The implication of this argument and the timing of the challenge was that, having usurped power in this manner, the government had used it to compromise the rights of victims by unilaterally arriving at a settlement and granting immunity to Carbide, against the expressed wishes of the victims.

The counter-argument to this plea was presented by the Attorney-General, who had represented the government in February 1988, and who had defended the settlement with Union Carbide in court and outside. In defence of the Bhopal Act, he argued that the disaster had been treated as a national calamity by the Government of India. The government had a right, indeed a duty, to take care of its citizens in the exercise of its *parens patriae* jurisdiction or in a principle analogous to it. In the course of the arguments he maintained that:

> Rights are indispensably valuable possessions, but the right is something an individual can stand on, something which must be demanded or insisted upon without embarrassment or shame. When rights are curtailed – permissibility of such a measure can be examined only upon the strength, urgency, and pre-eminence of rights and the largest good of the largest number sought to

> be served by curtailment. If the contentions of the petitioners are entertained . . . rights may be theoretically upheld – but ends of justice would be sacrificed . . . the consent of victims should be based upon information and comprehension of collective welfare and individual good.

It needs to be pointed out here that the issue of government acting as surrogate for handicapped people who are unable to make their own decisions has been widely debated in recent years. It is generally agreed that the surrogate has to apply a best-interest standard in making decisions on behalf of people declared to be judicially incompetent.[22] According to one interpretation, the best-interest standard requires a surrogate to do what, from an objective standpoint, appears to promote a patient's good, without reference to the patient's actual supposed preferences. This view has been challenged on the grounds that a surrogate is acting in the best interests of the patient only if he tries to replicate the decisions that a patient would have made had she been capable. The evocation of objectively determined interests, as against subjectively expressed preferences, can act as a mask for exercising power in the name of doing good.

The same question now presented itself before the Supreme Court. In its earlier judicial order, the Supreme Court had claimed it acted in the best interests of the victims. But the victims were contesting this. How could the court defend the actions of the government, as well as its own actions promoting the settlement, when the victims themselves were protesting against them? It was in this context that the 'suffering' and 'agony' of the victims seems to have found its *raison d'etre:* it allowed the judiciary to create a verbal discourse which legitimized the position of the government as guardian of the people and the judiciary as protector of the rule of law.

In their judgement, the judges upheld the constitutional validity of the Bhopal Act. They declared: 'Our Constitution makes it imperative for the State to secure to all its citizens the rights guaranteed by the Constitution and when the citizens are not in a position to assert and secure these rights, the State must come into the picture and protect and fight for the rights of the citizens.' This is a principle which expands greatly the power of the state to act as guardian and deprive people of their normal constitutional rights, including the right to petition a court of law. Aware of this contradiction, the judges further stated:

It is necessary for the state to ensure the fundamental rights in conjunction with the Directive Principles of State policy to effectively discharge its obligations and for this purpose, *if necessary to deprive some rights and privileges of the individual victims in order to protect these rights better and to secure them further* (emphasis added).

But in what way had the meagre settlement served to secure the rights of the victims or led to the 'greater good of greater numbers'– the utilitarian principle formulated by the Attorney-General and the judges at several times in the course of the argument?

The judgement said that the court had, in its earlier judicial order instructing both parties to settle, acted in the interest of the victims. 'The basic consideration', the court recorded, 'motivating the conclusion of the settlement was the compelling need for urgent relief, and the Court set out the law's delays duly considering that there was a compelling duty both judicial and humane, to secure immediate relief for the victims.' The court simply omitted to mention that the urgent need for immediate relief was precisely what the victims had asked for in their petition for interim relief, which had been upheld by the lower courts!

On the question of why the court had not found it fit to invite the opinion of the victims themselves about the proposed settlement before passing the judicial order, the judges noted that this had been because of a certain degree of unease and scepticism, expressed by the learned counsels of both parties, 'at the prospects of success in view of their past experience of such negotiations when, as they stated, there had been uninformed and even irresponsible criticism of the attempts to settlement.' So, we now discover that the first imperative to arrive at a meagre settlement was the 'suffering' of the victims. **The second imperative to do this with complete secrecy, and to present the victims with a *fait accompli*, was the irresponsibility and inability of the victims to understand the issues that affected their own lives.**

How had the court arrived at the particular sum of 470 million dollars as adequate compensation for the 300,000 victims known to have been affected? The fact is that medical examination of only half the claimants had been completed at the time that the court ordered settlement, and this through procedures highly questionable.[23] Similarly, medical folders which recorded the basis on which a victim's status was determined for purposes of compensation were not made available to them or to their representatives on grounds of medical secrecy. These arbitrary bureaucratic decisions could not be contested by the victims.

After the 22 December judgement, certain victim groups were able to secure some primary documentation on the procedures through which the extent of victimage was estimated. It was found that even the figures produced in the Supreme Court during a hearing by the Madhya Pradesh Council were arrived at after the settlement, and therefore could not have been the basis for the settlement. Further, the procedure by which the status of a claim was determined was based on a kind of scoring system: each symptom was given a score, and finally these scores were aggregated. Despite the fact that medical journals have constantly used the rhetoric of MIC being the most lethal gas known to man, the scoring system used the analogy of organ-by-organ injury rather than systematic damage as a result of toxic insult. To compound it all, patients who could not produce documentary evidence in the form of records of hospital admission, or proof of having been treated in the first few days of the gas disaster, were declared 'uninjured' regardless of the state of their health at the time of examination.[24] It does not require any familiarity with mass disaster to know that the immediate task at the time of a disaster is to reach help rather than keep meticulous individual records. Yet all this incredible and appalling disregard of human and medical ethics has been justified on the grounds of bureaucratic and legal necessity. When repeatedly challenged on how the court had arrived at its own particular sum for settlement, the court, in its own clarificatory orders, noted that the reasonableness of the sum was based not only on the individual quantification 'but the idea of reasonableness for the present purpose was necessarily a broad and general estimate in the context of a settlement of the dispute and not on the basis of an accurate assessment of adjudication'. In other words, whereas the victims were irresponsible and uninformed when they inquired about the basis on which the court had arrived at its estimate of victimage and the principles by which it determined compensation, the court itself had only been motivated by humane considerations in refusing to divulge medical information on the nature and extent of damage caused by MIC.

In its final transformation, then, the suffering of the victims was considered sufficient reason to justify the settlement and uphold the usurpation of power by the government. The principle on which this was defended was that the Bhopal Act could be upheld if it has been proved to be in the interests of the victims (the proof of the pudding is in the eating, as the learned judges stated). Therefore, although the judges conceded that justice did not *appear* to have been done (since the victims were not given a hearing), they also argued that justice was nevertheless *done* – on the principle that a small harm can be tolerated for a larger good. The 'suffering' of the victims was a useful narrative device which could be evoked to explain why victims had not been consulted; why their protests over the settlement could be redefined as the actions of irresponsible and ignorant people; to explain away the fact that the judges had not felt obliged to ask the government and its medical establishment to place for public scrutiny what it had accomplished by way of relief and help; to ignore the knowledge that had been generated on the impact of the deadly isocyanate on the health of people; and finally, to obfuscate the fact that they had completely failed to fix the responsibility for the accident and had thus converted the issue of multinational liability into that of multinational charity.

Outlook

In the course of the judgement, it was evident that there was no lack of concern for the impact of a hazardous industry on *society in general*; it was only the interests of these particular victims that could not be fully protected. There were acute reflections on the dangers arising from hazardous technology. The judges stated that there were vital juristic principles which touched upon problems emerging 'from the pursuit of such dangerous technologies for economic gains by multinationals'. The learned judges also noted the need to evolve a national policy to protect national interests from the ultra-hazardous pursuit of economic gain. Only the sufferings of people came in the way of evolving these juristic principles:

> In the present case, the compulsions of the need for immediate relief to tens of thousands of suffering victims could not wait till these questions, vital though these might be, were resolved in due course of judicial proceedings; and the tremendous suffering of thousands of persons compelled this court to move into the direction of immediate relief, which, this Court thought, should not be subordinated to the uncertain principles of law . . .

In all these discussions at the judicial and bureaucratic levels, 'victim' finally became a completely abstract category. The judges did not seem to have any clear idea of how many victims there were, nor the extent of havoc caused by MIC poisoning on their bodies and minds. In a moving speech I heard in Bhopal, protesting the settlement, one illiterate woman stated: 'We only ask the judges for one thing – please come here and count us.' In the judicial discourse, however, every reference to victims and their suffering only served to reify 'suffering' while dissolving the real victims in order that they could be reconstituted into nothing more than verbal objects.

THE SEQUEL

The judgement of 22 December had concluded on a note of judicial humility: 'It is well to remember . . . time has upset many fighting faiths . . . and one must always wager one's salvation upon some prophecy based on uncertain knowledge. . . . Our knowledge changes: our perception of truth also changes.'

The judges were not required to defend the settlement when giving their judgement on the constitutional validity of the Bhopal Act. Yet, they went to some lengths to defend the settlement on the grounds that suffering needed immediate amelioration. It is interesting to compare this judgement with the detailed 3 October judgement of Justices K.N. Singh, M.N. Venkatachalliah and N.D. Ojha on the review petitions filed on behalf of several victim organizations challenging the settlement on constitutional, legal, factual and humanitarian grounds. One of the main contentions of these review petitions was that the court had been misled by the Government of India regarding the number of victims and the type of injuries caused to them by the single-dose inhalation of methyl isocyanate. The petitioners contended that the ultra-hazardous nature and long-term impact of the lethal gas had not been understood by the court when it fashioned the settlement, and that the so-called medical examination carried out by the Directorate of Claims, Madhya Pradesh, on more than 3,00,000 people was superficial and likely to mislead.

The judgement by the three learned justices, it seems to me, conceded that the long-term hazards posed by methyl isocyanate had not been grasped, that the views of the victims had not been ascertained, and that the costs of medical supervision for victims exposed to the toxic gas – even if they were not showing present symptoms would be legitimately claimed by them. Indeed, for the judges to concede that methyl isocyanate caused injury to the immune system was a staggering admission in view of the fact that Carbide lawyers had maintained that it did not have any long-term effects. The judges even suggested that:

> What is, however, implicit in this stand of the UCC is the admission that exposure to MIC has such grim implications for the future; but UCC urges that the Union of India must be deemed to have put all these into the scales at the time it settled the claim for 470 million US dollars.

In view of the admission on the ultra-hazardous character of methyl isocyanate, how did the judges defend the amount for settlement? They made two major arguments in this regard. First, they conceded the point made by Carbide lawyers that any long-term effects of methyl isocyanate were known to the government at the time of the settlement, and therefore that the government must bear future costs. Second, the UCC had relied heavily upon an earlier affidavit of the Additional Director of Claims, Madhya Pradesh, that medical categorization of survivors was meticulous and reliable. The affidavit of the Additional Director of Claims had relied upon generalities and on an evocation of magnitude as metaphor.

> The Medical Documentation Exercise has been a unique effort . . . Hundreds of graduate and postgraduate doctors assisted by qualified and paramedical staff have examined the claimants with the help of sophisticated equipments. It cannot be reasonably contended that all of them have colluded with the government to distort the whole exercise?[25]

In this affidavit there was an extensive use of magnitude (hundreds of doctors), but no response to specific questions regarding pulmonary-function tests or exercise-tolerance tests was forthcoming. In the final analysis, it seems to me that the government used its very special position as *parens patriae* to obtain the right to represent victims; simultaneously, it used its police functions to declare the research being conducted by ICMR scientists as confidential, even having declared at one stage that giving victims access to their own medical folders would not be conducive to the maintenance of public order. This very secrecy protected the medical documentation from serious peer review and gave it authority in the eyes of the law. It is interesting that, because the experimental research conducted by Carbide scientists was available in medical journals, isolated doctors in their small laboratories, without commanding the resources of Carbide, could nevertheless set up experiments which contradicted the results obtained by Carbide's scientists.[26]

Similarly Dr Daya Verma, an expatriate Indian scientist teaching in Canada's McGill University, came to Bhopal out of sheer concern for the victims. He arrived immediately after the disaster and conducted a survey on spontaneous abortion following exposure to MIC in different localities around the Carbide factory, with the help of school children. Similarly, he conducted *in vitro* and *in vivo* studies on rats and guinea pigs showing that foetal loss was not only due to maternal distress but also because MIC directly enters the bloodstream of the foetus. Similar counter-arguments could not be adduced against the ICMR studies because these were presented to the courts as confidential documents. What gains the victims were able to make in having the courts recognize the seriousness of the disease were primarily a consequence of their being able to counter the claims of the official establishment, and often read the medical text produced by this establishment 'against the grain'. At the very least, the victims were able to challenge the monopolistic claim over knowledge by the ICMR establishment and the Director of Claims. Their defeat, paradoxically, was because the Government of Madhya Pradesh, having established both its sole authority over the documentation and categorization of claims through the Bhopal Act and the secrecy of the medical reports, was able to create a monopolistic control over knowledge. From the point of view of the victims, this way of dealing with the uncertainties of toxic hazard was not the best, since complete control over information could be established by the government on the plea that revealing information was not in the interest of the victims!

But there were two important gains that victim groups achieved by their insistence upon a right to be heard and to present the medical evidence, independently of how the government had presented it in court. From the point of view of public policy, the recognition by the court that populations exposed to an unknown toxic hazard had a right to recover costs of medical surveillance was important. The judges endorsed the views of the victims, stating that 'The exposed population may not have manifested any immediate symptomatic medical status. But the long-term latency period of toxic injuries renders the medical surveillance costs a claim even though ultimately the exposed persons may not actually develop the apprehended complications.' They endorsed an earlier judgement, in the case of Ayers vs. Jackson (525 A 21.287 [NJ. 1987]), that 'the claim for medical surveillance expenses stands on a different footing from the claim based on enhanced risk'. They set aside the plea of Nariman, the Carbide lawyer, that the only form of compensation known to common law is a lump-sum award – a once-and-for-all determination of compensation for all plaintiff losses, past, present and future. The judges seem to have been aware that the amount of settlement was not adequate to cover this, but, being constrained to defend a settlement they had themselves fashioned, they simply appealed to UCC and UCIL and received their consent to provide a hospital for the medical care of patients.

Similarly, it is of some importance that rights of unborn children and people who may become patients later were recognized through a kind of reopening clause, and by the direction to the government to provide insurance cover to the exposed population.

The important question in this regard then pertains to how the scientific profession, the bureaucracy and the courts respond to uncertainty. This crucial point was made by Reich when he said that, in the case of chemical disasters, bureaucrats and professionals speak as if certainty is possible, whereas the facts of the case are often that by the very nature of the event, certainty is an illusion.[27]

In some ways, the contrast set up by Schuck (1987) and many others, between traditional tort law which addresses the problem of injury, and mass toxic tort cases which may be more meaningfully modelled on public law, represents the two poles within which the question of justice to victims must be resolved. Clearly, there are questions of regulation of large economic and social interests in the case of mass toxic tort cases; these are not so evident in the case of personal injury cases. But the personal kind of injury, though experienced by individuals, reflects social conditions and choices regarding technology and production relations: witness, for instance, the increasing number of accidents sustained by agricultural labourers after the mechanization of agriculture. Conversely, though accidents of the kind witnessed in Bhopal involve a large aggregate of people, questions of justice to the individual cannot simply be ignored. The judgement of October 1991 was a movement between these two questions.

In the judgement on the validity of the Bhopal Act, the court tried to signal its legitimacy by using the suffering of the people as a trope for defending the settlement. And so they wrote:

> The whole issue, shorn of legal subtleties, is a moral and humanitarian one. What was transacted with the court's assistance between the Union of India and the UCC on the other is now sought to be made binding on the tens of thousands of innocent victims who, as the law has now declared, had a right to be heard before the settlement could be reached or approved .... Any paternalistic condescension that what has been done is for their own good is out of place. Either they should have been heard before a settlement was approved in accordance with the law declared by this Court, or it, at least, should have become demonstrable in a process in which they have a reasonable sense of participation that the settlement has been to their evident advantage or, at least the adverse consequences are effectively neutralized. The ultimate directions on point J that we propose to issue will, we think, serve to achieve the last mentioned expectation. Legal and procedural technicalities should yield to the paramount considerations of justice and humanity.

The Agent Orange case took on the dimensions of a morality play in which a cathartic drama was enacted about the Vietnam War and America's dismal treatment of soldiers who fought it. The Bhopal case did not serve this purpose, but the court's defence of itself did have the rudiments of a morality play. The case failed to provide an occasion for the interrogation of multinationals, as also of the scientific community and its responsibility towards victims of mass industrial disasters. Fortunately, the emphasis upon the irresponsibility of the victims, who were constantly under suspicion in the earlier judgement, was corrected in the later one. The court perhaps realized how seriously misled it had been on the long-term hazard of MIC for human health. Even then the Chief Justice, who gave a separate judgement from the one analysed here, did find occasion to comment adversely on a professor of law with activist orientations. If we think of these judgements as intended not only for an immediate audience but also for an audience located in the future, it may seem ironic that these very 'irresponsible' victim groups and law professors with activist orientations gave the judges one further opportunity to record their understanding of the nature of toxic hazards.

THE RESIDUE

In semiotic theory, we think of a residue as an unconnected moment, when the narrative could have taken a different direction. Even when a story is completed, the residue may become an important resource in memory

for reopening the narrative. There was one such unconnected moment in this whole episode when the contingency of the situation was frankly acknowledged and remedial action framed to take this contingency into account. This particular moment deserves special attention.

This was when, by administrative action, the Janata government which came into power in January 1990 took upon itself to provide relief to the victims. While submitting itself completely to the rule of law in the fight against Carbide, it nevertheless decided it would support the victims in various review petitions challenging the settlement. Further, it took its role as guardian of the victims with great seriousness, stating that there could be no conflict of interest between victims and government. Recognizing their urgent need for succour, the government evolved a scheme for interim relief that was not dependent upon litigational uncertainties or bureaucratic rationality. A sum of Rs 360 crores (amounting to a little more than half the settlement amount), required to support the scheme, was to come out of the government's own coffers and become adjustable only against the final settlement. The motive behind this was to do away with the kind of rationality by which victims, already destroyed by disease, are further victimized in the process of acquiring appropriate certificates to satisfy bureaucrats. At one stroke, the victims were transformed from incompetent, irresponsible people to those whose needs for survival were of paramount importance, even as the government acted as surrogate for them on account of the enormous legal complexities of the case. Above all, the limits of judicial and bureaucratic rationality were recognized by the state, and it decided to absorb the uncertainties itself rather than make victims bear the costs. The administrative example set by the government was not followed by the Supreme Court. Schuck (1987) had concluded his book on the Agent Orange case thus:

> The law of the future governing mass toxic exposures must receive extensive, probing, public debate. For exposures that entail the kind of causal indeterminacy, scale, spatial and temporal dispersion, and cost exhibited by the Agent Orange case, the law should look primarily look to non-tort techniques of deterrence, compensation and dispute resolution.

This recommendation came with the realization that in the Agent Orange case a methodology which was 'aggregative, probabalistic and policy-oriented' was sought to be fitted into a legal form that was designed for measures 'individualistic, moralistic and corrective'. In my formulation, I would say that the crucial question for us is whether, in face of the challenge to medical and bureaucratic certainties, the courts can now evolve a jurisprudence wherein the suffering of victims and the regulation of powerful entities takes primacy over a fine balancing of individual responsibility and corrective justice.

CONCLUDING COMMENTS

A semiotic understanding of law conceives of it as an ongoing conversation in which rules are not something 'out there', for they are not a collection of norms waiting to be applied. Instead, rules are seen as becoming meaningful even as they become integrated into a conversation. The peculiar feature of law as conversation is that it possesses subtle devices for filtering out valid arguments that are defined as 'outside the purview of legal arguments'. Yet we have seen that judges themselves use several rhetorical devices, including figures of legal speech, through which they signal that the judicial prose they produce is appropriate to the occasion: the narrative use of a victim's suffering is one such trope. As long as we look at law as conversation, particular judgements can be seen as temporary closures (law is valid as 'temporary frozen preference', as Luhmann puts it).[28] In the Agent Orange case, we saw that many Vietnam veterans regretted that the settlement with the chemical companies had brought a closure to the conversation before they had 'their day in court'. In the Bhopal case too, the judgement displayed an extensive use of paradoxes, plural connotations, and distensions of metaphor. The more suffering was talked about, the more it was used to extinguish the sufferer. Doctors were transformed from healers into bureaucrats whose job was to sort people into slots. Victims who drew attention to their pain were transformed into malingerers. In literature and poetry, the malingerer who lives on the peripheries of society, whose melancholy and physical disability is on display, becomes a sign of all that is wrong with *society*. In the case of modern medical science, bearing the stamp of industrial discipline, malingering becomes a moral fault. In the case of Bhopal, especially, victims whose suffering and disease challenged the certainty of a bureaucratically defined medical science, came to be themselves stigmatized. 'If we cannot understand your disease by the tools of our discipline, then you must be at fault': this was the message by which the melancholy malingerer of poetry became the slothful sinner against industrial and bureaucratic discipline.

The legal conversation on the meaning of suffering, undergone by people who are the bearers of risk within modern industrial societies, needs to be reopened again. What a pity if it were only to happen in the wake of another disaster. The Bhopal case has enough residues to create such a new understanding of suffering in relation to existing theodicies of the state. The most important of these was the responsibility, the direct responsibility that the Janata Government took: it is a rare instance of politically humane moment that needs to be recovered, for it affirms existence by its very 'irresponsibility'.

In his description of a victim, Lyotard says: 'It is in the nature of a victim not to be able to prove that one has been done a wrong. A plaintiff is someone who has incurred damages and who disposes of the means to prove it. One becomes a victim if one loses these means.'[29]

A struggle on behalf of the victim must always be a struggle to restore these means.

IN THE COURT OF THE 11th METROPOLITAN

MAGISTRATE, AHMEDABAD

MRS. ZAKIA AHSAN JAFRI

V/S

MR. NARENDRA MODI & OTHERS

PROTEST PETITION

ON THE COMPLAINT DATED 8.6.2006 &

AGAINST THE

FINAL REPORT

OF THE

SPECIAL INVESTIGATION TEAM DATED

8.2.2012

(PART I)

Civil rights activist Teesta Setalvad is one of the most prominent figures in the struggles for justice of those affected by perhaps the defining incident of the millennial turn – the 2002 Gujarat riots. This chapter deals with the legal and political aftermath of the riots that took place following the burning of a railway train in the city of Godhra, Gujarat, which resulted in the deaths of 58 Hindu pilgrims (or *karsevak*s) returning from the city of Ayodhya (where, in 1992, the Babri mosque had been demolished). The riots ended with over a thousand dead, nearly 80 per cent of whom were Muslim, along with rapes, looting and destruction.
The following decade saw a slow and tortuous process of finding legal retribution, the naming and punishment of the guilty. This text, in which Setalvad describes the nature of state harassment and victimization she underwent, also explains her commitment to the Constitution of India (as against to the nation).

This is excerpted with permission from the fourth chapter of **Foot Soldier of the Constitution: A Memoir** (New Delhi: LeftWord Books, 2017). Support of the author as well as LeftWord Books is gratefully acknowledged.

Images: Facsimile images of the protest petition by Zakia Jafri in the court of the Metropolitan Magistrate, Ahmedabad in June 2006, Enquiry Report of the Special Investigation Team (SIT) ordered by the Supreme Court in 2009, and documents submitted by Teesta Setalvad in support of her statement to the Ahmedabad police station in response to the April 2018 Mumbai High Court order. Images of Ehsan Jafri's house from Rakesh Sharma's landmark documentary, **Final Solution** (2004). Grateful acknowledgment to Sabrang Communications & Publishing Pvt Ltd. and Rakesh Sharma.

16

TEESTA SETALVAD

2017

BEING THEIR TARGET

I had a premonition on 24 July 2015, the day of the hearing before the Central Bureau of Investigation (CBI) court in Mumbai. I could see the stakes clearly: the might of the state and the hatred directed towards me. I was in the dock. I could go to jail, where the incarceration would have been in the hands of the foot soldiers of a hate-driven administration. Anticipatory bail seemed improbable given the attitude of the CBI and the courts.

The past ten days had been tense. The CBI conducted ignominious, clumsy and vindictive raids against me, both at my home and office, on 14 and 15 July. This agency is directly under the command of the Prime Minister's Office (PMO). It seemed motivated to harass me, to intimidate me into silence. The raids had drawn national and international media attention. The media wondered about the motives behind the raid. Was this to do with the Zakia Jafri criminal revision?[1] Zakia Jafri had filed her appeal against the rejection, on 26 December 2014, of her protest petition in disagreement with the (Special) investigating agency. Filed on 15 March 2014, that petition was to be heard by the Gujarat High Court on 4 and 5 August.[2] Weeks before that hearing, the state threw its might at me. Was this a coincidence or was this an attempt by the government to intimidate the persistent quest for justice into silence?

What was I being charged with? The accusations dripped with vindictiveness. Earlier it had been a criminal case by the Gujarat police. Now it was accusations of violations of the Foreign Contribution Regulation Act (FCRA) by the government. In both cases, for the first time both Javed[3] and I were being drawn into the web of state intimidation. Earlier, in four false criminal cases filed against me since 2004, I had been the sole target. We had turned over twenty-five thousand pages of documents to the investigating agency in the first case, and when we had whiffs of the second one, had written to the CBI offering full cooperation. There was nothing to hide. The government that denied a CBI investigation in the Vyapam scam case[4] decided to prosecute me with alacrity.

I don't wear the feeling of being a victim on my sleeve. That is not my character. But I did feel as I went into the courtroom that morning that the state's vindictiveness towards me was venal. I was a target of this government, which was hell bent on my incarceration at any cost. I did not share this premonition with anyone. The CBI had insisted on our presence in the courtroom. This is a requirement in the Maharashtra courts. The hearing went on interminably. The afternoon drew towards evening. I was sure that the judge would reject our bail application and send us, with little time to appeal, to a police lock-up.

Our lawyers were fully prepared to rush down the street to make a quick appeal at the High Court. But this was Friday and the day was almost over. When the judge finally rejected my appeal, I broke convention, walked to the front of the bench and addressed the court: 'M'Lord, I do hope that you know what you have done. Being a judicial decision, I respect it. But by taking this view, with the full knowledge of the vendetta directed against me, you have endangered the life of my family and myself.' What followed was a tense and chilling blur.

Friends and comrades – activist journalists, activists from the far left and from the Communist Party of India (Marxist) – had stood with us in the court. I knew they were there. I got immense strength from them.

We moved swiftly to the High Court for a stay on the CBI Court's order. Television cameras played out the drama. There was barely veiled and gleeful vindictiveness in their voyeurism. No one was sure of the outcome. These were difficult hours. Finally, just before the Bombay High Court concluded its work for the day, the judge hearing the matter stayed the order and granted us protection. It was an immeasurable relief.

The government has – almost obsessively – sought to cut me down to size. In 2004, I was accused of kidnapping and tutoring witnesses. The accusations of Zahira Sheikh[5] became the spear. By 2010–11, the accusations changed to 'submitting false affidavits before the Courts'. By 2014, it was 'financial embezzlement', in which both Javed and I were implicated. By 2016, we had become a threat to 'national security'. The ostensible reason was a consultancy with Ford Foundation, entered into after taking full legal advice between 2004 and 2009. It is ironic that the Modi regime wanted to 'book us for offences' that allegedly took place five years before 2016! Spokespersons of the ruling dispensation – possibly in a cheap bid to scare us off – said in June of 2016 on a commercial national television (Zee News) that they would get us one way or another. The edge of intimidation and violence should not be ignored. My car was stoned in Gujarat on 22 March 2002. In September 2010, a car tried to run me down on the premises of the old High Court buildings, where the Gulberg, Naroda Patiya and Gaam trials[6] were being heard. In the mid-2000s, powerful accused politicians Babu Bajrangi Patel and Maya Kodnani (former minister and elected MLA of the Bharatiya Janata Party [BJP]) burned effigies of me at the Holi festival. They have done all that they could to whip up hostile sentiments of the mob against me.

In Ahmedabad, within the courts, senior advocates have been known to hurl threats, such as 'We will ensure that she flees the country, never to return!' This was shouted by a senior lawyer with a known Rashtriya Sevak Sangh (RSS) background, who has enjoyed influential posts in the UPA II government. He enjoys a lucrative and influential practice even today in the national capital after the change of guard at the centre. The Shiv Sena mouthpiece *Saamna*[7] has reviled me long before social media appeared to take over the job. When the Best Bakery case was transferred from Gujarat to Mumbai, the Shiv Sena felt it had to take charge on its turf. Some of this go back to the days after 1992–93, when we had called for accountability based on Justice B.N. Srikrishna's Report[8] on the violence in Bombay. The Shiv Sena – as the rest of the supremacist right – does not easily forget.

I remember one such abusive call in the aftermath of the Gujarat carnage. My phone rang. It came from a landline. The gentleman tried to engage me in conversation for forty-five minutes. I kept my calm. That was itself an act of liberation. He hurled provocative gendered sexual abuse at me over the telephone. My colleagues in the office were aghast, upset, embarrassed and worried. I somehow felt it was crucial not to be the one who gives in. He was the aggressor, the *agent provocateur*, pushed into actions that were small as they were demeaning. Finally, in sheer frustration, it was he who disconnected the call. This was of course not the only call. They came like waves from the sea, looking furious but simply water pushed along by the political currents.

That kind of abuse came from all quarters. I was in the Supreme Court in December 2004 to answer allegations made by Zahira Sheikh. I was sentimental, going to visit the Bar Library where M.C. Setalvad's[9] majestic portrait hung. I wanted Dada (grandfather) to give me courage before facing the single-minded hate within the court. I sought succour and security. Within the court, after hearings began, senior advocate P.N. Lekhi sought me out and hurled horrific gendered and communal language at me. His daughter-in-law Meenakshi Lekhi – also an advocate – has now taken this abuse to even more vicious levels, first in the media and now in government.[10] P.N. Lekhi made crude allusions to my marriage by *nikaah* (an offence it would seem!). I was upset by his language, but more so by the senior counsel who appeared for me. He was a relative of my father. I had expected him to stand up to P.N. Lekhi's barrage. I remember thinking, 'He has known me since my birth. He knows I was married by a civil ceremony. He attended the party at Juhu after our marriage. Why did he not more firmly and aggressively counter the viciousness of Lekhi?' I have lived, and learned, now through hardened personal experience, that this is what proto-fascists (RSS) do; they paralyse even seemingly good people into silence. They insidiously penetrate institutions of democracy – wedded to inclusive and non-discriminatory governance under the Indian Constitution – with a deeply embedded majoritarian psyche.

That day in December 2004, I won my plea. It was neither the only time nor the first time that I came out of court, watery-eyed, bludgeoned as it were by the personal viciousness and vitriol directed at me. I expected the portals of the Supreme Court to be firmly resistant to, or against such outright vilification. Repeatedly since, and especially after 2010, members of the legal profession have been garnered to head the rapacious vanguard against me, because our struggle for accountability has been a legal one. Many of these men have abandoned all morality and ethics as they have shamelessly mouthed lies perpetrated by an indicted, insecure and vindictive state in Court. The portals of justice await redemption from such lies.

Soon after we filed an application in the Supreme Court in 2009 for a reconstitution of the SIT, the attacks became ferocious and more marked. By 2010, all manner of arsenal were garnered by a nasty state headed by a man who has vendetta and insecurity as his abiding credo. The media joined in. The media did not merely report the attacks on me. They participated in them.[11]

On 11 August 2015, the Bombay High Court granted us anticipatory bail. The court gave us a speaking order, which made specific observations about the freedom of speech: 'Holding views that are against *a government* does not amount to be *against the nation*'. This was in response to the half-baked arguments made by the CBI counsel on the activities of Sabrang Communications,[12] which it said was a 'threat to national security'. There is nothing anti-national about being critical of the actions of a government.

The Gujarat state apparatus did all it could to bury the narrative of its omissions and commissions in 2002. This attempt intensified during the Best Bakery case in Mumbai in 2004–05. It only increased when the SIT was finally appointed and operated from 2008 onwards, to date. It was a

Ehsan Jafri's home

dreary time. I had to protect myself and at the same time keep the spirits of the survivors up.

Dalit and Adivasi groups and mass organizations took me to their bosom when this attack was unleashed. At meeting after meeting in Mumbai, Kerala, Chhattisgarh, Wardha and elsewhere, they came out in my support when the Gujarat state unleashed its venom. I was struck by this show of solidarity. I asked friends and leaders closely what lay behind their understanding: why was it necessary to lend this support? How did the struggle for justice for 2002 matter in the overall scheme of things, for them? Their response was grounded and sobering. If a malevolent state gets away with this obviously motivated attack on you, our defences also get breached. It means that it could as easily, or more easily, get at us. It is the sheer depth of this kind of learning that has helped me to grow and mature politically.

The struggle for justice has become multiple things. It is to speak truth to power regardless of the consequences. It is to fight the good fight even when others tire. It is to relentlessly pursue, gather and cull through evidence while protecting my own back. The entire process has been exhausting. I have to look over my shoulder at every turn. I know that my mobile phone is tapped, my emails are being tracked. The police and other agencies of an increasingly desperate government are on my back. To battle the perverted demon that lurks behind narrow religion-based nationalism, that justifies well-choreographed mutilation and killing, let alone rape, is to lay yourself open both literally and figuratively to all means and manner of attack. It is to make yourself vulnerable and threatened.

Stamina and inner force remain my strength. From 2004 onwards, I was determined not to allow my work to suffer – whether it was the legal-aid work, the work with education in our schools, or my journalistic and academic writing. My heels dug into the ground. I have kept going.

The verdict of the Gulberg massacre case was delivered on 2 June 2016. It was a disappointing verdict. In 2002, 69 people were killed in the Gulberg Society, while thirty-one others went missing. This was the second largest massacre of the Gujarat pogrom. When the verdict was announced in the Gulberg case, most families of victims were deeply hurt and disappointed. Tanvir Jafri, son of Ehsan Jafri, said:

> The Gulberg Society is not *chai ki lari* (tea stall), which can be burnt by one person. It is a very big society. Fifteen to twenty bungalows were there. Ten flats were also there with 400 to 500 people staying there. Twenty-four people cannot burn the whole society, loot, kill, burn large numbers of people in such a brutal manner for over twelve hours. . . . It looks a little odd. Thirty-six

> people have been acquitted. We will decide on whether to go for further appeal or not.

The single largest massacre was at Naroda Patiya, where – according to the chargesheet – 96 people were killed, although our figures show 194 killed. The judgement in the Naroda Patiya case was delivered on 29 August 2012. Thirty-two people, including a former minister, were convicted. In the Gulberg case, eleven people received life sentence. A Vishwa Hindu Parishad[13] leader – Atul Vaidya – was sent to prison for seven years. This was a low sentence for the kind of atrocities that they conducted at Gulberg.

In his oral observations as he pronounced judgement in the case, special judge P.B. Desai said in open court that he had not accepted the idea of a wider conspiracy behind the Gulberg massacre, an argument that had been made rigorously since the start of the trial by advocates for the witness survivors. This aspect of the investigation was doggedly resisted by the SIT investigators and prosecutors. The SIT prosecutor R.C. Kodekar did not make a case for conspiracy at all. Yet, in his reaction to the media on 2 June, SIT chief Raghavan said that the 'judge did not buy the prosecution's conspiracy theory, but it was not because the evidence pointing to a conspiracy was weak. Possibly, in the eyes of the judge, it was not convincing enough to sustain a conviction.' Was this evidence actually weak? Or was it consciously not pressed by the SIT in its arguments before the trial concluded? The reasoning in the judgement provided on 17 June 2016 provided the answers.

On pages 778 and 779 of the 1345-page judgement, the special judge writes:

> No material has been considered even *prima facie* worthwhile to arraign such special police officer and government officials and politicians in power as accused in a number of proceedings including the present proceedings and in my opinion, therefore, it would be unsafe and improper to even have a further discussion on this aspect. The controversy, in my opinion, has been laid to rest and is required to be given its due burial.

Here lies the tale behind the weak and disappointing verdict. The Supreme Court-appointed SIT assigned with the worthy task of both investigating and prosecuting these trials, simply did not press hard enough to establish the charge of criminal conspiracy, never mind the availability of sustainable evidence.

In our desire to ensure that the SIT probe deepened and improved, senior counsel Mihir Desai argued for the arraignment of four officers as accused in the Gulberg case under section 319 of the Code of Criminal

Procedure. This was in January 2010. I first filed affidavits in the Supreme Court on 1 December 2009. Since then I have approached the courts on a number of occasions. These affidavits have been backed by documentary evidence procured through repeated applications in the Gulberg Society massacre trial. We revealed that the SIT has deliberately or consciously failed to investigate key aspects of documentary evidence from the documentary records procured after the trial began. What were these documents? They were charts showing arms and ammunition available with policemen stationed on duty (including the rounds of bullets they did not fire). They were records of the Fire Brigade register in Ahmedabad. They were the Police Control Room Records (PCR). They were the analysis of the CD of phone call records first presented before the Nanavati-Shah Commission by the then Deputy Commissioner of Police (DCP) Crime Branch (March–July 2002) in 2004.

These phone-call records placed before the court have assumed the status of a 'hot potato' that few want to touch or peel. They point to wider knowledge of the massacres executed in broad daylight. An analysis of the CDs made available by former IPS officer, then DCP Crime Branch Rahul Sharma, reveal a total of fifteen calls that day received and made by Pande with different officials from the then chief minister's office. Of a total of 302 calls received and made on his mobile by Pande on 28 February, he spoke several times to his boss, Director Genral of Police (DGP) Chakravarthi and eight times to the Joint Commissioner of Police. Despite the proximity of the commissioner's office, curfew was not declared in the Meghaninagar area till as late as 12:54 p.m., an act that is inexplicable.

Our advocates for the witnesses have argued (and at least four eyewitnesses from Gulberg have testified to this) that the high-level conspiracy behind Gulberg went beyond the bestiality of the mob attack. Tandon's role, callous and calculated, included the destruction of evidence. Around 5:30 p.m. on the evening of the bestial attack, when the survivors were being rescued by a police van, two survivors pleaded to be allowed to take the bodies of their near and dear ones who had been raped and killed with them. 'You look after yourself, we'll take care of the dead,' Tandon had reportedly told them. The *panchnamas*[14] of the site reveal how the embers were allowed to burn, undoused at Gulberg Society for three days after the attack, ensuring that any forensic evidence behind the killings was properly destroyed. When survivors buried the charred remains of their loved ones at the Kalandari Masjid Kabrastan[15] on 3 March 2002, these bodies had been reduced to ashes. There is little deliberation on this destruction of evidence in the judgement.

Part of the goal here seems to be to undermine the very idea of a criminal conspiracy in the Gujarat carnage. On 29 August 2012, the verdict in the Naroda Patiya case upheld the possibility of a wider conspiracy. It lauded Ashish Khetan's sting operation[16] as corroborative evidence (his tapes were examined and found to be genuine by the CBI following an order of the National Human Rights Commission in 2008). If, in the Gulberg trial, the SIT and its prosecutor had argued, as evidence demanded, for charges of criminal conspiracy to be upheld, it would have made arguments for Zakia Jafri in the High Court that much easier. The Zakia Jafri case is pending in the Gujarat High Court. Even here, the SIT refused to investigate the demands of criminal conspiracy into the three hundred incidents that took place across the state. The Gulberg-massacre case relates to one incident in 2002, in which sixty-nine people were killed. The Zakia Jafri case, on the other hand, relates to three hundred incidents across Gujarat. It would pin down the criminal culpability of the administration in the violence. The Zakia Jafri case is at the pre-prosecution stage. The 2 June verdict in the Gulberg case is among the last of those 2002-riot trials being monitored by the Supreme Court. By avoiding any admission of pre-planning and conspiracy in the Gulberg massacre case (especially after the special sessions judge hearing the Naroda Patiya case had made strong findings on criminal conspiracy), the motivation is clearly to weaken the wider claims of state-wide criminal conspiracy being made in the Zakia Jafri case.

An unfortunate hostility by the SIT towards the victim survivors and witnesses was observed as trials wore on. This hostility was even directed against us on more than one occasion. Chairman, SIT, R.K. Raghavan's intervention via senior counsel and amicus (in other cases) Harish Salve to push the Supreme Court to 'reprimand' me for communicating with the Office of the High Commissioner for Human Rights (OHCHR) on the issue of the safety of our lawyers, is a stark example. The letter I had written was to the OHCHR at the United Nations. India is a signatory of the treaty that governs the treaties that provide OHCHR with its mandate. It is therefore perfectly acceptable for a citizen or organization to interact with the OHCHR. 'We can't allow foreign interference in our affairs and we can't approve it,' said justices D.K. Jain, P. Sathasivam and Aftab Alam. They argued that my letters to the OHCHR constituted interference. 'We don't appreciate letters being sent to a foreign country,' said the judges.

It is an unfortunate fallout of the robust struggle for justice that human rights defenders have had such comments passed against them by the court. I believe we have the right to continued engagement with the courts within India, while exercising our rights to report in fairness of the progress of the trials. Our institutions remain trapped in an unfortunate double-standard: while corporations and financial institutions 'collaborate' and 'influence' all manner of public policy (including by senior Indian Administrative Service (IAS), Indian Police Service (IPS), Intelligence officials being actually employed and on the payroll of powerful Indian and international corporations), activists and organizations struggling for constitutional governance and the rule of law are often singled out for judicial reprimand and criticism.

I'm not always sure what motivates me to keep at it. Indira Jaisingh,[17] an old friend and comrade in arms, says that my parents named me after 'a river in Bangladesh which flows fearlessly across borders'. There is also a clearer motivation. Soon after the 1992 riots, at a public meeting in Mumbai, many of us human rights activists, including Indira and I, had agreed that if we had fought for justice against the perpetrators of the 1984 killings in Delhi, then the violence of 1992–93 might not have happened. It was the culture of impunity that had to be punctured. If, after 1992–93, the findings of the Justice Srikrishna Commission had been accepted, and if the courts had convicted all the killers – including the instigators at the highest level – then 2002 might not have happened. During my struggle for bail, Indira Jaisingh remembered this discussion:

> It is this understanding that compels her to continue with the fight against the killers of the 2002 carnage. What we are witnessing is the power of the state and its terrorising arm, the CBI, to mount a raid on Teesta's home and office to prove that she misused foreign funds versus the power of the courts to hold power to account. Who will win this battle? It is the courts of this country that are on trial, not Teesta.

My challenge is to fight the culture of impunity. That is what I have been motivated to do.

This long and dreary battle continues and when justice sometimes comes, it redeems our faith. One such moment was on 12 April 2004. It was the Supreme Court judgement in the Best Bakery case. The court said,

> When the ghastly killings take place in the land of Mahatma Gandhi, it raised a very pertinent question as to whether some people have become so bankrupt in their ideology that they have deviated from everything which was so dear to him. When large number(s) of people including innocent and helpless children and women are killed in a diabolic manner, it brings disgrace to the entire society. Criminals have no religion. No religion teaches violence and cruelty-based religion is no religion at all, but a mere cloak to usurp power by fanning ill feeling and playing on feelings aroused thereby. The golden thread passing through every religion is love and compassion. The fanatics who spread violence in the name of religion are worse than terrorists and more dangerous than an alien enemy.

He told the mob- *Spare these people*
I'm coming out...Do what you want with me

As this book goes to print (*Foot Soldier of the Constitution: A Memoir*), I was asked for a singular honour: to deliver the K.G. Kannabiran[18] Memorial Lecture in Madurai. Ending on a personal note, I quoted from a powerful piece this rare human being, human rights advocate and jurist had written for us in the April–May 2004 issue of *Communalism Combat*, after the historic verdict of the Supreme Court in the Best Bakery case. Titled, 'A Question of Justice', Kannabiran severely reprimanded our courts as only a person of his experience and understanding could do.

> What happened in Gujarat in March 2002, what happened in Mumbai in January 1993, and to members of the Sikh community in 1984 are genocidal trends, and courts, as enforcers of International Covenants, ought to have taken serious note of these blatant transgressions of human rights and devised jurisprudential and procedural tools to deal with this situation. A magniloquent attack on lawlessness is hardly a substitute for doing justice to the wronged. A court which innovatively protected propertied interests by devising the concepts of prospective over ruling and basic structure could have devised a concept for disqualifying a chief minister or other ministers as having been constructively responsible for the carnage by redefining a writ of *quo warranto* for meeting these situations. If the chief minister Modi had been disqualified on the principle of constructive responsibility, Rule of Law would not have become the fugitive that it has become now. Bal Thackaray's[19] Mumbai is not going to be any different. Seeing Rule of Law fleeing like a fugitive could invite private justice and the terrorist may say, 'I shall repay.'

Another critical aspect, where we come in, both individually and as Citizens for Justice and Peace, was how the apex court has dealt with the issue of rights' activists and groups intervening actively to be with the victims and to see their fight through. The Gujarat High Court had seen fit to pass scathing remarks against us. Even on this, the Supreme Court ruling has created a judicial precedent. By not simply expunging the remarks but doing so actively with stern observations on the baseless observations by the High Court, the judgement lends credibility and strength to legal interventions by human rights defenders in the future:

> The High Court appears to have miserably failed to maintain the required judicial balance and sobriety in making unwarranted references to personalities and their legitimate moves before the competent courts – the highest court of the nation, despite knowing fully well that it could not deal with such aspects or matters.

> Irresponsible allegations, suggestions and challenges may be made by parties. . . . But such besmirching tactics, meant as innuendoes or serving as surrogacy ought not to be made or allowed to be made, to become part of solemn judgements, of at any rate by High Courts, which are created as courts of record as well. Decency, decorum and judicial discipline should never be made casualties by adopting such intemperate attitudes of judicial obstinacy.

By ordering the historic transfer of this trial outside Gujarat to Maharashtra, the highest court has deliberated upon and accepted the arguments being made for decades – that were amplified a thousand times in the case of the Gujarat genocide – that such incidents underline the need for the system to operationalize areas and mechanisms of neutrality to avoid subversion of the process of fair investigation and justice, in short, due process of law. This judicial acknowledgement needs to be expanded to ensure institutional memory through reform. Be it Muzaffarnagar of 2013 or Assam of 2011[20] – if similar judicial standards are applied as happened during the intrepid Gujarat 2002 struggle for justice, will not justice become a more realizable norm? The unfortunate instances of communal violence that, in the past decade and a half, have taken the distinct character of pogroms against religious minorities – Muslims and Christians – reveal distinct patterns and similarities. These were evident in full-blown measure in the Gujarat genocide. The first is the months of insidious preparation by outfits committed to the politics of hatred and division. They initially use hate-speech and hate-writing to vilify and demonize a particular section, here a religious minority, and create a climate conducive to violent crimes against the demonized section. This technique, which has been well honed, and also proven by over two dozen commissions of inquiry after every bout of communal violence, has, after the Gujarat genocide, acquired even more vicious dimensions. Documented cases of such a bias guiding or rather affecting the conduct of the police are now legion. Those of justice being delivered are rare and few. Preparations for communal carnage are not now restricted to hate pamphlets and speeches though these form a vital ingredient to cooking up such a hate-filled atmosphere. As I personally experienced and witnessed in Gujarat, preparations are now taking the form of full-fledged training camps of young men and women, where violence is projected as the sole means to self-empowerment and weapons are openly distributed, unchallenged by wings of the state and the law-and-order machinery. The potent drug that intoxicates these camps is hate anecdotes against communities wherein history is interwoven with current-day politics and with the demonization made legitimate.

The system on its own does not intervene to deliver justice, condemn discrimination and slaughter; it has to be pushed to do so. It has been rare that our system has delivered in the case of communal carnage and crime. The pogrom against Sikhs in 1984 in the nation's capital or the post-demolition pogrom targeting Muslims in Mumbai has escaped judicial condemnation and correction. If the victims of earlier bouts of communal violence or pogroms did not have the satisfaction of a resounding judicial verdict in their favour, it does not speak well of the role of the police and the state and the existing legal and justice system. Our Constitution, then, remains on paper. Rarely do our courts initiate *suo motu* action on issues of mass homicide and rights atrocities. It was only after the country experienced Zahira Sheikh's sensational testimony in a press conference organized by Citizens for Justice and Peace, Mumbai that the true import of the situation in Gujarat became real and was addressed by the courts.

What became transparent before the Supreme Court was not simply that a huge human tragedy had befallen Gujarat in 2002. The tragedy was compounded by an unrepentant administration and executive that two years later were without guilt or remorse. All police officers who had functioned without fear or favour, and they were many, are today sidelined in Gujarat. The vindictiveness of Modi and his men against Rahul Sharma, Rajnish Rai, Satish Verma and R.B. Sreekumar continues to this day, an all-out effort to even deny honest officers their pension. The state, meant to rule by the Constitution, is being used – and abused – to target those engaged in risky truth-telling and documentation of a kind that is rare in post-Independence India. The role of the public prosecutor has been truly subverted by the state, with persons with distinct allegiance to the outfits who perpetrated the hatred and violence against the minorities being asked to represent the state! The struggle for justice has meant meticulously documenting all this before the courts so that any claim that we made was backed by irrefutable facts.

In February 2006, the Best Bakery retrial judgement of Judge A.M. Thipsay finally convicted nine persons (if the Gujarat police are to be believed, seven of the accused are still absconding!). On 30 October 2007, eight persons who were accused of rape and murder in Eral, Panchmahal, were sentenced for life, while twenty-nine were acquitted. They were part of a mob that had brutalized, raped and then killed seven Muslims. In January 2008, in the Bilkees Bano case,[21] also transferred to Mumbai, Judge U.D. Salvi sentenced eleven to life imprisonment. The case involved the brutal gang rape of Bilkees and the slaughter of her three-year-old daughter Saleha, during an incident in which fourteen Muslims had been massacred. Though a constable was convicted for destruction of evidence, government functionaries, including doctors, escaped the arm of the law and senior policemen who had orchestrated the subversion of the case were let off by the court.

It is in this overall context that the 9 November 2011 verdict in the Sardarpura massacre case[22] – which convicted thirty-one persons, all of them landed Patels responsible for assaulting defenceless agricultural labourers who had toiled in their fields for generations – must be viewed and assessed. Until then, this was the highest number of convictions ever recorded in a case of targeted communal violence in independent India. It is a tribute to the grit and courage of the thirty-three survivor witnesses, displaced from their homes, who testified in court, identified the accused despite threats and inducements and ensured that justice was delivered. That the case was one among those monitored by the Supreme Court, whose directives had ensured effective witness protection, enabled the impossible to happen. That the judge cleared CJP and its secretary of malicious and motivated charges of tutoring witnesses was another landmark. None of this would have been possible without the energetic and committed CJP team, especially its lawyers in Gujarat. In October 2016, the High Court pronounced its verdict on the appeal, acquitting fourteen of the thirty-one convicted and confirming the convictions of seventeen powerful accused. The next round of our legal interventions will now begin, appealing this verdict in the Supreme Court!

Remember that Gujarat 2002 was about 300 ghastly incidents in nineteen of the state's twenty-five districts. Evidence was led through witnesses who testified about significant preparations by politicians and leaders of the Bajrang Dal[23] who enjoyed state patronage and protection. Witnesses also sought to lead evidence on *Tehelka*'s courageous sting 'Operation Kalank' which revealed specific and relevant aspects concerning arms and ammunition being brought into Mehsana (the district in which Sardarpura is located) prior to the Godhra killings on 27 February 2002. At witnesses' insistence, the SIT did record the statement of *Tehelka*'s correspondent Ashish Khetan but they did not call him as a witness. Why? Though former DGP R.B. Sreekumar's affidavits, with annexed reports of the State Intelligence Bureau, corroborated some of this evidence, the SIT was reluctant to probe this aspect further.

Sharp and aggressive in its approach to the Godhra train-burning tragedy, the SIT and its prosecutor had not only bought the Gujarat police's shaky and shady version of conspiracy but had argued for the death penalty, which was imposed on eleven of the thirty-one accused. In the Sardarpura case, witnesses, being opposed to retributive justice, did not argue for the death penalty at all. And thus a niggling question remains: Do we view the incidents of Godhra and post-Godhra as qualitatively and quantitatively different kinds of crimes? This is a tough one, which the Indian system would do well to answer.

If the constructed narrative to justify targeted crimes in 1992 and 2002 related to 'retaliation against violence (of the victim)' or 'who cast the first stone', three other narratives have since then been built upon these, brick by brick. 'Love Jihad', 'Ghar Vapsi' and now 'Gau Raksha' are the new slogans of the storm troopers of the extreme right: their targets are girls and women who express autonomy in forging relationships, Dalits, Christians and Muslims who are accused of 'converting away' from the main faith, and culture and food choice as vegetarianism is sought to be imposed. All these terms are terminologies circulated to justify mass, targeted violence. They are also being used to test democratic institutions, especially Indian Courts, and actually bully them into accepting, as valid, a majoritarian and discriminatory governance and discourse. Slowly and surely what we are witnessing is a re-fashioning of the Indian republic.

Where, then, will the resistance emerge? What happens after the tale of mass violence is first told? Survivor's stories, narratives of neighbourhoods, all need not just re-telling but re-building. What happens to those who have been used as foot soldiers, fed on tales of enemy-othering and hate, even as the chief architects fast ascend the pyramid of state power? These are some of the questions that have lingered on, seeking resolution through further action, maybe of an even more intense and all-encompassing kind. For lasting peace, and harmony, an edifice of justice must exist or be created. But do the paths of the peace-maker, the harbinger of harmony need to be distant or parallel from those who seek justice? Can they not, through concerted action, merge?

From November 2011 to February 2012, despite being the centre of vicious attack, we planned the tenth memorial of the Gujarat carnage, differently. We drew in young students of schools and colleges as well as reached out to the media and filmmakers who had in some way been part of the journey. For a week before, we worked, cajoling and persuading workers at the Ahmedabad Municipal Corporation to help spruce up the society. When I say 'we', it was a large collective effort, of activists, academics, students, photographers, writers and artists. It was all to culminate in a one-day memorial at the Gulberg Society, where in the open, Shubha Mudgal[24] would render songs of resistance, and healing. For months, we toiled within the society and the neighbourhood that had seen such bloodletting and hatred. Deserted homes showcased narratives, banners with powerful words in Gujarati and English, proclaimed the tale. As night drew in and Shubha climbed on to the roof of Kasim Mansuri's home that was set as the dramatic, open-air stage with Aneesh Pradhan and Sudhir Patwardhan beside her, the strains of trial runs of the *tanpoora* and *tabla* filled the air. For an hour and a quarter soon after that, the voice of Shubha Mudgal, honed through the annual, 1 January performances at Safdar Hashmi Memorial Trust (SAHMAT) since 1990, rang through the neighbourhood. We had kept one of the side gates open; many 'others' from the neighbourhood crept in. Neighbourhood wedding processions

DOCUMENTS TO BE SUBMITTED WITHIN FORTNIGHT OF STATEMENTS RECORDED AT DCB CRIME POLICE STATION ON 6.4.2018. (F.I.R. NO 1/20/2018)

1. MEMORANDUM OF ASSOCIATION OF SABRANG TRUST.
2. MINUTES OF SABRANG TRUST RELATED TO APPLICATION, DECISIONS, BUDGET ETC OF MHRD - KHOJ PROJECT.
3. LIST OF EMPLOYEES OF THE KHOJ PROJECT DURING TERM OF DURATION OF KHOJ-MHRD PROJECT (2010-2013; Xtn till 2014) / ADDRESS/MOBILE ETC
4. ~~MHRD~~ NARRATIVE REPORTS/ ACTIVITIES REPORTS SENT TO MHRD BY SABRANG TRUST.

STATEMENT(S) OF TEESTA SETALVAD & JAVED ANAND RECORDED AT DCB CRIME POLICE STATION, AHMEDABAD (F.I.R. NO. 1/20/2018) AS PER ORDER OF BOMBAY HIGH COURT DATED 5.04.2018 IN ANTICIPATORY BAIL APPLN. NO. 627/2018.

quietened themselves for an hour, in what we believe, was a silent homage. Over one thousand survivors and friends from all over Gujarat, Mumbai and Delhi shared those precious moments and the journey. It seemed to throw open a pathway to the future. For Zakia Apa, Salimbhai, Sairabehn, Kasimbhai, Tanveerbhai, Nishrin, their precious Gulberg Society had, for some moments that day, become once again that dream bouquet of Indian pluralism that Ehsansaab had dreamt of.

There are a couple of favourite stories of mine that I share when I speak to young people, cajoling them to join the good fight, spare those precious few hours of every day to battle the politics of hate and deepen values of solidarity, equality and non-discrimination. One related to Khan *chacha* from Dharavi who, despite losing his elder son in December 1992, refused to divulge the identity of the assailants to his younger son. 'I want the cycle of killing to stop', was his simple rationale. Or Vimlabai Khavnekar, mother of Shiv Sena Shakha *pramukh*[25] from Kurla who confronted the mob led by her son, Bharat Khavnekar and prevented it from marauding and butchering Muslim residents of a building located in an 'all-Hindu street' (on the midnight of 7 December 1992). Can we build an India with foot soldiers of peace, harmony and justice in every mohalla and street? Can we reclaim this public space as our own – a space that belongs to the constitutionally created Indian republic?

A battle rages for the heart and soul of India out there and in our homes, and we do not know yet, who shall win. It needs to be fought on the streets, within our homes and classrooms armed with arsenal from history, culture, poetry, music, literature – both everyday-lived reality and a committed politics. But when in the Naroda Patiya of Ahmedabad – on 27 July 2016 – Dalits marched silently with candle lights quietly proclaiming 'Dalit–Muslim unity', survivors who had wept and fought, deposed in court and even won, received a powerful message: of an attempt to apologize for the brutalization of 2002.[26]

Maybe that then is one way into the future. Mass organization and mobilization on the path of reparation for crimes, affirmative action to ensure social justice, paved with attempts, at least, of a genuine reconciliation, based on the non-negotiable, equality and non-discrimination. Against the divisive politics of hate.

□

जय भीम
जयभीम कलैण्डर 2020
जय भीम

Feminist author Sharmila Rege (1964–2013) explored a new 1990s development in the subaltern public sphere: the Ambedkerite publics, celebrating their own pilgrimage sites, their own counter-history and their pantheon of religious and political figures in popular music, both recorded and live, and in new visual material such as calendars with their own sense of events to memorialize and festivals to follow. At this time, as India reinvents a new politics of Occupy, this text has renewed significance.

Earlier version published in *Economic and Political Weekly* (vol. 43, no. 7, 16 February 2008). Reprinted with permission of the journal. Grateful acknowledgement to Anil Saini for his support.

Images: Montage using an Ambedkarite 2020 Jai Bhim calendar in multiple locations, in one instance set against Navjot Altaf's major installation, **Links Destroyed and Rediscovered** (1994). Grateful acknowledgement to Navjot Altaf for permission and support.

17

SHARMILA REGE

2008

INTERROGATING THE THESIS OF 'IRRATIONAL DEIFICATION'

Mass gatherings on significant Ambedkarite dates are seen by some as irrationally deifying Ambedkar. In fact, on these days, Dalit history is remembered and reinterpreted, notably through the large sale of audio cassettes of compositions: from the 1930s extolling Babasaheb's struggles, to a current *I Love You Ambedkar* collection that celebrates selfless commitment to the community.

The commemoration of Babasaheb Ambedkar's' *mahaparinirvan* (death anniversary) on 6 December is usually followed by a stream of commentaries on the irrationality of the gathering at *Chaitya Bhoomi* in Mumbai.[1] The usual middle-class common sense reading of the annual Ambedkarite gatherings is that these events are irrational and emotional, and cause civic problems related to traffic and hygiene. Comments by social scientists on these annual gatherings suggest more continuity than differences with the common-sense view. There is very little in the way of sociological documentation of these gatherings, and social scientists (with notable exceptions) have continued to explain these publics through a thesis of either deification of Ambedkar or manipulation of the masses by the leadership. Some of them contrast the rationality of Ambedkar's thought and practice with the irrationality of these annual gatherings, and the public is then seen as undeserving to claim the legacy of Ambedkar. A documentation of Ambedkarite calendars, and the sociological mapping of annual gatherings of the popular masses that constitute the calendar, interrogates the easily drawn conclusion about the irrational deification of Ambedkar by the Dalit masses. It foregrounds the reflexive circulation of mudhouse representations[2] of Ambedkar, mapping thereby the contours of an Ambedkarite counterpublic.

I would like to begin by situating my engagement with the mudhouse writers and their literary representations in the formation of Dalit feminist groups in the early 1990s, and in the interrogation and revisioning of feminist politics that followed. For many like me, the alliances with democratic Dalit-Bahujan groups and cultural movements brought the realization of gross ignorance of histories and cultures that have been violently marginalized,along with the manufacture of ignorance with which academic practice is complicit. For some of us, curricular transformation became the immediate site for engagement and projects,when explicit pedagogical functions were undertaken. It is this context that began the documentation of the Ambedkarite calendar, and some of the gatherings that constitute it.

A DATE WITH HISTORY

The Ambedkarite calendar refers to those published yearly by several Dalit groups, which are visually distinct in establishing a historical lineage from the Buddha, Jyotirao Phule and Shahu Maharaj to Ambedkar.[3] The advertisements (mostly middle-level entrepreneurial efforts from the community) occupy a very small space at the bottom of the page. Each of these calendars is a documentation of history, in that while marking the days, each day is represented as a day in the history of Dalit doing. The calendars become a mode by which critical memory and the history of the Dalit movement is reiterated, reinterpreted and re-indexed. What is suggested by this empirically documented history from below, of the publics that constitute (and are constituted by) the Ambedkarite calendar?

A documentation over the last six years of the gatherings on 6 December at *Chaitya Bhoomi* in Mumbai, on 14 October at *Diksha Bhoomi* in Nagpur, on 1 January, at *Kranti Stambh* in Bhima Koregaon and on 20 March and 25 December in Mahad suggest that thousands of people repeatedly visit these places.[4] Can the visits be explained solely in terms of their special value in being connected with Ambedkar? Why do these places continue to be culturally and politically meaningful year after year? As a part of the empirical documentation, we asked people to tell us about what they do, why they visit these places, the cost of the visits, the way they are organized, and their experience of travelling without tickets that often places these groups in direct confrontation with the state. We also documented the trade in these gatherings – the activities at the different stalls exploring questions of: who puts up these stalls, what do they sell and what sells.

The stalls sell a wide range of items like brass vessels from Muradabad, *Jai Bhim* caps, statues, posters, calendars, prints of Ambedkar, statues of Buddha, lockets, watches, pens, key chains, ribbons and night lamps with images of Ambedkar. There are other stalls offering free medical services, stalls put up by various banks, those giving career advice and matrimonial data. The book stalls and stalls of '*gayan* parties' (singing troupes) with their audio cassettes, which sideline others by their very number, and the crowds that they draw were documented in detail.

Buying and selling of goods by Dalits at these gatherings has been commonly summarized as these events have been 'commercialized'. With very little information about commerce and cooperative building efforts among Dalit communities, buying and selling by subaltern groups at these gatherings has often been explained either through a thesis of alienation or resistance. I am not suggesting here a neat hypothesis that equates consumption of commodities that iconize Ambedkar to a form of cultural politics, but am making a case for exploring the interconnections between the expressive and symbolic issues and the practical.

The mass gatherings of Ambedkarites at Nagpur and Mumbai are viewed by the unmarked public as days of traffic nuisance – packed trains and days on which the Shivaji Park grounds in Mumbai get littered. These are reactions to unmarked public spaces being occupied (physically) on certain days in a marked manner. Space and spatial strategies of appropriation, deployment and control have been of crucial significance in maintaining hierarchical relations of caste. The Ambedkarite movement has contested this through claiming the right to public water resources, temples and educational centres by dropping negative rights to spaces such as the *watan*[5] and denouncing the space within Hinduism. At the level of ideology, the spatial strategies can be seen as articulating the physical, material and mental imaginative aspects of social space.

The Ambedkarite utopia (a community based on the call to educate, organize and agitate) represents a search for society in a perfected form but, like all utopias, it does not have a fixed address or determinate physical space. It may be argued that the Ambedkarite calendar events link the utopia to real places thereby constructing Dalit heterotopias[6] – real places that exist on a map, and which can be visited. They mediate in a mirror-like fashion between utopias and ideological subjects, and link popular masses with a possible political moral identity that they can assume. The printed booklet and the music perform considerable ideological labour in

जय
भीम

sustaining heterotopias. For the moment, setting aside the printed booklet which lends largely to the rational–critical dimension of the Dalit public, we shall explore further the sphere of music and *gayan* parties.

MUSICAL MEMOIRS

A dimension of social imagination and promise is lent by the *gayan* parties which constitute the second largest number of stalls at these gatherings. The *mahar*[7] community is traditionally associated with singing, and in the Ambedkar era, old forms of publicity like the community bhajan came to be thematically reformulated. The private forms of expression, like women's compositions of the 'ovi' (songs of the grinding stone), 'palana' (songs of the cradle), adopted overtly political themes of a caste society. Some of these compositions of the 1930s and 1940s, otherwise lost to history can be retrieved from the memoirs of an Ambedkarite teacher, Gaikwad Guruji.[8] Gaikwad recalls the verses in which women admonish the Congress for ignoring the *khoti* (a land tenure system) abolition bill, claiming Ambedkar as the sole leader of the peasants and the poor:

> The peasant toils day and night/Like a cobra that claims a readymade hole/The Khot with no efforts claims his share,
> My peasant brothers, do not lose patience/To your interests, the courageous/Ambedkar alone shall remain – always dedicated.[9]

In the 1940s, in the context of the struggle by Sambhaji Santajii Waghmare for houses for Dalits in the BIT(Bombay Improvement Trust) *chawls* (working-class housing), the compositions of women are centred on Rajgrih, the house that Ambedkar built in Mumbai.

> Come dear women –
> Let us go and see Babasaheb's palace/Ramabai is sprinkling water in the garden,
> As Bhaiyyasaheb plays with the cart/Let us go and see the first floor,
> Where, in the garden of roses/Ramabai plucks flowers.[10]

In the 1930s, even as older forms of publicity were being thematically reformulated, a new mode of publicity – the 'Ambedkari *jalsa*' emerged.[11] Commenting on the emergence of the *jalsa* (celebration of music), one of the early composers Bhimrao Kardak recalls how the poor turnout at meetings led a group of young Ambedkarites in Nasik to the idea of a *jalsa*.[12] In the *jalsa*, the structure of the tamasha (folk theatre) was radically reorganized as verses and dialogues became the central point of the performance, which began with a salutation not to Ganesha but to Babasaheb. One such popular salutation was:

> Bhimraya, I touch your feet/Give me the intellect to sing of your virtues.
> In this world, except for you, we have no saviour/You are the true mother of the untouchables/To emancipate the dalits –
> Give me the intellect to sing of your virtues.[13]

Shantabai Dani, a well-known Ambedkarite feminist in her testimonies, narrates at length Babasaheb's appreciation of the *jalsa* and particularly the dramatization, in one performance, of the entry of the Harijan into the Congress. She recalls how the *jalsa* sought to convey the message of Ambedkar through comic dialogues and parody.

The *jalsa* had one more incident where a person who is a Harijan enters the Congress. Having become a member of the Congress, he starts living in style. He walks with an affected gait. With obviously plenty to eat and plenty to drink, he becomes a great show-off. But there is a problem. This undreamed of comfort is very hard to get used to and proves to be too much for him. Finally, unable to cope with it, he kicks the bucket. The corpse is kept on the stage. The Congress members come, see him and go back. His wife is howling. It is not an ordinary funeral though. The howling is interspersed with dialogues. She says, 'O body, you were just as stiff before dying and you are the same even after death.' Babasaheb was guffawing loudly watching this.[14]

CONTESTING DOMINANT PERCEPTIONS

The first generation of Ambedkarite composers (1920–56)[15] while seeking to spread the message of Ambedkar used idioms that contested the dominant message of the day. A popular verse contested the category Harijan thus:

> All of us *mahars*, *mangs*, *bhangis* and *chambhars*/Let's condemn the name *Harijan*.
> Hearing the name – makes my mind sad/*Harijan* is a stamp – a stigma, a sign of slavery,
> And this dictatorial Congress government/It claims to run a democratic government![16]

V.D. Savarkar's[17] composition *Tumhi Amhi Bandhu Bandhu* (You and Us – we are all brothers) – is contested by Patitpavandas:

> You are human beings, We too are Hindu human beings, You too are Hindus, Yet when it comes to temples – It is always – you above and we in our place.[18]

Keruji Ghegde contested the claims of the political parties of the period in his composition *The Market of Indian Politics*. He imagines it thus:

> To the bazaar of Indian politics, goes the old congress woman, She is really obstinate,
> She is possessed by nonviolence, Has lost her principles – lost her path
> How can she get Swarajya (self-rule)? To the bazaar of Indian politics,
> Goes a Hindu Mahasabha woman/She is obstinate,
> She is possessed by Hindutva/Has lost her principles – lost her path
> How can she get Swarajya?[19]

In the 1930s – the Pune Pact[20] was the predominant theme in the compositions of the '*jalsakars*' (composers) of the period. One of the very popular verses was:

> Gandhi – what kind of Mahatma?/Fooling people with his pretences
> What kind of Mahatma is this?/He propagates the message of nonviolence
> But kills democracy in broad daylight/What kind of Mahatma is this?[21]

Keruba Gaikwad – also a first generation Ambedkarite *shahir* (poet-singer)[22] – addresses the tensions between modern education and community ties:

> . . . Babasaheb Ambedkar is so highly educated, Yet his life is committed to society,
> For his community, he sweats blood, Always seeking its prosperity.[23]

In the 1950s, as conversion to Buddhism became a political issue, composers contesting the critics of *dhamma* (Buddhist term for religious law) moved swiftly between the familiar and universal. Keshab Subha Aher claims:

> When they heard of it the new Dhamma, Dhamma of Equality, Independence, Fraternity
> The casteists lost their cool, When we lay in the hell of slavery
> Did they have no shame?[24]

EMBERS OF REVOLUTION

The second generation of Ambedkari *shahirs*[25] composing after the 1950s, while carrying on the earlier genres created a new genre of music: Bhimgeet and 'Buddhageet', which underlined the strong linkages between Ambedkar and the Dalit masses. The *palana*(cradle) of Phule, Ambedkar and Shahu became a popular genre with women, and printed booklets of these songs priced between Rs 2 and Rs 5 are among the most popular items. The primary theme in the compositions of the second generation is the message of modernity; to provide quality of life for Dalits as also to legitimize Buddhist practices as modernist expressions. Vamandada Kardak, one of the best known *bhimshahir* (composer of the Ambedkar movement) says:

> Throw off the skin of the Hindu Dharma/Take on the blue shawl of Buddha's Equality,
> Throw off the old one – worn out woven by threads of hatred/It's so patched, Why should anyone use it?
> When it has no trace of humanism Say no to Hindutva/For in it there is no place for fraternity By declaring some to be lowly
> And others as high, This culture has been blinded It has been rendered lame.[26]

Kardak's social imaginary[27] is one that at once recognizes the failure of modernity to deliver on its promises and invites it to deliver. He says:

> Bhima, your thought/It's like the shade of a peepal tree/A door to happiness, a storehouse of knowledge/a message for good living/ This is all a favour from you/A new house, a car at the door/Your community owes it all to you/We have the sword of your thoughts as sharp
> as ever/Your thoughts and new vows/We have to follow in your footsteps/Singing your song/For the poor you are the only support.
> There's hunger in my stomach/My face may look sad/But for Waman, the joys lie in your shade/In this shade, lie the embers of revolution/the door to happiness.[28]

The *jalsa* became central to the Buddhist conversion movement as well as the land grab movement led by Dadsaheb Gaikwad in 1959 and 1964. The decline of the *jalsa* in the late 1960s has been explained by scholars in terms of the political subordination of Dalit politics to the Congress. The neglect of the tradition by Dalit political leaders, the rise of the electronic media and of Dalit youth musical groups, are also seen as contributing

JAI
THE BEATS OF DALIT
जय

M!
STANCE

to this decline.[29] While the impact of these forces cannot be denied, our documentation of the cassette culture of the *gayan* parties suggests that the issues of tension between preservation and expansion of cultural forms cannot be settled at once.

As the *jalsa* troupes faced closure in the post-Ambedkarite period, a new generation of *gayan* parties or *quawal* parties emerged.[30] Buddhist *mahilamandals* (women's groups) formed local *gayan* parties which travel to perform at the calendar events. One such group articulates their relation to Ambedkar and his to the nation:

> They went away just the way they had come/All shattered to pieces/Who says our nation stands on the rupee note/You must say only that what is true/My Bhima lifted the nation,
> Just on the nib of a pen!
> My father called him father/My mother calls him father/I call him father/My son too calls him father/Try searching in the world
> One such relation/Does anyone share this kind of relation?
> Like the one we share with my Bhima?[31]

CASSETTE CULTURE

The compositions of these travelling troupes move across regions and generations so that often (unless mentioned in the composition or obvious by the individualized style) the original composition is difficult to trace. The rich genres of Ambedkarite music cannot be reduced to an organizing tool for politics or to something all too readily appropriated by market forces. In the late 1980s, the possibilities opened by locally produced inexpensive cassettes, have meant a revolution in quantity and variety of music and it has sometimes revitalized the *gayan* parties. The cassette culture has brought more women singers and parties into prominence and has not eroded the base of the live performances. At the *Chaitya Bhoomi* and *Diksha Bhoomi* the audio cassette stalls are the most colourful with posters announcing new cassettes with live performances of artistes at regular intervals.

A preliminary documentation of cassettes sold at *Chaitya Bhoomi* suggest that recurring themes include a re-reading of events in modern Indian history, a mapping of the struggles in the everyday life of Ambedkar and commentaries on contemporary issues in the sociopolitical domain. In re-rendering modern history, musical meanings centre on the Pune Pact while in articulations of contemporary politics, it is saving the Constitution that occupies the imagination of the composers. The intellectual war between the two great men, Gandhi and Ambedkar, is imagined to be an intellectual *akhada* (wrestling ground) and the interesting and repeated imaginary in the compositions is the request made by Kasturba Gandhi to Ambedkar to grant *jeevandan* (boon of life) to Gandhi.[32]

The compositions in the much circulated popular cassette *I love you Ambedkar* outline the contours of conjugal relations in the new Ambedkarite community. The four compositions present an interesting mix – the first one, *Ambedkar I love you Lucy Mhanali* (Lucy said, I love you Ambedkar), narrates the story of a British woman Lucy who expresses her love for Ambedkar. Her lack of control over her feelings and her plans to entice Babasaheb are underlined:

> She drops her books and/Then says sorry sorry

All these efforts of Lucy are lost on Ambedkar who tells her that she is like a sister to him, for fidelity and commitment are important to him. The second composition, *'Baba mhanto samaj mala – lagna konashi karu'* (The community calls me 'Father' – who can I marry), imagines the doctors advising Babasaheb to marry a second time after the death of his first wife Ramabai. Babasaheb replies that the welfare of his Dalit children numbering nine crores (ninety million) is his real aspiration and work. The whole composition places on record the reason why Ambedkar might have married Savitabai,[33] a Brahmin doctor, and the secondary importance of conjugality as compared to the community. The third composition outlines the condition that a young Dalit boy makes before agreeing to marry. He agrees to marry if the women can find him a bride like Ramai (Ambedkar's first wife) whose contribution to Babasaheb's work is then underlined. The fourth composition, *'Tumcha kahi nahi mala akaycha'* (I will listen to nothing you say) is the voice of a woman's determination to attend the *jayanti* (anniversary) celebrations at her paternal village where the celebrations are grander than at her conjugal home. She warns her husband that her mind has been made up. The four songs together weave patterns that contest upper-caste bourgeois ideals of conjugality. The ideals of faithfulness and loyalty of the man, of the priority of community over conjugality, of a supporting and giving wife – who can challenge the husband if he stands in the way of her commitment to the Ambedkarite ideology are grounded socially and in Dalit historical struggles.

CRITICAL MEMORY

The musical meanings, it is apparent, are grounded socially and historically in struggles and operate on an ideological field of conflicting interests, institutions and memories.This project of documentation with all its methodological and other problems, seeks to bring the *jalsa*, *gayan* parties and cassettes into the curricula thereby interrogating the uncritical classical anthropological gaze at Dalit publics and suggests that the analytical gaze of the publics be thrown back at academic practices in general and those relating to the analyses of recognition struggles and social movements in particular. It seeks to recover Dalit intellection erased by dominant frameworks in the academy, and interrogates the assumption of Dalit citizenship as incapable of thinking in universal terms and engaging only with everyday mundane problems.

The foregrounding of mud house literary representations brings up the significance of critical memory and passionate politics in studying Dalit identity and politics. An articulation of the present crisis through linking it to moments of the time past is a defining feature of the mud house literary representations. This work of critical memory is not to be confused with nostalgia – for nostalgia is selective and conservative, in that it does not link the past to the crises of the present. Critical memory of the mud house composers works in a cumulative manner, through a collective maintenance of a record that links time past and the crises of the present. Music plays a distinct role in organizing a Dalit counterpublic. A public (as also counterpublic) is notional and empirical, and is never just the sum total of persons. It has to have some way of organizing itself – for it is different from crowds or audience which require co-presence.

The Dalit counterpublic emerges as a distinctive social space through the reflexive circulation of the music; with texts not only asserting their own position, but also characterizing their relation to all other positions in the imagined horizons of circulation.[34] How do we understand the music as constituting a counterpublic – is it the claims to the oppositional that constitutes the 'counter'? Or is it the host of the alternate publishing and circulating institutions, practices and sites that make it counter? To some extent it is both: the claims and the institutions that make these publics counter. But more importantly it is also in the awareness of the subordinate status – and of the conflict of ideas, the modes of address, and the speech genre – that it marks itself off from the dominant public.

Exploration of the Ambedkarite counterpublic and the passionate politics that constitutes it not only opens up new dimensions of Dalit politics, but also brings emotional reflexivity into the analyses of Dalit assertion by allowing a mapping of the relation between representations of Ambedkar and the generation of subversive counter emotions. If gratitude and loyalty to Ambedkar and his ideology emerge as the predominant cementing emotions; moral outrage and anger against the leadership co-opted by the state play an important role in holding back cynicism or resignation – emotions that otherwise demobilize the popular masses.

□

Its also against our constitution words where we give "FREEDOM OF CHOICE" to every Indian.

Kindly take your decision back.

Your sincerely
Yogesh

प्रबं./SPP/HYD - 2013 पोस्ट कार्ड POST CARD

Philately: King Of Hobbies
COLLECT
INDIA POSTAGE STAMPS
CONTACT
Nearest Philatelic Bureau

The Chief Justice of India
The Supreme Court of India
Tilak Marg
New Delhi

पिन PIN | 1 | 1 | 0 | 2 | 0 | 1

(इस लाइन के नीचे न तो लिखें और न ही मुद्रित करें Do not write or print below this line)

Excerpt from the report Towards Gender Inclusivity: A Study on Contemporary Concerns around Gender, by Sunil Mohan, assisted by Sumathi Murthy who now chooses to be recognized as Rumi Harish. Written mainly in the context of a diverse and often invisible universe of sexual violence beyond conventional legal definitions, the text seeks to expand the field both in social and more specifically legal terms.

The report was originally published by Alternative Law Forum, Bangalore, in 2013. Reprinted here with permission. Grateful acknowledgment to the authors, Alternative Law Forum, Bangalore, and Arvind Narrain.

Images: Letters written during the campaign to remove the draconian Section 377 of the Indian Penal Code that refers to gay sex. Originally introduced in British India in 1861, Section 377 was declared unconstitutional by the Delhi High Court in July 2009 but overturned by the Supreme Court in December 2013. However, in August 2017, the Supreme Court upheld the right to privacy as a fundamental right, and in a huge victory for the lesbian and gay communities across the country, in September 2018 the court ruled that Section 377 was unconstitutional 'in so far as it criminalizes consensual sexual conduct between adults of the same sex'. The letters are from the collection of **Orinam**, an all-volunteer unregistered collective of LGBTIQA+ people and allies started in 2003, based in Chennai.

18

SUNIL MOHAN & RUMI HARISH

2013

VIOLENCE

In a general sense, the very word violence brings about an image of the use of physical force to cause injury, damage or death. Violence is regarded as an area of concern, not only for law, but also for medicine, and the state – all of which make attempts to regulate it. Violence is also often associated in its most extreme form with war and genocide.

What people may not recognize is that there are forms of violence that are not as visible and as obvious as this. Every manifestation of violence cannot be registered in law – violence requires different analytical categories for the offence to be punished by the law. Dominant conceptions of violence often ignore different sections of the population, and different root causes for violence, including caste, race, class, ethnicity, gender, gender identity, sexual orientation, etc. These dominant definitions are often influenced by funding sources – many of which come from the west which often constructs us as always 'victims' of physical violence, but rarely permit the space to consider other expressions of violence. In this piece, we want to highlight the types of violence that manifest themselves in more subtle and yet equally harmful ways. This type of violence may take the form of discrimination, exclusion, marginalization and the violation of rights of minorities. These types of violence are usually the ones that are addressed by social justice movements.

The idea of violence is constantly changing. It is difficult to identify one definition for violence. In order to better comprehend violence, one has to observe the ways in which people ascribe the term to different situations and contexts. This model of self-identification is more encompassing than one fixed definition. Social movements must move beyond a language of only 'legal' injustice and denial of 'rights,' and should instead seek to expand notions of violence and incorporate new bodies and scenarios into mainstream understandings of violence. Our communities are defined not only by our identities and by our possession of rights, but also by our experiences with violence.

VIOLENCE AND THE WOMEN'S MOVEMENT

What became evident to the women's movements early on, is that violent gender inequalities could not necessarily be addressed by the law. The law, as an institution, often has to rely on fixed and rigid definitions of complex phenomena: like 'violence' for persecution. Women's movements moved beyond the boundaries of the law and identified violence in private spaces of domesticity and questioned 'private' social institutions like the family and marriage. The women's movements were the first to draw attention to the politics of personal and private spaces. Landmark cases – including those of the Shah Bano case, the Mathura Rape case, the Bhanwari Devi case[1] – present an understanding of violence related to the violation of the female body and her right to consent.

Women's movements also expanded conceptions of violence by drawing attention to the violent exclusion that accompanies gender difference in our society. After the 1960s, the women's movement began to become critical of the way that 'biological sex difference' was used as a justification for the denial of equal access and opportunity for women. Feminists showed how different social institutions in both the public and private realm actually constructed gender roles for women. Feminism began to raise questions about social structures including the economic sector, family, marriage, divorce, child custody, housework, education and reproduction. In doing so, feminists showed how patriarchy predetermined spaces and roles for women and created a subordinate gender for women. Feminist analysis thus expanded a definition of violence beyond the physical and drew attention to the emotional and psychological violence that occurs from being in a marginalized position in society.

Respondents indicated that while issues of gender were initially only addressed by women's movements, the dawning of the human rights movement fundamentally changed this. Activists began to question both public and private spaces, and how they restrict individual worth and happiness. Over time, the rights of 'lesbian, gay, bisexual and transgender' people became apparent. However, as some of the feminists we spoke to said: the use of the human rights perspective became more about funding NGOs than actually addressing injustice on the basis of gender and sexuality. The more issues became framed as human rights issues, the more funds NGOs received. Human rights, as these feminists argued, has failed to really make people question their understandings of gender and sexuality.

It is important to recognize that some of the feminists we spoke to in Chennai and Bangalore were self-critical of the movement's unwillingness to interrogate a politics of desire, sexuality and pleasure. One of them spoke about how discourse around violence is marketable, and attracts sympathy from other people, but discourses around pleasure and desire do not attract similar sympathy. She conceded that the idea of the personal being political has not extended to the topic of sexuality rights. Another feminist remarked that, when we think about violence, the perception still remains in terms of the law and that our conceptions of violence are dictated by the politics of NGO funding – even for feminists. What became apparent is that the idea of the woman's body as sexual is only a new understanding for feminists. The only time feminists spoke about sexuality was in the context of reproductive rights. Issues like abortion and family planning became prioritized over the right to orgasm.

VIOLENCE FACED BY FEMALE-BORN SEXUAL AND GENDER MINORITIES

While feminism has politicized the personal, it has not pushed this analysis to the personal level of our bodies and their very desires. This is evident in the limits of feminism to accommodate the experiences of female-born sexual and gender minorities – bodies which are united in their common experience with violence after they assert a right to pleasure (being with another woman, changing one's gender).

What we discover from our interviews is that the heteropatriarchal marriage system in India leaves no choice for female-born sexual minorities to realize their pleasure, either in terms of having a sexual partner of their same gender, or in terms of wanting to identify with a different gender than the one they were ascribed at birth, or even expressing non-stereotypical gender behaviour, like cutting their hair. Indeed, one of the main attacks for both MTF (male-to-female transgender people) and FTM (female-to-male transgender people) is on the basis of hair. For FTMs cutting off the hair by force is common and sometimes it has led to even murder of the person by their family. On 8 November 2011, Kumara Velu, an MTF, was killed by her family for having long hair and the case was hushed up with no proof. Similarly, cutting of long hair by female-to-male transpeople is also punished; in fact many FTMs actually cannot even cut their hair till they come out of their family. Expression of any self-pleasure, let alone homosexuality, has no legitimate space.

This becomes evident with the interviews we conducted with parents of female-born sexual minorities. Very few parents even consider the rights of their children to experiencing pleasure.

One individual's parent refused to speak, stating that he would feel uncomfortable to speak about this issue with women! Another individual's parent refused to give an interview stating that her parents accept her because, in their perception, the girl is ugly and cannot be married off. Moreover, they exclaim that this acceptance is a 'private' thing and not public.

We did receive some favourable situations. Two parents responded, stating that they knew about their child's 'lesbian issue' and that they felt it is the right of their 'daughter' to have their choice of sexual orientation. One person's confused parent told us that, ultimately, it is her daughter, and her happiness matters. However, it is important to note that all these three people who gave interviews were from upper middle-class and middle-class families.

It is difficult to think about 'one' experience of female-born sexual and gender minorities in regard to issues of violence and pleasure because this community, like all communities in India, is divided by caste and class. The intersections of caste and class in the context of sexuality and gender are very complex. Restrictions on gender are more common in higher castes and classes, even though sexual diversity is rejected. In the lower class and castes, the gender expressions are sometimes seen as an upward mobility in female-born people, and acceptance often comes from economic contributions to the family. However, lesbianism is not accepted while being transgender might be accepted.

We interviewed two FTMs from Kerala, whose crisis cases I handled during my work with Sangama.[2] One person's poverty made his parents not even search for him when he ran away from Kerala. Not all FTMs experienced similar violence; some of them were able to receive tolerance from their parents by fitting into their heteronormative vision.

One FTM's mother approved of his gender and his relationship with a woman, because she viewed him as being a heterosexual husband with a wife. One of the parents who responded to the interview said that it was her child's right to have a choice of sexual orientation, but she did not know about transgenderism. Though the question of acceptance was not an issue, the concept that a female-bodied person would want to be a male was very difficult for her to understand.

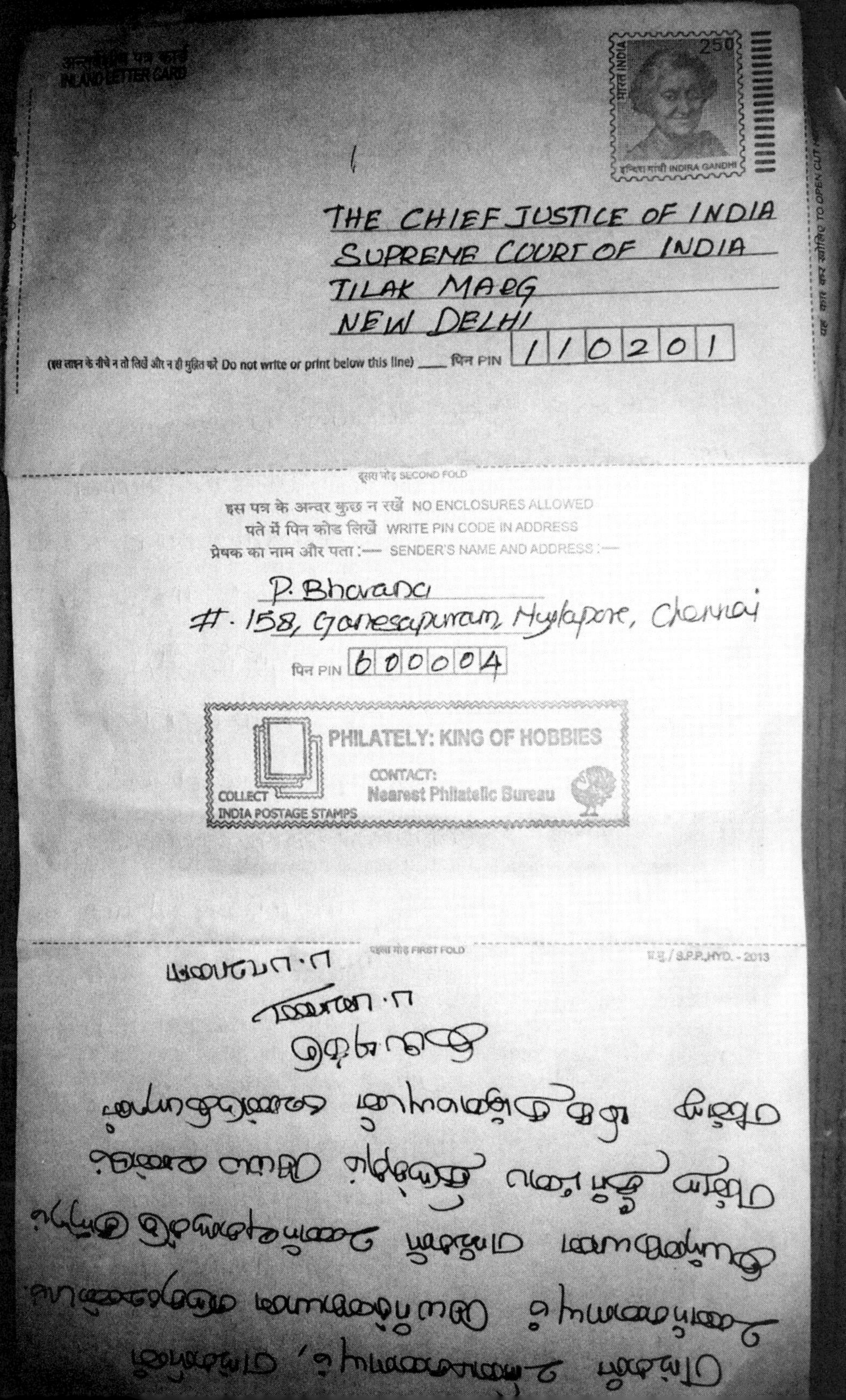

अन्तर्देशीय पत्र कार्ड
INLAND LETTER CARD

भारत INDIA 2.50
इन्दिरा गांधी INDIRA GANDHI

THE CHIEF JUSTICE OF INDIA
SUPREME COURT OF INDIA
TILAK MARG
NEW DELHI

(इस लाइन के नीचे न तो लिखें और न ही मुद्रित करें Do not write or print below this line) ____ पिन PIN 110201

यहां काट कर खोलिए TO OPEN CUT HERE

दूसरा मोड़ SECOND FOLD

इस पत्र के अन्दर कुछ न रखें NO ENCLOSURES ALLOWED
पते में पिन कोड लिखें WRITE PIN CODE IN ADDRESS
प्रेषक का नाम और पता :— SENDER'S NAME AND ADDRESS :—

P. Bhavana
#. 158, Ganesapuram, Mylapore, Chennai
पिन PIN 600004

PHILATELY: KING OF HOBBIES
CONTACT:
Nearest Philatelic Bureau
COLLECT
INDIA POSTAGE STAMPS

पहला मोड़ FIRST FOLD
म.मु. / S.P.P.,HYD. - 2013

எங்கள் உண்மையையும், எங்கள்
உணர்வையும் இயற்கையான அந்தரங்கம்.
இயற்கையான எங்கள் உணர்வுகளுக்கு குற்றம்
என்ற தீர்ப்பை திருத்தம் செய்ய வேண்டும்
என்று மிக தாழ்மையுடன் வேண்டுகிறாள்
இப்படிக்கு
ப. பவானா
ப. பாவனா

What one can see in these limited number of available responses is that there is very little space for approval and acceptance of female-born sexual minorities. Sexuality and gender as a choice and sex work as a choice challenges the structure of heteropatriarchal family and marriage system, systems that rely on restricting the agency of female-born persons.

From our interviews, we began to recognize that the experiences of female-born gender and sexual minorities present new examples of violence and assault. While sexual assault committed in the public space can be recognized by laws, this is not the case for female-born sexual and gender minorities. Forced heterosexual marriage in the private realm is violation of self. It is a type of sexual assault – an assault to dignity and pleasure – that has become normalized in our culture and happens every day.

In most cases, the moment the family comes to know about the homosexual orientation, heterosexual marriage is seen as a remedy to 'correct' the woman of her immorality, or disease. For various reasons, the family is also not equipped to handle homosexual orientation, especially within female-born people. This assault, this violence, has serious effects on the mental health and stability of female-born sexual minorities. Unlike male-born people, female-born people often receive punishment for behaving like a man or having a relationship with women. There are cases where women have been put under house arrest, without any connection to the outside world for months.

Many years ago, in Mumbai, there was a case of suicide by a Gujarati girl. It was a case of a Sindhi girl and a Gujarati girl in a relationship. The Gujarati girl underwent a sex change operation as the Sindhi girl insisted on this surgery to pass off as a heterosexual relationship. When the Sindhi girl refused the relationship due to the pressure of her family, the Gujarati girl committed suicide. The other part of the chawl that he stayed in, was indifferent to this suicide. Scenarios like this happen all over southern India. In our community research, we learnt that Sahayathrika[3] has recorded more than thirty cases of lesbian suicides in a span of ten years. We also estimate that between 2003 and 2009, there were six lesbian-suicide cases in Tamil Nadu. Sometimes these cases do not even get recognized as suicide, because of the individual's non-heterosexual orientation. One does not even know of any kind of such documentation some thirty to forty years ago. What this reveals is that compulsory heterosexuality can be lethal and cost one's life.

STRUCTURAL VIOLENCE

Structural violence is violence based on the systemic processes in which social, political, cultural and economic structures in the society prevent people from exercising their basic rights. Institutionalized elitism, ethnocentrism, classism, racism, casteism, sexism, adultism, nationalism, ableism, heterosexism and ageism are some forms of structural violence. Many times, these structures perpetuate violence which is overt, like family violence, racial violence, hate crimes, terrorism, genocide and war, but there are also forms contributed by these structures which are not as overt.

Many LBT people we spoke to shared their experiences with how they were forced to reveal their sexual orientation in the family and were consequently subjected to severe emotional trauma by being forced into heterosexual marriage, 'treated' for homosexuality by mental health professionals, physically abused and sometimes even put under house arrest.

In a case in Tamil Nadu, a Muslim girl and a Hindu girl had a relationship. They were classmates and when the family came to know about their relationship, immediately, the Muslim girl's mobility was restricted. The family fixed her marriage and she was kept under house arrest for four months without any connection to the outside world.

In another case in Bangalore, when the family figured out the relationship between the two girls, one girl was forcibly taken for treatment. The other girl was treated like she had a contagious disease to the extent that she was put in a different room, everything was given separately to her, including her plate for eating. One of the girls' fathers even asked the other girl if she had a penis and if she could satisfy his daughter.

The structure of our social system is based on violence if there is any sort of nonconformity. The structural violence goes with various levels of intersectionality like that of caste, class, religion, and gender and sexuality. Moreover, cultures are different in various regions, and this adds to complex structural violence especially against female-born/women. When an individual is located in multiple marginalized positions, they experience even more violence in their inability to question and pursue alternatives to the systems they have been forced into. Because of this, female-born sexual and gender minorities must make do with even the little acts of recognition they are given or granted.

A woman from Palakkad called on Sahayatrika's helpline asking if there were any spaces at all which could accept this kind of relationship. She said that both she and her lover just could not speak about their relationship before their heterosexual marriages. Though it did not come across as forced marriage, they felt like homosexual relationships could not exist and they had no choice. So this woman, when she read about Sahayatrika's work in the media, called them secretly, as she was extremely scared that her husband would find out about her sexual orientation.

There was a suicide case of an Adivasi lesbian women in Kerala in May 2002, which was portrayed as though they were committing suicide due to poverty. Their sexual preference never came into the picture. Ignoring the fact of sexual preference in such cases is a further example of structural violence. What we are confronted with through these cases of suicides is the intersections of class, caste and sexuality. Hate crimes occur in rural areas but do not get recognized as such.

One FTM transperson who gave an interview shared that he was ridiculed terribly by his family and people around using the word 'aanachankali' in Malayalam, which basically means a woman/female-born person taking on the role of a 'man'. This usage is usually in the context of a husband regulating the powers of a wife and this is not a derogatory word. In fact, the FTM stated saying that he actually liked being ridiculed in that name, even though it was very bad, only because the ridicule is also recognition of his male identity.

In my own experience, I played cricket – so I thought I could handle my expression of gender identity in terms of my masculinity in the name of sports. But that also came under fire though my father is a sports person. He tore my shirt, snatched away my cricket uniform and burnt it in front of me because I was not behaving like a woman. My father would beat me black and blue because of my gender expression. For me, the biggest question always was, why did I have to receive so much physical and emotional violence? I was wondering if I could ever file a legal case against my father and family.

What becomes evident from these instances and others, is that female-born sexual minorities also experience public violence but the violence in private spaces is built into the system. Private space is in the family or within relationships where you do not go public or to the police stations to lodge complaints. It is where you cannot go public in the name of family honour. It is a situation where police refuse to register the complaint in the name of 'family honour'. While state officials may come in to 'help,' they are often more concerned with morally policing LGBT people and women.

Though male-born sexual and gender minorities have restrictions and norms of heteromasculinity, they still have access to a space, no matter how small it might be. Sometimes, male-born (homo)sexuality and gender expressions get cultural sanction by religion. For this community, there is a history, there are mythologies. For female-born sexual and gender minorities, there is no such space – we are always under control of the system. Our sexuality and gender expressions are regulated according to a system that denies our existence. This system punishes female-born/women at every step and also has the power to block the outside world entirely. Moreover, female-born gender and sexual minorities are often not in a position to run away from an environment because they have been conditioned to be dependent (especially economically). While male-born sexual minorities might have economic mobility to escape from their families, female-born persons are often discouraged from education due to the context of poverty.

Violence in the context of a patriarchal system

We have shown how many forms of violence that previously did not have names came to be identified by legal, social and political systems due to efforts from feminist activists. The question then comes to us: once a form of violence is identified, how do we get it recognized? For example, dowry was unjust toward women, yet it had a cultural sanction. It was only because of the tireless advocacy of women's movements that dowry[4] got identified as crime. Indeed, if one looks at the legal system what gets identified as crime/violence is heavily based on male convenience and patriarchal structures.

Often the legal system also overtly refuses to identify crimes/violence based on morality (a word used to conceal patriarchal bias). For example, when a lesbian girl, forcibly married to a man, escaped to Bangalore from Tamil Nadu, her mother and ex-husband constantly tried to get her back and ultimately their efforts worked. They sedated her and abducted her back to Tamil Nadu. Sangama had earlier helped her resist her family's pressure to succumb to her marriage and children. While she was working at the Sangama office, she was abducted from her work space. When Sangama tried to give an abduction complaint to the police, the police refused to take the complaint stating that a mother and husband cannot abduct their own girl. Even after much persistence by the Sangama lawyer, the police refused to take the complaint. Finally, they agreed to take a missing complaint filed by a co-worker.

Thus, female-born sexual minorities find it difficult to receive support and validation from the patriarchal legal system. **However, they often face similar hostilities from women's advocacy organizations as well.** There is an example of a women's group in north India that helped the parents of the lesbian couple to find where they were, with disastrous consequences. In another case, a women's group in India refused shelter to lesbians out of fear. In another instance, a women's shelter home in south India could not take a decision, and forced counselling on a lesbian woman and advised her to go back to her family and husband.

Self-inflicted gender violence

Female-born sexual and gender minorities are also implicated within this system, evident in the extreme amounts of self-violence found in our communities. Our interviewees were marked by feelings of trauma, guilt and fear. These emotions sometimes lead to self-mutilation and, possibly, thoughts of suicide. Patriarchy has constantly justified violence and conditioned female-born people to not question violence nor recognize it as violence.

In a recent case in Tamil Nadu, a lesbian couple was exposed in the media by one of the girls' brothers. Later, the couple solicited help in Bangalore. During the negotiation process, the family of one girl took her back home and said that she could not be contacted. Her partner filed a habeas corpus case. Initially, the girl said that she wanted to stay with her partner. Then the court ordered the girl to stay in a shelter home, and take counselling and time to take a proper decision. After the given time, the girl stated that she wanted to get back to her family.

Now, one knows how she arrived at this decision, whether it was the counselling, or the coercion or blackmailing of the family. The advocate who was handling the case in fact asked the judge why the court did not give more time for the girl to take counselling to decide if she really wanted to go back to her family. This shows how state agencies and the judiciary actually do not even look at family spaces as sites of violence. This also shows how even female-born sexual minorities become agents of violence against themselves and their relationships due to pressure from a patriarchal system.

Concluding thoughts on structural violence

Everything cannot just be stated as gender violence, and similarly all LGBTI experience of violence cannot also be put together and be perceived as one form of violence. All these experiences cannot be addressed under one kind of law either. Violence comes into too many discussions – experiences of violence are different to various people based on the differences of caste and class. We have to undo the easy understanding of violence and also locate where sexuality plays a role and where gender plays a role and where both come together.

Male sexual and gender-minority communities are more vocal about their violence in public than female-born sexual and gender-minority communities. We engage with a community that hardly uses the state agencies like police or court. For the state to interfere in this issue, the biggest barrier is family – the honour of the female body as constructed by middle-class morals.

In our call for an analysis of new types of violence that are faced by female born sexual minorities, we do not mean to dismiss the very real and physical violence that our communities face. In fact, our status as female-born gender and sexual minorities increases our vulnerability to physical violence like rape and sexual assault as highlighted by women's movement.

FTMs are more susceptible to sexual violence in public, as the gender expression of FTMs is seen as challenging the masculinity of the male-born people. In a case in 2006, two FTMs were having a meal at a roadside restaurant in the evening. A male stranger came and sat at the same

Dear Chief Justice of India,

This one is to tell you that it is now hard to expect justice from you. Just to have the words "Justice" and "Supreme" doesn't make your decisions right.

You have crumbled people's rights, the right to love, live in peace and with dignity. And you have only added more disgrace ~~by~~ to your decision by calling them as "SO-CALLED" rights. Do you realize, you never even apologized!

Let me erase your misconceptions, you are not protecting our rights, but only helping the haters hate.

But I won't stop. This is my life and I will live it only once. I can't let a group of stubborn & ignorant people snatch it away from me.

लोगों को हक वापस दो, 377 वापस लो!

— Soumya [illegible]

POST CARD पोस्ट कार्ड

प्र.मु./SPP/HYD - 2013

Philately: King Of Hobbies
COLLECT INDIA POSTAGE STAMPS
CONTACT
Nearest Philatelic Bureau

The Chief Justice of India
Supreme Court of India
Tilak Marg
New Delhi

पिन PIN 1 1 0 2 0 1

(इस लाइन के नीचे न तो लिखें और न ही मुद्रित करें, Do not write or print below this line)

table. The stranger was drunk and picked up a fight with these two FTMs. When the fight got physical, a person in the restaurant screamed across the room exclaiming that both of them were not men and were actually women. The immediate response from the male stranger was to tear off the shirt of one of the FTMs. For the stranger tearing off the shirt meant exposing the female body to the public. When the FTM went to the police station to complain, the police and the stranger verbally abused the FTM. They asked him if he had a vagina? Did he have a hole in his vagina? What was the length of the hole in his vagina? Again society's focus on female-born people is on their vaginas and the need to keep this area 'pure'.

SILENCE AS VIOLENCE

In calling for attention to new forms of gender violence committed against female-born sexual minorities, it is important to think critically about the violence that accompanies silence in our communities.

Some forms of structural violence are not loud. Structural violence brings in a certain kind of silence, which amounts to complete non-recognition. Silencing occurs on all sides, including family and friends. Another type of silencing occurs because compulsory heterosexuality leaves no room for female-born sexual minorities to express any other preference. The difficulty with challenging this violence is that most forms of it are unstated, and not recognizable even by the victims themselves because they have become normalized in our culture. For example, we spoke to a female-born person who was forcibly married for seven years and experienced every possible type of violence in this marriage. He decided to suppress his desire for the sake of family honour and hence got married.

Many individuals might not even be aware that there are alternative ways of desiring, experiencing pleasure and creating relationships outside of a heteronormative system. This silence can be particularly isolating for female-born sexual and gender minorities. Unlike other minorities – including class, ethnic and caste minorities – sexual and gender minorities do not receive support from their families or communities. They became a minority within their family, state and society due to the silence around issues of gender and sexuality. In this context, the very first space where a female-born person attempts to express their preferred sexuality or gender expression is hostile. They get alienated by the family – a system conventionally thought of as the basic unit of society. The silencing of their desire and their difference begins here and extends to all other aspects of their life: work, education, marriage, etc.

LEGAL CONSTRUCT OF VIOLENCE AND POSSIBLE CHANGE

If we take the presence of this violence seriously, we must imagine new ways of creating and doing legal justice, as the law itself has been the cause of violence for female-born people across India. Currently, the construct of violence in law is much less about social justice and respecting individual and community rights, and is much more about defining crime and punishment. The criminal law is more lenient to those who are upper class and can access the law and all of its processes. The law never focuses on the victim's situation after the offence has already been committed; law is not empathetic, not truly concerned with what happens to the victim after the crime, and is rather only invested in punishment and law enforcement. One lawyer we spoke to remarked that even though law pretends to be objective and neutral, it is often exercised in a way that is more violent towards poor and other marginalized communities. For example, even when a wealthy person might commit a huge financial scam, they may receive a similar amount of punishment as a poor person who has committed a petty crime. We have also seen the ways in which the 'neutral' law is used as a tactic of violence and power against female-born sexual and gender minorities. For example, many of the people we spoke with talked about how officials in the state of Kerala have repeatedly claimed that there are no lesbians there.

Even though the law has been exercised as a tactic of violence against our communities, we do not believe that we should abandon the law in a struggle for justice. However, we need to drastically change how we imagine the ways that we think of and practice law to reduce the violence faced by gender and sexual minorities. We cannot think of law as the only solution for our communities. As we have expressed, the state and the legal system are both institutions of violence and cannot be trusted, therefore, to end all of our injustice.

Gender Expression: The Constitution guarantees this fundamental right – 'Right to freedom of speech and expression, assembly, association or union, movement, residence, and right to practise any profession or occupation (these rights are subject to security of the state, friendly relations with foreign countries, public order, decency or morality).' Gender expression is a form of expression and should be protected by the law. Therefore, any sexual or gender minority who is a target of violence for their gender expression should be able to pursue justice and report this violence as a violation of their fundamental right. In reality, though, this option is not really available and social morality governs every expression of gender and regulates and punishes anyone who does not conform. This punishment is not seen as a crime by the state and goes without redress.

Domestic Violence: In order to address the violence perpetrated against women within marriage and family, the state introduced the Protection for Women Against Domestic Violence Act in 2005. In this act, an 'aggrieved person' is any woman who is, or has been, in a domestic relationship with the respondent and who alleges to have been subjected to any act of domestic violence by the respondent. In this definition, the usage of 'has been in a domestic relationship' can be interpreted as domesticity that is shared in the parental house with family members like parents, siblings and relatives. Most female-born sexual and gender minorities undergo severe violence at the hands of their families. The definition of the 'aggrieved person' in the Domestic Violence Act, is broad enough to include the violence suffered by female-born sexual and gender minorities at the hands of their family.

Thus, while efforts to change the Domestic Violence Act was not intended to consider how to best address the unique circumstances of female born gender and sexual minorities, this legislation may actually be used to address these forms of violence. However, further legal analysis needs to be conducted to see how this law can be applied to all gender and sexual minorities. The definition of 'woman' in this act includes all people who are born female – so technically female-born gender and sexual minorities can fall within the definition of an aggrieved person. However, the current definitions of this law are still exclusionary. Firstly, we need to expand the definition of 'woman' beyond female-born to include hijras and other 'male'-born gender minorities who identify as women. Also, we need to realize that although they might be born 'female,' many FTM people identify strongly as male and, currently, would have to face the violence of being incorrectly gendered in the court as a 'woman' to receive justice for their violence. One suggestion that came up from our interviews was including transpeople in the very definition of 'aggrieved person,' while not taking away the special protection for heterosexual women against violence by their birth families and families they are married into. However, this strategy does not think about who will be considered in the category of 'transgender' and how they will be identified. We need to collectively think of ways to de-gender the 'aggrieved' person, but still simultaneously acknowledge the unique circumstance of violence faced by female-born people.

If the general legislations like physical assault and cruelty can be used against the family or public in the courts then, the gender specificity of protections for women need not be taken away, as one cannot at any cost compromise on women's rights. What one needs to look at is more about the act of crime, not the sex or gender of the person. Inclusion of transpeople should not mean making the law gender neutral as that would be dangerous in many senses.

House Arrest: In the situations of house arrest of female-born seyual and gender minorities, framing the issue as illegal detention and asking for remedy of habeas corpus works better as there can be an immediate action. Most of the female-born seyual and gender minorities have the experience of being under house arrest with absolutely no connections with the rest of the world. If it is a couple, one of the partners would be put under house arrest the moment the family comes to know about the homosexual relationship. If one of them identifies as a transperson and the girl manages to escape from the family and go live with him, then there might be an abduction case foisted on the transperson, and allegation that the transperson spoiled the girl.

In such situations, advocates in India have found one legal process useful: the habeas corpus petition where the state has to produce the details and information and the person in front of the petitioner. The partner is usually advised by activists to file a habeas corpus petition at the High Court because it is a more effective remedy. It is one of the most powerful writ petitions in India and has mostly worked effectively except for certain cases where 'social morality' gets brought up. For example, in Kerala, there was a lesbian case where the two girls, one Hindu and one Muslim girl, came out of the family and sought shelter in an NGO. When the Muslim girl was taken back by the family, the Hindu girl with the help of the NGO filed a habeas corpus petition. The High Court ordered that the two girls could live together because they were adults. Immediately after the judgement, when the girls came out of the court, the Muslim family, with the help of the police, kidnapped the Muslim girl and confined her in a place that was not accessible in any way. It was clear contempt of court, but the advocate at that point could not take further steps.

While habeas corpus petitions are useful remedies in any house-arrest situation, our interview participants suggested other laws from the Indian Penal Code as well:

> **Section 357, Assault or criminal force in attempting wrongfully to confine a person**: Whoever assaults or uses criminal force to any person, in attempting wrongfully to confine that person, shall be punished with imprisonment of either description for a term which may extend to one year, or with fine which may extend to one thousand rupees, or with both.
>
> **Section 339, Wrongful restraint**: Whoever voluntarily obstructs any person so as to prevent that person from proceeding in any direction in which that person has right to proceed, is said wrongfully to restrain that person. Eyception: The obstruction of a private way over land or water which a person in good

faith believes himself to have lawful right to obstruct, is not an offence within the meaning of this section.

Section 346, Wrongful confinement in secret: Whoever wrongfully confines any person in such manner as to indicate an intention that the confinement of such person may not be known to any person interested in the person so confined, or to any public servant, or that the place of such confinement may not be known to or discovered by any such person or public servant as herein before mentioned, shall be punished with imprisonment of either description for a term which may extend to two years in addition to any other punishment to which he may be liable for such wrongful confinement.

Section 345, Wrongful confinement of person for whose liberation writ has been issued: Whoever keeps any person in wrongful confinement, knowing that a writ for the liberation of that person has been duly issued, shall be punished with imprisonment of either description for a term which may extend to two years in addition to any term of imprisonment to which he may be liable under any other section of this chapter.

□

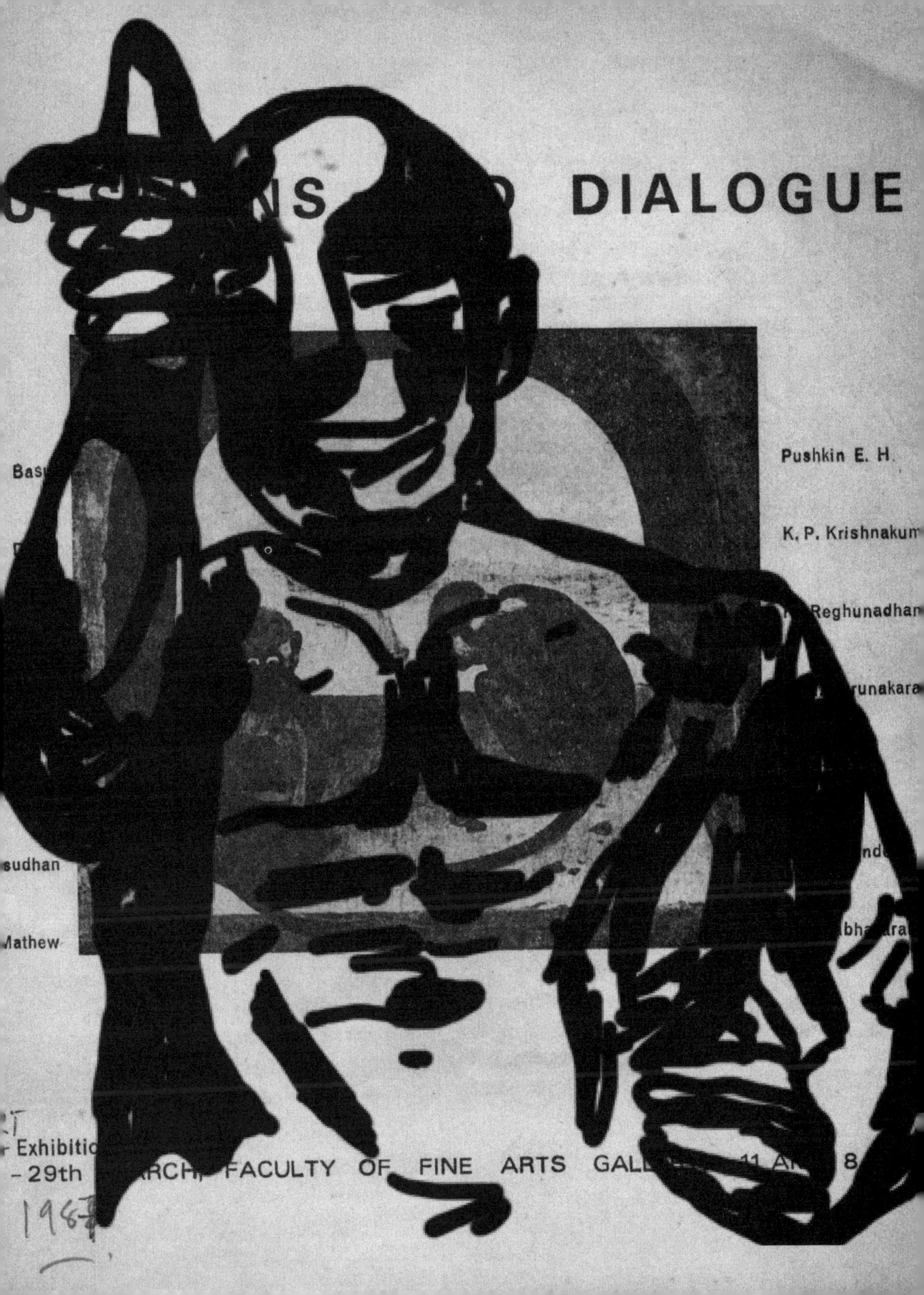
DIALOGUE
Basu
Pushkin E. H.
K. P. Krishnakum
Reghunadhan
runakara
sudhan
Mathew
Exhibitio
– 29th
FACULTY OF FINE ARTS GAL

In March 1987, an art exhibition was organized at the well-known Faculty of Fine Arts, at the M.S. University in Baroda. The exhibition was itself a staging ground to launch a movement led by radical artists primarily from Kerala, intended both as a critique of key prevalent tenets of contemporary Indian art and as a new, politically informed way forward. Briefly institutionalized as the **Indian Radical Painters and Sculptors Association**, the short-lived movement effectively came to a close following the suicide of its leading figure, the artist **K.P. Krishnakumar** (1958–1989). In its time, it mounted a critique against the kind of art that had come to be associated with the Faculty of Fine Arts and its major figures, leading artists and art historians K.G. Subramanyan and Gulammohammed Sheikh, more generally with the 'narrative movement' (see Editor's Note 13), and still more generally with the schools of painting associated with Indian nationalism (e.g., the 'Bengal School'). In opposition to this entire legacy was an art that would, in an effort to be differently informed and engaged, claim the inheritance of a global avant-garde ranged from the Soviet Union to Latin America, positioning the persona of the artist within a different, more heroic, expressionist mould.

The text, by artist and curator **Anita Dube**, was printed and circulated during the 1987 exhibition. Although authored by Dube and using the first-person pronoun, it was written following extensive debates within the group, and represented a collective vision.

Images: Reproductions of the original Questions and Dialogue manifesto with a meme of the pointing finger, along with the sculpture itself, one of K.P. Krishnakumar's best known works and perhaps the iconic image of the entire movement: **The Thief** (painted fibreglass, 1985). Image courtesy Geeta Kapur and Vivan Sundaram Archive, Asia Art Archive.

19

ANITA DUBE

1987

QUESTIONS AND DIALOGUE

A dialectical situation arises in the cultural arena. A group of artists consciously rejects the practices of the 'mainstream' and mobilizes a radical new-left collective to search for a pedagogy of art; an alternative 'philosophy of praxis'. This critical act turns the compound questioning eye on everything, seizes the present moment, stands crude, naked and knife-sharp, and will not allow anyone to pass.

Antonio Gramsci in his *Prison Notebooks* lucidly states our position:

> Creating a new culture does not only mean one's own individual 'original' discoveries. It also, and most particularly, means the diffusion in a critical form, of truths already discovered, their 'socialization' as it were, and even making them the basis of vital action, an element of coordination and intellectual and moral order. For a mass of people to be led to think coherently and in the same coherent fashion about the real present world, is a 'philosophical' event far more important and 'original' than the discovery by some philosophical 'genius' of a truth which remains the property of [a] small groups of intellectuals.[1]

The philosophical questions haunting history and the consciousness of artists – more acutely in modern times with the global expansion of capitalism – are what is man and what can man become. Inasmuch as man does not exist alone, but consciously and intellectually interacts with other men, with the natural world and the world of things to transform them, he is a political 'species being'[2] who creates history. History is therefore this process of becoming or humanization of man. In the swamp of class-society, the swamp-filled darkness of repression, all 'human substance' is petrified. Yet through the swamp voices have risen; vital potential voices of 'man' – in radical art, in radical thoughts, in radical philosophies, radical literature, radical scientific achievements, revolutionary struggles: pushing against the wall. A politics of resistance and discovery, a continuous human search for truth and knowledge to enlarge the world and its meaning, struggling for a classless freedom for every man – as a necessity and the ultimate freedom from that for a realization of true humanism.

In art, taken as aesthetic strategy and intellectual and philosophical struggle (located absolutely in the material and philosophical conditions of the present, carrying a national and global consciousness of today, to change this), the search for a persona and voice and a search for an authentic history, are interlinked. They demand an uncompromising consciousness of 'nationhood' through which an artist can speak to his people, and at the same time stand in the world arena shoulder to shoulder with the community of universal human and artistic truths. The criteria and meaning of 'nationhood' has become significant under the pressures of imperialism and social-fascism, especially if we see this not in a causal relation to history or as a populist slogan, but as closely connected to the idea of the freedom of 'man' which can only be realized within the concept of a nation.

Indian nationalism, for all its passion and sincerity, has been unable to develop this philosophical and revolutionary potentiality contained within the idea of nationhood. It has remained fatally attached to the limited perspective of gaining independence and preserving it. The Congress leadership, submissive to what George Steiner calls 'the imagined garden of liberal culture',[3] originating in nineteenth-century England, has failed to fully undertake the process of decolonization and radical independent modernization. In the tacit conviviality of private enterprise, government, national leadership, bureaucracy, educational institutions, cultural platforms, in the attitude of the bourgeoisie, the educated petty-bourgeoisie and the intelligentsia, there emerges under the veneer of liberalism, secularism, nationalism, quasi-socialism and scholarly practice, the philosophy of the dominant majority, the Hindu philosophy, which has turned the state, its supporters and its slogans into fascist ones.

Today, Indian society is a complex class and caste society, hooked onto the diabolic mechanism of world capitalism since the early nineteenth century; susceptible to its dominant logic in the political, economic and cultural arenas. It is therefore, I believe, a gross mistake and a view from across the line, to overlook this fact in any dialogue on Indian history, culture and art.

In the forty years of independence, our art reflects these very problems. Out of a colonized consciousness of fear, arises a concurrence of the bourgeoisie and petty-bourgeoisie classes (from which the artists are drawn) with democracy and its myth of progress and freedom, in which the role of an artist is marginalized and tolerated in the same fashion as the 'opposition', as a sulking pet dog. The artist learns to 'perform' as a juggler or a cynic the 'labour of Sisyphus'.[4] He struggles defensively without fully comprehending the forces he is struggling against and therefore what he is struggling for. The questions that arise are therefore formal or pseudo-questions, far away from the real issues.

During the national movement, an authoritative nostalgia was widely generated in the arts for the lost coherence of a centre that held over and above the objectivities of historical fact and processes. Notwithstanding the perspicacious and sensitive scholarship of Indologists like E. B. Havell and Ananda Coomaraswamy and artists like Abanindranath Tagore, they created an overpowering mythical vision of Indian cultural history and art traditions from a feudal bourgeoisie's point of view.[5] In the process, they rejected the most advanced humanistic thoughts of the time arising out of the philosophy of dialectical materialism, and turned instead to idealist organic streams of thought which were incapable of understanding the world under capitalism as a totality. The artists associated with such scholarship, in the Bengal revivalist movement, dispersed strategically to all the prominent art schools in India, at Shantiniketan, Lucknow, Delhi, Lahore and Madras to entrench this parochial vision on a national scale.

The afterlife of the same vision continues today in the philosophy of the 'living tradition', which seems to be a fetishistic form of the earlier nationalism. It contains an inability to live in one's own time, and is also a strategy to survive in it. K.G. Subramanyan, searching for a 'total' holistic vision of art as against the 'fragmented' sensibility of the modern,[6] locates his philosophy on the idea of an 'electric plurality' within the traditional hierarchic interpenetration of the 'little' and the 'larger' manifestations in art and culture. In an essay 'Do We Need an Art Movement'[7] he writes,

> If one walks through the state of Orissa, for instance, village to town, you can see a whole spectrum of these simple wall decorations of untrained tribal housewives, the work of the village potter, metal worker, muralist, with greater skill impulse the works of various skilled craftsmen like the silversmith, whose filigree work is no less refined than a (Richard) Lippold, and weavers whose geometricism

> and colour sense will do credit to any modern artist or designer, then the well-known temples with their astounding sculpture. You can see this in many parts of India. The ordered circuits of their activity as against the adventurous and self-defeating cross circuiting of the modern scene I have described should certainly make us think and recall Coomaraswamy's statement that while artists can be special kinds of men all men can be special kinds of artists (without each being a Michelangelo or a Cezanne). In fact, some of the specialities of certain levels of these activities come from their simplicity or unambitiousness, even unconcern, about being art.

Today, in our situation, it is difficult to accept Subramanyan's great nostalgia for the collective practices of proto-capitalist, moribund village and town economies. What is his idea of historical process? When he speaks of the potter, the weaver, the tribal woman as fixed in history, with no right to a choice of expression, all in the name of an 'electric plurality', a grand hierarchic design which should not be disturbed, he speaks with a paternal false-humanism of a feudal bourgeois. Obviously, for him, state capitalism and class society are eternal unchanging institutions.[8] Yet, capitalism, having destroyed at the root a collective way of life, has destroyed the *raison d'être* of folk art. Therefore, to speak of a living tradition in art and culture outside the perspective of socialism is to parody or make a pastiche of the same. This is increasingly evident in the cultural policies of today, where folk art and culture are being preserved and marketed as precisely a parody, to satisfy the increasing historical appetite of the bourgeoisie.

Folk art can no longer economically sustain, in any honourable fashion, the craftsmen involved in it. What then is the reason for its survival, if not as a political act of resistance against the phenomena of forgetting that capitalism entails? Organic historic memory is a preserve of these pockets of culture, one which cannot be seen to be formally appropriated, or sold in a sophisticated urban context outside the organized vulgarization of history, which has become a symptom of our times.

The other mainstream modern Indian art carries an ambivalent relationship, one of admiration and rejection, to the whole revolutionary drama of 'modernism' played out in Europe between the mid-nineteenth to the mid-twentieth century. Fundamentally, the resistance is located against the radical-intellectual strains within modernism, especially its apotheosis of science, its contemporaneity, its knowledge of the world made available through research in anthropology and sociology. [What is lost thus] is its objective materialist engagement with reality, history, truth, Utopia, its close connection to philosophy, literature and the other arts, its resistance to the freezing of the 'human substance' under

capitalism, expressed in psychopathological escape, moral protest to attempts at objectively and scientifically interpreting reality as a totality, in its multifaceted dimensions, both individual and typical. Art under modernism became a measure of humanistic concern, in the bloodstream of an artist engendering a clash with the old syntax of visual language, its untenable philosophic content, in changing times.

Indian artists, influenced by the sensibility of the older Victorian and post-Victorian bourgeoisie, could not fully penetrate this materialist humanist tradition. For them, its forms and ethos were 'variously ugly, dissonant, obscure, scandalous, immoral, subversive and generally anti-social'.[9] And yet this same has perversely fascinated them. By appropriating modernism's attractive features as a 'style' and a method of avant-grade art practice, its original spirit was in fact 'vulgarized'. Ironically, they have usurped the anarchic classless freedom of the modem artist, not as a struggle, but simply as a corollary to their profession. This conveniently places them outside the problems of 'real' history, outside questions in class terms, somewhere between the workings of subjective consciousness and phenomenology. From such a position, the imaginary, personal and historic events and characters are put in inverted commas, as part of their commodification which can serve the artist as 'referents' to make all kinds of critical gestures, even gestures of anarchy and protest.

This is related in fact to the canonization or institutionalization of 'modernism', its reduction to a set of dead classics in Europe around the 1950s when Indian artists contacted it. The waning of its effect was giving rise to a new phenomenon of postmodernism. This philosophy was the cultural logic of multinational capitalism, in which a new populist rhetoric was slowly taking over the older modernist, metaphysical concerns with truth and Utopia. Ideologically, it was celebrating a commodification of culture, and demonstrating that the omnipresence of the class struggle which had haunted modernism was now in retreat.

When we examine broadly the features of the postmodern (after Frederic Jameson's brilliant analysis of it in an essay 'The Cultural Logic of Capital'), we find that with the exception of a few artists, like Amrita Sher-Gil and Binode Bihari Mukherjee, the majority of our artists have submitted in a lesser or greater degree to the overpowering logic of the same. What is this philosophy then, which is freezing the blood of artists all over the world? Frederic Jameson writes,

> . . . aesthetic production today has become integrated into commodity production generally; the frantic economic urgency of producing fresh waves of ever more novel seeming goods (from clothing to airplanes), at even greater rates of turnover, assigns an increasingly STRUCTURAL function and position to aesthetic

> innovation and experimentation. Such economic necessities then find recognition in the institutional support of all kinds available for the newer art, from foundations and grants to museums and other forms of patronage.[10]

Postmodernism is therefore a triumph of capitalist aesthetics, one from which Indian artists have, without knowing it, been unable to escape. In a literal sense, postmodernism brings with it an obvious superficiality. It focuses on surface, and features of the surface, smoothness, or textures and marks and multiple surfaces which stubbornly resist an opening up into depth, even in a literal sense. Everything is as if held on the surface – a flatness, which is reminiscent of mechanical reproductions, prevails. Colour and principles of construction are apotheosized, and the art product begins to resemble a commodity in the market with a new anti-human autonomy over 'man'. All search for 'real' history is replaced by a pseudo-historical depth. In the absence of the old artist's monadic ego which compiled him to struggle for a distinctive subject and a style as unique as his own physiognomy, 'the producers of culture have nowhere to turn to but the past'.[11] There emerges a 'random cannibalization of all the styles of the past, the play at random stylistic allusion'.[12] Here, pasts or history become a mere referent, concerned with 'textuality' and the 'glossy qualities of the image'. All this is prompted by a growing consumer's appetite for "a world transformed into sheer images of itself and for pseudo-events and 'spectacles'".[13] In postmodernism then, parody and pastiche, kitsch and 'camp' tastes rule. In the assembly line, in the marketing copy, in the museums and galleries, all art, all philosophies, are made to look alike, to compete. Glamour irons out all radical differences. In the myth of individual freedom, individual choice reigns supreme and opportunities appear endless.

The narrative movement,[14] in India, in recent years, taking character from the British example and continuing a tradition of colonial patronage and approval, is the Indian version of an archaeology of historicism emerging from the postmodern.

Through the history of art, narration has been a special method which places the 'individual' in the 'historical' axis, i.e., it dialectically confronts the 'inside'/'outside' perception of reality of the artist through his protagonists, to face the special temper of his times. However, within the narrative mode also lies the danger of dramatic incidental storytelling, of creation of arbitrary situations and facts which deny the political and intend to surpass history. I believe, the great narrative tradition, whether Indian, from the Ajanta murals, to the sculptures at Sachi, Ellora und Mahabalipuram or European, from Piero Della Francesca to Michelangelo's *Last Judgement*, to Bruegel, to Courbet, right up to Beckmann and Leger, does not fall into a populist rhetoric by compromising individuals and events and history of their times. The narrative paintings of today do not seem to escape from this very populist rhetoric, which (I have mentioned earlier, is postmodernism's triumphant 'historicism') can consume and in the process devalue almost anything, even the past.

The paintings of this 'narrative' movement appear to stand in a critics' court to argue their social and political consciousness, their scholarship and painterly virtuosity. The events and characters portrayed are subordinated to principles of structuring and surface design, and carry a causal relation to historical processes. With the use of multiple references, what we have called 'textuality' with the use of pseudo-historical content, with the use of narration, with the use of a rhetorical tone, a myth is created which says that, that which is being portrayed is reality and the 'historical'. I fail to see how, without seriously examining the politics of visual language and subjects, (i.e. their particular existence under bourgeois aesthetics) it works, for whom and from whom, to attempt the 'historical' is to 'vulgarize' the same. Further, to pledge a preoccupation with the human figure and to be unable to draw and paint it freely and imaginatively, with a depth of observation and knowledge, certainly speaks for the shrinking sincerity and ability of artists, one that can never be justified with any theoretical argument.

Any art tradition, Indian or western, offers a philosophy of understanding 'man' in his surroundings. Within each exists a definite method of observation, of study, of gathering knowledge, a developed linguistic system by which this can be expressed. In any case, whatever their choice, an artist's skills must be sharp enough, their means viable enough, to penetrate the world around them in its material and philosophic truth.

Related to this whole new phenomenon of art practice is a growing cultural leadership that has acquired a determinist role in the arts. Pure intellectualism indulges in polemical complexities and exercise in thought in a rarified atmosphere. As professionals and specialists, they articulate their thoughts outside class terms. Antonio Gramsci, discussing the role of such scholars, writes,

> The pure intellectuals, as elaborators of the most developed ruling-class ideology, were forced to take over at least some Marxist elements to revitalize their own ideas and to check the tendency towards excessive speculative philosophising, with the historical realism of the new theory in order to provide new weapons for the social group to which they were allied.[15]

We do not want to see the relationship between intellectuals (artists as special kinds of intellectuals) and the masses in mechanistic terms. In a theoretical leadership of intellectuals of the faceless masses (outside any real contact) we see distinct fascist tendencies. The only alternative to these existing modes of art practice appears to us in a collective organization of artists to recover lost pedagogic-didactic values of art. By organizing radical activities outside the dominant cultural itinerary, we believe we may stand somewhere between mass consciousness and the pure intellectuals, directing in the process both towards a more meaningful and truthful engagement with reality.

In this brief critique of the postmodern and apotheosis of the spirit of high modernism, I do not in any way suggest a step backwards. In fact, features of the postmodern are definite cultural symptoms of our times on which we stand. Yet, we cannot deny within it a loss of values. Ideologically, the formation of our group is related to all these issues about which I have argued above.

Our group takes character on the decision of its members, not on anything else. In the crisis of our times, we believe that a philosophy of praxis, other than one of an isolated artistic search, is demanded of artists to avoid the inevitable purification of life and art under capitalist competition and the exercise of individual ambitions. Our commitment towards a political pedagogy in art places a heavy responsibility on us. It is no easy decision. Only via a politicization of consciousness and a reaffirmation of true nationalism perhaps, can we return to our real past, understand history outside the will of the dominators with the knowledge of the most advanced global philosophies and science. As artists, our real battle lies in our work, against all forms of kitsch; national kitsch, international kitsch, political kitsch, social kitsch, social-fascist kitsch, feminist kitsch. The jargon of generalizations is overwhelming. Sameness, mundanity, banality make us nauseous. The battle, as much as it is outside, is within us.

In such a large group of artists sharing a particular history, sensibility and vision, it is quite remarkable that there emerge distinct directions of individual enquiry. The old monadic ego is not dead. The search, and resistance of my friends, visible in their art, will clarify I believe, what I have written.

A sleepless wind is raising a sleepless song in sleepless heads in sleepless nights.

□

KEYWORDS

NOTES & REFERENCES

KEYWORDS

A list of names, terms and concepts used in the texts in this volume. While these are likely to be familiar to readers acquainted with Indian political theory, they are revisited here, in part as a ready primer for those less acquainted with these debates, but also to draw attention to their shifting and open-ended definitional status.

Aadhaar
Symbolically the single-point incarnation of the Government of India's digitization ambitions for digital delivery of services as well as, more visibly, for surveillance. At its most basic, it is a programme for creating a 'unique identity' for all Indian residents based on biometric data. Introduced in 2009, it was a cog in a giant wheel – the wheel being at that time the National e-Governance Plan (NeGP) – but it was the only cog that defined the wheel itself, defining how a data identity could become an essential tool of all governance. Aadhaar has repeatedly asserted that it is not a proof of **citizenship**. It has also repeatedly said that it is not mandatory but demand-driven: something economist Jean Dreze famously dismissed, saying it is 'like selling bottled water in a village after poisoning the well'. It has received increasing notoriety as the technological undergirding of an entirely new data environment in recent years that makes precisely opposite claims and requirements, including most recently the **National Population Register** and the **National Register of Citizens**, so far implemented in Assam but proposed, by numerous accounts, for the entire country. In 2017, a major Supreme Court case on Aadhaar declared **privacy** to be a right under Article 21 as well as Part 3 of the Constitution. Draft Privacy Bills as well as Data Protection Bills are currently pending in Parliament. See both the Introduction to this volume and Ravi Sundaram's essay, 'Beyond the Nationalist Panopticon'.

Adivasi
In her autobiography, excerpted here, Teesta Setalvad writes: '**Dalit** and Adivasi groups and mass organizations took me to their bosom. . . . I asked friends and leaders closely what lay behind their understanding: why was it necessary to lend this support? . . . Their response was grounded and sobering. If a malevolent state gets away with this obviously motivated attack on you, our defences also get breached.' Adivasi literally means 'original inhabitant', but both as a political and normative category it has had a difficult career in India. The term itself has been an enduring and potent signifier for many things over the modern era: valorized in romantic terms for *originality*, anthropologized as the autochthonous cultures of the subcontinent, criminalized for example by the Criminal Tribes Acts of the 1870s, and a significant political

presence in several uprisings across the subcontinent in the colonial period as well as after Independence. After 1950, it has often come to be equated with the constitutional category of **Scheduled Tribes**. See the essays 'Being Their Target' by Teesta Setalvad and 'Violence' by Sunil Mohan & Rumi Harish.

Ambedkarite
Term used especially by Sharmila Rege in this book, to distinguish the followers of Dr B.R. Ambedkar (1891–1956), a subset (and occasionally more radical version) of the more general category of **Dalit**. The Ambedkarite Public Sphere is defined around a series of events that defined Ambedkar's life and the figures of history he valorized, defined by music, theatre, poetry and pilgrimage, and often politicized (see **Dalit Panthers**). The practices are substantially based in the state of Maharashtra and evoke their proletarian saint-poets, of whom Ambedkar is seen to be one. It has become an important predecessor to several Occupy movements in Maharashtra. See Rege's essay, 'Interrogating the Thesis of Irrational Deification'.

Azaadi
Literally meaning 'freedom', used before Independence mainly to define the more radical elements of the freedom struggle, from Bhagat Singh to Netaji Subhas Chandra Bose. The cry for political independence was revived in the 2000s in Kashmir, where it also derived its current militant aspect. It was brought into national discourse by protesting students of the Jawaharlal Nehru University, Delhi, some of whom were accused of sedition in 2016. A part of militant popular culture after it was converted into a form of dub poetry and used in the hit Bollywood film *Gully Boy* (dir. Zoya Akhtar, Hindi, 2019), it has since become a rallying cry in political agitations, e.g., in the context of the anti-Citizenship Amendment Act of 2019.

Babu
Derogatory term to refer to government clerical staff, or an unenlightened, procedure-bound bureaucracy. Referenced by Sudipta Kaviraj in the essay, 'The Imaginary Institution of India'.

Bandh
Local word for a popular lockdown, when a city, or state, or sometimes even the country, closes down usually in protest. Bal Thackeray (1926–2012), founder and leader of the Shiv Sena (or army of Maratha king Shivaji), a political party in Mumbai, claimed to have invented the term in the early 1970s, boasting his ability to bring the city to a halt almost overnight.

Baniya
A caste term to refer to a trader class, associated sometimes with moneylending; occasionally used pejoratively to indicate narrow money-mindedness. See 'Hindu Death and Our Death' by Kancha Ilaiah Shepherd.

Brahmin/Brahminical
Priestly elites in a hierarchy of castes. Although the hierarchy of castes is one of the most controversial aspects of Indian society, and most caste (or *jaati*) definitions sit uneasily with what is often called the *varna* hierarchy

based on occupation, 'Brahmin' may nevertheless be the only articulate definition of caste in India. Historian Irfan Habib speaks of the Brahmin era as one that replaced the dominance of Buddhism, between 600 and 1200 CE:[1] a period defined by adherence to the ideology of the *Manusmriti*, a second-century BCE Sanskrit text sometimes seen as the origin of Indian legal theory (see **Manuvaad**). The social reform period also saw the rise of anti- and **non-Brahmin** ideologies in most parts of India, notably in central and south India. While the *political* displacement of Brahmin dominance may well have been one of the achievements of Independence, many argue that there has not been any parallel decline in *economic* dominance of the Brahmin castes, as we see in the autonomous private sector and in spaces where 'meritocracy' prevails (see also **Reservations**). See 'Interrogating the Thesis of Irrational Deification' by Sharmila Rege, and 'Hindu Death and Our Death' by Kancha Ilaiah Shepherd.

Caste
Although as both social identity and a means of defining social oppression the term goes back to the proletarian saint-poets who valorized 'low' gods and popular speech forms in opposing Brahminical dominance, the concept may have taken its modern definition under colonialism. The idea of *varna* (a defined hierarchy based on occupation, and dividing Indian society into four basic categories – of the priest, the warrior, the trader and the lowest caste of everything else, the **Shudra**) – took shape as a means of both enumeration and governance. Influential (if increasingly discredited) definitions include Louis Dumont's concept of *homo hierarchicus*[2] and sociologist M.N. Srinivas's concept of **Sanskritization**. Aspects of *varna* were also inherited by the constitutional category of **Scheduled Castes**, framing the debates around new definitions for enumeration under the Socio-Economic Caste Census (SECC), 2011. See **Dalit**, **Dalitbahujan**, **Reservations**.

Citizenship
Some time in the 1970s, writes Ravi Sundaram, the growing emphasis on national borders and the technologies of mapping underpinned a new political development, in which the state laid claim to 'a *monopoly over identity formation, citizenship and national representation*'. Citizenship remains a key concept in political science, and is also a word that, with **politics** and **narrative**, may have a specifically Indian meaning. Its recent history starts from the Constitution, whose Article 5 held all *residents* of India as well as those *born in India* at the time when it came into effect to be citizens – a provision directly contextualized by the Partition of the subcontinent. The original Citizenship Act of 1955 has been repeatedly amended, controversially (e.g., after the Assam Accord in 1985 restricting citizenship only to children of citizens). The 2004 amendment first envisaged the creation of a National Register of Citizens, so far implemented only in Assam. The 2019 Amendment, in which people from several neighbouring countries could qualify for citizenship if they were not Muslim, goes alongside the **National Population Register** and the technological base provided by the

Aadhaar biometric project, and has led to numerous nationwide protests. See especially Madhava Prasad's 'The Republic of Babel' and Ravi Sundaram's 'Beyond the Nationalist Panopticon'.

Congress/Congress-I
In the post-Independence period, writes Hamza Alavi, we need 'an understanding of the complex class basis of the Indian National Congress – the party which has been dominant in the Indian state, at any rate at the level of the central government. [Its] class basis . . . has not been an unchanging one; and its changes throw much light on the major shifts in agricultural development policy that took place at the end of the fifties'. The Indian National Congress (INC), founded in 1885, became the main liberal-nationalist force that negotiated Independence with the British, and was the dominant political party for the first forty years after Independence. It is increasingly viewed more as a large coalition than a party, and its ability to manage diverse political interests across the ideological spectrum as well as the individual ambitions of various politicians has been viewed as a key political counterpoint to the post-Independence Indian state. Its latter career is primarily associated with the Nehru–Gandhi family and with 'dynastic' politics. The Congress-I (for Indira), the best known of several breakaway factions, was created by Indira Gandhi after the **Emergency** (1975–77). See especially Hamza Alavi's 'India and the Colonial Mode of Production' and Sudipta Kaviraj's 'The Imaginary Institution of India'.

Creamy Layer
Term used to define the economically well-off among the 'backward' class/caste categories. The term was first used by Justice Krishna Iyer in 1975 in a major Supreme Court case,[3] when he said that the danger of 'reservation' is that 'its benefits, by and large, are snatched away by the top creamy layer of the "backward" caste or class, thus keeping the weakest among the weak always weak and leaving the fortunate layers to consume the whole cake.' While it has economic definitions, its main use has been to signal a social category that was historically oppressed by Brahmin domination but which, since Independence (or, by some accounts, even more recently, in the 1980s), has risen to economic dominance. See **OBC (Other Backward Classes)** and **Reservations**.

Crore, Lakh
Crore or *koti*, equivalent to ten million, is a term of Vedic origin. A *lakh* is equivalent to one hundred thousand.

Dalit/Dalitbahujan
A term used in practically all the texts in this book. *Dalit* is of Sanskrit origin, meaning 'divided, broken, scattered' – also by some etymologies the 'downtrodden'. *Bahujan* literally means 'the majority of the people'. Both terms were brought into contemporary usage by social reformer Jyotiba Phule (1827–1890) and more famously by Dr B.R. Ambedkar, as a radical counter to Mahatma Gandhi's preferred use of *Harijan* (people of God) to refer to India's so-called 'untouchable' castes. The emphasis on majority is used typically to oppose Hindu

majoritarianism. The Bahujan Samaj Party (party of the majority people) was formed in Uttar Pradesh in 1984. See especially the essays by Sharmila Rege and Kancha Ilaiah Shepherd, and the report by the Andhra Pradesh Civil Liberties Committee, in this volume.

Dalit Panthers
A radical **Ambedkarite** wing founded in 1972 in Maharashtra, closely linked to the Dalit literary movement in Marathi, that broke away from the more mainstream Republican Party of India (founded by Ambedkar in 1956). Among its founders were the major Marathi poets Namdeo Dhasal and Arjun Dangle. The name took direct inspiration from the Black Panther movement of the USA.

Democracy/Politics/Political Society
A critical troika of terms that appear at times to significantly depart from their dictionary definitions. Several political scientists in India have redefined the democratic process to refer to a combination of institutions, processes, mobilizations and negotiations actively created by the state to deliver social benefit in a way that shortcircuits the cumbersome modernist–pedagogical procedures of welfare. Rajni Kothari influentially spoke of diversified political centres through 'a network of benefits and obligations, and the mobilization of diverse sections of society in this network, thus closing the gap that has traditionally divided the village society from the polity'.[4] *Politics* here becomes the art of *negotiation*, *navigation*, or (as Partha Chatterjee says) a 'different *mediation* between the population and the state . . . that would not ground itself on a modernized civil society'. Chatterjee has influentially named the vast array of 'parties, movements, non-party political formations' as *political society*.[5] He makes two critical shifts: one, where he says the state, in actively working to enable this political society and as a means of negotiation, replaces the idea of citizen with that of *populations*; and two, that the political purpose of the mediation is to provide, not *welfare*, but rather *democracy*, interpreted as a means to 'channelize and order popular demands on the developmental state'. One question that has arisen is whether such an enumerative, population-driven apparatus of service delivery may have presaged the arrival of neoliberal biopolitics, and become (at the time of writing) precisely the tool with which to segregate people into different groupings and categories: as recipients of *benefit* rather than *welfare*, as well as, more dangerously, segregated in other ways including by religion and caste. Also see **Emergency**, **Modernism**. See Rajni Kothari's 'Democracy in Search of a Theory' in this volume.

DMK (Dravida Munnetra Kazhagam)/ DK/AIADMK
The DMK (Dravida Munnetra Kazhagam or Progressive Federation of the Dravidian People), a political party founded in 1949 by writer and politician C.N. Annadurai in Tamil Nadu, became, along with several mutant parties, the state's most influential political force. Its origins in the Self-Respect Movement and the Justice Party defined its diverse ideologies, which included, at various times, a commitment to atheism, **anti-Brahmin** politics and regional

statehood. It was later associated with a number of writers and actors who made major careers in the Tamil cinema, e.g. writer M. Karunanidhi and movie star M.G. Ramachandran, who founded the most recent breakaway iteration, the All-India Anna DMK (AIADMK). See M.S.S. Pandian's 'Void and Memory'.

Emergency
How is it, Rajni Kothari asks, that 'with the exception of 1975–76 [the Emergency years] . . . India [has] been able to remain democratic? Why, despite massive socio-economic problems and the prolonged incapacity of governments to resolve them, has democracy not been undermined?' He is referring here to the brief period when Prime Minister Indira Gandhi invoked Article 352 of the Constitution of India, that allows temporary suspension of civil rights under conditions that threaten the country's security, widely viewed as the only time when India saw itself enter a situation resembling totalitarian conditions. Such a view has however been challenged along three lines. One, that it may well be too early to tell, that the question Kothari asks above may yet not have received the final answer. Two, that while the Emergency may have seen the suspension of democratic processes in the national capital, several parts of the country – notably its North East, Kashmir, and several parts of central and south India where peasant insurgencies are being ruthlessly quelled – have seen such suspension both before and after 1975–77. Three, and perhaps a more significant critique in the light of the Hindutva challenge, is to consider a constitutionally Emergency-like 'new normal', in which *de facto* suspensions of rights are taking place as a permanent everyday reality rather than a temporary one. See Rajni Kothari's 'Democracy in Search of a Theory'.

FCRA (Foreign Contribution Regulation Act)
An Act brought in by the Government of India in 2010 for the regulation of all foreign monies used in India for non-profit purposes. Usually seen as a means to control non-governmental organizations and independent foreign funding agencies for supposedly anti-national actions, it is increasingly being used as a punitive measure to curb various forms of dissent. See 'Being Their Target' by Teesta Setalvad.

Hinduism/Hindutva
Widely used in several essays in this volume. Hinduism: conventionally and controversially described as a 'religion' and even as one of the world's oldest religions traceable to the 'Vedic' period, its categorization as such has been divisive and exclusionist – e.g., it being an 'Aryan' and **Brahminic** religion, and its exclusion of diverse groupings divided by **caste**. Its Orientalist approximation to a religion in the European sense, more or less coinciding with colonialism, may have also provided the long-term roots of its mutation into a far more militant ideology of *Hindutva*, a more articulately religious ideology adopted by the **Sangh Parivar**, often used to mobilize against diverse minorities and sought to be made into a state religion (or Hindu *rashtra*). See the essays

by Rajni Kothari, Sudipta Kaviraj, Teesta Setalvad, Sharmila Rege and especially Kancha Ilaiah Shepherd (as well as Ilaiah's book, *Why I Am Not a Hindu*, 1996).

Hindu Mahasabha
A pro-Hindu-nationalist political party that took its formal shape in 1921, initially created as a reaction to the Minto–Morley reforms of 1909 and the creation of separate Muslim electorates. Initially a moderate force, it took its aggressively right-wing form under the influence of the political activist V.D. Savarkar (1883–1966), considered by many to be the founder of **Hindutva**. It was replaced by the Jan Sangh in the early 1950s.

Kamma, Reddy, Kapu
Caste identities in Andhra Pradesh and Telangana, usually the landed elites and the most influential political castes in these states. Although the **Kshatriya** category is not commonly used in the states, in favour of the more common term **non-Brahmin**, these castes trace a similar imperial ancestry (e.g., the Vijayanagara and Kakatiya empires) as well as similar histories of land ownership. See the report by the Andhra Pradesh Civil Liberties Committee, 'The Chundur Carnage'.

Kshatriya
The 'warrior' caste, second in the *varna* caste hierarchy, beneath the **Brahmin**. Frequently tracing an imperial history which included land rights, this caste is often seen as having risen to power after Independence, as the most prominent **non-Brahmin** elites claiming **OBC (Other Backward Class)** status.

Kulak
Term used to define a class of 'small capitalist farmers'. Taken from Russian history, where this class often defined the revolutionary purpose of the USSR, in India it usually identifies the class that rose to economic and political power post-Independence, benefiting from a major infusion of capitalist systems of agrarian production. While this class has remained an important presence in political theory – e.g., in studies of post-Emergency politics and with the emergence of the **Reservations** question – the term itself has receded in importance, even as the USSR receded in significance as the key point of economic and political reference. See Utsa Patnaik's 'The Republic of Hunger' and K. Balagopal's 'Rich Peasant, Poor Peasant'.

Lathi Charge
A police-charge using long sticks (or the *lathi*), the local equivalent of a baton – a late colonial police practice but widely used even today. See the report of the Andhra Pradesh Civil Liberties Committee in this volume.

Madiga, Mala, Mahar
Among the most prominent of India's **Dalit** communities, in Andhra Pradesh (Mala, Madiga) and Maharashtra (Mahar); usually an artisanal caste associated with weaving and leather work (in turn related to animal skinning). See the Andhra Pradesh Civil Liberties Committee report, and the essays by K. Balagopal and Kancha Ilaiah Shepherd.

Manuvaad
Ideology ascribed to a **Brahminical** elite, drawing from the Sanskrit text

Manusmriti, viewed, especially by the British, as defining a Hindu jurisprudence after William Jones translated the text in 1794. Its defence of the caste hierarchy as well as sanctification of several practices of social discrimination led to Dr B.R. Ambedkar famously burning this text in 1927 during the Mahad agitation, when he led Dalits to access drinking water from a public resource from which they had been barred. The term *Manuvaad* (or, roughly, Manu-ism) as attributed to the ruling **Hindutva** ideology is more recent. See 'Hindu Death and Our Death' by Kancha Ilaiah Shepherd.

Maruti 800
A small, 800 cc motor car that became the face of Indian globalization. Originally a project of Indira Gandhi's son and heir-apparent, Sanjay Gandhi, during the **Emergency**, in 1983 the car was rolled out following a collaboration between the government-owned Maruti Udyog Corporation and Japan's Suzuki Motors. For almost twenty years this car symbolized the new Indian middle class. See the references to 'Maruti cars and VCRs' in K. Balagopal's essay, 'Rich Peasant, Poor Peasant'.

Modernism
To be read with **politics** and **democracy**, a term whose Indian usage may depart from its conventional definitions. 'Modernism,' writes Geeta Kapur, 'as it develops in post-colonial cultures, has the oddest retroactive trajectories, and . . . these make up a parallel aesthetics.'[6] While India shares several disjunctures with other post-colonial contexts, it has some specific issues that may be unique, including its special qualifications to be the Asian heir-apparent of the European project as the aesthetic counterpart of economic modernization. In the early years after Independence, the Nehruvian state indeed adhered to this inheritance, especially in the areas of architecture and urban planning, but also in setting up several major institutions of the arts along a mostly European model. Modern*ization* proved however to be a much more complicated and intractable business, not least because of difficulties in the accompanying process of modern*ity*. Kancha Ilaiah, for example, speaks of how 'modern **Brahmins** and **Baniyas** not only eat the best and most modern food available in India, but also have the best houses. Their styles of living have been modernized. They now have cushioned double beds, air-conditioned houses, air-cooled bedrooms. They have the most decorated houses. Even here, modernity has been cleverly Brahminized. The centrepiece in a well-decorated room is, not uncommonly, a painting of a Hindu god or goddess' – to reproduce a common critique of the superficies of Indian modernity as something to be adopted, imitated, even while keeping social hierarchies intact, leading to the view that while we are free to choose *our* modernity, we can make no intervention into modernity *itself*. We have, says Partha Chatterjee, 'a shrewd guess that given the close complicity between modern knowledges and modern regimes of power, we would forever remain consumers of universal modernity; never would be taken seriously as its producers'.[7] Referring to perhaps a related phenomenon, Geeta Kapur speaks of post-Independence India as

possessing a kind of soft modernism, existing 'without an avantgarde', 'buffered by a national and progressive state, so model and strategic action are less acutely positioned vis-à-vis each other; there is less dramatic confrontation than has been the case in Latin America'. India's artists have 'appeared . . . hamstrung over the progressivist as against "correctly" modernist definition of modernism', and thus have been 'tardy in making a direct avowal of modernism'.[8] See Geeta Kapur's essay, 'Contemporary Cultural Practice'. Also K. Balagopal's 'Rich Peasant, Poor Peasant' and 'Hindu Death and Our Death' by Kancha Ilaiah Shepherd.

Nari Adalat
Or 'All-Women's Court': a system for alternative dispute resolution (ADR), introduced in various Indian states in the late 1980s to address specific gender-related legal issues. Part of the larger **panchayat** system which includes several socially determined practices for ADR, along lines of caste, for example, and *Lok Adalat*s or people's courts. See the essay 'Violence' by Sunil Mohan and Rumi Harish.

Narrative/Narrative Contract
Term used in the social sciences and in disciplines ranging from law to medicine, in addition, of course, to the humanities, to mean a textual equivalent of the social contract. Its arrival broadly coincides with a post-structuralist turn in the social sciences, and the influence of Gramsci and, more significantly, Foucault. However, contrary to its usual meaning of making phenomena intelligible, here the term is used in conjunction with new concepts of **politics** and **democracy**, to bring to light the shadowy social negotiations that define state functioning, along with invisible political phenomena, 'fuzzy' communities and local knowledges. It is connected to the negotiations associated with **democratic** existence. See Sudipta Kaviraj's 'The Imaginary Institution of India' and Veena Das's 'Suffering, Legitimacy and Healing'.

National Democratic Alliance (NDA)
A right-of-centre political alliance led by the Bharatiya Janata Party (BJP), especially between 1998 and 2004. The term has receded now, although technically still in force, since the BJP has won a parliamentary majority on its own. See Utsa Patnaik's 'The Republic of Hunger'.

National Population Register (NPR)
A register started in 2010, merged with the Census of India, to list what were controversially named as the 'usual residents of the country', amending the Citizenship Act (1955). It defines a resident 'as a person who has resided in a local area for the past 6 months or more'. Initially viewed as ideologically in conflict with **Aadhaar** (which, unlike the NPR, is not officially mandatory), the merger of the two is what offers the single largest threat to uniform **citizenship** rights. Unlike the Citizenship Amendment Act, which primarily concerns those seeking asylum in India, or the National Register of Citizens, at the time of writing used only in the state of Assam, the NPR–Aadhaar combine is the one that is likely to most directly affect all of India's residents.

Naxalite/Urban Naxal
Naxalite is a term used for far-left political movements that first came into use in 1967, after the village of Naxalbari in West Bengal that saw a major peasant uprising that year. It has since come to define a broad Maoist coalition of parties and groupings across many parts of North East, central and south India, working typically with peasant and tribal groups. *Urban Naxal* is a pejorative term used to debunk all forms of dissent as coming from urban elites. See 'Media Trials and Courtroom Tribulations' by Shuddhabrata Sengupta.

NICNET
The digital network of the National Informatics Centre (NIC), established in 1976; the ICT and eGovernance backbone of the government, and a pioneer in diverse applications in social and public administration as well as electronic delivery of services. See 'Beyond the Nationalist Panopticon' by Ravi Sundaram.

Nikaah
Traditional Muslim marriage as defined under the Muslim Personal Law. While the Special Marriage Act of 1954 is a completely secular form with no religious identity, several forms of Personal Law defined by other religions are also recognized. A significant intervention into Muslim marriages however was the Muslim Women (Protection of Rights on Marriage) Act, 2019 which banned the controversial divorce practice of 'triple *talaaq*'. See Teesta Setalvad's 'Being Their Target'.

Non-Brahmin Movement
A late nineteenth and early twentieth-century reform movement attacking **Brahmin** dominance in various parts of the country but most influentially in Tamil Nadu, with the founding of the Justice Party in 1916 and the influence of Periyar E.V. Ramasamy Naicker. In many parts of south India, the category 'non-Brahmin' is an umbrella term including everyone who is not **Brahmin** or **Dalit**. This movement is often seen as insufficiently radical and led by non-Brahmin elites. See M.S.S. Pandian's 'Void and Memory'.

Non-Resident Indian (NRI)
An elite category of Indians who live overseas or a person holding Indian citizenship but who lives outside the country. Officially, the designation has to do primarily with taxation issues. While the categories of Indians who live abroad are diverse, including indentured and migrant labour, as are the several government programmes for 'persons of Indian origin', the 'NRI' has been culturally the most visible presence of the Indian diaspora, especially after the launch of globalization, and is sometimes viewed as the self-appointed guardian of neo-traditional values expressed in many ways, some moving in tandem with **Hindutva**. See 'Beyond the Nationalist Panopticon' by Ravi Sundaram.

Other Backward Class (OBC)
The Constitution of India enables the identification of socially and economically backward classes other than those 'scheduled' castes and tribes for **reservations**, i.e. mandatory reserved

places in the areas of education and employment. The question of who constitute the 'backward' sections and how backwardness may be defined – and especially whether criteria defining backwardness should be social or economic or a combination of both – remains controversial. In 1980, the Second Backward Classes Commission (or Mandal Commission) made its initial recommendations, which were sought to be implemented in 1989, leading in 1990 to major protests (see **Reservations**). In 2006, a revised list (commonly known as Mandal-II) increased the number of 'backward castes' by almost 40 per cent. Also see **Creamy Layer**. See Rajni Kothari's 'Democracy in Search of a Theory' and M. Madhava Prasad's 'The Republic of Babel'.

Panchayat/Khap Panchayat
Panchayat, meaning 'village council', refers to the traditional form of village self-governance under a village head (or *sarpanch*). It was given its current form in 1992 by the Parliament under the Panchayati Raj Act, as part of a drive for local government. The *panchayati* system has considerable political as well as economic power, including for alternative dispute resolution, but can also function extra-constitutionally, e.g., in *khap panchayat*s or caste groupings dealing summary justice, which are entirely illegal. See K. Balagopal's 'Rich Peasant, Poor Peasant'.

People's Union of Civil Liberties/ People's Union of Democratic Rights (PUCL/PUDR)
Major human rights organizations. Although the history of human rights in India goes back to the 1930s, its recent trajectory begins in the context of the **Emergency**, and specifically following widespread evidence of what came to be known as 'encounter' killings – cold-blooded murders dressed up to appear like shoot-outs, in which police claimed self-defence. The PUCL was formally set up in 1980 as an avowedly liberal, centrist and non-partisan organization (in tacit critique of some civil liberties organizations seen as 'fronting' for radical political parties), banning members of political parties from holding office. While the report by its first president, V.M. Tarkunde, titled *Encounters are Murders*, remains iconic, both PUCL and PUDR have sent fact-finding teams and published numerous reports on diverse issues across the country. See Gyanendra Pandey's 'In Defence of the Fragment', and also the report by the Andhra Pradesh Civil Liberties Committee.

Prevention of Terrorism Act (POTA)
A draconian Act passed in 2002 with the avowed objective of strengthening anti-terrorist operations, following the 2001 attack on the Parliament. It replaced the notorious Terrorist and Disruptive Activities (Prevention) Act (TADA) that existed from 1985 to 1995. POTA was repealed in 2004. See 'Media Trials and Courtroom Tribulations' by Shuddhabrata Sengupta.

Privacy Law
This became a major political issue especially following the arrival of digital governance and the tracking of GIS data from the early 2000s. There was some question as to whether Article 21 of the Indian Constitution on life and personal liberty included the right to

privacy, and what privacy actually meant in India. The issue came to the forefront with the introduction of **Aadhaar** and the **National Population Register**. Two Supreme Court judgements in 2015 and 2017, both in the context of the constitutional validity of Aadhaar, declared that Article 21 as well as Part III of the Constitution (on Fundamental Rights) declared privacy to be a right. Such a right has been primarily defined in terms of Data Protection. India presently has two draft bills, on Privacy and Data Protection, pending in Parliament. See 'Violence' by Sunil Mohan and Rumi Harish.

Reservations
The special allocation of seats for admission into educational institutions and employment for those defined as 'socially and educationally backward', as per the Constitution of India. The question of reservations has been a major issue of debate in the history of independent India: first around whether reservations should exist at all (at the cost of 'meritocracy'); secondly, around who should qualify and what criteria should be used to define 'backwardness'; and thirdly, concerning which institutions the law applies to and, notably, whether the private sector should be forced to adopt state rules in this regard. The debate took its most visible form following the recommendations of what is popularly known as the Mandal Commission, which used a complicated set of social, educational and economic criteria to determine that 52 per cent of the Indian population could be deemed 'backward' and thus qualifying for reservations. The effort by the government to implement these recommendations in 1989 led to major protests and student immolations in 1990. See also the keywords **OBC** and **Creamy Layer**.

Sangh Parivar
Literally translating as 'family union', it refers to a clutch of entities aligned to or under the Rashtriya Swayamsevak Sangh (or RSS; loosely, National Volunteer Organization). The RSS was formed in 1925 as a kind of paramilitary youth organization with the explicit ideology of creating a Hindu *rashtra* (or Hindu state; see **Hindutva**). The 'family' consists of the Bharatiya Janata Party (literally the Indian People's Party), currently in power in India at the centre and in several states, as its political wing; the Akhil Bharatiya Vidyarthi Parishad (All India Student Council) as its student wing; and the Vishwa Hindu Parishad (World Hindu Council) as its cultural wing – besides several other organizations. The BJP was preceded by the Jan Sangh (People's Union), founded in 1951. It was a part of the united opposition that came together in 1977 to form a political party then named Janata Party (People's Party) to defeat Indira Gandhi's Congress, but it broke away maintaining a part of that name in 1980. Currently, it is perhaps the most powerful political force in India. See the essay 'Being Their Target' by Teesta Setalvad.

Sanskritization
Term originally attributed to Indian sociologist M.N. Srinivas.[9] 'The caste system is far from a rigid system in which the position of each component caste is fixed for all time', he wrote. 'Movement has always been possible and especially

so in the middle regions of hierarchy. A low caste was able, in a generation or two, to rise to higher position in the hierarchy by adopting vegetarianism and teetotalism and by Sanskritizing its ritual and pantheon. In short, it took over as far as possible the customs, rites, and beliefs of the Brahmins and the adoption of the Brahminic way of life by a low caste seems to have been frequent though theoretically forbidden.' While usually used as aspirational, the term has also been used to indicate a reverse process of social cleansing – as texts, languages, social associations and even patterns of behaviour are purged of unsavoury caste associations. On Sanskrit and cultural elites, see 'The Imaginary Institution of India' by Sudipta Kaviraj.

Scheduled Caste/Scheduled Tribe (SC/ST)
Terms from the Constitution of India, arising from the First Schedule of the Scheduled Castes and Tribes orders of 1950, initially listing 1,108 castes and 744 tribes, adding up to approximately 17 and 9 per cent of the population respectively. The definition has been a matter of debate both politically and in terms of governance, leading to substantive questions around **reservations**, and procedural around criteria for definition, especially with the far more complicated and contentious addition of **OBC** to the list, expanding the number of 'backward' classes to well over half the population. See **Adivasi**. See also the essay in this volume by Gyanendra Pandey, 'In Defence of the Fragment', the report by the Andhra Pradesh Civil Liberties Committee and Hamza Alavi's 'India and the Colonial Mode of Production'.

Section 377
A notorious law in the Indian Penal Code introduced in 1861 by the British, making 'sexual activities against the order of nature' illegal. A major battle by the LGBT community in India saw an extraordinary victory in September 2018 when the Indian Supreme Court ruled Section 377 as unconstitutional, 'irrational, indefensible and manifestly arbitrary'. The law had been originally struck down by the Delhi High Court in July 2009, in what came to be known as the 'Naz Foundation' case. The 2018 judgement followed from the 2017 Supreme Court judgement on the **Aadhaar** case, which upheld the right to privacy as a fundamental right. See the essay 'Violence' by Sunil Mohan/Rumi Harish.

Sedition
An offence covered by Section 124A of the Indian Penal Code, enacted in 1860 by the British, as part of the larger set of 'offences against the Indian state'. It was used extensively in colonial India, most famously against the nationalist Bal Gangadhar Tilak in 1897 and Gandhi in 1922. In recent years, however, sedition has been used to stifle all forms of political dissent: against the human rights activist Binayak Sen, but also against journalists, environmentalists and others. In February 2020, when students of a school in the small town of Bidar did a play on the prevailing controversy around the **National Population Register** that apparently satirized the Prime Minister of India, the school staff were arrested for sedition.

Shudra
The lowest caste in the *varna* hierarchy, increasingly used more as a poetic remembrance of oppression and 'untouchability' than as a political entity. But also used sometimes to refer to professions such as manual scavenging.

Swarajya/Swadeshi
Swarajya means self-rule, and *swadeshi*, own-country. In her essay, Sharmila Rege quotes an **Ambedkari** poet Keruji Ghegde singing a song titled 'The Market of Indian Politics', which asks of various people entering the political bazaar what they understand by *swarajya*, and questioning their credentials to truly comprehend freedom. Both terms were popularized by Gandhi, but both effectively originate in the thinking of the nationalist leader Bal Gangadhar Tilak (1856–1920), who also led the *Swadeshi* movement in the early twentieth century as a call for economic nationalism through boycott of foreign manufactures. Their later relevance, especially in **Dalitbahujan** politics has been to interrogate the concept of freedom itself, and more particularly the kind of political freedom India received with Independence. See Rege's essay, 'Interrogating the Thesis of Irrational Deification'.

Zamindar
Literally landlord, refers to a form of land ownership instituted by Lord Cornwallis of the East India Company with the Permanent Settlement Act of 1793, in which ownership of vast amounts of land was legally permitted on condition that a certain proportion of the revenue would be deposited with the Company. While *zamindari* goes back to the Mughal period, it takes its best known form under the British, becoming a more properly feudal system. Its modification into new forms of tenancy, along with agrarian expropriation, define key aspects of what Hamza Alavi names the 'Colonial Mode of Production'. The abolition of *zamindari* after Independence following land reform movements has been a matter of further debate, around whether the role of the colonial mode simply replaced the *zamindar* with a new class of landed elites, or whether the arrival of modern capitalist systems of farming after Independence actually transformed the feudal system. See also **Kulak**. See especially the essays by Hamza Alavi ('India and the Colonial Mode of Production') and K. Balagopal ('Rich Peasant, Poor Peasant') in this volume.

NOTES & REFERENCES

Introduction

1 Partha Chatterjee, *I Am the People*, New York: Columbia University Press, 2020, p. 85.

2 The crucial legal judgements here being the *Justice K.S. Puttaswamy (Retd.) v. Union of India* (Supreme Court, 2017) judgement on privacy, the Naz Foundation judgement (*Naz Foundation v. Government of NCT of Delhi*, Delhi High Court, 2009) and its sequel judgement, *Navtej Singh Johar & Ors. v. Union of India* (Supreme Court, 2018), on the elimination of Section 377 of the Indian Penal Code. But there were several other judgements. See Gautam Bhatia, *The Transformative Constitution: A Radical Biography in Nine Acts*, Noida: HarperCollins, 2019.

3 From roughly the mid-2000s, India has seen a growing argument that *surveillance* must come together with the *direct targeting of beneficiaries*, especially in poverty eradication programmes. By 2006–07, there were at least 151 Centrally Sponsored Schemes entailing annual expenditures of about Rs 72,000 crores. It was widely believed that there was tremendous wastage associated with such schemes, and that only a small fraction of overall resources reached the poor due to, in varying degrees, inefficiency of targeting (inability to reach the poor), leakages (to the non-poor), participation costs (foregone earnings that are especially consequential in employment programmes) and large administrative costs. It was therefore considered that establishing the individual beneficiary's *identity* was in effect *almost more important than establishing her eligibility*. Towards this end, by the late 2000s, several kinds of smart cards were either proposed or already in place: the voter ID card, the BPL (Below Poverty Line) card and the NREGS (National Rural Employment Guarantee Scheme) job card, and in some states, a health insurance card under the Rashtriya Swasthya Bima Yojana (RSBY, or the National Health Insurance Scheme) and a PDS (Public Distribution System) smart card. See Devesh Kapur, Partha Mukhopadhyay and Arvind Subramanian, 'More for the Poor and Less for and by the State: The Case for Direct Cash Transfers', *Economic and Political Weekly*, vol. 43, no. 15, 12 April 2008, pp. 37–43.

4 The need for data protection began as a serious question, legally and politically, with the introduction of the national biometric project, or Aadhaar, in 2009 as a part of the National E-Governance Plan (NEGP) to digitally enable all government services. The problem arose when biometrics began to be mounted on several data resources for surveillance, most obviously the NATGRID (National Intelligence Grid) but including, in the words of former Home Minister P. Chidambaram, '21 sets of databases . . . to achieve quick, seamless and

secure access to desired information for intelligence and enforcement agencies'. These databases would include a DNA data bank, the NATGRID and a series of others such as the Crime and Criminals Tracking Network and Systems (CCTNS) and a National Counter Terrorism Centre, all of which could work together to make a devastating and unimaginable impact on surveillance. The 2017 *Justice K.S. Puttaswamy (Retd.) v. Union of India* case declared privacy to be a right under Article 21 of the Constitution, leading to the recommendations in the report of the committee of experts chaired by Justice B.N. Srikrishna: *Free and Fair Digital Economy: Protecting Privacy, Empowering Indians*, New Delhi: Ministry of Electronics and Information Technology, Government of India, 2018.

5 In February 2020, a small school in the district of Bidar, Karnataka, staged a play that criticized the Indian Prime Minister and the controversial Citizenship Amendment Act (CAA) introduced in 2019. The school was charged with sedition, a colonial-era law that, writes legal scholar Siddharth Narrain, appears 'bang in the middle of Chapter VI of the section in the Indian Penal Code that deals with "Offences against the State", a passage that deals with serious offences including waging war against the state'. In the colonial period, major nationalist figures including Bal Gangadhar Tilak and M.K. Gandhi were accused of sedition, but more recently, civil liberties activists, protesting students, people simply holding placards, and writers 'giving offence' in literature and theatre, have all been accused in a widespread and indiscriminate use of the law. See Siddharth Narrain, '"Disaffection" and the Law: The Chilling Effect of Sedition Laws in India', *Economic and Political Weekly*, vol. 46, no. 8, 19 February 2011, pp. 33–37.

6 This is notwithstanding Balagopal's often trenchant disagreements with the 'mode of production' debate and the economists who conducted it. In one essay he attacks unnamed antagonists speaking of 'feudal landlords, capitalist landlords, semi-feudal landlords and kulaks', and invites them to walk into any village of their choice and 'exhibit for our edification individual specimens of these well-defined classes'. 'Does such a differentiation really exist within the microcosm of a village?' he asks, arguing that the 'ensemble of social relations that define the rural rich have not differentiated into distinct classes'. 'If Indian capital had had to depend upon its internal strength and dynamism for its self-expansion it would have been forced to contend with and destroy, or at least totally subsume, pre-capitalist relations.' But there has not been, Balagopal says, a single instance of 'profit-maximizing capitalist farmers' fighting feudal landholders in the history of post-Independence India. 'There have only been agitations of all the rural rich for a greater share of the resources the state has borrowed from abroad or generated for itself.' K. Balagopal, 'Agrarian Struggles', *Economic and Political Weekly*, vol. XXI, no. 32, 1986, pp. 1401–05.

7 See the series of essays that come together in Geeta Kapur's book, *When Was Modernism: Essays on Contemporary Cultural Practice in India*, New Delhi: Tulika Books, 2000.

8 Phrase by cybersecurity activist Srinivas Kodalli, see https://medium.com/karana/videos-tv-debates-219145e98b76, accessed 15 April 2020.

9 Anita Dube, 'Midnight Dreams: The Tragedy of a Lone Revolutionary', *Afterall: A Journal of Art, Context and Enquiry*, no. 36, Summer 2014, pp. 40–53.

1 I Rajni Kothari

1 *Hindutva:* See Keywords.

2 I Sudipta Kaviraj

1 This can be derived from the common Marxist concept of ideology, though there are not many detailed arguments on this point or this part of the ideological process of creating and reinforcing similitudes.

2 I take the point Marx makes in *The German Ideology* about the French Revolution to be true of all successful ideological movements.

3 It is possible to argue that some movements gain a real universality, e.g., the bourgeois political formations in the French Revolution. In cases like the Indian national movement, bourgeois trends fail to achieve such discursive or political hegemony. However, they still aspire to it and try to create it retrospectively by slowly occupying the history of the nationalist movement as a whole.

4 **Editor's note:** *Bankimchandra Chattopadhyay* (1838–1894), Bengali novelist, poet and journalist. Bhudev Mukhopadhyay (1827–1894), educationist, writer and novelist. Both were key figures during Bengal's literary renaissance and in early nationalism.

5 A very detailed and textually scrupulous account of what the horizon looked like can be found in Tapan Raychaudhuri, *Europe Reconsidered*, Delhi: Oxford University Press, 1988.

6 '*Babus*': See Keywords.

7 Antonio Gramsci, *Selections from Cultural Writings*, London: Lawrence and Wishart, 1985, p. 235.

8 To do this was fairly common though systematic comparisons were rare. In Bengal, two eminent examples of such comparative sociology are the works of Bankim and Bhudev Mukhopadhyaya. Bhudev is more concise and systematic; cf. Raychaudhuri, *Europe Reconsidered.*

9 See Gellner's *Nations and Nationalism*, Oxford: Blackwell, 1983.

10 Using these terms in the sense given to them in social theory by the work of Ferdinand Tönnies, cf. *On Sociology: Pure, Applied and Empirical*, Chicago: Chicago University Press, 1971.

11 Literature, poetry and especially patriotic songs are good examples of this. In Bengali, a particularly telling illustration is the poetry of D.L. Roy, and his poem of ultimate excess: *Dhanadhanye puspe bhara amader ei basundhara / tahar majhe ache des ek sakal deser sera / se je swapna die tairi se des, smrti die ghera* (Blessed with wealth, adorned with flowers / This Mother Earth of ours, In her midst is a nation / Most famed of all nations, Oh that nation is made of dreams / Wrapped in memories)

12 The power of this idea is illustrated by Marx's hypothesis about an Asiatic mode. Even Marx, whose thinking is so scrupulously historical, was willing to believe in unchanging village communities. Marxist historians have found this hypothesis unhelpful.

13 Elsewhere, I have tried to critically analyse the standard narrative constructions of 'the history of Bengali literature', which seeks to confer this antiquity on the regional identity of Bengal. See Sudipta Kaviraj, 'Writing, Speaking, Being: Language and Historical Identity in South Asia', Keynote paper for the section on 'Identity in History: South and Southeast Asia', German Historical Congress, Bochum, 27–29 September 1990.

14 Indeed, one of the principal controversies in modern Indian politics has centred around a satisfactory arrangement of identities. Are other identities compatible with the identity of the nation?

15 Eric Stokes, *The English Utilitarians and India*, Rpnt. Delhi: Oxford University Press, 1964, is the most detailed account on the subject.

16 See *Kamalakanta* (by Bankimchandra Chattopadhyay, 1885).

17 See essay '*Bangadeser Krsak*' ('The Cultivators of Bengal', Bankimchandra Chattopadhyay, 1872).

18 Jawaharlal Nehru, *An Autobiography,* New Delhi: Allied Publishers, 1964 [1936].

19 **Editor's note:** *Abanindranath Tagore* (1871–1951), artist and writer. Best known as the founder of what came to be known as the 'Bengal School' of painting. Less well known is his equally significant work as a children's author.

20 This theoretical constitution of the object of historical enquiry is often done by other disciplines, or by the general intellectual culture.

21 This is done most notably in the work of Peter Winch: *The Idea of a Social Science and its Relation with Philosophy*, London: Routledge, 1990.

22 Historians have, along with other mainstream social scientists, traditionally neglected discourse in their immersion in the narratives of economic and political events. Anthropologists were, by contrast, more attentive to these questions. Consequently, it is not surprising that new forms of history writing, for instance *Subaltern Studies*, but also some others, use a large number of the anthropologist's tools.

23 E.g., Edward Said, *Orientalism*, London: Routledge and Kegan Paul, 1978.

3 | Gyanendra Pandey

1 See the many reviews of *Subaltern Studies* and of Ranajit Guha's *Elementary Aspects of Peasant Insurgency in Colonial India* (Delhi: Oxford University Press, 1983) which make the criticism that these works have concentrated too greatly on the moment of open revolt and violence. The criticism fits in with a more

general trend in 'peasant studies' and social history that has led to the recent emphasis on 'everyday forms' of people's existence and resistance: J.C. Scott, *Weapons of the Weak: Everyday Forms of Peasant Resistance*, New Haven: Yale University Press, 1985.

2 Lata Mani, 'The Female Subject, The Colonial Gaze: Eyewitness Accounts of *Sati*', paper presented at a workshop on 'Culture, Consciousness and the Colonial State', held at the Isle of Thorns, UK, 24–27 July 1989, which makes a similar point about agency and the moment of suffering among other propositions.

3 PUDR and PUCL: See Keywords.

4 **Editor's note:** *Asghar Ali Engineer* (1939–2013): a very well-known figure in India's human rights movement, primarily in the context of the 'communal' political history of India in the 1980s–2000s. Also known for his work to reform the conservative Dawoodi Bohra sect in India.

5 The same point needs to be made about the kind of historical and social science writing discussed in this essay. I have taken my examples deliberately from some of the best left and liberal scholars writing today. This is because it is among them, rather than among chauvinist 'Hindu', 'Muslim' or 'Sikh' historians and social scientists, that there is serious debate about 'secularism'/'communalism' and the meaning of sectarian violence. It seems to me also that a critique of their writings is not only harder to make but, in terms of building up an alternative to the dominant (chauvinist) political and ideological tendencies in India today, also the more necessary.

6 See, for example, *Ashis Nandy, 'An Anti-Secularist Manifesto', Seminar, no. 314, 1995; T.N. Madan, 'Secularism in Its Place', Journal of Asian Studies, 46 (4), 1987; Partha Chatterjee, Preface, in Bengal 1920–47: The Land Question, Calcutta: K.P. Bagchi and Co., 1984; Dipesh Chakrabarty, 'Invitation to a Dialogue', in Ranajit Guha, ed, Subaltern Studies, Volume IV, Delhi: Oxford University Press, 1985; G. Pandey, The Construction of Communalism in Colonial North India, Delhi: Oxford University Press, 1990.*

7 Bipan Chandra, *Modern India*, New Delhi: National Council for Educational Research and Training (NCERT), 1971. Reprinted in new version as *History of Modern India*, Hyderabad: Orient Blackswan, 2009. All references are to the original NCERT edition.

8 Ibid., pp. 305–06.

9 Ibid., p. 306.

10 Ibid., pp. 296–97 and passim.

11 Ibid., pp. 306–07.

12 Sumit Sarkar, *Modern India: 1885–1947*, New Delhi: Macmillan, 1983.

13 Ibid., p. 438.

14 Ibid., pp. 438–39.

15 Ibid., p. 439.

16 There is no equivalent, for example, to the debates in Germany about the meaning of the holocaust and the whole experience of National Socialism. German historians and philosophers have battled with the question, was this a one-time aberration or something produced by a German 'national character'?. Cf. Theodor Adorno, *Minima Moralia: Reflections from Damaged Life*, English edition, London: New Left Books, 1974 [1951]; Karl Jaspers (1967), *The Future of Germany*, Chicago: University of Chicago Press.

17 Muhammad Umar Memon, 'Partition Literature: A Study of Intizar Husain' (and the references he cites), *Modem Asian Studies,* 14 (3), 1980; Aijaz Ahmad, 'Urdu Literature in India', *Seminar*, No. 359, July 1989; Alok Rai, 'The Trauma of Independence: Some Aspects of Progressive Hindi Literature, 1945–47', and S.S. Hans, 'The Partition Novels of Nanak Singh', in A.K. Gupta, ed., *Myth and Reality: The Struggle for Freedom In India, 1945–47*, Delhi: Manohar Publications, 1987. **Editor's note:** At a moment of history that appeared to defeat historical understanding, the role of fiction writers extending their practice to take on the historian's responsibility has been well documented. Manto (1912–1955) remains perhaps the leading eyewitness and author of this epoch. *Rahi Masoom Raza (1927–1992) wrote Aadha Gaon (Divided Village or Half a Village, originally published in 1966, an autobiographical account of the rival halves of a zamindar family, set in the author's village in Ghazipur district on the fringes of Avadh, Uttar Pradesh – a book that defies generic classification).*

18 Tapati Chakravarty, 'The Freedom Struggle and Bengali Literature of the 1940s', in Gupta, ed., *Myth and Reality*, p. 329.

19 **Editor's note:** *Tamas (In Darkness), a television series by filmmaker Govind Nihalani based on a novel by Bhisham Sahni (1974), one of Indian literature's best known accounts of the Partition.*

20 The strife in Delhi (1984), Meerut (1987), Bhagalpur (1989) has been reported in this way. For a still more recent example, see Tavleen Singh's report regarding comments on the Gonda riots, *Indian Express,* 14 October 1990. **Editor's note:** *Delhi 1984*: the anti-Sikh riots following the assassination of Indira Gandhi. *Meerut 1987*: the 'Hashimpura massacre' of 22 May 1987, when around 45 Muslim men were taken away by the Provincial Armed Constabulary (PAC), shot and thrown into two gutters. *Gonda 1990*: September 1990, classic riot when the Vishwa Hindu Parishad (VHP) first conducts a deliberately provocative rally, then there is an attack by Muslims followed by retaliatory attacks. This happened in the Karnailganj township of Gonda.

21 The details in the next two paragraphs are taken from the People's Union for Democratic Rights (PUDR) report, *Bhagalpur Riots* (Delhi, April 1990), and the notes upon which it is based.

22 While many local people put the death toll at not less than 2,000, the official figure for the number of people killed as of April 1990 was 414. The most careful unofficial calculations suggested that 1,000 people lost their lives, over 90 per cent of these being Muslims; ibid., p. 1.

23 I refer here to our own efforts as a team of investigators. Satish Saberwal and Mushirul Hasan also note the 'Wholly unjustified confidence' of the mass media in the official version of events in recent instances of strife: 'Moradabad Riots, 1980: Causes and Meanings', in Asghar Ali Engineer, ed., *Communal Riots in Post-Independence India*, Delhi: Sangam Publications, 1984, p. 208.

24 As the PUDR report notes, the support given to its ten-member team by local activists of the Communist Party of India (Marxist) 'effectively doubled our strength'; PUDR, *Bhagalpur Riots*, p. 70.

25 It is worth noting, indeed, that we were repeatedly pressed to also go and see those places where Hindus had been the victims of attacks – notably, a village named Jamalpur and a few sections of Bhagalpur city. We had decided to visit these places in any case, even before our on-the-spot investigations began in Bhagalpur, precisely in order that we might see and hear 'both sides'.

26 PUDR, *Bhagalpur Riots,* p. 17.

27 Vishwa Hindu Parishad: See Keywords.

28 Ved Prakash Vajpayee, *Navbharat Times,* 19 November 1989 (translation mine).

29 Ibid. Here is an even cruder example of the same kind of argument: 'In India the basic material is very good, I mean, the people. They are honest, intelligent and generous. They are only waiting to be drawn into the national mainstream. What is absent is leadership of the right type.' A.S. Raman, 'Leaders to blame for communalism', *Sunday Mail,* 14 October 1990.

30 PUDR, *Bhagalpur Riots,* p. 6

31 Asghar Ali Engineer, 'Causes of Communal Riots', in Engineer, ed., *Communal Riots in Post-Independence India,* pp. 36–37.

32 Sumitra Kumar Jain, 'Economy of Communalism', in *The Times of India,* 1990, reproduced in *India Pakistan Times*, May.

33 PUDR, *Bhagalpur Riots,* pp. 32, 37

34 I should add that 'secularism' and 'communalism' are perhaps not the most useful terms to be applied in our investigations of the social and political consciousness of different sections of the Indian people. This is a point that is made by several scholars and also by me in my book. (Gyanendra Pandey, *The Construction of Communalism in Colonial North India*, New Delhi: Oxford University Press, 1990.)

35 A detailed newspaper report on the rape of two nuns teaching at a convent school in Gajraula, Uttar Pradesh, notes that the three rapists, wearing nothing but undergarments, addressed one another as 'ustad' and 'guru' while they held the nuns at gunpoint (*Hindustan Times,* 23 July 1990). This is the kind of brag commonly associated with young louts found teasing women and girls on Delhi buses and in Bombay films. It is worth pondering the question, how large is the step from this kind of molestation of women to the violent assault involved in rape.

36 This applies, of course, not only to constructions of the different religious communities, but also to stereotypes of different caste and tribal communities as 'dirty', 'mendacious', 'turbulent', 'ferocious', 'criminal' and so on, which have had wide influence since the nineteenth century if not earlier.

37 All of these instances are taken from Bhagalpur – see PUDR, *Bhagalpur Riots* – but the examples could be multiplied from elsewhere.

38 The rumour was, in fact, malicious and baseless. Most students living in the boarding houses left as soon as the disturbances broke out, if they had not left a little earlier, and many were helped to get away safely

by their Muslim landlords. The number of students killed or missing is now computed to be no more than six: of these the bodies of only two students (one Hindu, one Muslim) have been found (PUDR, *Bhagalpur Riots,* p. 12). However, in the disturbed and dangerous condition of the city and district in the first few days after the outbreak of violence, many students appear not to have been able to reach their homes directly. During this time, and indeed for long afterwards, the story of the massacre of students was neither investigated nor countered by the district or the university authorities. On the contrary, it was publicized in the press, even aired on the radio (both local and BBC), and was readily and widely credited. It was still widely believed when we visited Bhagalpur at the end of January 1990.

39 See Asghar Ali Engineer, 'On the Theory of Communal Riots', in Asghar Ali Engineer and Moin Shakir, eds, *Communalism in India*, Delhi: Ajanta Publications, 1985, p. 62; and leaflets and pamphlets collected by the PUDR team in Bhagalpur. The two preceding quotations in this paragraph are from a leaflet entitled *Bhagalpur ka Sampradayik danga kyon?* issued in the name of the 'People of Bhagalpur'; and V.D. Savarkar, *Six Glorious Epochs of Indian History*, trans. S.T. Godbole, Bombay: Bal Savarkar Publishers, 1971, p. 175.

40 *Hindu bandhuon, socho aur sambhlo* (translation mine; by Rajeshwar, Akhil Bharat Hindu Mahasabha), which is among the leaflets mentioned in note 39.

41 The English word is used in the Hindi text.

42 A. Shankar, *Chetavni 2 Desh ko Khatra,* Vishwa Hindu Parishad, n.d.. On some of the logical problems arising out of the declaration that Indian Muslims are converts (forcibly converted) and descendants of Babar at the same time, see Alok Rai, 'Only bigots feel that conversions follow invasion', *The Times of India* (Lucknow), 13 August 1990.

43 Lajpat Rai, *A History of the Arya Samaj*, New Delhi: Orient Longman, 1967 [1915], p. 120 (emphasis added).

44 Ibid., p. 120n.

45 On the impact of the Gait Circular, which suggested that separate tables be drawn up in the 1911 Census for 'debatable Hindus', see ibid., pp. 124–25, and Kenneth W. Jones, 'Religious Identity and the Indian Census', in N.G. Barrier, ed. *The Census in British India: New Perspectives*, Delhi: Manohar, 1981, pp. 91–92.

46 V.D. Savarkar, *Hindu-Pad-Padshahi or A Review of the Hindu Empire of Maharashtra*, Chennai: B.G. Paul and Co, 1925, pp. 272–73. The words in quotation marks are from Savarkar, *Six Glorious Epochs of Indian History*, pp. 154, 188, 192–93 and passim.

47 J.T.F. Jordens, *Dayanand Sarasvati: His Life and Ideas*, Delhi: Oxford University Press, 1978, pp. 170 and 322n.

48 Interview with Shri Arun, Bhagalpur, 20 January 1990.

49 Badaun and Bhagalpur provide instances in 1989.

50 Manaazir Aashiq Harganvi, *Ankhon Dekhi: Bhagalpur ke Bhayanak Fasad ko dekhne ke baad,* Bhagalpur: Maktaba Kohsar, 1989. Translations in the following paragraphs are mine.

51 Gramsci: 'Is it possible to write (conceive of) a history of Europe in the 19th century without an organic treatment of the French Revolution and the Napoleonic wars. . . . One can say, therefore, that [Croce's] book on the *History of Europe* is nothing but a fragment of history'. See Antonio Gramsci, *Selections from the Prison Notebooks of Antonio Gramsci*, edited by Q. Hoare and G.N. Smith, London: Lawrence and Wishart, 1971, pp. 118, 119. It will be clear of course that I am not advocating the kind of 'objective', 'integral' history that Gramsci called for.

52 I might add that given the very great difficulty, if not impossibility, of translating cultures and consciousness into alien languages, a new historiography also requires a more concerted effort to recover what we continue in India to call the 'vernacular' (and also the dialect) in terms both of sources and of the medium of historical debate. Along with that, there is the need to recognize that the 'vernacular' may also be the 'national', in more ways than one.

53 The Preamble, *Constitution of India.*

4 | Andhra Pradesh Civil Liberties Committee

1 **Editor's note:** *Kilvenmani*: Refers to the massacre that took place in the village of Keezhvenmani in Tamil Nadu in December 1968, when forty-four people from the families of striking Dalit village labourers were murdered by a gang allegedly led by their landlords.

2 **Editor's note:** Protection of Civil Rights Act, 1955.

3 **Editor's note:** *Kanchikacherla Kotesu*: Dalit youth set on fire and killed when upper-caste people accused him of stealing a bronze tumbler on 24 February 1968. Viewed as the first such incident in modern Andhra Pradesh, it became a national controversy, and Prime Minister Indira Gandhi issued a statement in Parliament.

4 **Editor's note:** *Kamma, Mala, Madiga* and *Reddy* are all caste names. Kamma and Reddy are traditionally upper castes.

5 **Editor's note:** *Telaga, Brahmin, Vaisya* families: traditional upper castes. Telaga, a community of agriculturists considered a sub-caste of the better known 'Kapus', concentrated in the financially powerful Coastal Andhra region. Vaisya are trading castes. Erukula (or Yerukala) and Yanadi (or Yenadi) are among the 'Scheduled Tribes' as per Article 342 of the Constitution of India.

6 **Editor's note:** A *'mandal'* is an administrative sub-district of a 'tehsil': both categories used for revenue collection. A Mandal Development Officer is thus a politically powerful category.

7 **Editor's note:** *Section 144* of the Indian Penal Code addresses the right to assemble in public .

5 I Utsa Patnaik

1 Ansley J. Coale, *Rapid Population Change in China, 1952–1982*, Washington, D.C.: National Academy Press, 1984; Judith Banister, *China's Changing Population*, Stanford, California: Stanford University Press, 1987.

2 First in the *New York Review of Books* and subsequently in his many lectures and books including A.K. Sen, *Development as Freedom*, New York: A Knopf, 1999.

3 A.K. Sen, *Development as Freedom*, p. 43.

4 Nai-Ruenn Chen, *Chinese Economic Statistics: A Handbook for Mainland China*, Edinburgh: Edinburgh University Press, 1966.

5 Utsa Patnaik, 'On Famine and Measuring Famine Deaths', in S. Patel, J. Bagchi and Krishnaraj, eds, *Thinking Social Science in India: Essays in Honour of Alice Thorner*, New Delhi: Sage India, 2002.

6 Utsa Patnaik, 'Export-Oriented Agriculture and Food Security in Developing countries and in India', *Economic and Political Weekly,* Nos 35–37, September 1996; reprinted in *The Long Transition: Essays on Political Economy,* New Delhi: Tulika Books, 1999.

6 I Hamza Alavi

1 Most of the contributions have appeared in the quarterly supplements, 'Review of Agriculture' (RA), of the *Economic and Political Weekly (EPW).* The main contributions include: Ashok Rudra, A. Majid and B.D. Talib, 'Big Farmers of the Punjab: Some Preliminary Findings of a Sample Survey', *EPW (RA)*, vol. 4, no. 39, 27 September 1969; Ashok Rudra, 'Big Farmers of Punjab: Second Instalment of results', *EPW (RA)*, vol. 4, no. 52, 27 December 1969; Ashok Rudra, 'In Search of the Capitalist Farmer', *EPW (RA)*, vol. 5, no. 26, 27 June 1970; Ashok Rudra, 'Capitalist Development in Agriculture: A Reply', *EPW,* vol. 6, no. 45, 6 November 1971; Utsa Patnaik, 'Capitalist Development in Agriculture: A Note', *EPW (RA)*, vol. 6, no. 39, 25 September 1971; Utsa Patnaik, 'Capitalist Development in Agriculture: A Further Comment', *EPW (RA)*, vol. 6, no. 52, 25 December 1971; Utsa Patnaik, 'On the Mode of Production in Indian Agriculture: A Reply', *EPW (RA)*, vol. 7, no. 40, 30 September 1972; Utsa Patnaik, 'Capitalism in Agriculture', *Social Scientist* (in two parts), no. 2, September 1972 and no. 3, October 1972; Paresh Chattopadhyay, 'On the Question of the Mode of Production in Indian Agriculture: A Preliminary Note', *EPW (RA)*, vol. 8, no. 13, 25 March 1972; Paresh Chattopadhyay, 'Mode of Production in Indian Agriculture: An Anti-Kritik', *EPW (RA)*, vol. 7, no. 53, 30 December 1972; Jairus Banaji, 'For a Theory of Colonial Mode of Production', *EPW,* vol. 7, no. 52, 23 December 1972; Ranjit Sau, 'On the Essence and Manifestation of Capitalism in Indian Agriculture', *EPW (RA)*, vol. 8, no. 13, 31 March 1973.

2 Similar questions have been raised elsewhere. In fact, a theoretical point of departure for the Indian debate is the well-known polemical exchange between A. Gunder Frank and Ernesto Laclau about feudalism and capitalism in Latin America. Andre Gunder Frank, 'Capitalism and Underdevelopment in Latin America', New York: Monthly Review Press, 1967. Ernesto Laclau, 'Feudalism and Capitalism in Latin America', *New Left Review,* 67, May–June 1971; reprinted in Laclau (1979), *Politics and Ideology in Marxist Theory: Capitalism, Fascism, Populism*, London and New York: Verso.

3 **Editor's note:** *All India Trade Union Congress (AITUC)*: India's oldest trade union, founded in 1920, initially not affiliated to any political party, since 1945 associated with the Communist Party of India (CPI). See Keywords for more.

4 **Editor's note:** *Trusteeship*: controversial philosophical view of Mahatma Gandhi, proposing ways by which the rich would become 'trustees' for people's welfare, widely denounced as being in favour of landlords, feudal princes and capitalists.

5 The overall result of the 'Land Reform' was summed by Ladejinsky recently; he wrote: 'Summing, up for India as a whole, by the end of 1970, the "declared surplus" was only 2.4 million acres and the "Area Distributed" just half of that, or 0.3 of one per cent of the total cultivated land of India.' Wolf Ladejinsky, 'Land Ceilings and Land Reform', *Economic and Political Weekly*, Annual Number, vol. 7, nos 5–6–7, 5 February 1972. There have been numerous detailed studies of land reform legislation and implementation in different states, one of the best of them being that for Bombay state by V.M. Dandekar and G.J. Khudanpur, *Working of Bombay Tenancy Act, 1948; Report of Investigation by V.M. Dandekar and G.J. Khudanpur*, Gokhale Arthasastra Sasodhana Sastha Prakasana No. 35, Poona: D.R. Gadgil, 1957. Also Daniel Thorner's well known lectures: Thorner, *The Agrarian Prospect in India*, Delhi: Delhi School of Economics, University of Delhi Press, 1956. The issue of class alignments in this context is examined with great clarity by Suhas Chattopadhyay, who writes: 'An all-out attack to smash the feudal and semi-feudal fetters on the land relations were necessary for the fulfilment of this (declared Congress) aim. But the land reforms were deliberately not directed towards this goal because the ruling bourgeoisie was not ready to sacrifice its class alliance with the landlords.' Suhas Chattopadhyay, 'On the Class Nature of Land Reforms in India since Independence', *Social Scientist*, no. 16, November 1973, p. 21.

6 Government of India, *Report of the Indian Delegation to China on Agrarian Co-operatives*, New Delhi: Planning Commission, 1957; also Government of India, *Report of the Indian Delegation to China on Agricultural Planning and Techniques*, New Delhi: Ministry of Food and Agriculture, 1956.

7 'To create an atmosphere favourable to the formation of agrarian co-operatives . . . (the) atmosphere should be one of equality and non-exploitation. In creating such an atmosphere, land reforms will play a vital role.' Ibid., p. 150.

8 Daniel Thorner, for example, wrote: 'But the success of rural cooperatives presupposes a modicum of social equality, political democracy, and economic viability among the villagers. These preconditions have not been present in village India. . . . Two things must happen: (i) the power of the village oligarch must be broken . . . and (ii) the government must become an instrument of the ordinary people'. See Daniel Thorner, 'Context for Cooperatives in Rural India', *Economic Weekly*, vol. 14, nos 4–5–6, 27 January 1962. Cf. also Daniel Thorner, *Agricultural Cooperatives in India*, Bombay: Asia Publishing House, 1964.

9 Barrington Moore, *Social Origins of Dictatorship and Democracy: Lord and Peasant in the Making of the Modern World*, Boston, Mass.: Beacon Press, 1966, Chapter VI.

10 F.G. Bailey, *Politics and Social Change: Orissa in 1959*, Berkeley: University of California Press/London and Bombay: Oxford University Press, 1963.

11 Myron Weiner, *Party Building in a New Nation: The Indian National Congress*, Chicago: University of Chicago Press, 1967, pp. 154–55.

12 Government of India, *Report on India's Food Crisis and Steps to Meet It*, New Delhi: Ministry of Food and Agriculture and Ministry of Community Development and Cooperation, 1959.

13 J.W. Mellor *et al.*, eds, *Developing Rural India*, Ithaca: Cornell University Press, 1968, p. 83.

14 The analytical and critical bibliographical essay by T.J. Byres, where he lists 104 items, is still the best guide to the main body of that literature. Cf. T.J. Byres, 'The Dialectic of India's Green Revolution', *South Asian Review*, vol. 5, no. 2, January 1972. The important contributions published since that article was written include: (i) Francine Frankel, *India's Green Revolution: Economic Gains and Political Costs*, Princeton, NJ: Princeton

University Press, 1971; (ii) Harry M Cleaver *et al.*, 'The Contradictions of the Green Revolution', *Monthly Review*, vol. 24, June 1972, pp. 80–128; (iii) Hari Sharma, 'The Green Revolution in India', in Kathleen Gough and Hari Sharma, eds, *Imperialism and Revolution in South Asia*, New York: Monthly Review Press, 1973. Also see the numerous contributions in the 'Quarterly Review of Agriculture' in the *Economic and Political Weekly* (Bombay).

15 Samir Amin, *Accumulation On a World Scale: A Critique of the Theory of Underdevelopment*, New York: Monthly Review Press, 1974, passim.

16 Laclau, *Politics and Ideology in Marxist Theory*, p. 28.

17 Utsa Patnaik, 'On the Mode of Production in Indian Agriculture: A Reply', p. A-146.

18 Perry Anderson writes: 'Political sovereignty was never focused in a single centre. The functions of the State were disintegrated in a vertical allocation downwards, at each level of which political and economic relations were, on the other hand, integrated. This parcellization of sovereignty was constitutive of the whole feudal mode of production.' See Perry Anderson, *Passages from Antiquity to Feudalism*, London: Verso, 1974, p. 148.

19 Cf. Hamza Alavi, 'The State in Post-Colonial Societies', *New Left Review*, 74, July–August 1972, reprinted in Kathleen Gough and Hari Sharma, eds, *Imperialism and Revolution in South Asia*; 'L'Etat Dans les Societes Post-Coloniales', *Les Temps Modernes*, no. 314–315, September–October 1972.

20 In the words of Henry Maine, 'Land in pre-British India was one of the aspects of rulership, whether viewed in the person of a *raja*, in the body corporate of a *bhaichara* (brotherhood) village, or in the person of the *zamindar*, the closest approximation to the Roman *paterfamilias*. Thus, the Indian view of land was also political.' Quoted in Walter Neale, 'Land is to Rule', in Robert Eric Frykenberg, ed., *Land Control and Social Structure in Indian History*, Madison: University of Wisconsin Press, 1969, p. 7. **Editor's note:** For *zamindar*, see Keywords.

21 S. Nurul Hassan, 'Zamindars under the Mughals', in Frykenberg, ed., *Land Control and Social Structure in Indian History*, p. 28; Also cf. S. Nurul Hassan, *Thoughts on Agrarian Relations in Mughal India*, New Delhi: People's Publishing House, 1973, and Irfan Habib's classic work, *The Agrarian System of Mughal India, 1556–1707*, Bombay and New York: Asia Publishing House, published for the Department of History, Aligarh Muslim University, 1963.

22 **Editor's note:** François Bernier, *Travels in the Mogul Empire A.D. 1656–1668*, trans. Archibald Constable, 2nd edition revised by Vincent A. Smith, Oxford: Oxford University Press, 1916, p. 204. He writes: 'It should be borne in mind, that the *Great Mogol* constitutes himself heir of all the *Omrahs*, or lords, and likewise of the *Mansebdars*, or inferior lords, who are in his pay', and further, 'what is of the utmost importance, that he is proprietor of every acre of land in the kingdom, excepting, perhaps, some houses and gardens which he sometimes permits his subjects to buy, sell, and otherwise dispose of, among themselves'.

23 Eric Stokes, *The English Utilitarians and India*, Oxford: Clarendon Press, 1959. The ideological debate amongst the colonial rulers is brilliantly examined by Ranajit Guha, *A Rule of Property for Bengal: An Essay On the Idea of Permanent Settlement*, Paris: Mouton, 1963.

24 For the concept of 'internal disarticulation' of colonial economies, cf. Samir Amin, 'Accumulation on a World Scale', passim.

7 | K. Balagopal

1 **Editor's note:** Refers to the strike between 8 May and 27 May 1974, by 1.7 million workers of the Indian Railways, considered then as one of the largest recorded industrial actions worldwide. Led by major trade unionist George Fernandes, it directly presaged the declaration of Emergency the following year.

2 **Editor's note:** *Buddhijeevi*: the intellectual (privileged/leisure) classes.

3 **Editor's note:** *Sharad Joshi* (1935–2015), founder of the Shetkari Sanghatana or Farmers' Organization mainly from the state of Maharashtra; Mahendra Singh Tikait (1935–2011), leader of the Bharatiya Kisan Union (Indian Farmers' Union) from the state of Uttar Pradesh. Both were widely viewed as representatives of the rich peasant category.

4 **Editor's note:** *Panchayat* or *gram panchayat*: village council, a form of rural self-governance legitimized by the 73rd Constitutional Amendment in 1993.

5 **Editor's note:** *Telugu Desam*, meaning Telugu land, a political party set up by the movie star–politician N.T. Rama Rao in the state of Andhra Pradesh in 1982.

6 **Editor's note:** *Zamindar, literally landlord, evoking a colonial-era system of a feudal elite that continues after Independence.* See Keywords for more.

7 **Editor's note:** *Benami*, literally 'unnamed', refers to property or transactions that are anonymous.

8 **Editor's note:** *Begar*, 'unfree' or bonded labour.

9 **Editor's note:** *Karamchedu* – 17 July 1985, six Dalits killed in confrontation with the Kamma caste; *Neerukonda* – two years later in July 1987, second attack on the Dalit Mala caste by Kammas; *Gudivada* – also in July 1987, a Dalit labourer killed in a dispute over a small patch of tankbed land by an upper-caste (Raju) Congress party leader; *Dontali* – the month after Neerukonda, on 27 August 1987, fourth attack. These are only the leading incidents, all in the same cluster of land in Coastal Andhra Pradesh.

10 **Editor's note:** *Ryotwari*, a system of land revenue implemented by the British that gave some rights of ownership to the actual cultivators. ILTD: Indian Leaf Tobacco Development, an arm of the multinational cigarette manufacturer, Indian Tobacco Company (ITC).

11 **Editor's note:** *The Vijayanagara empire* (1336–1646), one of the most influential in pre-colonial south India, has been something of a floating signifier for south India: defined on different occasions as an anti-Islamic empire that began as an effort to ward off northern invasions, as a Kannada empire (and thus a legacy of the Hoysala dynasty) and a Telugu empire (successor to the Kakatiya kingdoms). This nationalist-ethnicist attribution is especially important for one of south India's most prosperous regions, the Coastal Andhra belt.

12 **Editor's note:** Refers to *Tirupati*, one of India's wealthiest temple shrines, dedicated to an incarnation of Vishnu, in Chittoor district of Andhra Pradesh.

13 **Editor's note:** *Maruti cars and VCRs*: refers to the first range of small cars manufactured by Maruti–Suzuki from 1983, which, together with video cassette recorders (VCRs), were a sign of economic prosperity at the time.

14 **Editor's note:** *Ragi*: millet; *jowar*: sorghum; *bajra*: pearl millet.

15 **Editor's note:** *Lambada, Gond*: migrant and often 'tribal' labour. Both are Scheduled Tribes as per Article 342 of the Constitution of India. *Kushki* land: dryland as per revenue records, whose purpose has not yet been listed.

16 **Editor's note:** *N.T. Rama Rao* (1923–1996): a major Telugu movie star, founder of the Telugu Desam Party in 1982, and former Chief Minister of the state of Andhra Pradesh. Balagopal has written separately about Rama Rao in a famous text, 'A False Resurrection: The Rise and Fall of N.T. Rama Rao', *Economic and Political Weekly*, 10 November 1984. N. Chandrababu Naidu, Rama Rao's son-in-law who inherited leadership of the Telugu Desam Party, known also for having introduced one of India's early globalization experiments when he was the Chief Minister; also the subject of an essay by Balagopal, 'Chandrababu Naidu, The Man and the Times', *Economic and Political Weekly*, 26 June 1999.

17 **Editor's note:** *Karshaka Parishad*: Body set up in 1988 in Andhra Pradesh, ostensibly to look after farmers' rights, but actually to oversee agricultural revenue.

8 | Geeta Kapur

1 R. Srivatsan, 'Concept of "Seva" and the "Sevak" in the Freedom Movement', *Economic and Political Weekly*, vol. 41, no. 5, 4 February 2006.

2 **Editor's note:** *Swadeshi*, an anti-colonial movement for the economic boycott of imported goods, peaked in the period 1904–17. Its aesthetic aspects were primarily explored by the art historian Ananda K. Coomaraswamy in his influential 1910 essay, 'Art and Swadeshi'. This refers more generally to the influential 'Bengal School', an umbrella term bringing together the artistic and pedagogic practices instituted in the Government School of Art, Calcutta, the writings and teachings of the artist Abanindranath Tagore (1871–1951), the founding of the art school at Santiniketan by Rabindranath Tagore in 1921, amid the more general theories of reform associated with the Brahmo Samaj, a monotheist reform of Hinduism in Bengal.

3 **Editor's note:** Gandhi's deployment of tradition, especially in terms of his arguments to reform Hinduism through moral regeneration and a new system of ethics, a new *yugadharma* (or ethics for our times), has been a matter of ongoing debate, especially as it draws selectively from various strands of modernity, and from other religions including Buddhism, Jainism, Judaism, Islam and, especially, Christianity, along with ideas from Tolstoy, Ruskin and Thoreau.

4 **Editor's note:** Rabindranath Tagore's astonishing and trenchant opposition to several key aspects of *swadeshi*, especially as it related to the burning of foreign cloth and to the symbol of the *charkha* (spinning wheel, used for the making of *khadi* or homespun cloth), and his disagreement with Gandhi on this, are among the key components of the debates between these two figures. See Sabyasachi Bhattacharya, *The Mahatma and The Poet: Letters and Debates between Gandhi and Tagore 1915–1941*, Delhi: National Book Trust, 1997.

5 **Editor's note:** Filmmakers Satyajit Ray (1921–1992) and Ritwik Ghatak (1925–1976) were contemporaries but coming from two very different and, for many, opposed traditions in Bengal: one, a direct inheritor of the Bengal renaissance; the other, a Partition refugee from East Bengal (later Bangladesh). Both, however, extensively referred to and invoked Rabindranath Tagore in their films, to very different ends.

6 **Editor's note:** Refers to the invocation of the 'mother' archetype in Ray's films, and much more elaborately and expressively in Ghatak's films, usually with reference to 'mother-goddesses' from primitive religious forms, later also invoked by Ghatak's leading student, the filmmaker Kumar Shahani.

7 **Editor's note:** *Mani Kaul* (1944–2011), major avant-garde filmmaker. This statement in all probability refers to Kaul's famous documentary, *Mati Manas* (Mind of Clay, 1984).

8 **Editor's note:** *Kumar Shahani* (b. 1940), avant-garde filmmaker and contemporary of Mani Kaul. Both were students of Ghatak. Shahani's interest in epic structures derives as much from his conscious use of it in music, theatre and from the theories of Eisenstein and Brecht. See the book, *Kumar Shahani: The Shock of Desire and Other Essays*, ed. Ashish Rajadhyaksha, New Delhi: Tulika Books, 2017, for his writings on the subject of the epic.

9 **Editor's note:** *K.G. Subramanyan* (1924–2016) and *Bhupen Khakhar* (1934–2003), artists who provided extraordinarily influential new directions to contemporary Indian art, through accessing traditions from the folk to the popular, and forms deliberately dismantling modernist distinctions between high and popular art, between artists and craftsmen. Both were associated with the Faculty of Fine Arts, Baroda. Subramanyan was also an extremely influential art teacher in Santiniketan.

10 **Editor's note:** *Ravi Varma* (1848–1906), belonging to an aristocratic family related to the royal house of Travancore, was initially a court painter there and in several other courts, before choosing to turn into a popular artist, adapting conventions derived from the art school aesthetic and the courtly styles to the marketplace, inaugurating what would come to be called 'calendar' painting. Perhaps the most influential artist in modern India, especially for defining the contours of 'traditional' art in the way he painted gods and mythological figures.

11 **Editor's note:** *Upanishads*: ancient Sanskrit texts, part of Vedic literature, and a great influence on Tagore.

12 **Editor's note:** All the artists mentioned were members of, or associated with, the Progressive Artists Group (PAG), a group formed in 1947 with explicit political linkages to the Communist Party of India.

13 **Editor's note:** *Indian People's Theatre Association (IPTA)*, radical political theatre group affiliated to the Communist Part of India, formed in 1943 in the context of the Bengal famine, which later had a nation-wide influence on theatre, music and cinema. Like the PAG (see Editor's note 12 above), IPTA introduced a deliberately internationalist political vanguard aesthetic into Indian art, alongside a conscious exploration of peasant and proletarian performative traditions.

14 'Third-World literature in the Era of Multinational Capitalism', *Social Text*, no. 15, Fall 1986. The reply by Aijaz Ahmad, 'Jameson's Rhetoric of Otherness and the "National Allegory"', also in *Social Text*, no. 17, Fall 1987, provides a substantial part of the argument in this essay.

15 See Nelly Richard, 'Postmodernism and the Periphery', *Third Text*, vol. 1, no. 2, Winter 1987, for an excellent discussion on the subject.

9 I Ravi Sundaram

1 Sankaran Krishna, 'Cartographic Anxiety: Mapping the Body Politic in India', *Alternatives*, 4, 1994.

2 Henry Lefebvre, *The Production of Space*, Oxford: Blackwell, 1991.

3 Ashis Nandy, *The Savage Freud*, New Delhi: Oxford University Press, 1995.

4 One does not have to read Michel de Certeau to understand Gandhi but the former's book throws interesting light on 'sly' practices of resistance. Michel de Certeau, *The Practice of Everyday Life*, Berkeley: University of California Press, 1984.

5 As Deshpande points out, 'The construction of the national economy very soon becomes synonymous with the nation itself. This enshrining of the nation as the synechdonic representation of the nation was perhaps one of Nehru's distinctive personal contribution to the nationalist cause.' Satish Deshpande, 'Imagined Economies', *Journal of Arts & Ideas*, 25–26 December 1993, p. 24.

6 David Harvey, *The Condition of Postmodernity: An Enquiry into the Origins of Cultural Change*, Oxford: Blackwell, 1989.

7 This is what Zizek says, 'In Bentham's Panopticon one finds virtuality at its purest. You never know if someone is at the centre. If you knew someone was there, it would have been less horrifying. Now it's just a dark spot as Bentham calls it. If someone is following you and you are not sure, it is more horrible than if you know there is somebody. A radical uncertainty.' Geert Lovink, 'Civil Society, Fanaticism and Digital Reality: A Conversation with Slavoj Zizek', *Ctheory* (http://ctheory.net/ctheory_wp/civil-society-fanaticism-and-digital-reality-a-conversation-with-slavoj-zizek/), 1996.

8 Architecture never played an iconic role in post-Independence India. Nationalism, unlike colonialism, never sponsored major historicist buildings. It was content in importing some of the worst versions of the International Style which replaced traditional methods of construction. The only concession to the avant-garde was the invitation to Le Corbusier to design the city of Chandigarh – surely one of the most soulless urban sites in post-Independence India. For an interesting analysis of Corbusier, see Manfredo Tafuri, *Architecture and Utopia*, Cambridge, Mass.: MIT Press, 1976. **Editor's note:** The *Bhakra Nangal* dams in Himachal Pradesh are the showpiece of Nehruvian developmentalism. Conceived in 1944 and formally inaugurated in 1948, a year after Independence, they were referred to by Nehru as one of the 'temples of the future'.

9 The 1975 Emergency was in many ways the denouement of the Panopticon, the beginning of the end of the old centralized state of developmental nationalism.

10 During this period India was going though considerable political turmoil with challenges from ethnic/regional movements leading to a cycle of political violence.

11 Political leaders, led by the then Prime Minister Rajiv Gandhi, would insist on posing beside a desktop; most advertisements after the early 1980s were sure to include images of the computer as part of their sales pitch.

12 Early efforts were focused on developing a local telecommunications production base. These efforts were centred around the Centre for Development of Telematics (C-DoT). Led by the charismatic Sam Pitroda, C-DoT's efforts were later subverted by a section of the bureaucracy sympathetic to transnational capital. **Editor's note:** *Sam (Satyan) Pitroda* (b. 1942) is a telecom engineer, inventor and entrepreneur, founder of C-DoT, considered by many as the founder of the Information Technology revolution in India when, in the early 1980s, he oversaw Prime Minister Rajiv Gandhi's ambitious technology missions, aimed at extending digital telecommunications to every corner of the country.

13 Even though the computer campaign had started in the early 1980s, this writer saw his first computer in 1988, when he had to submit his first assignment as a graduate student in a US university!

14 **Editor's note:** *NICNET*: The digital e-resources arm of the National Informatics Centre (NIC) established in 1976. See Keywords.

15 There were ugly public slanging matches between NICNET and the state monopoly which acts as India's international gateway – Videsh Sanchar Nigam Limited (VSNL).

16 In an interview with this writer, the Director of NIC maintained that controls on the net were meaningless, and the state could do nothing to check the dissemination of pornographic and explicit material.

17 NICNET, *Ten Years of the National Informatics Centre*, New Delhi: National Informatics Centre, 1994.

18 Even in Delhi, the average period that this writer has managed to stay online is twenty minutes! The simple facts of third-world connectivity: phones break down, as does electricity.

19 Nandy, *The Savage Freud*, pp. 181–82.

20 This was in contrast with Marx's optimistic view. Marx tended to see the role of the railway in India very much as Buadelaire saw Baron Von Haussmann's reconstruction of Paris in the mid-nineteenth century – the process of destruction and opening up of imaginative modes of social action.

21 A comparative journey, though more focused in time and space, is the Long March undertaken by the Chinese Red Army in 1934–35.

22 Krishna, 'Cartographic Anxiety'.

23 The exhibition mode had a limited presence in India. The great nationalist exhibition was Expo 72 in New Delhi in 1972. In a space specially built for the purpose, various Indian states and, more important, foreign (mainly western) countries put up halls for visitors. This was the Third World and Nehruvian version of the Crystal Palace, and was a huge success at the time. Since then exhibitions have tended to be more focused, concentrating on commercial and business interests rather than recreate the spectacle-like quality of Expo 72.

24 James Clifford, *The Predicament of Culture*, Cambridge, Mass.: Harvard University Press, 1988, p. 167.

25 Arjun Appadurai, 'Patriotism and Its Futures', *Public Culture*, 5, 1993, pp. 411–29.

26 The state networks (NICNET, ERNET, VSNL) have around 10,000 users and the private providers (Axess, RPG-SPRINT, Dartmail, UUNET) have around 20,000 between them. This is an approximate calculation. We must also bear in mind that accounts, particularly in research institutions, tend to be shared by a group of users.

27 See 'Boom Time for Computer Networks' *Pioneer*, 4 May 1995.

28 'What's on at http://www.indiainc.com' by Sudha Nagaraj, *Pioneer*, 26 April 1996.

29 The political wagers of the upper-caste elite have shifted from the state to the Hindu nationalist movement; yet other sections support the Congress party.

30 This refers to periodic calls by groups for censorship of films with explicit sequences in the name of moral order. Most state attempts at widening censorship guidelines have been ineffective. In fact, a recent Supreme Court judgement struck down the verdict of a lower court preventing the screening of the controversial film *Bandit Queen*.

31 Walter Benjamin, quoted in David Frisby, *Fragments of Modernity*, Cambridge: Polity Press, 1985, p. 254.

32 Once again, very few telephone connections manage to stay online for more than twenty minutes.

33 To be sure, alternative sites set up by dissenting members of the expatriate community do exist. However these sites cannot compete with those of the right wing.

34 The website of the right-wing Hindu nationalist Bharatiya Janata Party, which puts out an aggressive brand of nationalism based on majoritarianism and anti-Muslim rhetoric, is in fact operated from the US! The irony of this was entirely lost on the leadership of the BJP. **Editor's note:** See Keywords for Bharatiya Janata Party.

35 It is important to remember that despite all the authoritarian and disciplinary initiatives of Nehruvian panoptics, the relationship to the democratic political sphere prevented the realization of a 'totally administered society'.

36 **Editor's note:** This text was written in 1996.

37 In addition, the computer introduced was the old IBM PC with a rather unattractive modernist architecture. Macs were too expensive since clones did not exist.

38 Developmental modernism does not entertain any dialectical doubt that was possible in Europe. Here, the emphasis was more on functional mapping of space based on the triad development/science/nation. Here, the pioneers of developmental modernism were neither artists nor philosophers but what Rabinow in his work on the French modern calls 'technicians of general ideas': anonymous state managers who painstakingly built the model. Paul Rabinow, *French Modern: Norms and Forms of the Social Environment*, Cambridge, Mass.: MIT Press, 1989.

39 Michel Foucault, 'What is Enlightenment', in Paul Rabinow, ed., *The Foucault Reader*, New York: Pantheon Books, 1984, p. 43.

40 *The demise of the aura of technology has also its flip side: the emergence of a technopia* of global consumption which has as its main address the elite of the second cyberpublic.

41 The rapid rise of a mass consumption culture in the urban areas has removed the older aura around 'technical' articles of consumption. Articles which the urban mass public previously saw only as exhibitionary items (where, as Benjamin pointed out, 'you could see, but not touch') are now available for daily use. These include (public and private) telephones, televisions, and, for the more affluent, VCRs and refrigerators. Though many activists who are into cyberspace may be ambivalent towards the new consumption space, this is a world in which they work and struggle.

42 Given the situation of widespread income inequalities of a country like India, some form of state funding is vital for the development of alternative networks. Private and multinational capital has shown little interest in developing alternative spaces – there is every likelihood that this attitude will continue in the near future. The struggle must be, however, to create a genuine public space where access to networks is made as open as possible, without state controls.

43 Fredriech Nietzsche, *The Will to Power*, ed. Walter Kaufman, New York: Vintage, 1967.

44 Even as perceptive an observer as Paul Virilio tends to miss the mediated character of this transmission. Arguing that cyberspace heralds a new global time which is going to lead to the end of local times, Virilio writes: 'For the first time history is going to unfold within a one-time system: global time. . . . [I]n the very near future, our history will happen in universal time, itself the outcome of instantaneity – there only.' Virilio counters this bleak scenario with possibility of the 'accidents of accidents' – the cyber-accident, when networks crash and capitalism 'collapses'. Paul Virilio, 'Speed and Information: Cyberspace Alarm!', *CTheory*, 1995, http://ctheory.net/ctheory_wp/speed-and-information-cyberspace-alarm/.

45 Donna Haraway, *Simians, Cyborgs and Women: The Reinvention of Nature*, New York: Routledge, 1991; Paul Rabinow, 'Artificiality and Enlightenment: From Sociobiology to Biosociality', in J. Crary and S. Kwinter, eds, *Incorporations*, New York: Zone Books, 1992; Alucquere Rosanne Stone, 'Will the Real Body Stand Up: Boundary Stories about Virtual Cultures,' in Michael Benedikt, ed., *Cyberspace: the First Steps*, Cambridge, Mass.: MIT Press, 1991.

46 Phrase from David Tomas, to describe the experience of cyberspace, quoted in Stone, 'Will the Real Body Stand Up'.

47 **Editor's note:** Haraway's original quote is: 'In short, the certainty of what counts as nature – a source of insight and promise of innocence – is undermined, probably fatally. The transcendent authorization of interpretation is lost, and with it the ontology grounding "Western" epistemology. But the alternative is not cynicism or faithlessness, that is, some version of abstract existence, like the accounts of technological determinism destroying "man" by the "machine" or "meaningful political action" by the "text".' Haraway, 'A Cyborg Manifesto', in *Simians, Cyborgs and Women*, pp. 152–53.

10 | Madhava Prasad

1 Charles Taylor, 'The Politics of Recognition', in *Multiculturalism: A Critical Reader*, ed. D.T. Goldberg, Oxford: Blackwell, 1994.

2 Kwame Anthony Appiah, *The Ethics of Identity*, Princeton, NJ: Princeton University Press, 2005. All quotations pp. 101, 102, 104.

3 Cited in Jyotirindra Das Gupta, *Language Conflict and National Development: Group Politics and National Language Policy in India*, Berkeley: University of California Press, 1970, p. 160.

4 T.V. Sathyamurthy , 'Language, Religion and Political Economy: The Case of Bangladesh', in David Taylor and Malcolm Yapp, eds, *Political Identity in South Asia*, Collected Papers on South Asia, No. 2, London: Curzon Press, 1979, p. 214.

5 Ibid., p. 215.

6 When it comes to be figured as Mother/goddess, the illusion of possession acquires a new meaning.

7 This is amply clear from the way in which Indian languages have struggled to adapt their rules of grammatical number to the new situation of democracy. The use of the second person plural is now at least

ideally regarded as mandatory for addressing a stranger. The history of the variation of pronoun use, and its relation to political history, is not taken into account by grammarians, whose accounts give no indication of the complexities involved in pronoun usage. The usage depends not only upon the rank of the person addressed, but also the upon the rank of the speaker. The right to address another with the second person plural is reserved only for people who are themselves of a particular social standing. The lowly farm worker cannot assume this privilege in speaking to his/her landlord without appearing presumptuous.

8 From the point of view of the effectivity of the solution, the wholesale relocation of all members of a language-identified community in another language, the dominant language of the territory, would serve the purpose equally well. There is no compulsion for every language to necessarily go through this process. Ultimately, it is the people who must go through the process of locating themselves in a linguistic universal, whether their own or some other. In theory, in India, the education of all citizens in English would bring about the same results as the universalization of its major languages. But it has to be quick enough to match the speed with which an existing language can come to embody the universal here and now. Until then democracy will remain unachieved.

9 Florian Coulmas, *Language and Economy*, Oxford: Blackwell, 1992.

10 For an illuminating inquiry into 'colonial bilingualism' in India, see Veena Naregal, *Language Politics, Elites, and the Public Sphere*, New Delhi: Permanent Black, 2001.

11 Léopold Sédar Senghor, cited in Coulmas, *Language and Economy.*

12 See Robert W. Stern, *Changing India: Bourgeois Revolution on the Sub-Continent*, Cambridge University Press, 1993, who regards this as a key element of Gandhi's strategy for the Congress: 'Dividing Congress into "linguistic provinces" was part of turning Indian nationalism into a mass movement' (p. 106). Of course, in Gandhi's mind, this may have been a strategic move that did not entail admission that these provinces were nations, but in time this division developed into an accepted reality and it was assumed that independent India would be divided into states along linguistic lines.

13 As Stern again points out: ibid., p. 109.

14 See R.V.R. Chandrashekhar Rao, 'Conflicting Rules of Language and Regionalism in an Indian State', in David Taylor and Malcolm Yapp, eds, *Political Identity in South Asia*, London: Curzon Press, 1979, pp. 151–69. Also, James Manor, 'Language, Religion and Political Identity in Karnataka', ibid., pp. 170–90.

15 Chandrashekhar Rao, 'Conflicting Rules of Language and Regionalism in an Indian State'.

16 Jyotirindra Das Gupta, *Language Conflict and National Development*, p. 135: 'Some of the vernacular literary movements, led by the Brahmin elite were far from being national movements in their own right and thereby posing a threat to Indian nationalism. The primary language question in India, as the nationalists perceived it was the one between Hindustani and Hindi: when the Hindi lobby, openly equating Hindustani with Urdu and Muslims, demanded that Hindi be the national/official language of India, the campaign for Hindi . . . was given a boost by the support of the Bengali, Kannada, and other Sahitya Parishads and individual writers. . . . Clearly the language question was being played out as a question of religion and the "Hindu" litterateurs were rallying behind "their language", Hindi, so far were the literary movements in the vernaculars from imagining a nationalism of their own.'

17 If countries like India have avoided the common fate of post-colonial countries, of being consumed by civil strife and inviting the UN peacekeeping forces in to restore order, it is because they have adopted English as the peacekeeping force.

18 **Editor's note:** *Karnataka Rakshana Samiti* (Karnataka Protection Forum) and *Shiv Sena*: Right-wing political groups in the Indian states of Karnataka and Maharashtra, dedicated to preserving their respective regional linguistic identities.

11 | M. S. S. Pandian

1 Andreas Huyssen, *Twilight Memories: Marking Time in a Culture of Amnesia*, New York and London: Routledge, 1995, p. 3.

2 A few years back (1996), Madras city, the capital of Tamil Nadu state (India), was officially renamed as Chennai.

3 **Editor's note:** *Silappathikaram* (or 'The Tale of an Anklet'), an ancient Tamil epic attributed to a prince-turned-monk Ilango Adigal, probably composed in the fifth century CE, telling the tragic love story of Kannagi and Kovalan: a founding text for Tamil nationalism.

4 **Editor's note:** Conference organized by the Tamil-nationalist political party Dravida Munnetra Kazhagam (DMK, Dravidian Progressive Federation) a year after it first came to power in Tamil Nadu. While the conference itself was an academic event held at the University of Madras, there was a more popular World Tamil Conference aimed at a wider audience, showcasing the art, culture and architecture of Tamil Nadu. As part of this conference, the statues of ten important figures from Tamil history were unveiled on the Marina beach. Only one of these was of a fictional character, Kannagi, and her image was mainly modelled on the image of actress P. Kannamba from the 1942 film *Kannagi*.

5 **Editor's note:** *DMK*: See Keywords.

6 **Editor's note:** Madras, Bombay and Calcutta were Presidency cities, leading to much debate, especially in the cases of Bombay and Madras, as to which Indian state they should belong to when the division of states took place – given the financial power of Gujarati capital in Bombay (later the capital of the state of Maharashtra) and Coastal Andhra in Madras (later the capital of the state of Tamil Nadu).

7 On Walter Benjamin's distinction between auratic and distracted receptions, see Mike Savage, 'Walter Benjamin's Urban Thought: A Critical Analysis', in Mike Crang and Nigel Thrift, eds, *Thinking Space*, London and New York: Routledge, 2000, p. 46.

8 At Tirunelveli, Valioor, Tuticorin, Alwarthirunagari and Kanyakumari.

9 **Editor's note:** *J. Jayalalithaa* (1948–2016), movie star and politician, heir-apparent to *M.G. Ramachandran* (or MGR: 1917–1987), Tamil Nadu's Chief Minister and a major movie star. MGR broke away from the DMK and founded the All India Anna DMK, which Jayalalithaa inherited. After his death she effectively ran the state as Chief Minister for five terms.

10 **Editor's note:** *M. Karunanidhi* (1924–2018) – writer, film scenarist, politician and major figure in Tamil Nadu politics – led the DMK for five terms as Chief Minister before he was replaced by his chief rival, Jayalalithaa.

11 *The Hindu*, 19 December 2001.

12 *The Hindu*, 27 December 1999.

13 *Dinamalar*, 26 December 2001.

14 Ibid.

15 **Editor's note:** *Bal Gangadhar Tilak* (1856–1920), major figure in the early history of the Independence movement, key ideologue of the *Swadeshi* movement calling for boycott of all foreign manufactures. *Subramanya Bharathi* (1882–1921), Tamil writer, poet, journalist and Independence activist, a major figure in Tamil literary history. The location of the space where Tilak gave a speech calling for independence, the subsequent building (and then demolition) of the podium on the Marina beach, and its further reincarnation as an auditorium, are among the more quixotic histories of the space and indeed of political nationalism.

16 *The Hindu*, 7 January 2002.

17 Michel de Certeau, *Practices of Everyday Life,* Berkeley: University of California Press, 1988, p. 108.

18 *Thuglak*, 2 January 2002.

19 *The Hindu*, 20 December 2001.

12 | Shuddhabrata Sengupta

1 I have relied extensively on the information (court records, deposition, etc.) and analysis undertaken, collected and collated by Nirmalangshu Mukherjee in *December 13: Terror over Democracy*, New Delhi and Chicago: Promilla and Co. Publishers in association with Bibliophile South Asia, 2005. I acknowledge my gratitude for the scholarly diligence and care with which Nirmalangshu Mukherjee unravels the 13 December case. I have also relied on the report of the meeting to discuss the media trial of S.A.R. Geelani held at Sarai, CSDS. I would also like to acknowledge conversations that I have had with Nandita Haksar and Vrinda Grover while thinking about the background to the 13 December case.

I would like to acknowledge the students and faculty of the Department of Film Studies, Jadavpur University for the opportunity to present some of the material and ideas in this text to them and for their feedback on the same.
For more information on the 13 December Case, please see the website of the All India Defence Committee for S.A.R. Geelani: http://www20.brinkster.com/sargeelani/ Also see Nirmalangshu Mukherjee's article on 'The Media and December 13', http://www.revolutionarydemocracy.org/miscl/dec13.htm; Nandita Haksar's article in *Sarai Reader 04*, 'Trial by the Media', www.sarai.net/journal/ 04_pdf/20nandita.pdf; Tripta Wahi's article in *Sarai Reader 05*, 'The Strange Case of Qays al Kareem', www.sarai.net/journal/05_pdf/03/04_qay.pdf; and an earlier posting by me (18 December 2002) on the Reader List titled 'The Worst is Always Precise', http://mail.sarai.net/pipermail/reader-list/2002-December/002080.html which has links to several newspaper reports relevant to the 13 December case.
The films I watched while thinking about this text were *Dil Se* (director: Mani Ratnam, 1998), *Mission Kashmir* (director: Vidhu Vinod Chopra, 2002), *16 December* (director: Mani Shankar, 2002), *Khakee* (director: Raj Kumar Santoshi, 2003), the Zee News telefilm on 13 December as well as the Zee News 'Inside Story' on the Al-Qaeda Terror Manual broadcast on 24 July 2005, and the News at 9 and Special Programme at 9:30, *13 December Ek Saazish*, also broadcast on Zee News on the evening of 4 July 2005. I also watched several news broadcasts on Aaj Tak, NDTV, Rashtriya Sahara and Zee News, through the course of the successive trials in the special POTA court, the Delhi High Court and the Supreme Court.

Readers interested in the murky history of the involvement of European state intelligence agencies under the ambit of 'Operation Gladio' to 'create' incidents of terrorism and sustain a 'strategy of tension' particularly in Italy are advised to refer to 'Fascism and the Establishment: Italy and the Strategy of Tension', http://struggle.ws/freeearth/fe3_italy.html. Google searches incorporating the words 'Gladio, P2, Italy, Belgium' are also likely to yield interesting results. An equally interesting though less candid account of the work of intelligence agencies in India, particularly the IB, by a former intelligence operative, can be found in Maloy Krishna Dhar, *Open Secrets: India's Intelligence Unveiled*, Delhi: Manas Publication, Delhi, 2005.
Editor's note: POTA: Prevention of Terrorism Act, a parliamentary Act passed in 2002.

2 **Editor's note:** The reference is to British architect Sir Edwin Lutyens, who designed the enclave of 'New' Delhi when it became the capital of the colonial British government, and the Indian architect Raj Rewal, known for major public architecture projects in Delhi such as the Asian Games Village.

3 **Editor's note:** *Nandita Haksar*, who represented Geelani, is a human rights lawyer, teacher and activist, and author of several books, especially on India's North East: e.g., *The Judgement That Never Came: Army Rule in North East India* (2011). She wrote *Framing Geelani, Hanging Afzal: Patriotism in the Time of Terror* (2009).

4 **Editor's note:** *Lal Krishna Advani* (L.K. Advani): co-founder and key 'Hindutva' ideologue of the Bharatiya Janata Party (BJP), former Deputy Prime Minister and Leader of the Opposition, Advani was born in pre-Independence Karachi in 1927.

5 **Editor's note:** *Sanjay Kak*, filmmaker, best known for his documentary *Jashn-e-Azadi: How We Celebrate Freedom* (2007). *Sampat Prakash*, Kashmiri trade unionist known for his 1969 landmark case when he challenged his detention under the Preventative Detention Act, Section (13A) of Indian Parliament for launching a mass agitation against the government for low wages, on the grounds that this Act was not applicable to the citizens of Jammu and Kashmir as per Article 370, under which Kashmir was entitled to its own legal system.

6 **Editor's note:** Refers to the attack on the modern temple of Akshardham in Gandhinagar, Gujarat, on 24 September 2002 by two armed men who killed thirty people before the National Security Guard laid siege on the temple and killed the attackers. Six people were accused by the Gujarat police, but were acquitted in 2014 by the Supreme Court.

13 I Jayant Kaikini

1 **Editor's note:** *S. Radhakrishnan*, the second President of independent India; Venkateswara: the image of the deity at the temple at Tirupati – common subjects for popular painting.

14 | Kancha Ilaiah Shepherd

1 Udaya Kumar, 'The Strange Homeliness of the Night: Spectral Speech and the Dalit Present in C. Ayyappan's Stories', *Studies in Humanities and Social Sciences*, XVII (1 and 2), 2013, pp. 177–91.

2 **Editor's note:** In popular Hinduism, *apsaras* or, more commonly, sexy seductresses.

3 **Editor's note:** *Kuruma*: a community of shepherds. *Kurumba* in Tamil Nadu, *kuruba* in Karnataka, *kuruva* in Rayalaseema and Coastal Andhra, and *kuruma* in Telangana.

15 | Veena Das

1 I am grateful to Upendra Baxi, Prashant Bhushan, Ranendra Kumar Das, Radha Kumar and Arthur Kleinman for detailed discussions on the issues discussed in this essay.

2 These two approaches are lucidly presumed in Giles Deleuze, *Nietzsche and Philosophy*, London: The Athlone Press, 1983.

3 Peter H. Schuck, *Agent Orange on Trial: Mass Toxic Disasters in the Courts*, Cambridge, Mass.: Harvard University Press, 1987.

4 Ibid., p. 4.

5 Michael R. Reich, 'Public and private responses to a chemical disaster in Japan: The case of Kanemi Yusho', *Law in Japan: An Annual*, 15, 1982, pp. 102–29.

6 See the report on the Bhopal disaster in *The Lancet,* 15 December 1984.

7 For a clear and concise picture of these issues, see Upendra Baxi and Amita Dhanda, *Valiant Victims and Lethal Litigation: The Bhopal Case*, Delhi: Indian Law Institute, 1990. This book puts together, in one place, all the legal records necessary for an understanding of the issues.

8 See, especially, M.D. Royce and J. Callahan, 'Isocyanates: An Emerging Toxic Tort', *Environmental Law*, 18, 1988; D. Rosenberg, 'The Causal Connection in Mass Exposure Cases: A Public Law Vision of the Tort System?', *Harvard Law Review*, 97, 1984; and S. Elliot, 'The Future of Toxic Torts: Of Chemophobia, Risk as a Comparable Injury and Hybrid Compensation Systems', *Houston Law Review*, 1988.

9 See Upendra Baxi and T. Paul, *Mass Disasters and Multinational Liability: The Bhopal Case*, Delhi: Indian Law Institute, 1988; and Upendra Baxi, 'The Bhopal victims in the labyrinth of the law: An Introduction', in Baxi and Dhanda, *Valiant Victims and Lethal Litigation*, pp. i–lxix .

10 On the inadequacy of the settlement, see, for example, the letter of the reputed tort lawyer Melvin Belli, characterizing the settlement as the most 'unethical' in his fifty-year experience of dealing with tort law, in *The Times of India*, 7 March 1989. My own calculations show that even if only half the claims were valid, the sum of 470 million dollars was just enough to sustain the affected households at the minimal income of Rs 700 per month, and a minimal subsidy for risk to life, for a maximum period of ten years. I have not included costs of medical care in these calculations. Thus, without even going into questions of rights, the sum was not even adequate to ensure the survival of severely affected households for twenty years.

11 Writ Petition No. 268 of 1989, No. 164 of 1986, No. 981 of 1989 and No. 1551 of 1986.

12 Schuck, *Agent Orange on Trial*, p. 174.

13 Compare Beck's formulation that modern societies have made a transition from industrial societies to risk societies. Ulrich Beck, 'From Industrial Society to Risk Society: Questions of Survival, Social Structure, and Ecological Enlightenment', in Mike Featherstone, ed., *Cultural Theory and Cultural Change*, London: Sage Publications, 1992, pp. 97–123.

14 For a fine discussion of this distinction, see Jean-Francois Lyotard, *The Differend: Phrases in Dispute*, Minneapolis, University of Minnesota Press, 1988.

15 Thus L.D. Loya, medical officer, Union Carbide India Ltd, stated at the time of disaster on 3 December 1984 that 'The gas is non-poisonous. There is nothing to do except ask patients to put a wet towel over their eyes.' Quoted in David Dembo *et al.*, eds, *Nothing to Lose but Our Lives*, New York: Council of International and Public Affairs and Delhi: Indian Law Institute, 1987.

16 Quoted in ibid., p. 42.

17 I would hazard a guess that doctors in the local hospital who were in daily contact with their patients responded to their suffering quite differently from those to whom the patients were part of a population on whom scientific data was to be produced for litigational purposes. The fact that the diseases defied cure, and the best that could be done for the patients was to provide symptomatic relief coupled with care, probably made these doctors defensive and anxious. But the most distant and arrogant in relation to patients were doctors whose job could be defined as that of certification.

18 See Y. Alaris *et al.*, 'Sensory and Pulmonary Irritation of Methyl Isocyanate in Mice and Pulmonary Irritation and Possible Cyanide-Like Effects of Methyl Isocyanate in Guinea Pigs', *Environmental Health Perspective*, 1987, pp. 159–67, for the toxic hazards of methyl isocyanate as compared to twenty-five other known isocyanates or diisocyanates.

19 See L. Gassert *et al.*, 'Long Term Pathology of Lung, Eyes and Other Organs Following Acute Exposure of Rats to Methyl Isocyanate', *The Lancet*, 72, 1987, pp. 95–103; for a description of the three patterns of toxicity, see N. Anderson, M. Kerr Muir, V. Mehra and A.G. Salmon, 'Exposure and Response to Methyl Isocyanate: Results of a Community-based Survey in Bhopal', *British Journal of Industrial Medicine*, 45, 1985, pp. 469–75.

20 The long-term effects are lucidly summarized in N. Anderson, 'Long Term Effects of Methyl Isocyanate', *The Lancet*, 3 June 1989. See also, Daya R. Verma, 'Hydrogen cyanide and Bhopal', *The Lancet*, 2 September 1989, for an account of how the long-term effects of methyl isocyanate were sought to be obscured by a clever manipulation of the suggestion that the deaths had been caused by hydrogen cyanide, which is much less lethal than methyl isocyanate, but in the popular imagination is considered to be the most lethal poison since it is associated with cyanide deaths.

21 S.K. Jain and S.K. Dave, *Working Manual I: On the Health Problems of Bhopal Gas Victims,* Delhi: ICMR and DST Centre for Visceral Mechanisms, 1986.

22 See *Deciding to Forego Life-Sustaining Treatment: Ethical, Legal and Medical Issues in Treatment Decisions*, Report of the President's Commission for the Study of Ethical Problems in Medicine and Biomedical and Behavioural Research,U.S. Government Printing Office, March 1983.

23 To mention only one fact, although clinical studies with survivors showed development of small airway and large airway obstructions which worsened with the passage of time, tests of pulmonary functions were done on a minuscule number of claimants. Mostly, it was assumed that survivors were exaggerating their symptoms.

24 For a reasoned critique of the procedures of evaluation of health status by the Directorate of Claims, see C. Sathyamala, N. Vohra and K. Satish, *Against all Odds: The Health Status of the Bhopal Survivors*, Delhi, 1989.

25 Affidavit dated 5 December 1989 of the Additional Director of Claims, in W.P. No. 843 of 1988.

26 I am not suggesting that there was any misrepresentation of scientific data by Carbide's scientists. But often, the parameters of an experiment can give a direction to the results. For instance, if animals exposed to methyl isocyanate in small-dose concentrations were sacrificed after a period of time, there would be no opportunity to observe long-term consequences of MIC. This point was made by Doctors Anderson, Mackenzie and Verma in their numerous publications.

27 Michael R. Reich, 'Environment and Science: The Case of PPBB Contamination in Michigan', *American Journal of Public Health*, 73, 1983, pp. 302–13.

28 Niklas Luhman, *Ausdzferenzeirung des Rechts*, Frankfurt: Suhrkamp, 1981.

29 Jean-Francois Lyotard, *The Differend: Phrases in Dispute*, Minneapolis: University of Minnesota Press, 1988, p. 8.

16 | Teesta Setalvad

1 **Editor's note:** *Zakia Jafri, Ehsan Jafri, Gulberg Housing Society, Special Investigative Team* (SIT). On 28 February 2002, former Member of Parliament Ehsan Jafri was killed by a mob, along with 69 others, at the predominantly Muslim Gulberg Housing Society in Ahmedabad. A Special Investigative Team (or SIT) was appointed in April 2009 to inquire into this and other major incidents of violence which later absolved the (then) Chief Minister Narendra Modi of complicity. Zakia Jafri, widow of Ehsan Jafri, filed a review petition in the Supreme Court which was rejected in 2014.

2 The battle was fought zealously on social media as well, where journalist friends were made and alliances were forged. Here is what Amir Rizvi, a dear friend with the most crazy sense of humour, wrote on Facebook on 24 July 2015, 'From the 27th of this month final arguments in the Zakia Jafri case will begin. The new FIR by the CBI (directly under the PMO) needs to be seen in that light!!! "CBI books Teesta Setalvad and her husband for 'illegal' foreign aid" [Note: Teesta Setalvad is the first and only person in India who has sent 117 killers to jail, including the closest friends of Modi. On 27th of this month, final arguments in the Zakia Jafri case will begin. Modi is the prime accused in this case].'

3 **Editor's note:** *Javed Anand*, journalist, husband of Teesta Setalvad and, with her, co-founder of the organization *Sabrang Communications* and the journal *Communalism Combat.*

4 **Editor's note:** *The Vyapam scam*, a major scandal in Madhya Pradesh in 2013, involving politicians, senior and junior officials, and businessmen, in which impostors were employed to write examination papers, manipulate exam-hall seating arrangements and supply forged answer sheets by bribing officials.

5 **Editor's note:** *Zahira Sheikh*: Survivor of the 1 March 2002 attack on the Best Bakery, a small outlet in the city of Baroda, in which a mob killed fourteen people. The Best Bakery incident, which was first tried at the Baroda Sessions Court, in part based on Zahira's testimony, fell apart when Zahira, along with thirty-seven of the 73 witnesses, repudiated their testimony. The National Human Rights Commission (NHRC) moved a Special Leave Petition in the Supreme Court in July 2003, asking for a retrial outside Gujarat since the witnesses were not safe. The Supreme Court agreed, accusing the state government of judicial failures, but then Zahira once again changed her testimony, claiming that she was being coached by Teesta Setalvad. Later, the Gujarat government filed an amended appeal in the High Court seeking a retrial of the case that saw seventeen of the accused retried.

6 **Editor's note:** *Gulberg, Naroda Patiya*: Major incidents in the 2002 Gujarat riots. Gulberg, see note 1 above. The Naroda Patiya massacre, also on 28 February 2002 in Ahmedabad, saw 97 Muslims killed by a mob of approximately 5,000 people over ten hours. In July 2012, an Indian court convicted thirty people including former state minister Maya Kodnani and Hindu leader Babu Bajrangi. For the first time, the verdict acknowledged the role of politicians in inciting Hindu mobs.

7 **Editor's note:** *Saamna*: Newspaper run by the pro-Hindu right-wing political party Shiv Sena, which had electoral arrangements (until 2019) with the BJP.

8 **Editor's note:** *Justice B.N. Srikrishna Report*: The Justice B.N. Srikrishna Commission of Inquiry, was constituted to investigate the causes of the 1992–93 Bombay riots and bomb blasts.

9 **Editor's note:** *Motilal Chimanlal Setalvad* (*c.* 1884–1974), jurist, first Attorney General for independent India, Chairman of First Law Commission of India, first Chairman of the Bar Council of India, and Teesta Setalvad's grandfather.

10 **Editor's note:** *P.N. Lekhi/Meenakshi Lekhi*: P(ran) N(ath) Lekhi, Supreme Court lawyer; Meenakshi Lekhi, Member of Parliament representing the BJP, also Supreme Court lawyer.

11 Manoj Mitta, 'Is SC seeking to shore up SIT's lost credibility?' *The Times of India*, 28 May 2010.

12 **Editor's note:** *Sabrang Communications and Publishing*: Organization started by Teesta Setalvad and Javed Anand, which runs the journal *Communalism Combat* and *Khoj*, a secular education programme. See https://www.sabrang.com/

13 **Editor's note:** *Vishwa Hindu Parishad* (VHP): 'Universal Hindu Front', Hindu-nationalist organization founded in 1964, part of the *Sangh Parivar* or 'family' of organizations that make up the pro-Hindu right: the parent organization, the Rashtriya Swayamsevak Sangh (RSS); the political wing, the Bharatiya Janata Party; the students' front, the Akhil Bharatiya Vidyarthi Parishad (ABVP); the lower-caste militant group Bajrang Dal; and the workers' union, the Bharatiya Kisan Sangh.

14 **Editor's note:** *panchnamas*: police witness records.

15 **Editor's note:** *kabrastan*: burial ground.

16 **Editor's note:** Refers to a report (dated 7 November 2007) in the news magazine *Tehelka*, which conducted an extensive 'sting' operation of covertly recorded conversations over six months, proving that the Gujarat 2002 violence was enabled by the support of the state police and the then Chief Minister.

17 **Editor's note:** *Indira Jaising*: Supreme Court lawyer, feminist human rights activist and founder of Lawyers' Collective.

18 **Editor's note:** *K.G. Kannabiran*: Lawyer in the Andhra Pradesh High Court, major human rights figure and co-founder of the People's Union for Civil Liberties (PUCL).

19 **Editor's note:** *Bal Thackeray*: Maharashtra politician who founded the right-wing Shiv Sena in 1966.

20 **Editor's note**: Refers to major 'communal' incidents of political violence: the Muzaffarnagar riots of August 2013, and the attacks on Bengali-speaking Muslim migrants in Assam in 2011.

21 **Editor's note:** *Bilkees Bano*: Victim of gang rape in the Gujarat riots of 2002, in an incident that killed her family members. In January 2008, eleven men were sentenced to life imprisonment for rapes and murders and a policeman was convicted of falsifying evidence, later upheld by the Bombay High Court which also set aside acquittal of seven accused including police officers and doctors charged with suppressing and tampering with evidence.

22 **Editor's note:** *Sardarpura Massacre*: riots in which thirty-three Muslims were killed on 1 March 2002 in a village close to Ahmedabad.

23 **Editor's note:** *Bajrang Dal*: Part of the *Sangh Parivar* (or 'family' of organizations that make up the pro-Hindu right). See note 13 above.

24 **Editor's note:** *Shubha Mudgal, Aneesh Pradhan, Sudhir Patwardhan*: Mudgal is an eminent classical singer; Pradhan is her percussion (*tabla*) accompanist and himself a noted historian of Indian classical music; and Patwardhan is a visual artist. All three are associated with progressive secular-radical ideologies.

25 **Editor's note:** *pramukh*: chief.

26 https://www.sabrangindia.in/article/dalit-revolt-hindutvas-successful-laboratory-gujarat; accessed 11 March 2020.

17 | Sharmila Rege

1 **Editor's note:** *Chaitya Bhoomi*: The temple in central Mumbai which forms B.R. Ambedkar's final resting place. Designed as a Buddhist temple or prayer hall, it is a major location for pilgrimage annually, when hundreds of thousands of Dalits arrive and occupy the nearby middle-class Shivaji Park area, to camp and to sell their wares.

2 See Gopal Guru, *Dalit Cultural Movement and Dialectics of Dalit Politics in Maharashtra*, Mumbai: Vikas Adhyayan Kendra, 1997. **Editor's note:** Guru speaks of a cultural hierarchy that emerged in the 1980s between a modernist Dalit literary camp and 'mudhouse' activists, as the former blindly imitated a literary modernity at the cost of the Dalit popular. See Sharmila Rege, 'Of Mudhouse Cultural Activists and Cultural Hierarchies', *Economic and Political Weekly*, vol. 33, no. 7, 14 February 1998.

3 **Editor's note:** This is widely depicted as the popular lineage of Ambedkar. The Buddha after Ambedkar called for the conversion of India's Dalit peoples into Navayana Buddhism in order to escape the evils of Hindu oppression. Shahu Maharaj (1874–1922), hereditary descendant of the Bhonsle royal dynasty in the city of Kolhapur, Maharashtra, was a major reformer dedicated to overcoming caste inequalities, and was a follower of the reformer Jyotirao Phule (1827–90), an iconic figure in the reform movement fighting for both caste and gender equality.

4 **Editor's note:** The four locations that have become key pilgrimage sites of the popular Ambedkari movements. For *Chaitya Bhoomi*, see note 1 above. *Diksha Bhoomi*, Nagpur, is the location where Ambedkar converted 600,000 followers to Buddhism on 14 October 1956. *Kranti Stambh* (Revolutionary Pillar) refers to the afterlife of the 1818 Battle of Koregaon, when the British East India Company fought a Maratha faction, part of the Anglo-Maratha wars that led to the consolidation of the British empire in western India. The British put up a pillar in acknowledgment of the fallen soldiers, among whose listed names several appear to be from the Mahar caste. On 1 January 1927, Ambedkar visited this pillar and declared the battle as also a battle of Dalits against upper-caste Marathas. On 1 January 2018, on the anniversary of that visit, Dalits clashed with right-wing Hindu groups, making the location a flashpoint of violence ever since. On 20 March 1927, Ambedkar led a movement of all castes to use water from a public tank in the city of Mahad, Maharashtra.

5 *Watan* refers to lands that the Mahars received in return for the discharge of caste-based village duties. This was not fixed on individuals but on the entire community. Ambedkar introduced a bill for abolition of *mahar watan* in the Bombay legislative council in 1927. **Editor's note:** This practice, which continued through colonialism, was first formally abolished in 1918 in the princely state of Kolhapur by Shahu Maharaj.

6 The term 'heterotopia' is a medical term, introduced in the social sciences by Foucault. See Michel Foucault, 'Of Other Spaces', *Diacritics*, 16 (1), 1986, pp. 22–27.

7 Gopal Guru, *Dalit Cultural Movement.*

8 R.D. Gaikwad, *Ambedkari Chalvalitil Athvaani*, Pune: Sugava Prakashan, 1993.

9 Ibid., p. 62.

10 Ibid., p. 64. **Editor's note:** Ramabai (1898–1935), Ambedkar's first wife. Bhayyasaheb, Bhima, Bhimaraya: all terms of endearment for Ambedkar.

11 **Editor's note:** *Ambedkari jalsa*: *jalsa* is a word commonly used to refer to public concerts, fairs or other celebratory events. It was adapted into a specific form of popular live musical events, adapting traditional folk forms and musical styles to sing the praises of Ambedkar.

12 Bhimrao Kardak (1978), *Ambedkari Jalse: Swarup va Karya,* Bombay: Abhinav Prakashan.

13 Baban Londhe (2001), *Ambedkari Lokgeete,* Mumbai: Akshar Prakashan.

14 Sharmila Rege (2006), *Writing Caste/Writing Gender: Narrating Dalit Women's Testimonies*, New Delhi: Zubaan.

15 The first generation of Ambedkarite *shahir*s include Patitpavandas, Bhimrao Kardak, Keriji Ghegde, Arjun Hari Bhalerao, Keruba Gaikwad, Keshav Sukha Aher, Ramchandra Sonavane and Amrutbhawa Bavaskar.

16 Kardak, *Ambedkari Jalse*, pp. 86–87.

17 **Editor's note:** *V(inayak) D(amodar) Savarkar* (1883–1966), one of the founders of the ideology of Hindutva. He was a member of the right-wing Hindu Mahasabha (or Hindu Grand Assembly), a political front formed in the context of the 1909 Morley–Minto reforms that proposed separate Muslim electorates.

18 See Krishna Kirwale, *Ambedkari Shahiri: Ek Shodh*, Pune: Kalpana Kirawale, 1992, p. 66.

19 Ibid., p. 83

20 **Editor's note:** *Pune Pact*: Pact arrived at between Ambedkar and Gandhi on 24 September 1932, on the need for separate electorates for Scheduled Castes and Tribes following the British declaration of a 'commual award' that Gandhi opposed.

21 Gaikwad, *Ambedkari Chalvalitil Athvaani*, p. 93.

22 **Editor's note:** *Ambedkarite shahir*, or *Bhimshahir*: While *shahir* (or *shayar*) conventionally translates as 'poet', this is a tradition of bardic performance, of rousing songs of heroism, sometimes in the tradition of public performance, such as the *powada* – songs of the valour of the seventeenth-century Maratha king Shivaji.

23 Gaikwad, *Ambedkari Chalvalitil Athvaani*, p. 248.

24 Kirwale, *Ambedkari Shahiri*, p. 93.

25 The second generation includes Wamandada Kardak, Sridhar Ohol, Rajanand Gadpayle, Deenbhandu Shegaonkar, Annabhau Sathe, Dalitanand and Vithal Umap.

26 Baba Borade, *Ambedkari Lokshahir Waman Kardak*, Kolhapur: Prachar Prakashan, 1995, p. 21.

27 In over 4,000 compositions, Wamandada articulates the popular Dalit social imaginary and we are at present trying to document this – both through a collection of the texts and memories of the context of their production and reception.

28 Baba Borade, *Ambedkari Lokshahir Waman Kardak*, p 19.

29 Guru, *Dalit Cultural Movement.*

30 **Editor's note:** *Jalsa*: see note 11. The gradual erosion of traditional theatre and the arrival of new forms of popular music (*gayan*) troupes also signalled a new popular economy from live to recorded music. *Qawali* is a more specifically Sufi tradition of popular music.

31 These compositions are a part of the audiovisual documentation of songs of *mahila mandal*s (Mahad 2005); this and other compositions will soon be accessible on the digital archives housed by the CSS, University of Pune.

32 Listen to, for instance the song, '*Vachava Gandhi*' (Save Gandhi) in the popular cassette 'I love you Ambedkar', Wings, Mumbai, 2000.

33 **Editor's note:** *Savita Bhimrao Ambedkar* (1909–2003), social activist, doctor and Ambedkar's second wife.

34 My understanding of counterpublics draws upon Michael Warner, *Publics and Counter Publics*, New York: Zone Books, 2002.

18 I Sunil Mohan & Rumi Harish

1 **Editor's note:** Major legal cases in relation to violence against women. In the Shah Bano case (*Mohd. Ahmed Khan v. Shah Bano Begum*, AIR 1985 SC 945), the Supreme Court delivered a judgement favouring maintenance given to an aggrieved divorced Muslim woman in 1985. The Mathura rape case was an incident of custodial rape in March 1972, in which a young tribal girl was raped by two policemen at the compound of a police station in Gadchiroli district of Maharashtra. The Supreme Court acquitted the accused, but the outcry led to amendments in the Indian rape law. Bhanwari Devi, a social worker from Rajasthan was in 1992 gang-raped by upper-caste men angered by her efforts to prevent a child marriage in their family. Once again, the court acquittal of the accused became a landmark episode in India's women's rights movement.

2 **Editor's note:** *Sangama*, a Bangalore-based human rights organization started in 1999 dedicated to sexual minorities, sex workers and people affected by HIV. See http://www.sangama.org

3 **Editor's note:** *Sahayathrika*, started in 2002 and registered in 2008, is an organization catering to lesbian, bisexual and transgender persons from Kerala, working on counselling, community-organizing and survival. It was formed in the backdrop of rising lesbian suicide rates in Kerala.

4 **Editor's note:** *Dowry*: Payment made by a bride to the groom (or his family) as a condition for marriage. Historically a cause for disputes leading to violence (e.g., 'dowry deaths'), the practice was banned by the Dowry Prohibition Act, 1961, but continues and has wide social sanction.

19 I Anita Dube

1 **Editor's note:** Antonio Gramsci, *Prison Notebooks*, eds. Quintin Hoare and Geoffrey Nowell-Smith, New York: International Publishers, 1985, p. 325.

2 **Editor's note:** This is a reference to Karl Marx, and to the concept of man as a 'species-being' as explored in *The Economic and Philosophical Manuscripts* of 1844.

3 **Editor's note:** George Steiner, *No Passion Spent: Essays 1978–1995*, New Haven: Yale University Press, 1986, pp. 1–2.

4 This phrase is used by Rosa Luxemburg to describe the trade union struggle, which she considers a defensive struggle, in which the proletariat seeks to achieve the best conditions possible but within the capitalist system. The labour movement and parliamentary reform movements, she feels, occupy themselves only with one side, i.e. the formal side of democracy, without questioning its 'real' content. **Editor's note:** Rosa Luxemburg, 'Co-operatives, Unions, Democracy', in *Reform or Revolution*, London: Militant Publications, 1986 [1900], available at https://www.marxists.org/archive/luxemburg/1900/reform-revolution/ch07.htm, accessed 11 March 2020.

5 **Editor's note:** This and the following paragraph primarily stage the manifesto in opposition to what came to be known broadly as the 'Bengal School' of painting. It combines an aesthetic and pedagogic strategy framed in the Government School of Art, Calcutta, and attributed to the arts administrator E.B. Havell (1861–1934) and the artist Abanindranath Tagore (1871–1951), and later exported to art schools across British India, primarily in the Presidency cities. The polemic includes the art school at Santiniketan that was founded by Rabindranath Tagore in 1921. A leading figure at Santiniketan was the artist K.G. Subramanyan (1924–2016), whose art and writing, notably the book *The Living Tradition* (Calcutta: Seagull Books, 1987), forms a particular target of this text. It also includes the art historian–philosopher Ananda Coomaraswamy (1877–1947). Lumping all of these together into a single category, or naming such a category 'Indologist' and 'revivalist', is of course a simplification, but it is central to the polemic.

6 This is an unnecessary polarization since the modern with all its fragmentation is constantly preoccupied with the Utopia of 'total' man. The fragmentation Subramanyan refers to is probably a symptom of the postmodern, and its waning of values. But Subramanyan's own works, his murals, his teracottas and his glass paintings, for all their wit and clever references to the 'little' tradition, paradoxically do not escape many aesthetic features of the postmodern: namely, flatness, impenetrable surfaces, a turning to the past as a search for historicism, etc. – which I will discuss a little later.

7 **Editor's note:** This refers to Subramanyan's controversial lecture, 'Do We Need an Art Movement?', Xth Coomaraswamy Lecture, delivered at the Lalit Kala Akademi, New Delhi, in 1983.

8 According to Rosa Luxemburg, 'The necessity of determining the final goal of socialism provides the teleology by which it becomes possible to understand the present as a process of becoming. Without this teleology, bourgeois society would have to be accepted as essentially eternal, and social analysis would be reduced to empirical inductive methods which are incapable of dealing with capitalism as a totality'.

9 Frederic Jameson, 'Postmodernism, or The Cultural Logic of Late Capitalism', *New Left Review*, 1 (146), July–August 1984; reprinted in Frederic Jameson, *Postmodernism, or, The Cultural Logic of Late Capitalism*, Durham: Duke University Press, 1991. This quote is from Jameson, *Postmodernism*, p. 4.

10 Ibid., p. 5.

11 Ibid., pp. 17–18.

12 Ibid., p. 18.

13 Ibid.

14 **Editor's note:** This refers to a movement widely viewed as reintroducing narrative and figurative art into Indian modernism with the major art exhibition, *Place for People* (1981). A key interlocutor for this was the British artist and art historian Timothy Hyman, and his interpretation of the artist Bhupen Khakhar and several artists associated with the 'Baroda Group' and the Faculty of Fine Arts at the M.S. University, Baroda, as furthering his own preoccupations with figurative painting.

15 Antonio Gramsci, *Marxism and Modern Culture*, quoted in Maynard Solomon, ed., *Marxism and Art: Essays Classic and Contemporary*, Brighton: Harvester Press, 1979.

Keywords

1 Irfan Habib, *Medieval India: The Study of Civilization*, New Delhi: National Book Trust, 2007.

2 Louis Dumont, *Homo Hierarchicus: An Essay On the Caste System*, Chicago: University of Chicago Press, 1970.

3 *State Of Kerala & Anr vs N. M. Thomas & Ors* on 19 September 1975; equivalent citations: 1976 AIR 490, 1976 SCR (1) 906.

4 Rajni Kothari, *Politics in India*, New Delhi: Orient Longman, 1970, p. 11.

5 Partha Chatterjee, 'Beyond the Nation? Or Within?', *Economic & Political Weekly*, vol. 32, no. 1–2, January 1997.

6 Geeta Kapur, 'When Was Modernism in Indian Art?', in *When Was Modernism: Essays on Contemporary Cultural Practice in India*, New Delhi: Tulika Books, 2000, p. 297.

7 Partha Chatterjee, *Our Modernity*, Rotterdam/Dakar: SEPHIS/CODESRIA and Kuala Lumpur: Vinlin Press, 1997.

8 Geeta Kapur, 'National/Modern: Preliminaries', in *When Was Modernism*, p. 288.

9 Term originally used by M.N. Srinivas in M.N. Srinivas, *Religion and Society Among the Coorgs of South India*, Oxford: Clarendon Press, 1952.

ACKNOWLEDGMENTS

Grateful acknowledgments first and foremost to all the text and image makers – academics, activists, novelists, artists, filmmakers and photographers – for their generosity in giving permission to reprint (and occasionally to do things with) their work in this book. This project would be inconceivable without such support.

This is also to formally express my deep indebtedness to Johnson Chang Tsong Zung. He has steered the trailblazing West Heavens project for a decade now, in which time his leadership and support in both initiating and enabling several major projects, have opened new and paradigm-changing opportunities and made possible tough cultural crossings.

Tulika Books has been a leading presence in the ever-challenged space of independent publishing in India. This multi-volume project could not have been imaginable without Tulika's expertise, and I thank the entire team there. I especially thank Nilanjana Dey and Basantarani Haobam for holding the complex editorial process together. Thanks also to the Sher-Gil Sundaram Arts Foundation, and Gayatri Uppal, for help, advice and multiple courtesies.

Grateful acknowledgments to Liang Jie for seeing through the complex process of overseeing the translation and to Shen Ziling for opening the world of Chinese publishing to us.

As always, to Geeta Kapur and Vivan Sundaram. And to Tejaswini Niranjana. For everything.

To Gauri Nagpal for her extraordinary creativity, her work and her patience.

And finally, to Chen Yun and Indira Chandrasekhar, without whom nothing of this would have happened.

Ashish Rajadhyaksha
Bangalore, 11 May 2020

Ashish Rajadhyaksha is a film historian, and an occasional art curator. He is the author of *Ritwik Ghatak: A Return the Epic* (1982), *Indian Cinema in the Time of Celluloid: From Bollywood to the Emergency* (2009) and *The Last Cultural Mile: An Inquiry into Technology and Governance in India* (2011), and editor of *Encyclopaedia of Indian Cinema* (with Paul Willemen) (1994/1999). He co-curated the Bombay/Mumbai 1992–2001 section (with Geeta Kapur) of *Century City: Art and Culture in the Modern Metropolis at the Tate Modern* (2002), the *You Don't Belong* festival of film and video in four cities in China (2011), *Memories of Cinema* at the IVth Guangzhou Triennial, 2011, '*Make-Belong:* Films in Kochi from China and Hong Kong', Kochi-Muziris Biennale, 2015, and the exhibition *Tah-Satah: A Very Deep Surface: Mani Kaul & Ranbir Singh Kaleka: Between Film and Video* at the Jawahar Kala Kendra, Jaipur (January–March 2017).